Nollywood

Nollywood

THE CREATION OF NIGERIAN FILM GENRES

Jonathan Haynes

The University of Chicago Press CHICAGO & LONDON

The University of Chicago Press, Chicago 60637
The University of Chicago Press, Ltd., London

Printed in the United States of America

25 24 23 22 21 20 19 18 17 16 1 2 3 4 5

ISBN-13: 978-0-226-38781-9 (cloth)
ISBN-13: 978-0-226-38795-6 (paper)
ISBN-13: 978-0-226-38800-7 (e-book)
DOI: 10.7208/chicago/9780226388007.001.0001

Library of Congress Cataloging-in-Publication Data
Names: Haynes, Jonathan, author.
Title: Nollywood : the creation of Nigerian film genres / Jonathan Haynes.
Description: Chicago ; London : The University of Chicago Press, 2016. | Includes bibliographical references and index.
Identifiers: LCCN 2016007480 | ISBN 9780226387819 (cloth : alk. paper) | ISBN 9780226387956 (pbk. : alk. paper) | ISBN 9780226388007 (e-book)
Subjects: LCSH: Motion pictures—Nigeria.
Classification: LCC PN1995.67.N6 H39 2016 | DDC 791.4309669–dc23 LC record available at http://lccn.loc.gov/2016007480

∞ This paper meets the requirements of ANSI/NISO Z39.48–1992 (Permanence of Paper).

FIGURE 1. Top: Filming on location near Asaba with Mercy Johnson (center). Bottom: Shopping for films at the entrance to Ebinpeju Lane, Idumota Market, Lagos.

For Onookome Okome,
who is my friend,
and for
Sandra, Jesse, and Chloë,
who mean the world to me

CONTENTS

ACKNOWLEDGMENTS

Materials in this book have been drawn, in more or less altered form, from the following previously published essays: "Political Critique in Nigerian Video Films," *African Affairs* 105/421 (2007): 511–33; "African Cinema and Nollywood: Contradictions," *Situations* 4, no.1 (2011): 67–90; "The Nollywood Diaspora: A Video Genre," in *Global Nollywood*, edited by Matthias Krings and Onookome Okome (Bloomington: Indiana University Press, 2013), 73–99; and "'New Nollywood': Kunle Afolayan," *Black Camera* 5, no.2 (2014): 53–73. I thank all those whose editorial work polished the earlier versions.

My research on Nigerian film began through a friendship with Onookome Okome, formed shortly after I first arrived in Nigeria in 1991. He was a newly minted PhD in film studies—Nigerian film studies, about which I was wholly ignorant. I listened and began to go around with him, looking up Nigerian filmmakers. We wrote a book (*Cinema and Social Change in West Africa*, 1995) with three chapters by each of us, one of mine ("Nigerian Cinema: Structural Adjustments") being about the transition of Nigerian filmmaking from celluloid to video (also published in *Research in African Literatures* in 1995). Together we wrote the first full-scale attempt to describe the new video industry, "Evolving Popular Media: Nigerian Video Films" (1997, 1998). When I was back in Nigeria in 1996–97 he suggested that I edit what became *Nigerian Video Films* (1997, 2000), lining up many of the contributors, contributing himself, and facilitating its publication in Ibadan. In the following years he played an indispensable role in keeping me in contact with Nigeria, with the film industry, and with the emerging community of academics working on it, through his prodigious activity in co-organizing half a dozen conferences in Nigeria and Germany. Okome's personality—vibrant, open, generous, loyal—has been an essential factor in the establishment of this field of study. No one owes him more than I do or is more grateful.

This book is the fruit of conversations with Nigerian filmmakers, who have my everlasting gratitude for their generosity. I'm heavily indebted, as will be obvious, to a few directors for many hours of friendly talk over the years: Zeb Ejiro, Tunde Kelani, Bond Emeruwa, and Kunle Afolayan. In the acknowledgments to *Nigerian Video Films* I singled out Amaka Igwe because I owed so much of my understanding to her powerful clear intelligence. We had occasional conversations for another fifteen years, and I mourn her premature death. I thank the other people in and around the industry who spoke with me at some length informally or agreed to interviews that were usually recorded and sometimes repeated: Tunde Adegbola, Daniel Ademinokan, Afolabi Adesanya, Gbenga Adewusi, Adeyemi Afoloyan, Bethels Agomuoh, Chiwetalu Agu, Larinde Akinleye, Mahmood Ali-Balogun, Emeka Amakeze, Fred Amata, Jeta Amata, Andy Amenechi, Peace Aniyam-Osigwe, Ejike Asiegbu, Ola Balogun, Bankole Bello, Teco Benson, Franca Brown, Chike Bryan, Madu Chikwendu, Sam Dede, Oluchi Dikeocha, Vincent Dubem, Joe Dudun, Felix Dukor, Albert Egbe, Chico Ejiro, Keppy Ekpenyong-Bassey, Hyginus Ekwuazi, King-Richard Ekwegh, Joe Emordi, Abel Success Erebe, Ojiofor Ezeanyaeche, Femi Fatoba, Kenneth Gyang, Shaibu Husseini, Charles Igwe, Chris Ihidero, Lancelot Imasuen, Emmanuel Isikaku, Emem Isong, Ademola James, Mercy Johnson, Precious Kalu, Kanayo O. Kanayo, Jide Kosoko, Ladi Ladebo, Femi Lasode, Chike Maduegbuna, Emeka Mba, Oliver Mbamara, Kene Mkparu, Richard Mofe-Damijo, Kenneth Nnebue, Felix Nnorom, Charles Novia, Chidi Nwokeabi, Chris Obi-Rapu, Don Pedro Obaseki, Omoni Oboli, Roseline Odeh, Tade Ogidan, Uduak Oguamanam, Okechukwu Ogunjiofor, Wale Ogunyemi, Zik Zulu Okafor, Osita Okeke, Obi Okoli, Tunde Okoli, Felix Okoro, Andy Amadi Okoroafor, Moses Olaiya Adejumo, Segun Olusola, Francis Onwochei, Zach Orji, Tom Rowlands-Rees, Brendan Shehu, Joke Silva, BobManuel Udokwu, and Ugezu J. Ugezu. They tried to enlighten me; I hope I've listened well. Of course all my sins of omission and commission are on my head alone.

My research was helped along in various ways by Abdalla Uba Adamu, Afolabi Adesanya, Alex Andrade, Jahman Anikulapo, Emevwo Biakolo, Hyginus Ekwuazi, Jibo Ibrahim, the late Sam Kafewo, Bic Leu, Abdul Rasheed Na'Allah, Sylvester Ogbechie, Nduka Otiono, Charmaine Pereira, Maria Pereira, and my fellow jurors at the 2012 Zuma Film Festival: Duro Oni, Sam

Dede, Molara Wood, and Anouk Batard. Warm thanks to them all for their aid and friendship.

A Guggenheim Fellowship in 2011–2012 coupled with a sabbatical leave from Long Island University allowed me desperately needed freedom to think and write—a tremendous gift. My work continues to be informed by the three years I spent in Nigeria as a Fulbright lecturer, and I continue to feel lively gratitude to the Fulbright program and to my host institutions, the University of Nigeria-Nsukka, Ahmadu Bello University, and the University of Ibadan. Thanks to the University of Cologne and my hosts there, Matthias Krings and Heike Behrend, for a stimulating guest professorship. The National Endowment for the Humanities provided a grant in aid of my research. At Long Island University, my thanks to a series of English Department chairs (Sealy Gilles was especially resourceful), Dean David Cohen, and Vice President Jeff Kane, who have all been supportive. The Nigerian Film Corporation, the University of Lagos, and Pan-Atlantic University bought me tickets to Nigeria; Delta State University and Kwara State University have done so twice each. My research greatly benefited from these trips and I am grateful.

Being part of the flourishing international academic community dedicated to studying African film has been one of the best experiences of my life. I won't begin hailing friends and mentioning people to whom I feel indebted since I wouldn't know when to stop. The references in the text tell some of the story. But it's a pleasure to name and abundantly thank those (in and out of academia) who carefully read the whole manuscript—Brian Larkin, Ken Harrow, and Sandra Dunn—and those who read parts of it and made helpful comments: Jahman Anikulapo, Linda Bamber, Jane Bryce, Carmela Garritano, Lindsey Green-Simms, Tunde Kelani, and John McCall. I repeat the usual caveat: they are not responsible for my mistakes.

My deepest gratitude is to my beloved Sandra Dunn—my editor-in-chief and indispensable partner—and to our *ibeji* Chloë and Jesse for putting up with all the times that I or my mind have been elsewhere.

PREFACE

"Surulere is nice," Bond Emeruwa said, and I agreed. It's the Brooklyn of Lagos: a relatively low-density neighborhood and therefore neighborly and relaxed, and it's full of creative people—the concentration of Nollywood filmmakers like Bond, longtime president of the Directors Guild of Nigeria, is what draws me there. It has the buoyancy of a neighborhood on the way up, with money pouring into it. Generally, it's a fine place to have a beer in the cool evening while the conversation flows, to run into friends and acquaintances, to laugh and float in the current of news and gossip.

But Surulere is shaped by the same forces and structures or lack of structures that produce a dreary monotony across the whole city and all Nigerian cities: burglary bars, imposing metal gates, embedded glass topping cinderblock walls, concrete blackened by urban pollution and tropical mold, informal commerce and parked cars crowding the cement aprons of businesses and sidewalks (in the rare cases where sidewalks exist), motorcycles weaving through stalled traffic so that walking is taxing and hazardous. A thick tangle of electrical wires hangs overhead and cobwebs the sides of buildings—illegal connections that overload and short out the grid and keep it from economic viability. Not that anyone feels sorry for the electrical power authority. Nigeria's electricity problems are legendary: twenty billion dollars have been invested in the sector since the end of military rule at the turn of the new millennium without visible results. Power blackouts are constant in Surulere, like everywhere else. Businesses have to create their own infrastructures for water, sewage, and security as well as power, which increases their expenses by at least a quarter—a tremendous drag on the economy and a deterrent to investment. Since Surulere is a middle-class neighborhood, many people can afford to have generators, so the roar of traffic is supplemented by the roar of thousands of generators. This background din is hard to keep off the soundtracks of Nollywood films, which is one problem they have in getting into international film festivals.

The population of Lagos has grown to about twenty-one million. Even Victoria Island, once the green and pleasant part of the city that the British colonial elite claimed for themselves, has been relentlessly built up and paved over, gleaming bank towers and car dealerships replacing comfortable bungalows with their surrounding vegetation. But no amount of investment buys insulation from the ambient chaos just beyond the marble steps and wrought-iron fences. The city has grown without planning (or, to be exact, without enforcement of plans) and no sense of the common good, of public space. One night in the pouring rain, lurching and floundering through the flooded, potholed streets of Victoria Island looking for a way around a particularly intractable "go-slow," I noticed that the small street next to the Lagos residence of the Delta State governor—a position that permits unregulated and unlimited access to oil money—was choked with an eight-foot-high mound of garbage. On another occasion I was being put up for a few days at a fancy hotel on the Lekki Peninsula, a sandbar stretching east from Victoria Island, inhabited by a few fishermen twenty or thirty years ago and now a vast construction site of McMansions. The hotel was said to be owned by the former vice president Alhaji Atiku Abubakar, and inside the marble was kept admirably polished. But the road to it hadn't been completed—there was a story about the work being suspended immediately after the last election. As our car entered the gate its oil pan hung up on the threshold, the threshold between public and private, and we had to get out and walk.

Adeniran Ogunsanya Street is one of the main thoroughfares of Surulere. At the southern end, fast-food restaurants on the American model cluster around the roundabout. Such fast food is expensive in Nigeria, and these places have doormen and are settings for dates in romantic films. Near the roundabout, a dilapidated old open-air shopping mall has been replaced by an enormous, spiffy enclosed and air-conditioned one, anchored by a Shoprite grocery store, part of a South African chain. The new mall has a first world sense of space utterly unlike anything seen in Surulere before. It stays open late for weary shoppers who have been stuck in traffic. Families bring their children to stroll around the mall's wide smooth corridors. In 2013 a multiplex cinema opened in an adjacent, still-newer mall.

The current governor of Lagos State, Babatunde Raji Fashola, and his predecessor and mentor Bola Ahmed Tinubu have been pioneering a novel (for post–oil boom Nigeria) form of governance: collecting taxes from citizens (as opposed to running the state on the federal government's allocations of oil revenues) and visibly delivering services in return. Most neighborhoods have not yet profited much from this—half the population lives on less than two dollars a day, and their lives have hardly changed—but Adeniran Ogunsanya Street has been resurfaced and its gutters fitted out with neat covers from one end to another. The northern end terminates in another traffic circle, this one under the flyover of Alhaji Masha Road. The Surulere Central Mosque with its bulbous minarets stands on one side of the circle, and Hausa money changers occupy the sidewalk on the other side. The supporting walls of the flyover used to be plastered with film posters, but the government now rigorously scrubs them off.

A few years ago Adeniran Ogunsanya Street was dotted with cybercafés, which often doubled as international Internet telephone call centers. Now they are almost all gone, since wireless modems and Internet connection plans have become affordable, laptops are common, and smartphones are essential status symbols. In 2010, $2 billion was invested in transatlantic fiber optic cables into Nigeria. Satellite television is cheap and ubiquitous. Apartment buildings sprout dishes down their sides like orderly lichens. Every bar and restaurant, most hotel lobbies, and many offices have plasma TVs tuned to the Africa Magic channels from M-Net, part of a South African media conglomerate that also owns the satellite television provider MultiChoice. Africa Magic broadcasts Nollywood films twenty-four hours a day, seven days a week, transfixing the population. This is bad for the film business: why buy films when they are always on television for free? Nollywood's business model is in perpetual crisis even as it has achieved hegemony as a cultural force.

Western Avenue soars, sometimes elevated, over the eastern side of Surulere, part of the ambitious highway building of the oil boom era of the 1970s. As it sweeps south over the bridge onto Lagos Island (the oldest part of the city, the business and administrative center), it provides panoramic views of the skyline of high-rise office buildings and, across tide-roiled waters, ocean-going freighters tied up to the Apapa wharfs. This is the biggest port in West Africa, feeding the vast industrial areas of Ikeja in northern Lagos and filling the trucks that, at night, sit parked lining for miles and miles the road north to Ibadan and the interior of the country. The ships arrive heavily laden and leave high in the water; to balance the trade, oil flows out of Niger Delta ports, Port Harcourt, Bonny, and Escravos.

When I was first learning to pilot my way around Lagos in the early 1990s the highways were horrific. Where the guard rails hadn't been stolen to be melted down into cooking pots, they recorded a history of appalling vehicular violence, yard by yard, smashed, twisted, blackened. When traffic reached the speed for which the highways were built, the potholes became lethal. The signature vehicle was the *moluë*, a bus locally constructed on a truck chassis, packed solid with passengers, belching black smoke. One assumed they didn't have functioning brakes. Young men hung precariously to the outsides as the vehicles careened along. A school of literary critics named itself *bolakaja* after the challenge shouted by the rough bus conductors: "Come down and fight!"

Not the least of the problems on the roads were the many roadblocks manned by the menacing foot soldiers of the military regime and predatory police. They extorted money and shot people to death with impunity: "Sorrow, tears, and blood / dem regular trademark," Fela sang. The nation seemed to be in a death spiral under the malign auspices of the self-styled "evil genius" General Ibrahim Babangida. The economy collapsed, and in the general social disintegration armed robbery depressed nightlife (putting an end to cinema-going, for instance). The soldiers and police were not being paid enough to live on so they had little choice but to turn to extortion, and they were probably under orders to kick back money to their superiors. It was generally understood that the police were often in league with the armed robbers.

Now, more than a decade after military rule ended in 1999, the roadblocks and military personnel are almost all gone, contracted into dark, silent riot vehicles parked at strategic locations—closed up and so ominously dark they seem to absorb all the light and sound around them. The armed robbers have mostly been chased off into other parts of the country. The *moluës* are gone too, replaced by big red and blue buses with their own express lanes. A company given a contract to put up street signs actually did so. A few vehicles now track their progress with GPS navigation systems. But Lagos is still a city that wears its citizens out in traffic. Bone-weariness from hours of buffeting by fumes and noise and nervous tension is a fundamental Lagosian sensation.

Just south of Surulere, the National Arts Theatre sits on swampland. It is also an expression of the oil boom, of the era when Nigeria, "the giant of Africa," flush with cash and self-confidence, hosted FESTAC, a lavish celebration of world black culture. The theater's sweeping curved lines recall Eero Saarinen's TWA terminal at JFK airport. Some say it looks like a military officer's hat; it also suggests a crowned head, the dark glass facades seeming to veil something potent—an imposing presence in the cityscape, as it was meant to be. Water rises from the sodden ground to have its way with the pavement, at one point the roof leaked and the air-conditioning didn't work, and the institution has been repeatedly threatened with neoliberal privatization. But it is still the national theater. On Sundays, families troop in as they have always done to watch new Yoruba films.

What has gone on in the grounds around the theater has been as important as what happens inside it. The Actors Guild has its headquarters in a bare outlying building. Casting calls take place under the trees. Under the trees—*Abe-Igi*—actors from theater, television, and film meet to drink beer, gossip, and talk shop. (Or they used to: in 2013 a new director of the National Theatre, evidently a person with no sense of the ecology of creative communities, ordered everyone but staff employees away from the area. The actors relocated to a bus stop nearby.) In 1991, in the immediate prehistory of Nollywood, Okechukwu ("Okey") Ogunjiofor, then a recent graduate of the Nigerian Television Authority's training program but unemployed because of budget cuts and a hiring freeze and reduced to hawking things in the street, happened upon a group of actors rehearsing a play under those trees and began offering unsolicited advice. So began his integration into the social network that would produce the first Nollywood film, *Living in Bondage*, based on his own story.

The National Stadium is just to the east of Western Avenue, where Alhaji Masha Road crosses under a flyover. The adjacent Stadium Hotel was for years an epicenter of highlife music, the soundtrack of the independence era. In 1991, Okey Ogunjiofor got a job videotaping a social event at the stadium; the celebrants cultivated his acquaintance and he eventually discovered they belonged to a secret cult—the germ of the story of *Living in Bondage*. Babangida's henchman and successor as military dictator, Sani Abacha, demonstrated with brutal clarity the principle that as long as a military ruler controlled the oil wellheads, could make deals with complicit foreigners for the oil's immediate export, and was willing to shoot protesting citizens down in the streets, he could stay in power almost indefinitely. Babangida's way, by contrast, was to expand the already robust cohort of corrupt Nigerian politicians and organize them into an elaborate masquerade of democracy. The oil money kept flowing as the country sank into misery, finding its way through secret channels to fund the kind of display of wealth and social power that Ogunjiofor was filming. Gaudy arrogance, with barely disguised roots in corruption and dark wickedness, dominated the public scene.

The western side of the stadium structure, facing Surulere, now houses O'Jez Restaurant, with an open-air courtyard below where beer and pepper soup are served. The owner, Joseph Odobeatu, is a businessman dealing in industrial equipment with a strong interest in sports and show business, and the nightclub was established as a celebrity hangout. A swirl of stories surrounds O'Jez, like everything else in Nigeria. With Chinese partners, Odobeatu built factories in Lagos to replicate Nollywood films on video compact discs (VCDs), which replaced VHS cassettes as the standard medium for Nigerian films. (Until these factories were built, Nigerian producers took their films to Singapore for digital duplication.) But Odobeatu was cheated by his Chinese partners and nearly ruined. Jahman Anikulapo, who for years was arts editor of the Lagos *Guardian* and is the doyen of Lagos's cultural nightlife, worked with Odobeatu and the veteran broadcaster Benson Idonije to organize a series of highlife nights at O'Jez from 2000 to 2008. This was a work of cultural reclamation: Nigeria is reckless with its history, and the great musicians of the sixties and seventies were mostly growing old in poverty and obscurity. The concerts returned them to the limelight, if only briefly, and resurrected a whole bygone era. But finally Jahman and Idonije got fed up with Odobeatu's refusal to share his fat profits with the musicians and angrily withdrew.

Once when I was leaving for the airport, Western Avenue and the other main roads were clogged so the taxi driver took the back route, north and west through Surulere to Itire Road. The driver was an old Yoruba man, thin with a gnarled hand on the gear shift, wearing Yoruba-style clothes sewn from boldly printed fabric and hoarse from his constant commentary to other drivers and pedestrians. His spare, angular VW was like him, not yet a rattletrap but weathered, of a piece with the whole environment of Lagos's streets and roadways. His driving was aggressive and highly skilled—he was a master of the art of pushing through crowds.

I was noticing the architecture of the buildings along the streets, which for some reason was emerging out of the blur of the cityscape as if for the first time in my experience. I was noticing the buildings *had* architecture: the fabric of the neighborhood was detached two- or occasionally three-story buildings, each one different. The structures had common elements: shallowly gabled, soffited tin roofs, louvered or casement windows with burglary bars, water tanks mounted high up behind the buildings on rough metal piping, the dreary electrical wires draped around everywhere recording a history of failed and makeshift connections. The predominant style was distinctly modernist in its cheerful use of standardized industrial materials and its clean, functional geometries, window frames popping out of subdued flat stucco surfaces. But this deck was constantly reshuffled, and many buildings were fanciful and original, with bold asymmetries and the same kind of curved poured-concrete architectural shapes found in the extravagant mansions Nollywood likes to use as sets.

There are blocks of uniform, government-built housing units in Lagos and even some high-rise apartment buildings (though living nine floors up in a building where the elevators often don't function because of power outages is a problem), and new corporate architecture—an unbelievable number of bank buildings, mostly—lines some streets. But overwhelmingly Lagos is composed of small structures, built in an unplanned, unregulated environment for private use or by a landlord for rental. Each construction is an individual project, an independent, small-scale initiative.

Old buildings in the Yoruba style began to appear amidst the modernist urban structures along Itire Road. Heavy-walled, with the pitched, rusted corrugated tin rooflines so redolent of the colonial era, they could have been transported from Oshogbo or Ibadan—J. P. Clark's "Ibadan": "running splash of rust / and gold—flung and scattered / among seven hills like broken / china in the sun." Here the sunlight had trouble reaching them, it being the rainy season, with thick rolls of cloud slowly lifting over the city. They were also a bit overshadowed by the buildings around them, though they seemed impressively solid and enduring—not relics, still very much part of life. My taxi driver might live in such a place. Through the open front doors, over high sills that had been worn and darkened by the passage of many residents, I could glimpse cavernous rooms below street level; what daylight made its way in through the doors splashed color from the clothing of those gathered within. Later, they would light hurricane lamps. Then a street of shops selling car parts. We followed a line of vehicles through a rupture in the barrier separating the neighborhood from the Apapa-Oworonsoki Expressway, a chunk of concrete in the adjoining ditch making this unofficial on-ramp navigable, and so up into a prospect of warehouses and billboards and, in the distance, the airport, with a plane glinting above it.

It occurred to me that the basic character of the Lagos urban fabric was the same as the structure of the film industry, which also is gigantic, astounding in scale, filling the horizon farther than the eye can see, but all generated by small-scale independent producers. They can work quickly and cheaply because of the stock of interchangeable elements, but each product is unique. The predominant style is resolutely modern, but there are enduring, much older structures and occasional gleaming postmodern edifices. The film industry also, in its way, provides a place for Nigerians to live.

*

Living in Bondage appeared in 1992. In 1994, in recognition of the "video boom," the Nigerian government reorganized and renamed the Federal Film Censorship Board as the National Film and Video Censors Board. By the end of 2010, the NFVCB had registered more than fourteen thousand Nigerian feature films made on video.

FIGURE 2. A video shop in Surulere, Lagos. Nollywood has produced thousands of films.

This is a very, very large number. In contrast, Nigeria produced a total of about one hundred films on celluloid between 1970, when the first Nigerian film appeared, and 1992, when celluloid production ground to a halt. The rest of sub-Saharan Africa (excluding South Africa) produced fewer than four hundred celluloid fictional feature films between 1964 and 2006 (figures compiled from Armes 2008). In twenty years, Nigeria has indisputably created one of the largest film industries in the world.

The Nigerian film industry is not synonymous with Nollywood. The term "Nollywood," which was coined by *New York Times* reporter Norimitsu Onishi in 2002 (Onishi 2002), refers primarily to the English-language films emanating from the production and distribution system based in Lagos and in the eastern Nigerian cities of Onitsha, Asaba, Enugu, and Aba. Nollywood is sometimes said to be an Igbo thing, and it is true that the marketers who have always been the dominant force in the industry are overwhelmingly Igbo. *Living in Bondage* and the other earliest Nollywood films were in the Igbo language. English-language films did not begin to appear until 1994, after which they quickly eclipsed Igbo-language films. The medium of English allowed people from many southern Nigerian cultures to enter the industry, and they have played such important roles that Nollywood can certainly not be thought of as "owned" by the Igbos. (In general, Nigerians often talk as if the country were divided among the Igbos, Hausas, and Yorubas, the three largest ethnicities, but there are two hundred and fifty ethnic groups in the country, and the "big three" together amount to only half the population of 170 million.) Under the aegis of Nollywood, films are made on a small scale in "minority" southern languages such as Bini/Edo and Efik.

In northern Nigeria, there is a quite separate film industry making films in Hausa, which few people would include as part of Nollywood. Most Hausa filmmakers see their films as an expression of specifically Hausa (and Muslim) culture and values, and one can read Hausa film culture as a reaction to and against Nollywood. The aesthetics of Hausa films resemble those of Nollywood in some respects but are different in others, most obviously the Hausa films' obligatory song-and-dance numbers in the Indian style. Nollywood and Hausa films are never carried in the same distribution systems, few personnel cross over, and Nollywood filmmakers and audiences tend to have only a dim awareness of Hausa films.

A large and sturdy tradition of filmmaking in Yoruba descends, for the most part, from the Yoruba traveling theater by way of television appearances and celluloid films. The relationship of this segment of the industry to Nollywood is ambiguous. Yoruba filmmaking exploits specifically Yoruba cultural resources and has a core of distinct social and business networks. The Yoruba, Hausa, and Nollywood branches of filmmaking all have their own separate professional associations. But many people cross over between the Yoruba and Nollywood industries, their aesthetics overlap a great deal, and mutual awareness is strong. The Yoruba branch of filmmaking is recognized as different, but out of courtesy and recognition of its historical priority and continuing vitality, it is often treated as part of Nollywood.

Yoruba filmmaking has continued fairly steadily as the English- and Hausa-language industries have gone through cycles of boom and crisis, so the ratio among the three branches has fluctuated. Over the last twenty years the total number of films in Yoruba has been somewhat lower than those in English, with Hausa production at about half the level of the other two.

Yoruba and Hausa films are carried to wherever there are people who speak those languages, in adjacent countries and throughout the African diaspora. But it is Nollywood that has become the powerful international brand—"the Pan-Africanism we have," in John McCall's resonant phrase (2007)—watched across the African continent on the same Africa Magic satellite channels that Surulere tunes into and sold to Caribbean immigrants in Brooklyn who probably have no inkling that Nigeria makes films in languages besides English. The Nollywood brand is now so powerful it is sometimes used to refer to all Nigerian filmmaking.

This book follows the contours of "Nollywood" as I have just outlined them. English-language and Pidgin films are its subject. I take a friendly interest in the Yoruba tradition but do not pretend to anything like a complete treatment of the topic. I cheerfully leave Hausa films to those who are qualified to talk about them. (See the excellent works by Abdalla Uba Adamu, Brian Larkin, Matthias Krings, and Carmen McCain.) Because films from Ghana's film industry, which closely resembles Nollywood, are carried in the same distribution system and many actors cross over, I refer to them occasionally. (On Ghana, see the excellent works by Birgit Meyer and Carmela Garritano.) I do not discuss the earlier celluloid films except incidentally. (Readers should consult the proper authorities, including Hyginus Ekwuazi, Frank Ukadike, Françoise Balogun, and Onookome Okome.) Nigerian video film culture has effectively become Nigeria's film culture: a generation has grown up in a world saturated with video films but with little or no chance ever to see the films made in the period of celluloid production, though those films do perhaps continue to exercise some gravitational pull, like a dark star.

First and last, my interest in Nollywood has sprung from a fascination with Nigeria itself. The films are a record and interpretation of contemporary Nigeria, a social and emotional history. Nollywood's characteristic themes and its distinctive and original set of genres arise out of Nigerian society and address its values, tensions, and historical experiences. Africans have had to struggle to get their stories told on film as well as in other media, and in this respect Nollywood is a triumph of enormous proportions, all the more impressive and interesting because it is a popular art form whose perspective must stay close to that of its broad audience of ordinary Nigerians or risk commercial disaster. Of course the stories Nollywood tells and the way it tells them don't spring spontaneously from the mind of "the people"—they are mediated by the complex nature of the film industry itself. My story about the unfolding of Nollywood's central themes and genres is intertwined with an account of the nature and evolution of the industry.

The Nollywood business model is to produce movies cheaply (the average film budget is about $65,000) and quickly (often just a few months from start to finish) and to recoup the investment within another month or so. This model is enforced by the glut of films on the market and widespread piracy, both of which limit the shelf life of films and potential profits. The resulting movies are inherently and essentially generic: individualizing a film costs time and money, and a film that does not give off strong generic signals will get lost in the market. Even beyond such necessities, Nollywood's culture is conservative, working and reworking a durable set of themes and plot types. (The conservatism coexists with a relentless quest for novelty, varying or recombining existing forms and exploiting topical material. The quest for novelty also has commercial motives.) Individual films almost all disappear from the market to make room for others after only a very few weeks, so if a story hits a nerve with the audience, it needs to be retold to stay in public consciousness. The stories that are repeated, that don't wear out or that do so only after almost infinite repetition, have a special power: they are the most motivated and essential, the most deeply embedded in the tensions of contemporary Nigerian life. Much of the films' meanings lie in their common forms and thematic complexes, and these are what I try to map and explicate.

In naming genres I have followed common usages of the film industry and fans. (The one exception is what I call "diasporic films," which seem to have no generally accepted name.) These usages are not altogether consistent or systematic. Internet sites selling Nollywood films often dump them into Hollywood's generic categories, which is usually misleading (Haynes 2010b). The terms I have adopted from the parlance of video shops in Nigeria indicate how different Nollywood's genres are from Hollywood's, how profoundly they express the intentions of Nigerian society.

I understand genre to be a messy business, not a matter of neat taxonomies. My shifting methodological approaches reflect that sense—you can't see a masquerade by standing in one place, as they say. I dwell on origins, borders, and the evolution of genres as they react to changed circumstances and generate new genres by dallying or mating with one another. Nollywood genres are often defined by their settings, so something like a sketchy social geography will emerge as Nollywood opens out a succession of social spaces for representation.

By now a lot has been written about Nollywood,[1] but nothing like a full-scale survey of its genres. I have tried to be comprehensive but the results seem (even to me) to be personal and essayistic. There are simply too many films and too many kinds of films. Other writers naturally will draw lines, name things, and place emphases differently. At least I have made a start.

The same is even truer for the book's historical dimension. Originally I didn't intend a historical dimension, in part because I appreciated how little had been done along those lines and how much work it would be. I provide a rough scaffolding at best, certainly not the thorough, detailed history Nollywood deserves. As I repeat on every possible occasion, the materials for such a history urgently need preservation, beginning with the films themselves, many of which exist only on videotape now decomposing in tropical heat and humidity. Memories also decay and those who hold them disperse and die, so personal testimonials need to be gathered systematically and preserved in permanent form.

We are still close to the beginning of one of the world's important film cultures. Nollywood has grown and changed at a phenomenal rate, but some solid foundations appear to have been laid. "No condition is permanent" is a phrase often emblazoned on Nigerian vehicles. I've tried to remember this even as I've searched for what seems enduring in the young Nollywood tradition.

My accounts of the genres place a proper African emphasis on foundings and seniority. Of course people love to argue about such matters, so unfortunately this is not a terribly effective method of avoiding complaints that I have favored some films and filmmakers over others. I am certainly not attempting to discuss all the important ones and I beg for understanding and forgiveness from those whose contributions are overlooked here. My purpose is to outline some basic aesthetic forms, historical shapes, and social meanings, to provide some aids to navigation in this vast sea of stories.

The book's first part describes the foundations on which the industry was built and the initial genres, which remain hallmarks of Nollywood: the "money ritual" film, in which occult practices become a figure for social predation under military rule; films about "senior girls," independent career women hungry for power, money, and sex; and the "family film," often about a marriage threatened from within or without. These early chapters contain extended readings of several key films and accounts of the artistic visions of important founding filmmakers, including Kenneth Nnebue and Amaka Igwe. An entire chapter is devoted to Tunde Kelani's films. The chapters in part 2 reflect a partial shift in Nollywood's center of gravity from Lagos to Igbo southeastern Nigeria. The village is the crucial horizon of the imagination in "cultural epics" about the precolonial past and its values, and in some of the other genres emerging around the turn of the millennium that dealt directly with the crisis levels of violence and disintegrating governance as well as with the anxieties attending longer-term historical changes. "Political films" became possible after the end of military rule in 1999, and comedies reprise some of the same themes in a more buoyant spirit. Part 3 describes genres about Nigerians living outside of Africa and on university campuses—far removed from the rooted culture of village films. The Internet, satellite television broadcasting, and new multiplex cinemas, along with other factors, have unsettled the economic basis of the industry and led to segmentations of filmmaking and audiences. As it enters its third decade, Nollywood continues as a vigorous popular art, while a "New Nollywood" aspires to escape the constraints of the old Nollywood marketing system.

From the time Nollywood began I've believed that it deserved sustained, respectful attention as an expression of popular consciousness. Karin Barber laid down the principle that the products of African popular culture are no less complex as signifying systems than other kinds of art and that if we don't see this, it is because we are not understanding what these arts mean to those who produce and consume them (Barber 1987). I find complexity in Nollywood films and even certain kinds of subtlety and delicacy—subtlety not so much of emotion or characterization or technique, but as a wisdom that comes from a shared experience of living with multiple cultures and frames of consciousness, the assumption that individual lives have layers and a whole repertoire of potential responses shaped by a history of rapid, uneven development. The delicacy is that of the balance of contending forces, of wavering battle lines or the quick, precise movements of straining wrestlers.

I'm annoyed by simple and often dismissive generalizations about Nollywood being this or that. However we choose to value the films, in order to understand them well enough to make judgments we needed a more differentiated view of the movies and of the industry they come from. Genre provides such differentiation: each genre creates a different world, seen through a different lens. There are also segmentations, duly noted, along cultural, class, and generational lines. But there is an overarching unity to Nollywood based on the bedrock values of its audience: moral purpose and the sense of community. I try to always keep in sight and in mind the world that Nollywood films emerge from, the rough cement, the turbulent, disrupted circulations of vehicles, electricity, and trade goods, and have no wish to ignore the whole mass of motives, high and low, that brings the films into being, or the consequences of working on astonishingly low budgets. I keep watching the films because they are addictively entertaining, but also because I take Nollywood's values seriously—not just those of a few exceptional films, but the values embedded in basic generic forms across the whole range of production. I believe Nollywood deserves credit for its roles as a chronicler of social history, as an organ of cultural and moral response to the extreme provocations and dislocations of contemporary Nigeria, and as the bearer of a true nationalism. It arose in Nigeria's hour of need, when everything was crumbling, including the ideologies on which the state was based. In the midst of a general retreat into exclusionary, Manichaean forms of religious and ethnic thinking and—most of all—into a sheer head-down struggle for survival, Nollywood managed to stage debates about fundamental issues and sustained an image of the nation as resilient, grounded, tolerant, plural, certainly tormented and suffering but also managing to laugh and to get on with life. The films were always good at expressing aspirations, and now that things are better—for some people, at least—Nollywood is a symbol and source of Nigerian pride, the most visible dimension of the new buoyancy, projecting Nigeria's self-image across the African continent and beyond.

* Part 1 *

CHAPTER 1

Creating Nollywood: Conditions and Foundations

CINEMA IN AFRICA AND THE VIDEO REVOLUTION

Africa had been integrated into international cinema circuits since the beginning of cinema—there were film screenings in Lagos in 1903 (Ekwuazi 1991). But Africa was integrated on the worst possible terms. Cinema was a one-way street: Africans watched films but could not make them for lack of capital to fund productions and because of the complex and expensive training, infrastructure, and technical apparatus celluloid cinema requires. The films that were imported were chosen to appeal to the colonial elite or because they were the cheapest thing that could be dumped on the market. They were often racist and were always estranged from African realities. As Brian Larkin puts it, "Until recently, in African postcolonies like Nigeria, a trip to the cinema has always been translocal, a stepping outside of Africa to places elsewhere" (2008, 124). Onookome Okome relates that when he was growing up in Sapele, in the Niger Delta, the Pidgin phrase "na cinema be dat" ("that's cinema") meant that something was unreal, impossible. Nevertheless, Africans were and are avid filmgoers. Cinemas were one of the prime attractions of urban modernity. Hollywood movies sank deep into the popular imagination. Africans were subjected to a second kind of film, besides the commercial imports: the instructional and propaganda films created for African audiences by the British, French, and Belgian colonial film units, which were taken by mobile cinema vans into villages and neighborhoods that had no other experience of movies. Usually these films were unbearably condescending, but they left an important legacy: postcolonial African governments and many filmmakers continue to conceive of cinema (and television) as a tool for modernizing and shaping society (Larkin 2008, chapter 3; Garritano 2013, chapter 1).

In the scholarship on African cinema, the contrast between French and British modes of support for cinema in the colonial and postcolonial epochs is a familiar theme (Martin 1982; Diawara 1992; Ukadike 1994; Shaka 2004). The French restricted African film production during the colonial era but afterwards vigorously provided financing, technicians, and noncommercial distribution channels, resulting in a strong if small corpus of feature films but very little filmmaking infrastructure on the ground in Africa. The African filmmakers in this system (which is no longer overwhelmingly French, but still dominated by Europe) have needed not just the technical and aesthetic education necessary to make films but also the sophistication to negotiate this complicated international system. They are perforce members of the intellectual elite, conscious of managing a scarce resource and burdened with the full set of responsibilities that African intellectuals carry.

Their films are seldom seen by Africans in Africa because film distribution in Africa has always been dominated by foreign companies that make money by importing third-run Hollywood or Chinese movies, which are far cheaper than African films that need to recoup their production costs. Shut out of the distribution circuits, African cinema has never been able to reach African populations in a sustained manner and so has failed to become a real industry that makes films from the profits of previous films. It has always been clear that a celluloid film industry would be nearly impossible in Africa without substantial government support, which has never materialized.

The British Colonial Film Units did create a filmmaking infrastructure in Africa, including the training of a cadre of African technicians, but from the 1950s on the British did little or nothing to encourage feature film production. The Nigerian government founded the Nigerian Film Corporation amidst cultural nationalist rhetoric about strengthening, defending, and propagating African values and the national image but, like the British, effectively left feature filmmaking to the commercial sector (Ekwuazi 1991).

This situation changed abruptly in the 1980s and 1990s. The "video boom" in West Africa springs from two intersecting developments that radically altered media environments around the globe: the advent of new video technologies and the neoliberalization of media environments. "Small media"—videocassette recorders, video cameras, video projectors, satellite television receivers, DVD players, and computers—are far beyond the capacity of African governments to control. Moreover these governments, which previously had tried to control the media tightly out of some mixture of anti-imperialist cultural nationalism and political paranoia, were now distracted by the economic crises of the 1980s and 1990s and were under pressure from bodies like the International Monetary Fund and World Bank, which had acquired enormous leverage in those crises, to liberalize their media environments.

The result was an uncontrolled deluge of imported media of many kinds, from Julia Roberts movies to Pakistani recitations of the Quran. Suddenly African audiences had a very wide choice of what to watch. The foreign content is, for the most part, not being foisted on them by transnational corporations. It is being pirated, which annoys the transnational corporations when they bother to think about the African market. Audience choices are mediated through small-scale African entrepreneurs who pirate what they judge their clientele will pay for.

The same situation that allowed for the flood of imports also created the possibility for an eruption of African popular culture into the realm of recorded audiovisual media. Video is cheap and easily operated and so fits the model of the "African popular arts" as defined by Karin Barber: art forms created by small-scale entrepreneurs who need little equipment, training, or capital (Barber 1987). But the possibility has been realized unevenly in different places, depending on contingent factors.

Nigeria created the behemoth of African entertainment for specific reasons. First and foremost is size. A quarter of the whole population of sub-Saharan Africa lives in Nigeria, giving it an enormous internal market and therefore the same advantages that have worked in Hollywood's favor: bigger audiences allow for bigger budgets, which allow for higher production values, which attract bigger audiences in a self-reinforcing spiral towards dominance.

THE YORUBA TRAVELING THEATER

Nigeria's Yoruba traveling theater tradition (Clark 1980; Jeyifo 1984; Barber 2000) provided a ready-made basis for the video film industry. On stage since the 1940s, this syncretic theatrical form commanded a broad popular audience wherever Yoruba was understood. The performances mobilized deep Yoruba cultural forms—religious mythology, historical themes, the highly prized verbal arts, traditional drumming—as well as electric guitars, microphones, and topical contemporary subjects. By the 1960s, Nigeria supported a hundred traveling theater troupes. As soon as television was introduced in Nigeria (1959), they were on television. When celluloid film production began in the 1970s, they made movies. The Yoruba actors found their way around the problem of being shut out of the cinema distribution system by continuing to travel as they had always done, setting up in schools, city halls, and hotel courtyards as usual, but now they showed their films rather than put on live performances (Ricard 1983). Sometimes they worked with trained directors to produce the most distinguished and popular Nigerian films of the celluloid era. Often they were justly accused of simply pointing a camera at their stage plays. In any case, they demonstrated their ability to adapt to one medium after the other, reorganizing themselves each time. Each time they brought their loyal fans along with them.

Yoruba traveling theater actors made most of the roughly one hundred celluloid films produced in Nigeria between 1970 and 1992 (Balogun 1987; Ekwuazi 1991; Adesanya 1992; Okome and Haynes 1995; Haynes 1995). The others were a hodgepodge: Wole Soyinka's unsuccessful (as he admits) experiments (*Kongi's Harvest* (1970), *Blues for a Prodigal* (1984)); a few government-sponsored projects like *Shehu Umar* (1976), from a Hausa novel by Nigeria's first prime minister, Tafawa Balewa; Eddie Ugbomah's commercial thrillers (*The Mask* (1979), *Death of a Black President* (1983)), modeled at least in part on the American Blaxploitation films of the 1970s; Ladi Ladebo's ameliorative social dramas (*Vendor* (1988), *Eewo* (1989)); the Adesanya brothers' search for a formula that would combine authentic African culture with commercial viability (*Vigilante* (1988), *Ose Sango* (1991)). Nigerian celluloid film production was almost entirely detached from the Pan-African institutions of African cinema, such as the biennial FESPACO film festival and the filmmakers' organization FEPACI, and from the European support that was so crucial in Francophone Africa. The exemplary career of this period is that of Ola Balogun, a French-trained director who was the most prolific of all African film directors, making some ten feature films between 1973 and 1984. He both worked with Yoruba traveling theater artists, which was lucrative but irritating since the theater people had their own ideas about how to make films and were not sufficiently respectful of Balogun's expertise, and shot his own projects, which reflected many of the more advanced artistic and ideological tendencies of the period but languished for lack of an audience and a distribution system (Balogun 1987).

The Structural Adjustment Program (SAP) of the mid-1980s brought a precipitous devaluation of the national currency, the naira. Anything involving hard currency was suddenly beyond any filmmaker's budget, including importing film stock and going to London to process footage and do postproduction work, neither of which could be done in Nigeria. At the same time, most of the cinema houses closed. Armed robbers terrorized the night, a strong reason not to go out to the movies, and the theaters were sliding into ratty disrepair. And there were other reasons for the demise of cinema houses. The ascendance of both Pentecostal Christian and Islamic fundamentalism sharpened social disapproval of the culture of the theaters, strongly associated with disreputable young men smoking marijuana; when the electricity went off, as it did more and more often, and the theater's generator wore out or ran out of fuel, which was also increasingly likely, the audiences tended to vent their rage on the infrastructure they could get their hands on, the theater itself; the unsettled political climate made the behavior of the censors board dangerously unpredictable; and frequent political crises and other forms of unrest made scheduling the premier of a new film risky (Uchenunu 2008).[1] Public life was under general assault. Video permitted a retreat into private spaces. Celluloid film production ceased in 1992, the same year video production took off.

The professional celluloid directors rejected the advent of video filmmaking with bitter vehemence. Actors passed easily from one medium to the other—it had never been possible to define oneself as primarily a film actor, given the low level of film production; actors always made their livings from television and the stage. But apart from the Yoruba traveling theater element (and Tunde Kelani—see chapter 5), there is little continuity between Nigeria's celluloid and video directors.

The Yoruba traveling theater artists forged on through the downward spiral, finding ways to make do. They discovered a cache of reversal film stock (which produces a single, unreproducible positive print rather than a negative), and they used it up, though the unique prints would soon wear out, dooming the films to rapid oblivion. Hyginus Ekwuazi notes "the disenchantment by the audience at this kind of film that always got stuck in the projector" (2008b, 138). The next shift born of desperation was to shoot on video and transfer the films onto 16 mm celluloid. Video projectors arrived in the nick of time. The filmmakers were now operating in an all-video environment. The honor for first Nigerian video film seems to be shared between Ade Ajiboye ("Big Abass"), who made *Sonso Meji* (*Two Pointed Ends*) in 1988, and Muyideen Alade Aromire, who shot *Ekun* (*Tiger*) in 1986 but did not screen it until 1989 because he had taken it to the Nigerian Film Censors Board, where, according to reports, the legendary founder of the traveling theater Hubert Ogunde, who had turned to filmmaking and been named a member of the board, told Aromire that a video would be given the status of a film over his dead body. As Akin Adesokan dryly observes, "It turned out to be an exact, if unintended, prophecy: Ogunde is no more, and videofilms are here with us" (2008).

These films were still screened in improvised venues. The audience for the first film shown with a video projector, *Ekun*, rioted, but finally everyone had to settle for what they could have. In spite of the volatile behavior of spectators gathered in theaters, many observers have noticed that Nigerian audiences care about the story a film is telling above all else—if they are happy with that, they will ignore all kinds of technical and other deficiencies.

Yoruba films also began to be sold as videocassettes, though usually as an afterthought to public screenings. Yoruba society had a strong tradition of going out to see films, often in families, and screening of films continues to be an important aspect of the Yoruba video film business and culture. Opening a new film at the National Theatre has been a standard practice. Aromire, who did not come out of the traveling theater (he began as a writer and cartoonist (Adesokan 2008) and later opened a television station), appears to have been the first to make cassette sales the primary means of releasing his films, though his sales were modest.

It was Kenneth Nnebue, an Igbo electronics dealer who imported and sold videocassettes, who fully grasped the potential market for Nigerian films on video. Though he did not speak Yoruba well himself, in 1989 he produced a film with Yoruba traveling theater troupe leader Ishola Ogunsola, *Aje Ni Iya Mi/My Mother is a Witch*, shooting with an ordinary VHS camera and editing with two ordinary VCRs. *Aje Ni Iya Mi* cost Nnebue ₦2,000 (less than $200) to make, and he turned a profit of hundreds of thousands of naira. He immediately produced a string of similar Yoruba-language video films.

TELEVISION

The most important factor that enabled and shaped Nollywood was Nigerian television. Nigeria had the first television station in sub-Saharan Africa, WNTV (later named NTA-Ibadan when it was taken over by the national network, the Nigerian Television Authority), on air since 1959, an initiative of the progressive Yoruba political leader Obafemi Awolowo. After independence in 1960, Nigeria set about constructing by far the largest and strongest television network in Africa. At first a television set was something only the elite could afford, but by the early 1980s television was no longer a novelty and had spread through the middle class. Oluyinka Esan writes that it "became the focal point in homes." In 1984 the NTA boasted 30 million viewers per night (Esan 2009, 129); fewer than 50,000 were in the cinemas (Olusola 1986, 163). By 1991 the national NTA had twenty-four production centers and there were fourteen state-owned television stations, all managed and operated by Nigerians (Esan 2009, 130).

The NTA was arguably the single most powerful force in creating a sense of Nigerian identity. In 1983 an Organization of African Unity study found that Nigerian television had the lowest percentage of foreign content of any nation in Africa (cited in Lasode 1994, 166). The national news, watched simultaneously all over the vast country, has been an obvious unifying force, no matter how stultifying it usually was. In the early 1960s, the Nigerian artistic community was relatively compact and the surge of creative energy accompanying independence produced a cross-fertilization of cultural forms and a golden age of the performing, visual, and literary arts. Television was hungry for content, and much of this cultural efflorescence found its way onto the airwaves. All the most famous Yoruba traveling theater actors and their troupes appeared on WNTV in Ibadan. What happened at WNTV paralleled and intersected with what was going on across town at the University of Ibadan School of Drama, where—in a kind of cross-class collaboration that has become rare (Jeyifo 1984, 57)—the traveling theater artist Kola Ogunmola was invited for a residency during which he created a landmark stage production of Amos Tutuola's novel *The Palm-Wine Drinkard*, which was broadcast. Actors and writers associated with the University of Ibadan provided WNTV with regular dramas in English. A full roster of Nigerian writers had their work adapted for television: Wole Soyinka, Chinua Achebe, J. P. Clark, Cyprian Ekwensi, Bode Sowande, Adebayo Faleti, Akinwumi Ishola, D. O. Fagunwa, Abubakar Imam, Elechi Amadi, and Umaru Danjuma, to name some (Adesanya 1990a).

Segun Olusola, the most important Nigerian television producer, points out that, unlike in most of the rest of the world, in Africa television production did not follow (and follow from) cinema production, it preceded it; even more remarkably, he claims that "In this country, it was television that provided the impetus for the flowering of the modern theatre." The Yoruba traveling theater artists did not merely appear on television—some of the most important ones (including Duro Ladipo) got their first exposure and developed their art in the studios of WNTV and NBC-TV.[2] Olusola continues with a contrasting example from the early days of the elite/literary English-language dramatic tradition: "Experimentation and learning with the new medium were foremost in the minds of the motivators of the first ever television play—*My Father's Burden*—written by Wole Soyinka, when it was televised live mid-1960" (Olusola 1986, 174–75).

In the 1970s and 1980s, the NTA broadcast immensely popular serials. These shows, designed to create a common national culture, indigenized the transnational form of the television serial, which settled over the Nigerian cultural landscape, adapting to its contours. Olusola's *The Village Headmaster*, which ran from 1968 to the mid-1980s,

> portrayed a range of domestic and social dilemmas stemming from the need for a re-alignment of old ways to new lifestyles endorsed by Western education, hence the headmaster's prominence and the superiority of his counsel despite the presence of traditional political structures. According to the original headmaster, played by Ted Mukoro, it was a testament to the teachers and civil servants who took over from the colonialists. (Esan 2009, 89)

The cast reflected "a cross-section of socially recognizable types and exhibit[ed] the nation's ethnic diversity. This was federal character in action, long before the term was officially coined" (Esan 2009, 90). O. O. Oreh points out that

> all the [television] plays without exception inject the vernacular—Yoruba, Igbo, Hausa, or pidgin English—into the dialogues of the play which are usually in English. This common language denominator, more than the contents of the plays, makes them *classless* in the sense that they are neither highbrow, for the few educated elite, nor popular, only for the mass audience. One can therefore say that they constitute a unifying cultural experience. Next to this admixture of English, pidgin and vernacular languages, which produces a seemingly mother-tongue effect, is the spectators' natural fondness for familiar scenes and ways of life or indigenous norms and mores. (1985, 108)

The Masquerade, produced in Enugu and then in Aba, began as an attempt to make Igbos laugh after the trauma of the Biafran Civil War (1967–1970) (Ebeogu 1987; Oreh 1985). It often turned around topical social issues like the scarcity of kerosene for cooking, with abundant comic byplay and commentary in Pidgin, the unofficial national language and the great demotic vehicle of popular consciousness. The central character, Chief Zebrudaya (Chika Okpala), was a fountain of comic linguistic invention. Many of his coinages entered general speech. When the show was revamped as *New Masquerade*, it had a new urbanity. *Cock Crow at Dawn* (from 1980), produced and directed by Peter Igho, about a middle-class family that moves back from the city to a rural village in northern Nigeria and introduces modern farming techniques, was directly tied to government purposes (Esan 2009, 115). Ken Saro-Wiwa's *Basi & Company* (from 1985) made genial comedy out of its characters' greed, laziness, and unlikely get-rich-quick schemes. Lola Fani-Kayode's *Mirror in the Sun* (from 1984) opened a new horizon of artistic ambition for serials and created an idealized vision of an affluent, sophisticated society. It was an inspiration for Amaka Igwe, whose *Checkmate* (from 1990), along with Zeb Ejiro's

Ripples (from 1988), dominated the airwaves in the period immediately before video filmmaking began. Peter Igho made, and inspired others to make, high-quality made-for-television movies that complemented the serials.

The late 1980s were an exceptionally fertile period for Nigerian television. Nigerian content had decisively bested *The Cosby Show* and *Dynasty* for the attention of television audiences. Young people flocked into television production from the universities, or returned (like Lola Fani-Kayode) from studies abroad, as well as coming through the Television College that the NTA had established in 1980. In 1985 the NTA sponsored a now-legendary screenwriting workshop—a year's diploma course crammed into three months. The seasoned British instructors Victor Pemberton and David Spencer instilled a strong sense of professionalism. According to Mahmood Ali-Balogun, they taught an international standard form of screenwriting, without concern for the Nigerian cultural context. Those being trained included a remarkable galaxy of figures who would go on to create a new generation of television serials and then become major figures in Nollywood, including Ali-Balogun, Zeb Ejiro, Andy Amenechi, Bond Emeruwa, Richard Mofe-Damijo, Ralph Nwadike, and Charles Owoyemi.

VIDEOCASSETTES

During the oil boom Nigeria became saturated with videocassette recorders, like no place else in Africa. In 1984, an estimated 20 percent of television owners also had VCRs (Tudesq 1992, 256). Owning one became a defining feature of the Nigerian middle class. Pierre Barrot cites a 2003 survey that found that 67 percent of urban households had VCRs or DVD players, more than had refrigerators or potable tap water (Barrot 2009, 22).

The prevalence of VCRs led to the importation of video cameras and the business of making "social videos"—professionally made recordings of private events such as funerals, weddings, and chieftaincy and naming ceremonies. This form sprang from the "social diary" segments that have been a source of revenue for Nigerian television stations from the beginning, broadcasting tapes of such events for a fee paid by the celebrant (Esan 2009, 46–47).

More consequentially, an "infrastructure of piracy" (Larkin 2004) was created by businessmen like Kenneth Nnebue to service these VCRs, importing blank cassettes, pirating foreign films, reproducing them locally, and distributing them through a network of shops, peddlers, and rental clubs. The military governments of the day, preoccupied with maintaining their rule, pillaging the nation, and themselves routinely flouting the law, had little interest in or ability to control this new economic activity. It was on this foundation that Nollywood would be built (ibid.).

It was a treacherous foundation to build on, and piracy has been the great limiting structural factor of Nollywood's development since the beginning. "Piracy is our AIDS," Nnebue wrote (1997). Nnebue was well aware of the danger when he released *Living in Bondage*, which is preceded by a warning against unauthorized use that runs to two full screens of small type, stipulating among other things that the film is not to be shown without permission in schools, prisons, or on oil rigs. From the beginning of Nollywood the government has been constantly called upon to do something about piracy, but in practice it has turned a blind eye to the pirating of Nollywood films, as it did to the pirating of foreign films.

CRISIS, 1992

The NTA and the independent producers that provided it with content had created what by African standards was a very large cadre of trained professionals working behind as well as in front of the camera. Nollywood was born when crisis conditions forced many of these people to find work elsewhere, like Okey Ogunjiofor, who had come out of the NTA's training program with high marks but could not be employed because of a hiring freeze.

The whole audiovisual entertainment sector was in crisis in 1992, the year *Living in Bondage* appeared. As already mentioned, violent street crime caused cinemas to close. Video rentals were in serious decline, no longer profitable because of collapsing incomes. Television had always been an attractive medium but an unreliable business partner for the Yoruba traveling theater troupes. Karin Barber reports examples of how the NTA would cheat the theater people and says the Yoruba artistes found making films preferable because with films they maintained control over their product (2000, 245–46, 259). But celluloid filmmaking had become impossible, and traveling to put on either film screenings or live performances was difficult because of chronic fuel shortages and the deteriorating security situation on the roads and in the cities. In any case, audiences seemed to have lost their taste for live theater. When the great comedian Moses Olaiya Adejumo ("Baba Sala") organized some stage productions in Ibadan in 1997, almost no one came, and I watched people walk away when they realized he was putting on a play rather than showing a film.

Broadcasting was also unsettled. In line with the neoliberal deregulation that international institutions were calling for, the Nigerian government had announced that it would allow private television broadcasting, and jockeying was underway to secure licenses. But the government's careful rigging of the process of liberalization managed to demoralize the NTA while stunting the new independent media. Private owners could establish individual stations but not networks, which might rival the NTA. The result was that private stations had little money to create original content or, for that matter, to do much of anything besides worry about generating their own supply of electricity. Satellite distribution services had begun operation, but without obtaining redistribution rights from program suppliers; licenses for these services would also be issued by the government the next year (Bourgault 1995, 133–34). Producers of English-language television serials left the NTA throughout the early 1990s in response to deteriorating conditions there (Lasode 1994, 179). Bob Ejike remembers the wretched payments the NTA made to actors and musicians (2005), and a new and strangely misguided policy introduced at this time forbade NTA employees from acting in serials broadcast on NTA, which put an end to some of the most popular shows and led to the exodus of many personnel. Moradewun Adejunmobi describes a particular dispute in 1992 between the NTA and soap opera sponsors that led the latter to cancel their sponsorship, driving some of the leading directors, such as Zeb Ejiro, towards video film production (2003, 54–55).

This crisis in audiovisual production and distribution coincided with a general failure of the formal sector in Nigeria. The Structural Adjustment Program had devastated the economy, crippling industrial production and throwing many people out of work. Infrastructural breakdowns and blockages cascaded: the erratic supply of electricity made private generators necessary, but then often there was no gasoline to run them. Newspaper editorial pages liked to vent their outrage at this chronic fuel scarcity in one of the world's largest oil producers, which was due to catastrophic breakdowns in the refineries (whose maintenance budgets always disappeared), to rampant illegal exporting to neighboring countries of what gasoline there was by military officers and the politically connected, and so on and so forth—"the Nigerian factor." Civil servants (including teachers and even policemen and soldiers) were not receiving a living wage and often were not paid at all; their choices then were to turn to corruption or to do something else when they should have been doing their jobs. Schools on every level were starved for resources, frequently closed by strikes, or shut down following student riots. There was a permanent crime wave and the government lost its last vestiges of legitimacy and credibility as the frantic political manipulations of the Babangida regime led to the annulled elections of 1993. As a result of all this, people turned to the informal sector to get by: university lecturers ran their cars as taxis, those who could afford generators bought them and found fuel on the black market, and neighborhoods gated their streets and hired watchmen.

NOLLYWOOD IS BORN: *LIVING IN BONDAGE*

This was the moment Kenneth Nnebue seized. Nollywood was based on an unregulated technology and a largely informal sector of commerce, a form of popular culture expressing the energies of the nation when all else was failing—a true grassroots phenomenon. The cultural establishment was vehement in its denunciation of the video boom as an "all-comers' affair," complaining of people with no qualifications rushing to make films without asking anyone's permission and, in fact, sometimes not meeting any particular standard. But the Nollywood industry always harnessed larger, more powerful forces. *Living in Bondage* is considered the film that inaugurated Nollywood not because it was the first film made on video or sold on cassette—it was not—but because the cassette's full-color jacket and cellophane wrapper made it look comparable to an imported Hollywood film. It moved through the same national distribution system that carried Hollywood and Bollywood films and was sold alongside them. The term "Nollywood" would not be invented until a decade later, but *Living in Bondage* announced a competing entertainment industry, another "wood." It "opened the market," as people say, demonstrating spectacularly that the market was there and that a lot of money could be made from it.

Integral to this sense of an industry was its star system. Nollywood, like Hollywood and other commercial film industries, realized from the beginning that the way to make consumers recognize they wanted to buy a unique product that by definition was new to them is through celebrity actors. (In the festival and art house–oriented structure of celluloid African filmmaking, it is the auteurist director's name that brands the film.) The actors in *Living in Bondage* came from television serials: they had been on Zeb Ejiro's *Ripples*, Amaka Igwe's *Checkmate*, and *New Masquerade*.[3] Mostly they had not been playing major roles—it was *Living in Bondage* that catapulted them to real fame. But they were handled like stars. Their images appear in photomontage on the jacket of *Living in Bondage* and their names in the opening credits are accompanied by video clips of them, as if to give an immediate assurance to viewers of the film's star power.

On the set of *Living in Bondage* no one knew where this experiment would lead, but there was an excited sense of doing something different and better than the serials the actors were used to, according to one of them, Kanayo O.

Kanayo. Nnebue was spending his money to give them time to work more slowly and carefully, rehearsing scenes repeatedly, judiciously setting up the lights, controlling the look of the film. Nnebue showed it to Amaka Igwe before its release, and she predicted it would be a hit in part because it had what in the business is called "dimension": swank locations, a performance by a large cultural troupe of singers and dancers, beautiful designer clothes from fashion houses, and elaborate head ties that women viewers would discuss afterwards.

NOLLYWOOD AESTHETICS

Still, television was the standard of comparison, not cinema. The influence of television was massive. "Nigerian Video as the 'Child of Television'" is the title of an essay by Don Pedro Obaseki (2009). Nollywood films are sometimes projected in cinemas or elsewhere, but for the most part they are watched on televisions, and visually they are tailored for the small screen: the visual dimension that makes cinema cinematic is attenuated. They are talky, dialogue driven, spending most of their time watching people in conversation, as in soap operas. For that matter, Nigerian television serials are unusually talky. Peter Igho, one of the key creative people at the NTA, told Amaka Igwe this was because the first television producers, hurriedly given their positions when television broadcasting was introduced, had been trained as radio producers by the BBC and so had little visual sense. There are additional sources for this talkiness. The heritage of the voluble Yoruba traveling theater is often cited, but the training of many Nollywood actors, directors, and scriptwriters in university theater arts programs, which emphasize literary drama, is at least as important, as Awam Ampka suggested to me (cf. Oreh 1985, 109). And a general cultural bias directs attention to human beings and their social relations at the expense of anything else, in contrast to Western cinematography, which inherited traditions of landscape and genre painting, and to a naturalistic stagecraft that used scene painting, props, and lighting to establish characters in relation to a carefully delineated environment.[4]

The duration of Nollywood films typically exceeds the international norm for cinema, to the point that it suggests a television serial. *Living in Bondage* is in two parts, with each part filling a three-hour VHS cassette (part 1 is 158 minutes, part 2 160 minutes), for a total of almost five and a half hours—nearly four times the standard length of a film from Hollywood or almost anywhere else. (Indian films are long, distended by their song and dance numbers and digressive plotting, but do not have the typical two-part structure of Nollywood.) The two parts are not a free-standing film and then a more or less independent sequel, in the Hollywood manner, but one continuous narrative arc. Part 1 of *Living in Bondage* ends at a climactic moment, but the story is obviously incomplete at that point. The two-part structure remains standard (though not invariable) in Nollywood, and there is more or less universal agreement about the reason: marketers can make more money by selling two films rather than one. From the beginning, most producers chose to fill two-hour cassettes rather than three-hour ones. Around 2000, video compact discs (VCDs) were introduced and gradually became the standard medium. (VCDs are inferior in quality to DVDs but cheaper to produce; used in wealthier countries for data storage, they are a medium for films in the Far East as well as Africa.) A VCD disc holds about an hour of video, so each of the two parts is put onto two VCD discs or sometimes onto a single "2-in-1" disc.[5] Around 2007 shorter films began to appear, with each of the two parts about an hour long, fitting onto a single VCD disc. The two parts are packaged separately but usually sold together. They are normally shot at the same time (for reasons that will become clear from the story about the making of *Living in Bondage* below), and the division into parts often comes at an arbitrary point in the story, though part 2 will begin with its own credit sequence. Some films continue with parts 3 and 4, released later. The continuation may have a different but related title: *Rush Hour* 1 and 2 is followed by *Final Hour* 1 and 2, for example.

Moradewun Adejunmobi suggests we think of the Nollywood multipart format as a "short serial," designed to addict customers to a continuing story as in a soap opera, but in this case they pay for new installments. The instabilities of the market, as opposed to the institutional solidity of television broadcasting, limit the number of episodes a consumer can be expected to follow (Adejunmobi 2003, 2005). Soap operas of the American and British varieties are structured to go on forever, whereas Latin American telenovelas, which invaded Nigerian television in the 1980s, have a foreseen narrative closure that takes many episodes to get to, making them a closer model. Adejunmobi's idea captures essential continuities with television serials but needs qualification. *Living in Bondage*, at less than six hours, is still closer to the hour and a half of Hollywood than to the twenty hours or so of a telenovela, and its formal properties and the conditions of its consumption are closer to cinema: The film is normally watched in one or two sittings, rather than on many occasions scattered over months. The film does not need to be designed with a huge amount of redundancy in order to accommodate viewers who miss episodes or watch them distractedly because they cannot choose the time of viewing. *Living in Bondage*'s opening sequence of the protagonist soliloquizing clearly establishes him as the central character around whom the story will unfold, not as just one of a cluster of interacting regular cast members, and we immediately feel caught up in a narrative arc based on his desires and conflicts.

On the set, the influence of television was embodied in the person of Chris Obi-Rapu, then the most powerful director at the NTA, who directed the first part of *Living in Bondage* under his wife's maiden name (Vic Mordi) because of the NTA's strict rules against "private practice" by its employees. Obi-Rapu had worked as assistant director on Ola Balogun's celluloid film *Muzik Man* (1976) and was conscious of the differences between cinema and television. For instance, as he told me, he tried to move away from the constant shot/reaction shot pattern tied to dialogue, typical of the television serials, and since he did not have a dolly or crane with which to move his camera, he directed the actors to move within the frame.

Still, his whole career as a television director informed his work on *Living in Bondage*. Space is handled in the same manner as on, say, *New Masquerade* (which Obi-Rapu had directed). The film opens directly in the protagonist's sitting room (Nnebue's office was used as the set), with no establishing shot; we will never see anything of his flat besides the half of this one room visible from the camera setup, sofa to the right, to the left the door and two matching upholstered chairs pushed together to form a loveseat, dining table in the foreground when the camera pulls back. Nollywood films typically spend most of their time trapped inside rooms. Other characters will walk into this sitting room as they would walk onto a soap opera set—a kind of dramaturgy laid down in Nigeria by *The Village Headmaster*, whose early episodes were, for technical reasons, shot in one single take with no editing (Esan 2009, 90). Following the rhythm of a soap opera, after a few minutes we will cut away to another household, tangentially related to the protagonists' household in more than one way, though the plot will never connect them as closely as it would do over time in a serial. In this case there is a strong thematic continuity underlying the cut, as there would probably not be on television. Five and a half hours is a lot of time to fill, and the protagonist's story is actually pretty simple; anyway, as Nnebue said to me, "It will be boring if you have just one story without mixing it up with other stories. Even life is not like that." Amaka Igwe explained this as a fundamental principle of African aesthetics: "Africans don't like to listen to just one story at a time." So the film expatiates, moving from place to place, and it does so using the mechanisms of soap operas, recycling the same establishing shot for each familiar location, often zooming into a particular window behind which we will find the familiar characters.

CHAPTER 2

Living in Bondage: Money and Values

The 1992 Igbo-language film *Living in Bondage* inaugurated the video boom. It also established the first great Nollywood thematic complex—"get rich quick"—and its signature genre, the money ritual film, in which human sacrifice magically produces wealth. The movie was the product of an unstable collaboration among three men, who with symbolic precision represented the basis of the new industry: Kenneth Nnebue, a major player in the "infrastructure of piracy"; Chris Obi-Rapu, an established figure at the NTA dabbling in the informal sector; and Okechukwu Ogunjiofor, NTA-trained but living the SAP crisis. The film itself was a business experiment if not a get-rich-quick scheme, but it carries a deeply rooted and serious-minded popular discourse on values, intertwining what would remain fundamental Nollywood themes: economic morality and marriage.

LIVING IN BONDAGE 1

The film opens with Andy Okeke (Kenneth Okonkwo) soliloquizing: "What have I done to deserve this miserable existence?" He has resigned from five jobs because they paid him badly and went into trading, but he has gotten nowhere while his age-mates have Mercedes Benzes and beautiful houses and make large donations at social occasions. He suspects his problem has a spiritual dimension. "My God, did you bring me into this world to suffer? Am I bewitched or is this my destiny?"

His wife (Nnenna Nwabueze), tall and handsome like him and allegorically named Merit, has entered with a tray of food and now kneels to comfort and steady him: "Andy, I've told you this before: no one has bewitched you. God has not said that you won't ever be rich. . . . Every time you torment yourself with negative thoughts about money. . . . Do you know what these people do to make money? Some are money doublers [a well-known scam], some drug pushers. Andy, I've become afraid you might follow your get-rich-quick friends and plunge into evil." He leaps up, indignant. "God forbid that I, Andy Okeke, should soil my hands because of money!" She tells him to be content: peace and happiness are the most important things in life. They smile and kiss; she serves him food, a fundamental symbolic connection between husband and wife, shown here in the form Nollywood has adopted as a standard representation of marital romance: she feeds him with a spoon.

We move from this image of monogamous contentment to the turbulent polygamous household of Chief Omego (Kanayo O. Kanayo). This subplot may owe something to Chief Fuji and his three wives from Amaka Igwe's serial *Checkmate*, a source of comedy so popular it was spun off into its own serial, *The Fuji House of Commotion*. Chief Omego is conspiring to have sex with his pretty young third wife when it is by right the turn of the second. The enraged second wife catches the third trysting with Chief Omego in the guest bedroom. Attracted by the resulting noise, the first wife shows up too. The room is full of vehement unhappy people. When the husband threatens to beat all of them for disrespecting his authority, the eldest finds herself too disgusted to play her role as patient peacemaker. The scene ends with the kind of physical comedy on a stock domestic situation perfected by the Yoruba traveling theater: the jealous rivals wrestle on the bed while Omego struggles futilely to separate them.

On the street, by chance Andy is recognized by his old school friend Paul (Okechukwu Ogunjiofor), who now drives a Mercedes and takes him to a fancy restaurant. Andy complains about his money problems. Paul tells him money is indeed "the Emperor of the World. Whoever does not have it, is as good as dead." Paul promises to make Andy rich: "I'll show you how to make money and how to spend it, but, you must promise me that you must be strong-hearted. To become rich, you must be ready for very strong things."

Andy comes home ebullient. An acquaintance comes to their door, proposing a dubious business deal: if Andy will put money down on a shipping container full of engines and electronics that has just arrived from overseas, he is promised 700 percent profit. As the man leaves, a relative of Andy's known only as "Aunty" (Chizoba Bosah) crosses his path; she and Merit trade descriptions of the visitor as a demonic figure with shining "torchlight eyes" and a wagging tongue. Merit appeals to Aunty to help her dissuade Andy from the deal, explaining that she has already given Andy everything in her savings account as well as the last of the money her parents had given them. She worries because Andy is always thinking of his friends with their cars. (Andy breaks in restlessly to name the brands of Paul's vehicles.)

Aunty is glad to take up the task of giving Andy advice. She addresses Merit as "my wife," since according to Igbo custom their lineage, not Andy alone, would have paid Merit's bride price. The term is also clearly meant as an endearment and an expression of solidarity. From a society acutely aware of even slight gradations of seniority, she speaks with the authority of an elder though she is not at all old. Sure of her values and judgments, she is peremptory and stern, dominating the conversation with ironic jabs. "Andy, be quiet! . . . Look at the beautiful wife you have. Rather than settle down and live a good life, you're cataloging those who have Pathfinders and Mercedes. . . . She's giving you all she had for the sake of peace, you are not happy. Do you want to be like Chief Omego?" "God forbid!" he exclaims. "Then better listen to your wife." Andy argues that he wants money so he can buy Merit a car, repaying her for everything she has done for him. Merit counters that there should be no talk of repayment between husband and wife; if she wanted a car, she could have bought one with her own money rather than giving it to him. She repeats her central theme: "All I desire is your happiness, that we live in peace."

The discussion of values and proper behavior in this scene is rooted in the deepest levels of African culture. A cogent exposition of values is always prized, and the searching application of values to an individual and his situation is the true measure of intelligence and wisdom. The universal premise of African aesthetics is that stories should teach something, have a moral, a purpose.[1] This is bedrock, and much of Nollywood is built on it.

The scene develops a strong ideal of marriage. In Igbo society, women have always had a considerable degree of economic independence, gardening and trading for themselves. The strong-willed individualism this independence sponsors perhaps appears in the quarreling women of Chief Omego's household, shorn of its economic basis and rationale in a rural agricultural society, shorn in fact of everything except bitter sexual jealousy. Merit blends her money with her husband's in an economy of love but repeatedly reminds him of the money of her own that she brings to the relationship, both through her job and through her family's donations to the young couple. She is a full partner in every way, in spite of her unfailingly modest demeanor, and it is already clear she has the stronger personality. Contrasting with Chief Omego's polygamous family, this is a companionate marriage of the kind Christian missionaries preached, as against the welter of marital forms they found in Africa.

Merit is the ideal Christian wife, submissive but an indispensable spiritual as well as material helpmeet. The connection with specifically Christian values is left implicit, however; she is also the perfect wife in an Igbo cultural frame of reference, and the Igbo idioms captured by the subtitles sometimes highlight this—later her family will call her "a prize eagle of a woman." The cultural origins of her ideal qualities are thoroughly blended: she embodies them, so they become indistinguishable.

Andy has left his village to come to the city, measuring himself against the city and facing its temptations as he seeks to find his place in life (Okome 2003), but he is still surrounded by his family, which is to say his village society, held to account by it, judged by its standards, enmeshed in its texture, navigating by its landmarks. He brings the conversation back to Chief Omego, who is evidently from the same village as Andy, Merit, and Aunty. "How can someone use his mother for money medicine? . . . That sort of person deserves to be stoned to death. I, Andy, I can't eat from the same plate with that sort. I can't even get close to him at all. That's my life. But why is it that his elder brother cannot bring him to the King's Palace for trial? There's so many grounds for his trial." Aunty: "How can he, when they all eat and drink together? Who will try who? It's the end of the world. Things have fallen apart."

The forces of darkness have overrun the land. The evil that is in the city is also in the village, represented by Chief Omego, who maintains a social presence in both places—a normal practice. Andy looks to the senior male of Omego's lineage and the king's palace for justice, but they have been enveloped in the social network of corruption. We shall see that there is still sturdy legitimacy in the most basic institutions of village society—in fact we have been hearing that sturdy legitimacy in this conversation. It is embattled but not defeated. Central as the opposition of village and city is to *Living in Bondage*, then, that opposition is not entirely clear. The film does not polarize "tradition" and "modernity," either, any more than it tries to distinguish Merit's Christian virtues from her Igbo cultural ones: she is the pride of her village relatives and works in a Lagos office at an electric typewriter. Modernity in Africa, as Birgit Meyer writes, "is not represented as an option to reject or adopt, but as a context of life in the big city. The problem rather is how to handle modernity's promises and temptations" (2002b, 75).[2]

What is polarized is good and evil, good and bad persons, legitimate ways to make money and illegitimate ones. As we have already seen, Andy is surrounded by people who have no trouble making these distinctions and pointing them out to him, and Andy himself is vociferous in denouncing wickedness in general and, in particular, Chief Omego. Polarization does not mean social segregation. The film suggests the density and ambiguity of social relations (and perhaps also strains plausibility as it strives for efficiency in dramatic organization) by making Merit already acquainted with three of the wicked characters Andy is about to meet.

Everything turns, then, as the film's opening sequences clearly indicate, on Andy's character, his clarity of perception and strength of personality, his restless ambition, envy, and susceptibility to temptation. In the next scene, when tempted and tested, he promptly fails. Paul takes him to the birthday party of Ichie Million (Francis Agu) to meet the members of a "millionaire's club," "the grandees of the land." By later standards the display of luxury in this scene is modest, but we get the essentials of "enjoying," a Nigerian term that encompasses living the good life. The host tends bar and puts on music so his guests can dance. (Hyginus Ekwuazi points out the music is the "national anthem" of this sort of people, Oliver de Coque's "*Ana Enwe Obodo Enwe*," "we are the owners of the world" (2000, 139).) As in the earlier restaurant scene with Paul and Andy, the camera makes the eating of chicken as palpable as possible, trying to let the audience share in the pleasure. Andy exclaims when Paul points out Chief Omego and his third wife but looks deeply impressed when told Chief Omego imports eight shipping containers of car parts every week. Andy declares that he wants in. He asks after Ego (Ngozi Nwosu), the woman accompanying Paul's girlfriend Caro (Ngozi Nwaneto), and Paul promises to give her to him, saying, in English, "I have power over women."

Merit undergoes parallel temptations. She is, coincidentally, the secretary of the same Ichie Million who hosted the party. He plies her with compliments and gifts. Merit visits Paul's girlfriend Caro at her boutique to complain that Andy has given all their money to the dubious man offering the container deal, in spite of her warnings, and has lost it all. She reveals that Chief Omego is also trying to seduce her. Still she loves Andy. Caro is the spokesperson for marital and economic ideologies opposite to Merit's: "Don't you know there's nothing binding between us and men? As a friend, I tell you, your boss, gird him to yourself. Give him what he wants and get his money. And Chief Omego whom they said used his mother for money medicine, if his money is blood money, what's your business? Were you there with him? If he gives you money, it becomes genuine money in your hand." Once Caro reveals her true nature Merit breaks with her, as she quits her job when her boss chases her around the office and humiliates Chief Omego when he accosts her.

Andy visits Paul after the party. Paul carefully tests his resolve: Is Andy willing to do anything for money? Would he carry drugs through the airport? Andy declares he would do anything. Caro shows up with her friend Ego.

"Ego" means "money" in Igbo, and Andy tells her he likes her name. Her name and these sequences, intercut with Merit's distress over her husband's absence, interlock the themes of money and marital relations. Andy and Ego have a quick discussion about whether he can meet her needs for money; they dance; they wake together on Paul's sofa. Afterwards, Caro and Ego are jubilant. They are loud, brazen, incarnating the mercenary and the profane. Ego vows, "He is my prisoner. . . . I'll put Andy's account in the red. I, Ego, I eat money."

Finally, Paul's "millionaire's club" is revealed to be a secret cult practicing black magic. The cult members, bare-chested men with black wrappers tied around their waists, enter walking backwards to eerie electronic music. Andy is led in wearing a candidate's white wrapper. The Initiator has him swear secrecy and eternal loyalty "in the name of our Lord Lucifer." The Chief Priest (Daniel Oluigbo) tells Andy he will now become a full member of their cult and all their secrets will be revealed to him. The Initiator asks him, "Now, tell us, whom do you love most in this world?" Andy: "It's my wife." Chief Priest: "Tomorrow, you shall bring her here for the last sacrifice."

Andy turns to Paul in shock, but Paul tells him to shut up. Didn't he say he wanted to be rich at all costs? Andy plaintively asks to be counted out, but the Chief Priest tells him it is too late. "What will you get out of this life if you don't have money?" The cultists speak in turn to say they have all sacrificed loved ones. Ichie Million: "I did it. I used my child. Today, I ride V-Boot, ride Pathfinder." Chief Omego: "I used my dear mother, today I'm money myself."

MONEY RITUALS

A body of recent anthropological literature demonstrates that witchcraft is not a primitive, residual element in African life but is integral to African understandings of modernity and Africa's insertion into the world capitalist economy (seminal texts are Comaroff and Comaroff 1993 and Geschiere 1997). That a person can, through occult means, sacrifice or devour another and thereby gain power is a basic element in witchcraft discourses. Admission into a coven or cult often depends on making such a sacrifice. Belief in "money rituals" of the kind Paul's cult practices, in which a human sacrifice (often of a child) produces a cascade of cash, is widespread in West Africa. In a 1982 article about how the "petro-naira" of the Nigerian oil boom was interpreted in the popular imagination, Karen Barber discusses the Yoruba traveling theater's use of the money ritual to figure the mysterious, unearned wealth that was transforming Nigerian society. In Yoruba experience there had been a direct connection between wealth and visible agricultural labor, but the oil boom created a new dominant center of capital creation: the triangular relationship among government officials who gave out contracts and licenses and generally controlled the levers of the economy; the contractors angling for these things; and the middlemen who made connections between the two other groups. Fierce competition ensured that bribery and the formation of cliques and cartels were basic features of the system.

> In this situation there is no hard-and-fast distinction between legitimate and illegitimate wealth. Since the "normal" running of the economy requires faked accounts and clandestine deals, the line between standard procedures and embezzlement, fraud, and corruption is blurred. None of the wealth is produced by labour; all of it is acquired from the petro-naira boom by a variety of methods, none fully admissible but all in varying degrees condoned by the elite. (Barber 1982, 436)

Meanwhile, the decline of agriculture and a drift toward the cities amid stark extremes of impoverishment and the conspicuous accumulation of wealth in a few hands led to armed robbery on an entirely new scale.

> These two dominant themes—the armed robbers and the gigantic, baseless fortunes—seem to have coalesced in a popular image which appears constantly in Yoruba drama, namely: the child-stealer who uses his victims to conjure up boundless riches. It is widely believed that there are people who abduct children—in one version, by turning them into goats—confine them in a secret room, make medicine from their blood, and then by uttering the right incantations, cause unlimited quantities of naira to shower down into a calabash placed on the child's head. This image captures the violent and mysterious aspects of the new wealth . . . (Barber 1982, 438; cf. Watts 1994)

Witchcraft beliefs often stipulate that sacrificial victims must come from the sorcerer's kin (Bastian 1993). *Living in Bondage* makes a crucial shift from kin affiliation to the affective: Andy is told to sacrifice not a member of his lineage but the person whom he loves the most. The shift allows the socially symbolic figure of the money ritual to be spliced into the idiom of domestic drama as developed in television serials, which dwells on extreme emotional situations within the nuclear (or slightly extended) family and, especially, within marriages based on love. Larkin among others has observed that Nigerian videos register the social, economic, and political strains and tensions of the era by injecting them into the context of the family (Larkin 2008, chapter 6).

The money ritual became the hallmark of Nollywood, repeated in many films and almost always mentioned immediately in public discussions of the new video film phenomenon. (Rituals continue to figure prominently in commentary on Nollywood, even though Nollywood now only occasionally makes films about them.[3]) The sensation *Living in Bondage* caused was due partly to the fact that it represented something that was widely rumored to be happening but naturally occurred in secret where it could not be seen or proved to be true. This was one of the kinds of stories people told that embodied the wickedness that seemed to be washing over the country. Stories about money rituals were and are reported in newspapers and figure in popular novels and the Yoruba traveling theater repertoire, but they would not be allowed into television serials like *Checkmate* or *Ripples* or into celluloid filmmaking, which carried (according to the official Film Policy promulgated in 1994) the burden of providing positive images of Nigeria. *Living in Bondage* and the video films in general were scandalous—a revelation of the scandalous truth for their popular audience, a scandalous revelation of dark superstitions, retrograde mentalities, and shameful secrets for the official custodians of the Nigerian national image.

Andy objects, "Please, I go to church, o! If I do this, I will go to hell." The Chief Priest replies with specious theological argument: "The church tells us, falsely, that there is hell fire. The Holy Bible proclaims God's kindness. Let me ask you, would you condemn your beloved to hell fire? Yes, we will wrong him but he will forgive us." He concludes with another prayer to Lord Lucifer. This is very like Christopher Marlowe's *Dr. Faustus*; a black mass inverting Christian ritual, it does not sound or look indigenously African, in spite of some African elements like the bare chests and wrappers. The theology and the liturgical cadences of sermon and prayer are continuous with the visual decor: candles on the altar, the cult members standing in rigid isolation.[4]

Assimilating all indigenous African spiritual beliefs, forms, and practices to the works of the devil—the Christian Satan—is an ideological move often made by foreign missionaries in Africa and by African Christians. Everything, including magical practices like money rituals, is seen as part of one grand Satanic conspiracy.[5]

Filmmakers also have prudential reasons to adopt this strategy for representing secret cults. As Ogunjiofor and several other filmmakers have pointed out to me, representing cults creates a double danger. The public will suspect the filmmakers must themselves be cult members, else how could they know how to represent things that are by their nature closely guarded secrets? And actual cult members may feel that their secrets are being betrayed and retaliate. Moreover, a general anxiety or even terror may fill the set when occult scenes are being filmed, for fear that the occult forces might somehow affect those representing them. Obi-Rapu had to lay on hands and invoke the name of Jesus to get some of his actors back to work on this scene.[6] Obi-Rapu, Ogunjiofor, and the actor BobManuel Udokwu (who played a cultist) say that Nnebue feared for his life and took refuge in his car.

At home, Andy is lost in thought, flashing back to a romantic scene with Merit in a garden. That night, he picks up a prostitute named Tina (Rita Nzelu). In Merit's place she is brought, drugged or entranced, into the cult chamber, but she calls on the blood of Jesus and the Chief Priest reacts as if he has been struck. Paul reveals the deception and the Chief Priest orders that Andy be prepared for sacrifice. Andy gets Paul to help him beg for mercy. Andy is told he will die if he does not bring his wife to the next meeting. Tina tells her roommate her story. "That name Jesus, that's the name I shall worship." She throws her things together, resolved to go back to her parents' house.

Merit arrives home from her parents' house, bearing money from them and her brother. "We'll start life afresh," Andy says, but then remembers the threat against his life and looks stricken. He coaxes Merit out of the house in spite of her fearful premonitions. She enters the cult chamber dressed all in white, with a veil like a nun's wimple. She is laid on the altar and the Initiator takes blood from her arm with a hypodermic needle, squirting the blood into two calabashes. A cock crows as the Chief Priest raises the calabashes like a chalice and passes them around. The cultists drink eagerly. Andy grimaces as he drinks.

Aunty comes to Merit as she lies in a hospital bed, an IV in her arm. Merit exclaims against Andy for having killed her. "If there's reincarnation, I would want to come back with all the love I have for my fellow human being, but if there's not let your Kingdom be my reward, O God." And so she dies.

The syncretic overlaying of cultural forms in these last two scenes is remarkable, though the film does not seem to mean to call attention to contradictions. With her last breath, Merit is virtuous in both the Igbo system of religious beliefs, in which she would expect reincarnation, and the Christian one, in which she would not. This religious ambiguity is present from the beginning of the film. Ekwuazi has suggested that in his opening soliloquy, Andy is addressing his "chi"—his personal god or spirit, who is, or shapes or controls, his destiny (2000, 144–45).[7] But we have seen the power of calling on Jesus, and the dramatic structure surrounding Andy from the beginning is a psychomachia—a

Christian form in which a central character is surrounded by figures exemplifying virtues and vices, amongst which he must choose.[8]

The calabash from which Merit's blood is drunk is closely associated with money rituals—an indigenous element. The hypodermic needle with which the blood is drawn could not have been better chosen to illustrate the theme of "the modernity of witchcraft" (the title of Peter Geschiere's book) that at just this time, across the Atlantic, was becoming a hot topic in Africanist anthropology.

CONSEQUENCES

Andy's new mansion gleams in an establishing shot. Aunty enters the gold sitting room. "So it's true." She delivers her message: God saw what Andy thought he was doing in secret. They know he killed Merit.

In the village, Andy's father (Benjamin Nwosu) comes out of the family house, irritably complaining about the bleating goats. Andy's new chauffeur-driven Mercedes Benz makes its way down a dirt road, Andy emerging with an attaché case and wearing a *baban riga*—a voluminous robe of embroidered cloth, the dress of "big men."[9] The camera wanders to the jumbled cooking area behind the house, finding Andy's mother (Grace Ayozie) grieving over a framed photograph of Merit. Out front, Andy's father reprimands him for not writing and responds angrily when Andy announces his new marriage, warning him not to bring shame to their house, whose character has always been unimpeachable. It is too soon after Merit's death. The family mourns Merit—Andy's mother has joined them, weeping and extolling her virtues. They will not be part of his new marriage. Andy wants to take his sister to Lagos with him so she can get better schooling and leave behind her village ways, but both she and their parents refuse the prospect of the devouring city, whatever the supposed opportunities and advantages found there. "You want to take someone else to Lagos. Where is Merit whom you went with?" When Andy tries to give them money, his father refuses it, and Andy beats a retreat to his Mercedes.

Just as the camera does not aim at showing us a rural idyll, Andy's father's rapid, unbroken flow of irritability does not encourage us to sentimentalize him. But this scene powerfully conveys the dignity, deep emotion, and unshakeable principles of the family. They cannot be fooled or bought. Their response is carefully calibrated: while they do not disinherit Andy, they will not bring his new wife into the family.

A display of Igbo tradition can, however, be bought or rented. A cultural troupe sings and dances to the accompaniment of percussion and flute. The cultists and their women, guests at Andy's traditional wedding to Ego, make their entrances through this spectacle. Her father rises behind a table packed with bottled drinks to present kola nut to the guests, making the expected speech. Chief Omego plays the role Andy's father refuses to play.

At the reception afterward, Andy and Paul step outside. Paul says, "You see you've forgotten your wife now. Money is the emperor of this world," but Andy blinks as Merit's ghost appears to him. She reappears as they discuss increasing the number of containers he imports, and when she calls to him, he collapses. Pandemonium breaks out as he is carried inside.

So ends part 1.

INTERMISSION

Living in Bondage 1 caused an immediate sensation when it came out in late 1992, its reputation spreading like wildfire and entirely by word of mouth—there was no advertising, no publicity, no grand launching. The sensation was partly because it was the first movie in Igbo (apart from the early celluloid film *Amadi* (1975), which made very little impression).[10] Some Igbo television dramas and serials were made in Enugu, and comic sketches by Mike Orihedimma circulated on videocassette in Onitsha, but in spite of their immense economic and cultural vitality, until this moment the Igbos had had little comparable to what the Yoruba traveling theater artists had produced on stage and screen. The Igbo masquerading tradition had not evolved into a modern theatrical form. If *Living in Bondage*'s themes were not exactly reason for ethnic pride, they were central to this moment in Igbo society and were the occasion for self-recognition and intense debate.

The themes were of national interest too, and the film reached far beyond the Igbo community. A version subtitled in English was released in 1993. The actor Sam Dede recalls walking the streets of Port Harcourt—not an Igbo city—and hearing the soundtrack of the movie wafting from houses on all sides. The film's astonishing popularity was due to its timeliness—several mutually reinforcing kinds of timeliness, some of which have already been touched upon. It was a novel form of entertainment, an improvement on what television was providing, and it gave people something to watch and talk about as they spent their evenings confined to their homes, afraid to go out.

Above all, it was the story of *Living in Bondage* that was electrifying, a kind of story that swirled through popular consciousness as rumor and now surfaced in the new medium. As a piece of filmmaking it might be judged in different ways—though better than Nigerian television, those coming to it with the standards of international cinema might find it slow and sometimes wooden—but it had the power of myth, independent of the vehicle. In its reception, it crackled with strong currents of energy.

THE COLLABORATION

Just before they were to start shooting the second part of *Living in Bondage*, the collaboration between Nnebue, Ogunjiofor, and Obi-Rapu blew up—the first instance of the turbulent relationships that have characterized Nollywood, the sharp dealing and chronic tensions between marketers and the creative side of the industry. According to Ogunjiofor, his deal with Nnebue was that he was to be paid for his expenses (he collected ₦3,000, worth around $200, for his months of work) and was to get half the profits once the film was released. But when he asked to see the books to learn what his share would be, Nnebue refused, and Ogunjiofor quit in anger. He had not asked for a written contract, so he had no recourse. Obi-Rapu had been paid ₦10,000 for the month he spent shooting the film and was also expecting a cut of the profits, which he didn't get; he too left in disgust.

Nnebue told me there were no profits because the film had almost immediately been pirated, most of the pirating done by the distributors to whom he had entrusted the film. He reaped nothing except praise and encouragement, he said, but learned his lesson and prepared for the release of the second part by increasing his duplicating capacity and opening his own distribution outlets in Onitsha, Aba, Kano, Jos, and other major cities so he could flood the market with copies all at once, before the pirates had a chance to catch up with demand. He says he sold over 200,000 copies of the second part in the first week of its release and made a lot of money. He was secretive about how much duplicating machinery he had and where it was located. At an officially sponsored workshop on the film industry in Kaduna in 1997, members of the audience shouted at Nnebue in frustration as he stood at the front of the room refusing to say anything about his business—his years in the rough and tumble of Nigerian informal markets had led to an ingrained habit of suspicious silence about business matters, which defeated the policy purposes of the occasion.

Obi-Rapu and others do not believe the piracy story, since after part 1 was released Nnebue had the money to expand his business, to release the second part with an unprecedented publicity campaign including billboards and television spots, to move to fancier offices, and generally to be "living large."

Ngozi Nwosu (who played Ego) and Kanayo O. Kanayo (Chief Omego) also left the production before the second part was shot. Kanayo says he did not leave in anger but simply because he realized he could make much more money elsewhere. Nnebue paid a pittance, which the actors took out of enthusiasm for the novel project and because the business was untried. The stars got ₦500 ($40) or ₦1,000, according to Kanayo (BobManuel Udokwu says it was not quite so bad), the neophytes as little as a tenth of that, but everyone was happy—until they got a sense of how much money the new art form could generate and of how crucial the role of stars would be in selling films. Actors in television and the Yoruba traveling theater were badly paid even when beloved, and their social status was low. Nollywood's new generation of stars brought a new prestige to the profession.

Living in Bondage was like a seed pod: when it burst open it inseminated a whole industry. Ogunjiofor, Obi-Rapu, and Kanayo immediately made another film with a new sponsor, *Circle of Doom* (1993), which was released before the second part of *Living in Bondage*. Ogunjiofor produced two other important early films, *Nneka the Pretty Serpent* (1994, part 2 in 1995) and *Brotherhood of Darkness* (1996). Obi-Rapu (still working under the pseudonym Vic Mordi) shot *Taboo* 1 (1993) and *Evil Passion* (1993). Kanayo established himself as one of the biggest stars in the new industry, and BobManuel Udokwu also appeared to have an indispensable face: by 1995, three years later, he had been in seventy films (Husseini 2010, 49). Nkem Owoh, who did the English subtitles for *Living in Bondage*, would become Nollywood's greatest comic actor. Cast members Daniel Oluigbo, Francis Agu, Sydney Diala, and Nnenna Nwabueze all started production companies and made films. Almost everyone involved in the production was young, generally around thirty, most of them already successful but still near the beginnings of their careers. Sometimes the flush of success did not continue for long. Obi-Rapu retired from the NTA in 1995, won the US visa lottery, and moved to Minnesota. Ogunjiofor faded out of the industry after 1996. Nnenna Nwabueze married a rich man who insisted she stop acting. Others did not survive the transition to English-language filmmaking after 1994 and the sharp increase in competition as the industry expanded. But the initial efflorescence had created a whole new landscape.

The collaboration between Ogunjiofor, Nnebue, and Obi-Rapu was contentious, their break was bitter, and they give conflicting accounts about the division of labor among them—unsurprising, given the momentous importance of *Living in Bondage* in historical retrospect and the spontaneous quality of events as they unfolded. Nothing was formalized in writing. All three men seem to have come independently to the idea of making a film on video. Ogunjiofor, as an unemployed graduate of the NTA Television College, was used to video cameras and understood that celluloid filmmaking was far out of his reach.

Obi-Rapu had wanted to make movies since working on Ola Balogun's celluloid film *Muzik Man* in 1976, and he used ENG video cameras every day. In the 1980s he had gone to Sierra Leone as director of *New Masquerade* and learned the show was being recorded in the Sierra Leonean embassy in Lagos and flown to President Siaka Stevens, a fan, cassettes then trickling down through the elite. Obi-Rapu also noticed NTA employees making money on the side by dubbing cassettes of the Latin American telenovelas that had become a staple of television broadcasting. He says he urged Nnebue to think big about the potential of video filmmaking. Nnebue was already producing Yoruba films on video and selling them as cassettes, but these were cheap, rudimentary productions, a static camera filming actors from the Yoruba traveling theater performing plays from their repertoire and improvising around stock situations. He made more than twenty such films before *Living in Bondage*. The first was shot in a couple of hours, as Nnebue told me; in another case, he banged out two such films in a single day.

Nnebue had left school after six years of primary education and was apprenticed to his brother, who made handbags. He started trading in Onitsha Market before getting into electronics and relocating to Idumota, the central market for electronics in Lagos, which would become the center of the video film marketing system. Those who have worked with him acknowledge his powerful intelligence and ability to learn quickly, as well as his exceptional shrewdness as a businessman. On film sets, he was always watching and learning; he told me that when shooting the Yoruba films he already "directed my directors." After *Living in Bondage* he wrote and directed *Dirty Deal* (1993). There is no question that Nnebue deserves full credit for realizing the potential of the market for Nigerian films on videocassette. He was already a major marketer of cassettes of American, Chinese, and Indian films and dominated Nollywood in its first years, working on a scale no one else could match. Other marketers tried to avoid releasing their films the same week Nnebue released his.

Living in Bondage began as Ogunjiofor's project. He calculated he needed ₦150,000 (about $12,000) to make a film on video and set about trying—unsuccessfully—to raise that amount by street hawking when all else failed. When he met Nnebue, he asked for a Super-VHS camera (which Nnebue flew to Japan to buy) and the ₦150,000. This turned out to be what it took to make the film, not including the costs to reproduce and market it. Ogunjiofor claims that the film's story was his—he brought it to Nnebue, and it was the story of his own life as a young man trying to make his way, faced with choices about what path to take. It was inspired by his encounter with the Reformed Ogboni

Society when he filmed their public celebration at the National Stadium (see the preface) and discerned secret meanings behind the display. Later, a member of the cult tried to recruit him; the things Ogunjiofor says when he is playing the part of Paul are the things that were said to him. "The story of *Living in Bondage* is the story of what I passed through while I was trying to become somebody, how I narrowly escaped the hands of this occult group. It's my story. It's what I have seen . . ." He worked with Nnebue to produce the story outline (for both parts, not just part 1), which was written in English. Neither they nor any of the cast were used to reading and writing Igbo. He says the dialogue was developed through a month of rehearsals Ogunjiofor led, with the actors improvising on the basis of the story outline and Ogunjiofor coaching them in Igbo idioms and proverbs. He had thought of directing as well as producing and acting in the film but realized that it would be too much. Obi-Rapu, who had been his teacher, was invited in.

Nnebue took credit for both the story and the screenplay of *Living in Bondage*, making the claim prominently in the film itself and on the cassette jacket. In 1997 and again in 2002 he told me that the story of *Living in Bondage* came to him one evening; he picked up a pen and stayed up all night writing in a fit of inspiration until the scenario was done, surprised when his house help arrived in the morning and disturbed him. In an interview with the journalist Fred Iwenjora, Nnebue said, "When I did the scripting, I was serious. I didn't want any improvising. I put everything down and made sure that it was followed to the letter. That is not to say the actors didn't add their own nuances and colour to the script to make it current" (Iwenjora 2001). BobManuel Udokwu agrees that there was a full shooting script; he and Kanayo both told me they have copies in their houses, though neither was sure exactly where.

Obi-Rapu, however, denies that a proper full script existed—nothing that could be used, for instance, to gauge in advance the length of the film or guide the editing. He says he imposed his own sense of storytelling on the material, completed the casting, and guided the actors through further rehearsals, sometimes encouraging them to improvise scenes on camera and developing the dialogue from one take to the next. It is easy to imagine Obi-Rapu taking over. He is a tall, commanding figure, with a booming bass voice. He had seen combat as an officer in the Biafran Army. He was older than anyone else, much better paid, and, as the top director in the prestigious NTA hierarchy, infinitely senior in professional terms. Obi-Rapu was replaced as director of part 2 by Chika Onukwafor, another senior NTA staff director who had to use a pseudonym (Christian Onu). The actors tried to negotiate a better deal for themselves with the formidably shrewd Nnebue.

When I asked Nnebue where the idea for the story of *Living in Bondage* had come from, he said from conversations around him, the newspapers, and the radio. Ogunjiofor is even more categorical in rooting the story in real life. Because of my training as an historian of cultural forms, I believe works of art come in large part out of other works of art, and I go around trying to establish such filiations. But in Nigeria I am often met with responses like Ogunjiofor and Nnebue's, dismissing my line of questioning and insisting that their stories come straight out of social reality. (Meyer 2003a notices the same reaction from Ghanaian audiences.) "Based on a true story" is a frequent notification at the beginning or end of Nollywood films. Ogunjiofor went on to say that *Circle of Doom* was based on the experiences of a friend and that his other films, and Nollywood films in general, were also based on true stories, "embellished to make them entertainment," with a "surplus to teach other lessons." Nollywood has professionalized itself, creating a system of guilds and a habit of casting the same faces over and over that make it difficult for aspirants to break in. But the industry remains open to stories from the outside, which stream in unsolicited. As the writer and producer Chidi Nwokeabi told me, people often offer their stories or even completed scripts to producers for free; all the compensation they look for is the thrill of seeing their story on screen. Sometimes this means the thrill of authorship, their name in the credits; sometimes it just means sharing their experiences with the public. The sense that Nollywood tells true stories, and that personal experiences may find expression through the film industry, are powerful elements in Nollywood's popularity.

However, I notice that Andy's situation is actually quite different than Ogunjiofor's was. Andy has a comfortable flat, a perfect wife, and voluntarily resigned from five jobs. Personal ambition and envy motivate him—psychological and spiritual issues, character flaws, exacerbated by the conspicuous consumption he sees around him. Ogunjiofor's own story is centrally about the crisis of the Nigerian structural adjustment program: educated but unable to find any job at all, he admits he looked weather-beaten and hungry from his hawking in the streets when he appeared at the National Theatre, a thoroughly dislocated individual. A documentary or documentary-like film of his story would be rawer, with more exterior scenes, with national institutions in view, and, generally, with contemporary history more directly visible.

Nollywood's characteristic ideological and generic framings are fully evident in this transformation of Ogunjiofor's personal story into *Living in Bondage*. Nothing is more fundamental to Nollywood than understanding situations in moral terms. This tends to occlude other kinds of understanding, though it also exerts a constant pressure to look behind social appearances.

LIVING IN BONDAGE 2

Part 2 begins with Caro bringing Andy home from the hospital, where he has been for a week after his collapse at the wedding reception. Caro explains that Ego has left, embarrassed by this debacle and having heard rumors that Andy killed Merit. She ran off with ₦2 million of his money. Caro has in tow her friend Chinyere (Jennifer Okere)—"Chi"—and sets her up to comfort Andy. Chi appears demure and full of domestic virtues and immediately moves into the role of Andy's new wife.

In the village, a delegation of Merit's male relatives comes to Andy's parents' house. Social conventions are carefully observed, but their purpose is stern: they think Andy's remarriage before the end of the three-month mourning period for Merit is an abomination, and it makes them suspect he knows something about her death. They want Andy to return to explain Merit's death to them. It is understood that he will be asked to swear an oath as to his innocence—swear on an *ofor*, a sacred staff that will kill him if he lies, a standard juridical instrument in Igbo villages. Andy's father defends him and points

FIGURE 3. *Living in Bondage.* The jacket of part 1 displays Andy living the high life with his women and cultist friends on the front; the back of part 2 shows Andy as a mad beggar, Merit's ghost, and the born-again former prostitute Tina.

out how deeply the family mourns the sterling Merit. His wife sits by weeping. They agree to send for Andy. Like Andy's visit to his parents in part 1, this is a scene of quiet dignity. The speeches are what custom requires, but they are full of meaning and strong feelings.

In Andy's Lagos mansion, Chi dresses down for housekeeping and dresses up for an intimate meal she's cooked for her man. This culminating moment of domestic romance is disrupted by a blast of wind, a spiritual wind that blows a painting off the wall and the water out of the kettle on the stove, making the guilty couple cower and flee.

Incidental scenes in Chief Omego's house and Ichie Million's office develop the theme of gender relations. Chi comes to visit Caro in her boutique, as Merit had done in part 1. Chi and Caro are both jubilant about what they are getting out of their men. Chi is moving in with Andy, and Paul[11] has just given Caro a car—"It's now I know I've come to Lagos," she says triumphantly. Chi drops her demure mask for the occasion. When Caro asks how she can thank Paul, Chi is explicit: "You're asking? What other weapon do you have? There's only one gun, and one bullet inside. Once you miss that bullet, you're on your way out of Lagos to the backwoods. . . . Posture—variation, that is the key: you give him right, then left, then bang in the middle."

Andy, wearing his hangdog look, goes to the cult's Chief Priest for pastoral counseling about Merit's apparitions. The Chief Priest tells him not to worry: Merit was only a woman; he can have any woman he wants; his wealth is infinite. Andy picks up a girl and takes her to a luxurious hotel. After sex Andy notices her reflection does not appear in the mirror—a sign she is a spirit. He flees down the stairs in terror and collapses in the lobby, where a press photographer snaps his picture. Chi is furious to find her husband's sex scandal on the front page of the paper and berates him as he spins lies. Merit's three relatives from the village arrive into this unhappiness, unhappy themselves that Andy did not show up to justify himself to them. His behavior forces them to suspect him. Andy insults the eldest, wrestles with Merit's brother, and throws them out of his house.

The cult arranges for Andy to be awarded a chieftaincy title. This ceremony resembles Andy's traditional wedding to Ego in part 1: a full-scale cultural display with extended performances by a dance troupe and formal speeches. The master of ceremonies recites Andy's large donations to the village. Andy and others of his party "spray" the dancers, dealing out banknotes over their heads in a sign of approval, until the ground is littered with money. This is all about money: it is not Andy's own community that is awarding the title—it could not overlook the scandals around him—but another one that sees him as a source of cash. As the king presents him with the red cap and eagle feather of a chief, Merit's ghost appears to Andy again, and again he collapses.

Tina, whom Andy tried to sacrifice in Merit's stead, appears to her former roommates as they sit drinking, Flora regaling them with a raunchy tale of her sexual conquest of an unnamed rich man who will turn out to be Paul. Now Tina is dressed conservatively and announces she has brought them something nice: the word of God. Her sermon on the evils of prostitution seems to fall on stony ground. Her former colleagues laugh uproariously when she leaves.

But the tide is turning. In Andy's mansion, Merit's ghost appears to Chi as she eats alone at a gold table. Chi complains to Caro about her misery, in spite of the opulence of her life. Her speech reverses the earlier triumphant conversation between them; it also recapitulates, in a different key, Tina's sermon. "Caro, it's true that women aspire to marry rich men, but I tell you: those people are suffering deeply inside. Take me as an example. . . . Just get their money, but don't marry them. Caro, you can't even attend the meeting of the women's club, not because you don't want to but because your name will top the agenda." But Caro sticks to her guns: "The days are gone when marriages are for better or for worse. Today's marriage is like Abuja marriage,[12] a matter of convenience." Caro advises Chi to look around her husband's house for money and valuables against the day she will want to leave him.

Merit's ghost keeps reappearing, despite a cult ritual that covers Andy in a sacrificial animal's blood. Andy fires a pistol at it, also without effect. In despair, Andy gets out of bed and prepares to hang himself from the ceiling fan. "So this is the end of a strong man! God, please keep my soul in safe repose." Chi, who has been feigning sleep, cracks open an eye and murmurs, "Amen." Outraged that she would watch him die like this, he takes the noose from his neck and falls to beating her as she cries out hysterically—a grim comedy of psychological and spiritual degradation.

The cult meets again to hear the Cult Mother address Andy. Possessed and oracular, she announces that Merit's spirit refuses repose because she was blameless. The only thing Andy can do is sacrifice his two eyes and his genitals. Andy—stricken, naturally—demands to know why he alone faces such a fate. Is not death preferable? He threatens to expose the cult. The Chief Priest turns to assess the threat. "Don't dare trifle with us. This cult has been in existence before even your grandfathers."

Out of resentment, Andy hires thugs to kill Paul. Caro mourns his loss, but mostly mourns the loss of his money. Chi appears at Caro's door dragging a suitcase and a cardboard carton, both stuffed with cash. Chi had remembered

Caro's advice from the other day. "But where would I get solid money from? I remembered that there is a room in the house that Andy allows no one. I've always pondered: What could be in that room? I bade my time, stole the key at night and waited until his departure in the morning, determined. I saw a sculpture holding a woman's breast on its hands. When I saw this, I grew heads, but I managed to hold myself together determined to find out what was in the other room. When I unlocked the door, do you know what I saw inside? Money. If you saw the volume of money. You see this thing here? It's nothing. It's just what I could manage to gather with fear."

The secret room that no one is allowed to enter is a standard element in stories about money rituals. *Living in Bondage* avoids showing the mechanism of wealth creation, instead foregrounding Chi's description. Her experience—a mixture of fear and determination—is not unlike Andy's, and she too is betraying her spouse for wealth. Once again the film brings the issue into focus on the plane of marital relationships.

Chi plans to get visas and tickets for herself and Caro and leave the country. Caro celebrates the strength Chi has finally shown: "I like women who are strong-hearted like myself. No one can withstand Caro. You're the kind of person I like for a friend." In fact Caro is the strongest personality in the film (except, arguably, Merit). The men pride themselves on their willingness to stomach strong things and are organized into a cabal that gives them the means to prey on women—to sacrifice them, to sleep around with them, to marry them in large numbers. But Andy is weak, powerless in the face of his true wife's force, which interrupts his attempts to marry other women and finally requires his emasculation. Women lack solidarity, however. Chief Omego's wives quarrel among themselves while barely questioning his authority, and now Caro unexpectedly turns on her friend when Chi goes out to get the visas: "This is my opportunity. If I travel abroad with Chinyere and all that money, she'll likely turn me into a servant. No, I know what I'll do." Caro is the principle of pure egotism, individual ambition that dissolves all bonds. She poisons Chi's celebratory glass of champagne. Their talk over the wine is the chatter of the damned, false on one side, on the other shot through with the ironies and exhilarated inanities of one caught up in her doom. Off on an errand, Chi clutches her stomach and collapses, vomiting, close-ups of her vomit intercut with close-ups of her dead staring face.

We return to the three prostitutes, Tina's former colleagues. Flora laments the death of Paul, her best customer; like Caro, what grieves her most is her lost investment. Suzy has a revelation, remembering Tina's sermon on prostitution. She wants to retire and go back to the village.

Caro comes out of her boutique looking rushed and furtive, lugging the big suitcase and a bag full of cash. A car hurtles down the deserted street and hits her as she hesitates, reaching back for the bag she has dropped. In close-up, Caro's head bleeds onto the pavement, her eyes staring wide in death like Chi's.

Around a polished boardroom table, a deal is being signed for Andy's company to build a bank headquarters. But when it is Andy's turn to sign, Merit's ghost again interrupts. He tears off his flowing gold-embroidered robe and rushes out. He reappears in a motor park, mad, barefoot, and in shorts, wearing a torn woman's top. Food vendors drive him off. In the following shots he is wearing different bits of women's apparel, as if to ruin all distinctions, or to signal acceptance of his emasculation or identification with his victim. He eats out of the garbage. The born-again prostitute Tina recognizes him as he sits under an overpass amid his trash, wolfing down his food. "Was it not this man who wanted to use me for ritual? Is this the way the world is? So this is the way he has ended up. God, please forgive him." He chases her away, gesticulating.

Andy's mother comes to him with Aunty, calling his name in an ecstasy of grief. He urinates into a can and offers it to her, calling it English wine from Yugoslavia. He drinks it down himself. For the rest of the film there will be no more normal spoken dialogue. A battered van pulls up and Tina and three men pile out, hauling Andy into the vehicle.

Underneath a banner proclaiming "Jesus is Lord," a pastor prays over Andy, who tries to bolt once but then lies inert as the pastor speaks in tongues. Tina sings in a close-up: "Andy Okeke, Andy Okeke, confess all your sins to God, He'll forgive you . . ." and the camera pulls back to reveal the tiny congregation—Andy's mother, Aunty, and the three men who seized him—clapping and picking up the refrain, gathered around Andy as he sits catatonic. This is the "bethel" where Tina worships—just the corner of a room with the banner and the simplest of altars. The flat simplicity of the space recalls the cult scenes, but this simplicity is more radical. As Andy has humbled and humiliated himself through his madness, the means of his salvation are as humble as they can be: the little group of singers, Tina's hand on his forehead, the pastor's incessant prayers. He calls on Andy to confess his sins and Andy slides onto the floor. "It was I who killed Merit." Andy's mother leaves, distraught, trailed by Aunty. The singing continues over his supine body.

Andy's mother comes to Merit's burial plot. This too is as humble as it can be, a rectangle of fresh cinder blocks enclosing dirt marked with a cross. She sings, a singing that is also wailing: "Please, my daughter, spare Andy, please. Look at my face. Merit, you know I love you. Please forgive my son. I know your anger is justified but please, forgive, please." Merit's ghost flickers over her grave, assenting. Tears stream down the mother's face as she continues to sing and plead. The subtitles give out. We are at the heart of melodrama, *melos*, song, heightening emotion past words or action. Two women, mother and wife, are suffering infinitely, brokenhearted, but bonding in and through their pain, across death, to redeem the man who wronged them. Finally, Andy's mother gets up and walks away, having done what she could do.

Andy sings in close-up, released: "God has done it for me / He has done it for me / What no person can do for me / What my mother cannot do for me / God has done it for me." Wasn't it his mother who did it for him? And Merit, and Tina? There is more than one logic to his redemption. The camera pulls out to show him in clean clothes, his eyes focused nowhere, surrounded by the little clapping chorus. So the film ends.

REPRESENTING THE SPIRITUAL

Pentecostalism has swept across southern Nigeria and much of the rest of Africa, the most important religious, social, and cultural movement of the last generation (Marshall 2009; Piot 2010). Ogunjiofor and Obi-Rapu were strong Christians and Nnebue would become one, eventually abandoning the film business for preaching. Within a few years of *Living in Bondage* a genre of video films arose known as "Christian videos," growing out of church drama groups, distributed at least in part through churches, and conceived of as an extension of evangelizing ministry (Oha 2000, 2002; Ogunleye 2003a, 2003b; Okome 2007a; Ukah 2002, 2003, 2005, 2011). Nnebue's company NEK Video Links reissued *Living in Bondage* on VCD (no date) with the label "Bro. Kenneth Nnebue Film Evangelism." Outside of this more or less autonomous sector of the video film industry, many films end with pastors exorcizing evil spirits.

Ghana has not produced a separate genre of Christian videos the way Nigeria did, but Birgit Meyer argues that the Ghanaian video industry as a whole is deeply influenced by Pentecostalite culture, which immediately made major inroads into the spaces opened up by the liberalization of the media environment in the 1980s and 1990s. The register of representation created by the videos, she argues, is a revelation of what is normally or by its very nature unseen. The video camera conveys God's vision, revealing a world of spiritual forces surrounding and interpenetrating the reality we see. Pentecostalism's combat with evil spiritual forces calls attention to them, sponsoring their endless, obsessive representation (Meyer 1998, 1999a, 2002a, 2002b, 2003a, 2003b, 2004, 2005a, 2005b, 2006a, 2006b, 2006c, 2007, 2010a, 2010b).

Living in Bondage conveys this conception of the spiritual dimension in a restrained, simple way. Merit's ghost appears and disappears through elementary double exposures, and the spirit wind blowing through Andy's mansion was clearly created by an ordinary fan. Computer generated imagery would come to Nollywood later, but the modesty of the supernatural phenomena in this film seems to spring from its intentions at least as much as from lack of means or imagination. The strong, even lighting keeps us in a solid world. Andy is given to falling into trances, to abstraction, and to strong imagination, but the camera rests on the planes of his face rather than following him where he goes when he seems absent. Andy's psychology is the film's fundamental subject. As Lindsey Green-Simms argues in her analysis of how the supernatural leaks into the film, Merit's ghost does not appear in order to call attention to an invisible world but to draw Andy's attention (and ours) to his transgressions in this one (2012b, 38).

As became normal in Nollywood, his psychology is explored not by probing his deep emotional interiority but through showing the moral and spiritual choices he makes and the resulting disintegration of his intimate relationships and social position. Nnebue pointed out to me that Merit's apparitions may be seen in two ways, either as projections of Andy's guilt or as a "real" supernatural phenomenon. Nnebue himself seemed to prefer the former interpretation. The spirit wind terrorizes Chi and the ghost appears to Andy's mother as well, but in these cases, too, the women have their own powerful motives for hallucinations. The only other instance where the supernatural is made visible is when Andy picks up the woman who turns out to be a spirit (her nature also revealed through the most basic camera trickery). This incident is parallel to Tina's experience of being picked up by Andy, a symbol of the dangers of the anonymous city and of sexual commerce with strangers, an urban version of the famous folktale of the handsome stranger seen in the market who, when followed home by a smitten young woman, gradually divests himself of his borrowed limbs until he is nothing but a skull.[13] This is a folkloric moment poking through the fabric of the film.

The film's central instance of the occult is, of course, the money magic, but the secret chamber full of cash is only reported on, not seen. What we see and hear about throughout the film is not money appearing out of nowhere but consistent luck in business and the benefits of membership in a clique. Ichie Million still sits behind his desk; the cultists are always talking about importing containers of car parts and electronics. Business goes on, marriages go on, society goes on, and the film remains devoted to this immanent plane of social reality, despite its religious dimension.

"Making a complete break with the past" is a central precept in Pentecostalism for both the born-again individual and for the community of believers, often conceived as an army engaged in spiritual warfare. It is truly a radical agenda and has radically altered African cultures, sweeping away or weakening much of the indigenous heritage. Nollywood is sometimes explicitly allied with Pentecostalism and is almost never explicitly opposed to it. But most fundamentally, Nollywood is imbued with the African values of compromise, inclusion, and negotiation. So *Living in Bondage* is built on clearly Pentecostalite structures—the cult is Satanic, only the pastor can counteract its power, only being born again can redeem Andy and conclude his story—but the film never loses sight of other values and value systems.

Society is where Andy's desires lie. He is not an individual consumer like Caro, who understands that money is the universal solvent, nor is he tempted to take the money and run off to a new life abroad like Chi. Andy cannot be without a spouse, that indispensable element of Igbo adulthood. When the Cult Mother declares he must suffer emasculation, the loss of his ability to reproduce is stressed—implicitly, the end of his lineage—not his loss of sexual pleasure. Two of the three climactic moments in his career that Merit's ghost interrupts are occasions defining his social status within the Igbo traditional framework, his wedding to Ego and the chieftaincy ceremony. The corruption of Igbo society allows him to buy his way into these displays, but they remain his horizon, the markers that matter most to him. He is wrong about a lot of things, of course, but the film does not make us feel he is wrong about this.

FAST MONEY

"Get rich quick" was the first great Nollywood theme. Sacrificing a spouse and everything she signifies for money is the central symbolic and emotional instance in *Living in Bondage*, but subplots take up the theme in various ways and a discourse on money permeates the film. Money is polarized into a good and legitimate kind and a corrosive and wicked "fast money."

Merit stands for the good kind, and again she stands for more than one kind of goodness. She makes money in Lagos at her typewriter, content with her income as an urban wage worker. She also goes home to the village to bring back money from her family. Good money comes from the village and gets squandered (by Andy) in business transactions in the city, but making business investments in Lagos seems in principle to be a good idea. Her brother claims he traveled abroad on business before Andy did. We are not shown righteous agricultural labor or anything like it. What legitimizes the money from home is not its ultimate economic origin but that it is shared in the family, in love. Merit is confident she can go back to her family for more cash because they love her, and she tosses it all into the economy of love that is her marriage with Andy.

Caro and her friends Ego and Chi stand for the bad kind of money, with Caro as theorist. Caro argues money is fungible, abstract, characterless, outside of all social bonds and questions of legitimacy: the blood will come off Chief Omego's money if Merit takes it from him. So conceived, money dissolves any moral or emotional connection between husbands and wives, men and women. There is nothing but calculated, mercenary sex, prostitution in one form or another. The psychological and social damage from selling oneself is masked by absolute egotism and predatory aggression.

Caro's boyfriend Paul articulates two principles as he vets Andy's candidacy. The first, "the way a person pursues money determines how much you get," expresses a ratio between what the world will provide and inner strength of personality and moral orientation. It is a version—a perverted version—of the individualism and personal dynamism for which the Igbo are famous, values springing from an essentially egalitarian agricultural society in which wealth was directly related to work in the fields. These values are expressed symbolically through the *ikenga*, a statue representing a man's personal strength to which he offers sacrifices, and through the concept of *chi*, the personal daemon that is also one's destiny, though of a malleable sort that can be bent by the will: as Achebe writes in *Things Fall Apart*, "When a man says yes, his *chi* says yes also" (1994b, 27).

These values underlie Igbo village democracy—everyone has a *chi*, a piece of the divine spirit within them, and therefore is in principle worthy of respect—and the whole traditional system of social status and prestige. As Achebe tells us immediately about his hero Okonkwo, "His fame rested on solid personal achievements. . . . among these people a man was judged according to his worth and not according to the worth of his father. . . . Age was respected among his people, but achievement was revered" (1994b, 3, 8). There is a natural affinity between this conception of individual potential and money, which is also pure potential—a point made by Karin Barber and Christopher Waterman in their discussion of the Yoruba concept of *ase*, which is somewhat similar to the Igbo *chi*. They argue persuasively against the assumption that money, mobility, and individual dynamism—central features of Western modernity—were introduced to Africa by colonialism. They were already there (Barber and Waterman 1995). Class formation in Africa is incomplete, and the cultures of southern Nigeria strongly encourage individual ambition and self-realization through money, with the result that nearly everyone imagines getting rich someday (Barber 1987).

For Paul, the question is not how hard a man is willing to work but what moral and psychological lines he is willing to cross. Paul's second principle, "he who has people is greater than he who has money," is a wicked turn on another basic tenet of a kinship-based agricultural society (Guyer 1993). The African continent was underpopulated until the twentieth century, and the tsetse fly (bane of draft animals) ensured that all muscle power came from humans. The way to increase agricultural productivity and hence wealth was to increase the size of the family unit by paying the bride price on more wives and having more children. Security depended on a robust network of kin and social alliances. Moreover, as Jane Guyer points out, African currencies have been radically unstable for hundreds of years (2004). The situation of the Nigerian structural adjustment era, in which the devaluation of the naira made civil servants' pensions suddenly worthless and threw them back on family resources, was only one instance of a long-standing pattern. In the six months after *Living in Bondage* was released, the price of basic foodstuffs doubled or tripled—one constantly heard conversations that were mostly recitations of outrageous new prices, the outraged mixed with wonderment at how the world people knew was coming unglued. In the long run, kin and social networks are the most reliable form of capital. But for Paul, "he who has people is greater than he who has money" means that the key to wealth is membership in a cabal—a cabal that sacrifices people, and family members at that. The rupturing of Andy's ties with his family is momentous in this symbolic aspect as well as in the more obvious psychological and social ones.

The opening of the film quickly sketches in some other dimensions of the discourse on wealth and fast money. Merit refers to "money doubling" and drug dealing—a landscape of familiar criminal practices. She and Aunty see Andy's dubious friend with the deal on the shipping container as the economic equivalent of the spirit Andy picks up and has sex with.

Tina also discourses on the nature of money when she delivers her sermon to her former colleagues: "How can young women like you occupy yourself with nothing else but selling your body to men for money? What sort of money is that? Let me tell you: This is not work. It leads to nowhere else but hell. . . . Prostitution is not work, just management." (In Nigeria, a strong meaning of "management" is scraping along, managing to cope with a difficult situation.) Tina's words are recalled in the later scene in which her lesson comes home to one of the prostitutes, Suzy, who stresses the religious side of the lesson less than the perception that the economy they are in does not permit accumulation. "This is no business, it's only management. I'm tired; I don't see what I'm really gaining. So, I'm retiring, going back to the village." One of her friends says, "This is the wrong time for that. We have enough responsibilities. You're the one that looks after parents, your brothers and sisters, yourself! I went to school. I'm a graduate. All of us. But there is no work. [In English] Use what you have to get what you want." She adds, "What would you do in the village? Farm alongside your parents?" "I wonder," Suzy says, without losing her determination. This little scene humanizes the prostitutes and adds a note of realism—in the sense both of showing that life does not always offer simple, polarized moral choices and of opening a window onto a period of economic and social distress, during which (among other profound social catastrophes) Nigerian society reneged on the promise that university education would guarantee a comfortable career. The prostitutes had been shown throwing themselves headlong into the pursuit of money and pleasure; here we see that they have arrived at their profession through bitter experiences, hard choices, and even a self-sacrificing sense of responsibility to their families.

IMAGES OF WEALTH

A central tension in Nollywood films—frequently noticed because it is so central—is between a rooted moral perspective of the kind we have been exploring and the display of objects of desire, catering to the audience's longing for things that can hardly be acquired honestly. In some cases, the organizing principle is actually hypocrisy, the moralizing merely a gesture while the real point is rude lust for women, cars, and huge garishly furnished houses. Carmela Garritano, qualifying Meyer's claim that Ghanaian videos are determined by a Pentecostalite vision, argues that consumer desire, which motivates shots and whole sequences, is not reducible to that framework. (Meyer has also written on consumerism in video films but links it to the Pentecostalite prosperity gospel (2002b, 2007).) The videos are not necessarily the expression of one coherent kind of vision: the earliest Ghanaian videos, Garritano finds, are sometimes radically heterogeneous (Garritano 2013, chapter 2).

The video boom occurred in the moment of neoliberal capitalist triumphalism after the collapse of communism, experienced in Africa as general distress and instability because of structural adjustment, accompanied (because of deregulation) by a flood of imported consumer goods available only to a privileged few and a flood of images of consumer goods, which washed over everyone. Garritano stresses how maddening these images were (2013, chapter 2).

Nollywood's audience prefers Nigerian to American films even though the local products are somewhat more expensive to buy and the American films' budgets may be more than a thousand times greater. Part of Nollywood's appeal is that it provides images of specifically African forms of wealth and consumption: embroidered cloth, food served in covered plates, pampered African bodies, walled compounds with gatemen, expensive cars driven through familiar tropical landscapes, African languages or African-inflected English spoken into the latest cell phones. This Africanization of the pleasures of vicarious consumption helps drive Nollywood's phenomenal success across Africa and the African diaspora.

Nollywood's deployment of images of wealth also has a special character because it is produced outside of corporate control. Often a gross disjunction between the poor quality of the images and the shiny products they represent makes it clear that they cannot both be from the same system. Brian Larkin, in his marvelous reading of the materiality of media under third world conditions, evokes the qualities of degradation that come with VHS tape technology, smeared images common to pirated imported media and the West African videos created through the infrastructure of piracy. Viewers were necessarily watching "a dub of a dub of a dub."

> Pirate images have a hallucinogenic quality. Detail is destroyed as realist representation fades into pulsating light. Facial features are smoothed away, colors are broken down into constituent tones, and bodies fade into one another. Reproduction takes its toll, degrading the image by injecting dropouts and bursts of fuzzy noise, breaking down dialogue into muddy, often inaudible sound. . . . Distortion on an audio tape, dropouts on a video, and a slow connection to the Internet are the material conditions of existence for media. While media infrastructure creates the reality of being ever more connected to a globalized world, it does so by emphasizing Nigerians' marginalization at the same time. Electricity blackouts, snowy television images, difficulty getting international phone lines, and distorted loudspeakers on cassette players all create a technological veil of semiotic distortion for Nigerians. (Larkin 2008, 237, 239)

This "technological veil" overlays the objects of desire, expressing the distance from them, palpably locating the desiring subject on the periphery of the world system.

The transition from analog to digital technologies has partially lifted the veil (digital video has its own phenomenology of breakdown, of course), enabling the infinite reproduction without loss of cheap, scrubbed, gleaming images, as late capitalism further compresses time and space, bringing the images of tantalizing objects closer. But Garritano, building on Larkin's insight, describes other ways in which poverty inscribed itself in the early Ghanaian videos. The circumstances of production—borrowed locations and drastically limited time—are apparent, and the untutored filmmaking is sometimes agog with desire for commodities the production has managed to borrow, stopping the action of a scene, for instance, while the camera systematically explores a luxury car from bumper to bumper, not omitting to have a look inside the trunk. She describes a transition in Ghanaian video filmmaking from an initial stage of "amateur" delirium, redolent of the poverty from which it sprang, to a "professional" style that mimics the manner of international consumerism (Garritano 2013, chapters 2 and 3). In Nigeria the pattern of evolution is not quite the same: *Living in Bondage* is relatively cool and controlled, and Amaka Igwe's fully commercial style has been on prominent display from early on, her upscale television serial *Checkmate* evolving into the lavish settings of her early video film blockbuster *Violated* (1996) (see chapter 4).

A telltale exorbitance is typical, however. The camera captures an unmoored, desiring subject's point of view, not that of a whole integrated capitalist system where advertising and consumption are part of a package that includes disciplined wage labor and a large middle class. Capitalism is devilishly broad-minded in its manipulation of desire, but it is fundamentally pragmatic: advertising is directed at those who might actually consume—who have money, or at least the prospect of getting credit from a predatory lender.

Nigeria, like Africa in general, remains only partially integrated into the global capitalist system, even after half a millennium on its periphery as a source of brutally extracted labor and raw materials. That system has otherwise tended to see Africa as more trouble than it is worth, partly because of its poverty but also because of its determined resistance, its dense obstructions (Cooper 1981). Anyone trying to sell things in Nigeria has to cope with Nigeria's own aggressive marketing culture, its genius for improvised imitation (of car parts, for instance), and its piratical disregard of intellectual property rights. Foreign investors are scared off by the overhead expense of building their own infrastructures, the relatively high cost of African labor, and by Transparency International reports. This situation changed dramatically if not entirely in the early twenty-first century, as many African economies boomed, including Nigeria's, and high profit margins attracted foreign direct investment. But in the early 1990s when

Nollywood was born, international capitalist development seemed simply to be abandoning Africa as not worth exploiting, casting it adrift from the global economy.

Nollywood was formed around these disjunctions. Some producers get corporate money for product placements in their films—Amaka Igwe, already experienced in finding sponsorship for her television serials, sometimes financed films entirely in this way. But—as in the examples from Nnebue's *Glamour Girls* noted in the next chapter—these placements tend to be so obtrusive that they rupture the flow of the film, exposing the cash transaction rather than inviting the viewer into a seamless vision of an alluring lifestyle. Even as we're sold the goods, we are reminded that we are not in a smoothly functioning capitalist system.

INFORMAL COMMERCE, NOT CAPITALISM

Nollywood is whole-heartedly commercial, but it is not a capitalist industry, and this is profoundly important on stylistic, thematic, ideological, and other levels. It is commercial in the sense of the commerce of African markets, out of which it grew and of which it stubbornly remains part—trading, under "informal" conditions, largely without formal records. As John McCall explains, following the work of the economist Hernando de Soto,

> capitalism can only be mobilized under conditions of economic formality—official records and documentation make capitalism possible. A business owner cannot generate collateral without records documenting ownership of property, corporate inventory, equipment, payroll, etc. These records make it possible to transform property into equity, equity into credit. Informal markets lack the bureaucratic oversight required to fully mobilize modern capital creation. . . . To put it bluntly, Nollywood is not capitalist. (2012, 10, 11)

Nollywood began with Nnebue's $12,000 investment and an unwritten agreement with his collaborators, and the industry has grown to enormous size without fundamentally changing its character. As it became enormous, Nollywood began to be recognized by and to interact with formal institutions. Corporations use Nollywood stars for publicity, hire Nollywood directors to make commercials, and have sponsored a few films. Foreign embassies compete in organizing training programs for filmmakers. The Nigerian government always worried about Nollywood's power in forming the national image at home and abroad; by 2006, when the Nigerian film industry's annual revenues were being estimated at $200 million (Vasagar 2006), the government had to recognize the industry's contribution to the economy and to employment. President Obasanjo (1999–2007) and then President Jonathan have offered their patronage. But these are examples of attempts to tap the money and power of Nollywood rather than signs of actual economic structure.

The government's interest in Nollywood led to the establishment in 2010 of a $200 million loan fund to support the entertainment industry. But the formidable paperwork requirements, particularly the demand for collateral, were such that three years later no Nigeria-based filmmaker had managed to access the funds. Banks make occasional personal loans to filmmakers who put up their houses as collateral, but no bank tried to establish a serious relationship with the film industry until 2007, when EcoBank's "Project Nollywood" ended badly because of similar deep differences in business culture.

Also in 2007, the National Film and Video Censors Board introduced a "New Distribution Framework," a frontal assault on the informality of the business of Nollywood (National Film and Video Censors Board 2007; Obiaya 2012). It required that film distributors show the basic trappings of a formal business that would allow them to interact with banks and other institutions: an address where they could be found, books to record transactions, a certain level of capitalization, and legal representation. This was understood as an attempt to put out of business the people who had built the industry—the traders in the Idumota and Alaba markets of Lagos and Iweka Road in Onitsha. These marketers have regularly been denounced as "stark illiterates or semiliterates with a herd mentality" (Novia 2012, 8), mere traders with no sense of how to properly promote a film or of the possibilities of film culture and unable to think their way past their habits as informal-sector traders to a larger, rationalized business model that could begin to tap the enormous potential of the market. They are therefore seen as an impediment to the development of the industry. For their part, the marketers were incensed that the government, which had never done anything to help them, was now trying to take away their business. The result was an angry crisis and a standoff, followed by years of slow accommodation and negotiation. It became clear that more or less no one besides the existing marketers had the money and the requisite knowledge of how things actually worked to get into the film business. The imagined rational, capitalist, deep-pocketed investors never appeared. (The introduction of the new framework unfortunately coincided with the global financial meltdown.) Idumota, Alaba, and Onitsha remain the centers of power in the industry, the major sources of financing for films as well as the principle points of wholesale distribution.

Alaba Market, which became important in the video industry around 2000, is on the western outskirts of Lagos. The Alaba marketers are said to be even worse pirates than those of Idumota. When the actor/singer/producer/director Gbenga Adewusi came there with a contingent of police to confront marketers who were pirating his work, the policemen were beaten, Adewusi was stabbed in the arm and head, the whole entourage was driven away, and the police feared to send in reinforcements to make arrests (Kupoluyi 2004).

Idumota Market is where it all began—Nnebue and other early video film producers were electronics traders there. Busy commerce in cloth and housewares surrounds the video business. John McCall tells the story of Idumota's transformations:

> Idumota Market rose from the ashes of Nigeria's post-oil-boom economic collapse. Petty marketers and small-time operators of various sorts set up shop as squatters in the abandoned buildings where bankers, oil executives, and architects once had offices. Hope had been high for Nigeria's future in the 1970s when a booming petroleum market buoyed Nigeria's initial embrace of political independence and economic autonomy. Back then, the Idumota district of Lagos Island was planned as a center for commerce and high finance. Lagos' gleaming new financial district was intended to be the commercial nexus of the continent. . . . The Idumota district, once the crown jewel of Nigerian hope, fell into disrepair. Rather than maintain the crumbling business district, the surviving corporate residents fled to neighboring Victoria Island—a swank neighborhood designed for residential and retail uses. . . . The Idumota district is still a commercial center, but not the one it was intended to be. (2012, 13)

When I first visited Idumota in the mid-1990s, the streets were almost impassable because of mud and water, the vendors blocking sidewalks and spilling into the roadways, and the sheer press of people, many of them carrying things on their heads. A few vehicles were stuck in the crowd, swaying on their shock absorbers as they were buffeted by the bodies pushing past them. Since then the government has repaved the streets and now a remarkable number of men wearing various uniforms ruthlessly keep traffic moving.

Ebinpeju Lane is the epicenter of the Idumota film market, a name resonantly pronounced on trailers for thousands and thousands of films. But it is only a small alley, its entrance hard to detect as one walks by, an irregular tunnel with open gutters between four-story buildings. Shafts of sunlight rarely reach the ground. Little one-room shops with metal burglary bars line it, plastered inside and out with film posters. Some shops have rough wooden display cases set up outside. Bundles of films are carried in on men's heads—the lane is far too narrow and irregular for vehicles of any kind—and are handed up to the balconies of shops and offices on upper floors. The marketers leave their shops in the care of their apprentices. Sometimes they have an office somewhere else, up uneven cement stairs, or they may make deals out of their homes.

More often than not it is marketers who put up the money to make a film. These days they use bank cards to transfer funds, but in the first decade of the industry they were liable to pull a bag full of naira out from under a counter and hand it over to a producer or director. The marketers didn't believe in banks and didn't have accounts. ₦10 million ($65,000), an average budget for a film, fills a Chinese plaid woven plastic bag of the kind Nigerians call "Ghana-must-go." (Ghanaian workers in Nigeria, suddenly driven out by decree in the early 1980s, packed their belongings in such bags as they fled.) These Ghana-must-go bags of money are the heart of this mercantile system. The money whirls through the production of a film, unencumbered by paperwork, and is meant to return within three months or so. Then it will whirl again.

The traders' engrained demand for immediate profits is a frequently-heard complaint, but other potential sources of investment for independent productions are hardly different. McCall writes, "Nigerians do not cling to informal commerce because they are conservative traditionalists. They cling to it because it is the most reliable option they have available" (2012, 12). Bond Emeruwa told me:

> At the beginning there was no loan in Nigeria that was more than three months, including from banks, because all the banks did was buy and sell. They would calculate your loan period by what else they could be doing with the money—by how long it would take to get a shipment of sugar from Brazil. Everyone you went to for money to make a movie would figure on that basis. And three months was magnanimous. That imposed a production and distribution schedule, all in one. And if you get money from family and friends, every morning, whether you're religious or not, you'd better start by saying a prayer for the people you got the funds from. If the man gets sick or dies, the family will demand the money back immediately. If the man's wife has a baby, he needs to do a naming ceremony, so he needs the money back now.

Numerous marketers and producers can set such sums in motion, but they are all small-scale—no one has many productions going at once. The whirling leaves remarkably little in the way of infrastructure behind it, and given the "informality" and the deliberate opacity of everything to do with the business, it is hard to get a sense of what these operations consist of.

I asked Kanayo O. Kanayo, who had starred in a number of films from the leading producer and marketer OJ Productions, to describe the company. He warmly praised Ojiofor Ezeanyaeche—"OJ" himself[14]—for doing what a producer should do, standing by with ready cash to meet emergencies, like when a caterer didn't provide the promised food for the cast and crew or an actor needed to make an unexpected trip home. He could name half a dozen people who normally worked with OJ, but otherwise was vague—the recurring image was of the man himself standing there, pulling cash out of his pocket. He faulted him for not continuing to upgrade the equipment he had and confirmed that OJ pulled most of his profits out of the film business and invested them in hotels.

This failure to reinvest in the film industry is a familiar pattern. I have written elsewhere about how few physical spaces of any kind Nollywood has created for itself (Haynes 2007b). It has built no studios. There are sound stages in Lagos used for shooting television serials, advertisements, and music videos, but Nollywood productions cannot afford to rent them and most producers and directors do not know how to operate in them efficiently. Production outfits seldom own much equipment, renting it as necessary from a network of suppliers. The premises of marketers, producers, and directors never seem to exceed four or five rooms and tend to be quite modest if not battered. Lancelot Imasuen, for fifteen years perhaps the busiest director in Nollywood, operates out of a few dark, cavernous rooms in a building shared with a Pentecostal church, with dusty odd objects lying around and the warning "This house is not for sale" written on the outside walls to deter fraudsters from pretending to sell it. Amaka Igwe ran her multifarious projects out of the ground floor of the house where she lived in a gated, upper-middle-class neighborhood of Ikeja. People were constantly streaming through. At times her living room was piled with furniture because it was being used as the set of a television serial.

Individual film productions draw on a shifting population of specialized workers organized into a guild structure that reflects their industrial division of labor.[15] This system operates with remarkably little visible infrastructure beyond the many cell phones that litter the tables wherever film people meet. Like other Nigerians, they spend an inordinate amount of time staring at their phones, maintaining the social networks that keep them afloat in a permanently mobile, precarious environment and looking for that message that will transform their circumstances.

A constant state of waiting for opportunities comes with the film business almost anywhere, but it is intensified by and congruent with the whole character of life in the informal sector, which is how most Nigerians get by. AbdouMaliq Simone is a powerful theorist of how life in African cities is organized around networks that allow for survival, resilience, temporary stability, and a measure of creativity and play, even in situations of extreme poverty, uncertainty, provisionality, and marginalization (Simone 2004). Larkin uses Simone's work to describe the culture and psychology that Nollywood springs from and expresses: an anxious sensibility based in a constant state of preparedness to take advantage of any opportunity that may arise, a readiness to experiment given the lack of any clear model for success such as those that used to be provided by formal structures like the educational system, government jobs, or industrial labor, a worldliness that comes from manipulating far-flung networks to maintain some stability at home (Larkin 2008, 170, 179, 181).

IDEOLOGY

A film industry's economic basis largely determines its ideological character, of course. Hollywood is completely integrated with the structures of American (now, transnational) corporate capitalism, and television soap operas, as the name indicates, are even more directly linked to capitalist purposes—in the classic instance, the corporate headquarters of Procter & Gamble in Cincinnati exercised constant, detailed, iron control over the products of its soap opera empire. A familiar critique of mass culture sees it as designed by its corporate sponsors to train its audience to be consumers in a capitalist society and to systematically misrecognize their problems, becoming habituated to modes of thinking that block analysis and prevent effective political action. Latin American theorists working on Latin American television serials have emphasized this training in consumption and in the habits of wage labor in the context of "development" (Allen 1995).

Nigerian serials also had corporate sponsorship and were designed to create consumers and citizens. *Mirror in the Sun*, *Ripples*, and *Checkmate*, the most popular television serials of the period preceding the birth of Nollywood, celebrated the affluent lifestyle of an urban elite made possible by the oil boom, following the romantic entanglements of independent young people with good jobs, nice cars, and attractive places to live—models of stylish consumption. When I asked Francis Onwochei, who starred in both *Ripples* and *Checkmate*, whether these shows registered at all that things were turning very bad on the economic and political fronts, he said, "Either we didn't have the time, or the consciousness, or the confidence at that time. . . . Don't forget it was a military era. Even if you shared thoughts in the public space, even as we were all drinking, you could be taken in to State Security Services for questioning for two or three days. Nobody wanted that. It was that bad, not to talk of reproducing things like that on television. You could not dare to do that."

While the military regimes maintained tight control over what was broadcast or shown to the public gathered in crowds in theaters, Pierre Barrot emphasizes that it was much less concerned with the "home videos," as Nigerians often call them, since they were viewed in private spaces. A whole critical perspective from a popular point of view was permitted to the video films that would have been impossible in the more public media. Barrot also makes the point that unlike the mass culture industries that produce American soap operas or Latin American telenovelas, Nollywood does not turn away from social issues, the "wounds" of society, the sources of anxiety—indeed, it probes them constantly (Barrot 2009, chapter 5). Nollywood models consumption, but it also harbors—in fact makes central—the darkest suspicions about the wealth that often makes consumption possible, mounting a searing critique and denunciation. One may fault its moralism in addressing these issues, or agree with Karin Barber that using money rituals to represent the mysterious wealth and violence of the oil boom "translates them into a set of terms which makes further questions about the nature and origins of this wealth pointless and, indeed, unaskable" (1982, 438), but in any case Nollywood is not trying to anaesthetize its audience.

There is little difference in perspective between the people producing the films and those consuming them—we are not dealing with mass culture industrially produced by one class of people for consumption by another class, with an intermediary set of marketing experts. The actors and directors of Nollywood film are generally better educated than their audiences, but the marketers, who strongly control what kinds of films get made and distributed, are not. Everything depends on their instinct for what people will buy. Barrot's favorite theme is how directly and entirely Nollywood responds to the desires of its viewers.

To a remarkable extent, then, Nollywood expresses its public's view of the world. What that public experienced in 1992 was not rational modernity based in an integrated capitalist system. Industrial production, the educational system, and government employment were all collapsing. The commanding height of the economy—the oil sector—was opaque, corrupt, dysfunctional, and provided very few jobs for Nigerians. The financial sector was riddled with spectacular malfeasance. Nigeria was a prime example of "the criminalization of the state in Africa" (Bayart, Ellis, and Hibou 1999). Apart from oil exports, the brain drain, and remittances from Nigerians abroad (suddenly much more important), Nigeria's relationship with the world economy was defined by its emergence in this period as a major transshipment point for the international narcotics trade, a major supplier of prostitutes for Europe, and the home of the advance-fee fraudsters who would colonize the Internet as soon as it reached Nigeria. Nigeria experienced the opportunities of globalization not through the churn of regulated, macroeconomic developments—assembly plants opening or closing, back-office work being shifted around the world—but as an aleatory, individual free-for-all in a context of general desperation, where what mattered were individual initiative, luck, and social connections. Nigerian society had always been largely organized around kinship, patron-client relationships, and customary or voluntary associations. These reemerged in force as the institutions associated with the modern state decayed. Access to the informal or criminal possibilities of the new economy came through such relationships. This is the world Nollywood tells stories about and whose moral challenges Nollywood addresses.

In the Nollywood universe, there is an absolute requirement of ideological closure: good must triumph over evil at the end. BobManuel Udokwu:

> The concept of the law of retribution was one of the things in *Living in Bondage* that was copied and became a standard for the films coming out of Nollywood. God will punish. There's always a message. This doesn't always happen in real life—some people get away with it. But there is that belief in the African school of thought that if you can't challenge a person physically or in the law courts because of the influence he has, you throw up your hands and say, "let God judge." And in the traditional sense, if perchance something bad happens to that individual, you will feel vindicated, that God is there and has seen the person wrong-do and has passed a judgment. That concept came into the movies from *Living in Bondage* and stayed, which more or less gratified the viewers, especially the older generation. People say we glorify violence, but the criminals get killed or arrested.

The NFVCB policy states "If an illegal and criminal act is not punished in the first part of a film, the Board approves it on condition that such act will be adequately punished in the sequels" (Martins 2001). This official stricture is seldom necessary since filmmakers have internalized the idea that their stories should have a moral and, like other African popular artists, they like to position themselves as teachers of lessons (Barber 1987). But overwhelmingly, the demand for moral closure comes from the audience's aching need for order and justice. The reality of contemporary Nigeria does not provide either order or justice. Nigerians have faith in God, and they can depend on Nollywood to make sense of the world. Nollywood renovated stories about justice-dealing indigenous spiritual forces, and the rise of Nollywood coincides with the spectacular spread of Pentecostalism and Islamic fundamentalism, both of which, like Nollywood, offer narratives that explain and find consolation in a world of hardship, evil, and social disintegration.

So the "fast money" theme, like other Nollywood themes, is strongly rooted in a local popular discourse and pressing emotional needs. The moralizing is kept real because it is lived all the time. The temptations and instabilities that make the theme prominent are built into the structure of the industry itself. What created Nollywood was the spectacular commercial success of *Living in Bondage*, but Nnebue's business career has been rocky. In 2000 he invested much of his capital in a scheme to release films directly through video rental clubs, which involved locating and registering thousands of such clubs across the country at his own expense. The scheme failed completely because the video club owners didn't return the money they owed to him. He then invested profits from his films in properties, as OJ did, but was ruined in 2003 when he was swindled by fraudsters (Fair 2003). Meanwhile Ogunjiofor, who felt cheated by Nnebue, says his sponsor for *Circle of Doom* "cheated me after a very long time but the first batch of 50,000 films we did, he gave me ₦800,000. That was a lot of money. Instead of me to use that same money to sponsor films, I bought a brand new Mercedes Benz and a Toyota Corolla. Before long, I was broke again" (Abone 2009). Obi-Rapu says Ogunjiofor and Kanayo blew the money that was supposed to be used to edit *Circle of Doom*, and that Daniel Oluigbo blew the money for editing *Taboo*. There is no end to such stories.

MORE EARLY IGBO-LANGUAGE FILMS

Both Nnebue's next film, *Dirty Deal*, and *Circle of Doom* continued the theme of fast money in other topical forms. *Circle of Doom* is about a group of criminals who traffic in drugs and practice "419"—various kinds of fraud covered under article 419 of the Nigerian criminal code that had begun to flourish spectacularly and occupy a central place in street rumors and in cultural commentaries (A. Smith, 2001, 2009; D. Smith, 2001b, 2007; Utoh-Ezeajugh 2008). The scams and the drug dealing in the film are international as well as local operations. The character played by Francis Onwochei is an affluent businessman with investments and houses in the Far East and high government connections. An international dimension was already present in *Living in Bondage*—importing goods is the basic business of the cabal members, and late in his career Andy boasts of having factories in Italy and California producing clothing and accessories for him. *Circle of Doom* takes another step in suggesting the criminalization of Nigeria's relationship with the global economy and the corruption of national politics.

The circle of criminals is doomed because they will eventually turn on and destroy one another, following the logic of the stories of Caro and Chi and Andy and Paul. This theme of evil-doers betraying one another remains standard in Nollywood and is indeed indispensable given the axiomatic need for a restoration of moral order and justice at the end and the glaring absence of social institutions—like an adequate police force and court system—interested in and capable of doing the job. The world is corrupt, but there is an immanent moral structure that applies to the individual soul and therefore governs relationships among the wicked.

Nnebue's *Dirty Deal* is a topical response to the so-called "mushroom banks," irresponsible and often fraudulent institutions that flourished under the Babangida regime and were closed down in large numbers a few years later by a Failed Banks Tribunal. Nnebue directed as well as wrote and produced it; embarrassed by some faults in the direction, he let the film slip out of sight after its initial success. Like *Circle of Doom*, it is set in eastern Nigeria rather than in Lagos. Nnebue abandoned the marital, supernatural, and spiritual dimensions of *Living in Bondage* for a story about the intrigues of a Mephistophelean antihero, Chief Ogbu-Orie, who opens a "community bank" and uses it to pillage his town systematically. The focus is entirely on the mechanisms of power. The film begins with scenes of Ogbu-Orie expropriating land, burning a house and its occupants, and refusing the king's authority—violently and brazenly uprooting the settled order of things. Ogbu-Orie's basic mode of operation is to make loans and then have his gang of thugs rob his customer so he can foreclose. He has corrupted or cowed the local officials and is a consummate hypocrite, chairing the Police Public Relations Committee.

At his bank's opening ceremony his humanitarianism is praised, but we know the talk is poisoned. The dark satirical wit with which the whole scene is observed has a new edge. In *Living in Bondage* the climaxes of Andy's career are interrupted by Merit's ghost, bringing the underlying truth of the situation crashing in, but here the ceremony just runs on at length, letting the ironies pile up. The ironies extend very far—by analogy, to the nature of the Babangida regime itself, which also, under the trappings of legitimacy, deployed a system that operated through a mixture of terror, systematic corruption, and fraud. Breathtaking amounts of money disappeared from the national treasury, and it became normal for anyone in charge of the disbursement of salaries to delay payment while the money collected interest in their own personal bank accounts. The mushroom banks were only one of myriad examples of institutional scamming that flourished with the regime's blessing or participation. The term "419" is applied to Ogbu-Orie's regime, and it was frequently applied to Babangida's.[16]

The town riots against Ogbu-Orie, but with the connivance of the district police officer his regime lasts for six more years. Then John, son of one of his victims, returns from his studies abroad. Ogbu-Orie's daughter, also returning from studies abroad, falls in love with him. Ogbu-Orie accidentally kills her with a bullet intended for her lover; a second attempt to kill John is prevented in the nick of time by the police, John having persuaded the police commissioner to replace the corrupt DPO with an honest man. This suggests there is still some structure of responsible governance that will eventually deal with criminality. Ogbu-Orie is taken off to prison hissing threats against John. (The implied sequel was never made.)

The next film Ogunjiofor produced was *Nneka, the Pretty Serpent*. *Nneka* continues the get-rich-quick theme, and the supernatural and gender themes of *Living in Bondage* reappear in stronger and hotter forms. The film begins with a woman praying to a river goddess, complaining of her childlessness and promising that, if granted a child, it will serve the goddess. The imagery of prayer and sacrifice on the bank of the river is timeless, and the brief prelude establishes the supernatural dimension as the fundamental, underlying reality of the world. After the credits, we follow nice cars through Lagos traffic, leading to a heated confrontation in front of Nneka's house as the wife of the wealthy man she is having an affair with warns her to leave him alone. Afterwards, Nneka (Ndidi Obi) and a friend have a conversation like that between Caro and Ego, reveling in their power over both men and women. Nneka promises to suck the rich man dry before dumping him. She sometimes morphs, through video magic, into a cat as she destroys his family. She then sets her sights on Tony (Ogunjiofor), a rising young banker with a born-again fiancée (Rita Nzelu, who was Tina in *Living in Bondage*). During Nneka's first night in Tony's bed her spirit rises out of her body (a classic image in Yoruba witchcraft films), hails her spirit husband—a water spirit, as we will learn later—and asks him for the power to control Tony. She breaks up Tony's engagement and marries him herself. He commits fraud at his bank in an attempt to meet Nneka's incessant demands for money and is fired. He ends up working as a waiter in her restaurant, a drunk, while she goes out with other men. She eliminates two of his age-mates from his village, but another friend teams up with Tony's spurned born-again fiancée and a pastor to free him from Nneka's clutches and break her power.

The parallels with *Living in Bondage* are clear. The great shift is to give so much power to the female figure—not Merit's virtuous power over Andy's psyche but Caro's kind of power, carried to shocking extremes: the power to push past a secretary into a man's office, to push past a househelp into a man's house, to eject his sister and then his mother from his house, to face down his wife or fiancée. The film is full of confrontations between women in which a man is powerless. Nneka uses her sexuality brazenly, and she uses her mind-controlling special-effects eye beams on occasion, but mostly she just uses the force of her personality. She is a nightmare of pure will power, emasculating for men and humiliating for everyone, her occult powers supplementing an aggressive independence that is scary enough.

This figure of the alluring, predatory, devouring good-time girl, the independent city woman, was thoroughly familiar in popular culture—from the Onitsha market literature that flourished from the 1940s to the 1970s (Obiechina 1971; Thometz 2001), for instance, and from highlife songs. In *Glamour Girls* (1994), Nnebue embedded this figure in the kind of film he was moving toward, which was analytical about how power works in his society.

CHAPTER 3

Nnebue's *Glamour Girls*: Scandalous Women

FROM IGBO TO ENGLISH

Glamour Girls 1, which came out in 1994, was the first video film made in English. This was an event no less momentous than the appearance of *Living in Bondage*, and its importance was better understood at the time: it was heralded by radio, television, and billboard advertisements (Shaka 2003). It opened up a huge new market—a national Nigerian market, in the first place, and also, as an unintended consequence, an international one.[1] Nollywood's hegemony across Africa, its deep penetration of the Caribbean, and its inroads among African Americans would be unlikely if its medium were not the most powerful world language.

It was not obvious that filmmaking in English would work. At the end of the celluloid filmmaking era, Afolabi Adesanya concluded (after poor returns on his English-language film *Vigilante* (1988)) that while Nigerian audiences would watch television programs in English, they would not go out and spend their own money to see English-language films (Adesanya 1990b). In fact there had been only a handful of celluloid films in English, in contrast to the outpouring in Yoruba. Films in Nigerian languages have a cultural depth and resonance, an immediate emotional power and a communal adhesion that films in English cannot match. Moreover, Nigerian actors tend to sound like they are reciting lines when they perform in English; they are more spontaneous, lively, and authentic in their mother tongues.

But "English is the language of success," as Moradewun Adejunmobi puts it. It turned out Nigerian audiences did not see English as a foreign language, in the sense of unpleasantly alien to them: it is, after all, the national language, the language of education past the primary level, and it has been indigenized through a whole spectrum of Nigerian Englishes from a lightly accented Queen's English to Pidgin, which is as much African as European in its grammatical structures and which soaks up loan words from every locality. English is part of the Nigerian cultural landscape, and in that context it signifies an elevated class status and a desirable cosmopolitanism. It stands for making it (Adejunmobi 2002; 2004, chapter 3). These connotations compensate for the lost emotional immediacy. The adoption of English as the medium of the films shifts their horizon away from cultural depth and particularism and toward the multiethnic nation. That move in turn is crucial in allowing Nollywood films to travel throughout the African continent and diaspora. This shift of horizon is not absolute: English-language films embody specific cultural references to a greater or lesser extent. But English suggests an orientation that has pervasive effects.[2]

In literary circles, whether African writers should work in their mother tongues or the colonial languages was debated for half a century; the video film marketers saw that English films sold better than Igbo ones and within months the industry was transformed, even though the film medium entails special difficulties. The thoughts and words of Achebe's Okonkwo are transcribed transparently in English—a work of literary genius, but lesser writers also learned to write in English or French about African cultures without serious incongruity. In the serial drama the NTA made of *Things Fall Apart* in 1986, however, the English dialogue seems in jarring relation to the carefully reconstructed settings. Also, the literary debates turn on a binary opposition between a particular African cultural localism and the universality that comes with the languages of the colonizers, but Nollywood's situation is not exactly binary. An obstacle to the penetration of Nollywood films into the American mainstream is that many Americans find Nigerian accents in English hard to understand to the point that they are unable to follow the stories. The Canadian documentary *Nollywood Babylon* (2008) subtitles all Nigerians speaking English, including Onookome Okome, who is a professor of English in Canada. Foreign film festival audiences are liable to have an easier time with a subtitled Yoruba film than with an English-language Nollywood one.

The shift from Igbo into English greatly expanded the reservoir of filmmaking talent as well as the potential audience. A number of the most important directors and actors of Nollywood's next phase are not Igbo, including the *Glamour Girls* stars Liz Benson, Sola Fosudo, and Golda John. (*Nneka, The Pretty Serpent*, in Igbo, was cowritten by Joe Dudun, an Itsekeri, and Zeb Ejiro, an Isoko who also directed part 1; part 2 was directed by a Yoruba, Bolaji Dawodu. But this was unusual.)

More than fifteen other producers had immediately followed Nnebue into the business of making Igbo films, but filmmaking in Igbo proved to be a flash in the pan, declining very rapidly once English-language production began and sputtering since then. Some years the censors board registered no Igbo films. Yoruba and Hausa production, in contrast, has steadily flourished. Even Edo (or Bini) filmmaking, with a much smaller population base, has established a healthy modest market. There were strong reasons to turn to English, but there were also reasons to turn away from Igbo.

One of the two standard explanations for this relies on the Nigerian stereotype of the Igbo as being less attached to their language than, say, the Yoruba, normally illustrated by the supposed difficulty most Igbos have of getting through a sentence without throwing in some English. (Most Igbo-language films were in fact titled in English, like *Living in Bondage*.) The other explanation relies on the stereotype of Igbo marketers as having no motivation except profits, which are higher in English.

But there were other factors, including a general weakness of cultural infrastructure. Yoruba and Hausa both evolved strong central standard dialects out of many local variations, in a process resembling the formation of the major European languages. These standard dialects became the bases for literary languages and for substantial literary output, journalism, drama, and broadcasting. A standard Igbo dialect was created but never took strong hold. Little is written in Igbo. The scenarios and scripts for all the Igbo films were in English because neither the writers nor the actors were used to written Igbo. "Among the Ibo the art of conversation is regarded very highly," Achebe wrote in *Things Fall Apart* (1994b, 7), but many Igbos, including actors, feel they do not meet this high standard, having spent their formative years being educated in English rather than mastering proverbs at the feet of elders. Outside of Enugu and Aba, where the television stations broadcast dramas and other programming in Igbo, there was no established pool of actors who were used to working in Igbo.

Casting *Living in Bondage* was a slow, careful process because of the language issue, and Ogunjiofor spent hours coaching actors on their lines, introducing adages, flowery turns of phrase, and a style of light bantering sarcasm. Capturing these nuances in subtitles was impossible. Because so few actors could perform well in Igbo, almost immediately the industry had a problem with the same faces appearing over and over. Amaka Igwe discovered that once her actors began speaking Igbo they enjoyed it so much they wouldn't shut up, lost in the elaborate metaphors and philosophical dimensions of the language. The first part of *Rattlesnake* (1995) was supposed to run two hours but she ended up with eleven hours of material, which she cut laboriously down to three. She also found it difficult to assemble a cast that spoke the same dialect. At the extremes, northern and southern Igbo dialects are almost mutually unintelligible. If the actors were supposed to be members of the same family, they had to sound the same. And she pointed out to me that subtitling not only added a new expense, it also meant degradation of image quality as the videotape went through a further generation of reproduction when the subtitles were added.

The brief efflorescence of Igbo films crystallized many of the themes that would be fundamental to Nollywood. Igbo marketers remain the most powerful players in the industry, a fact that is often grumbled about in ethnic terms, and Igbo culture is represented more often than any other. But the contribution of the founding Igbo films passed into the whole Nollywood film culture without creating a particular style or genre that is recognized as specifically Igbo.

GLAMOUR GIRLS 1

Living in Bondage is solid, even stolid, in its foursquare moral and formal organization, firmly centered on the drama of its protagonist, unafraid of redundancy as it establishes symbolic parallels, locking down its meanings in a polarized universe. The first part of *Glamour Girls*, directed by Chika Onukwufor (who directed *Living in Bondage* 2, again working under the pseudonym Christian Onu) but conceived and written by Nnebue, is loose jointed and free swinging, composed of shards of narrative organized into a whole that has an exploratory, experimental feel about it, an adventurousness that would decline as Nollywood settled into more predictable generic forms.

The film opens with a sequence of a woman, Doris (Gloria Anozie), driving on an open road. She talks business on her cell phone and nothing else happens, but the image of a well-dressed businesswoman driving herself in her own car indicates the film's subject: independent modern women on the loose, outside patriarchal control. Nigerian newspapers and magazines, which take an obsessive interest in such women, call them "senior girls"—women who have chosen careers over marriage and pursue their own sexual interests.[3] Films about them are sometimes called "aristos," after a 2003 film of that name.

Sandra (Jennifer Okere Ossai), Doris's friend from their university days, turns up on her doorstep, having failed to find a husband or a livelihood—every man wants to sleep with you before he gives you a job, she complains. An ingenue, Sandra is stunned and nervous around the luxury of Doris's house and profoundly, repeatedly shocked by Doris's conversation with her friend Thelma (Barbara Udoh).[4] Doris tells Thelma she's got a new multimillionaire, and the two chat cynically about the rich older men they see. Sandra thought Doris's money came from her boutique, but Doris explains the real money comes from men. Thelma gets money from her father-in-law and her husband in America but still needs to go out with other men. She assumes her husband will abandon her for a foreign woman. Sandra asks, "Who will marry you after all of this?" She is told, "Husbands are no longer the important thing—you've got to make money for yourself, then you can buy yourself a husband." These lines, shot in the usual static way as the women sit on sofas, are featured in the trailer for the film, as nothing the film shows could be more scandalous than this statement of principles. The pattern of women occupying themselves with their own small businesses while men control the serious wealth reproduces the typical relationship in a traditional Igbo marriage, but for the woman in effect to pay the bride price for a man upends everything. The managing director of an airline arrives and invites them to a millionaires' cocktail party. Sandra will need a makeover.

In the next scene a tall young woman, impeccably bourgeois in appearance, asks a gentleman in a Mercedes for a lift to the next bus stop. As she gets out of the car she starts railing at him, claiming to the bystanders that he promised to pay her ₦2,000 ($35) for two nights' sex but now is trying to get rid of her with ₦500. The poor guy is innocent—in fact, he's almost the only person in the film who has nothing to do with prostitution. He was just on his way to the airport to pick up his daughter. But threatened by the crowd, he has to pay.

Two cool young rich guys banter over the bar in the host's home. In high spirits, the host sends his driver out to pick up a girl. The driver comes back with the beautiful tall prostitute we've just met. The host agrees to her ₦2,000 price, samples her wares, and sends his friend in to her. When the friend turns her over on the bed, kissing her, he discovers she is his own sister.

This is a classic bit of urban folklore, classic because the sexual irresponsibility flourishing in the city collides with the ultimate principle of sexual order, the incest taboo. The accusation against the man in the Mercedes comes from another genre, anecdotes of witty scams, perhaps an urban version of the venerable trickster tale. In this case, the edge to the incident comes from the woman's calculation that the urban masses would defend the sanctity of her contract, even for prostitution, and even though the sum involved was far beyond them.

Later in the film this woman reappears in a flashy red sports car with a man whose wife waylays them. She fights with the wife; the wife hits the husband.

Later still, we find her in a moment of postcoital tenderness with a politician. She convinces him to take a nude photo with her but then demands ₦50,000, saying she's sure his wife or the press or his political opponents would double the price. It's business. In the end, she takes what he has, ₦25,000.

This incident and the other hard little kernels of narrative involving this woman drive home a point the film has been making repeatedly through its extended melodramatic plotlines: prostitutes are not to be trusted and any sentimental involvement with them is dangerous. But the last time she appears the effect is different. She has a name now, Helen, she is clearly enjoying sex with the man she's with, and they are getting more than casually interested in one another, even as they haggle over the price of a longer-term contract (she'll waive the value-added tax). We learn by the way that she'll have to miss classes to spend time with him. When he asks what drove her into this life, she tells her story. She grew up wealthy; while she was in secondary school, her father would invite her friends into his bedroom and give them money, but he wouldn't give her any and she began to look tattered. Her urge to go with men grew; she wanted to know what it felt like. The first man gave her ₦500, and she made it a habit.

What are we to make of this? Brian Larkin, who is interested in the way this character "is periodically inserted to inject sexual havoc and bursts of sheer outrage," follows Adejunmobi (2002) in finding that while the actions of the women in *Glamour Girls* are presented as wrong, "their actions are justified as necessary responses to the violence of everyday life" (Larkin 2008, 189). He comments on Helen's choice to "boycott classes" to make money as a prostitute: "The scandalous world of Nigerian film is often erected over the much more quotidian struggles of everyday life, and it is the contrast of the one with the other that gives these films their charge" (ibid., 190). As in *Living in Bondage*, the life of a prostitute gets anchored in very recognizable real-life difficulties and the prostitute herself is humanized, given a name, a history—in the earlier film, even a soul. Larkin sees Helen as a trickster. I would go further than he does in arguing that the response to her outrageous behavior is always tempered by the traditional ambivalence around the trickster. She is witty, courageous, free, a worldly, practical satirist. And then this last scene is softening; no external judgment comes into it, and she disappears from our view unpunished, unscathed. If men fall in love with prostitutes it is because they are lovable—their hearts are not gold, but they do have hearts. *Glamour Girls* is set up to demonize its characters in obvious ways, but subversive understanding and sympathy may creep in.

Doris and her friends attend the millionaire's cocktail party, the camera surveying the room full of people. Muzak plays on the soundtrack, drowning out dialogue for long periods. What we see resembles the "social diary" segments on Nigerian television, in which rich people display their importance. Men are picking up women. Jane (Liz Benson), eyes and teeth flashing, is approached by Alex (Raymond Johnson), who says he's running for president. "That will cost a lot of money," she responds. Doris and Thelma arrive with the transformed Sandra in tow. Sandra is shy and tentative, not sure she likes the scene. Soon a managing director hooks up with her.

It turns out Jane already has a man, of the ideal type. As Desmond (Sola Fosudo) departs from their home, he tells her he will go from his oil company directors meeting to her parents to settle their traditional marriage ceremony. Jane telephones Thelma, who is delighted to hear the news.

Sandra has also hit the jackpot: her new man, Chief Esiri, offers her a banking job complete with car and driver, furnishes a duplex for her, and proposes marriage. She thanks Doris, who tells her to use her connections and influence well, now that she's come "to the top class of senior girl," and refers to the basis of Sandra's career, which we haven't actually seen—"No more hawking in the night, no more standing in the road for a pick."

Meanwhile Jane gets a call from home, saying that her father's second wife has told Desmond her secret: she has been a streetwalker all her life. It is a long way from the street to Desmond's mansion, whose two full sets of living room furniture the camera pans over, but as already noted, social mobility and incomplete class formation are characteristic of Nigerian society, and there seems to be an affinity between the ruling elite and the prostitutes with whom they mingle. The stigma of the street should be disastrous, but it isn't: Desmond comes home cheerful, forgiving, and high-minded. If Jane has a ten-year-old son, as he has been told, it's a sign that she did not get an abortion, as 95 percent of women have had. "I know you can change. We are sometimes forced by circumstances to lead a certain life. . . . Jane, promise me you'll never go back to your past rough life, and I promise to stand by you forever."

Doris is planning to marry Daniel, a very young man. Everyone comments. One of Daniel's friends thinks she is too old for him, in spite of her money. Another says size or age would not stop him from marrying a woman if she were rich. Daniel maintains he is a full-grown man and will always be in control. Sandra is appalled: "Everything you've risked from AIDS from old men you're going to throw away on a young boy?" Doris says she is in love with him. But then in sequences scattered through the rest of the film we watch her dominate him with merciless tongue lashings: "That's the only way to handle small boys like him. You always have to be one step ahead or they will break you." She continues her relationship with her wealthy old chief in spite of Daniel's objections and subjects him to symbolic humiliations including washing her underwear.

Jane's mother has a stroke. Desmond gallantly flies off to see to her medical care but passes out himself on the way home, is hospitalized, and has to have his legs amputated. Meanwhile Alex, the man Jane met at the party, besieges her. He discusses huge transactions on his cell phone while she listens. "What makes a man popular in the country besides money? If you have money you can buy the so-called elites and the masses." He wants her to divorce Desmond and become the next first lady of the country. He claims he has a passport for her with an American visa and a dress for her to wear to dinner with the President of Nigeria. He sends his lawyer to help her mobilize all her assets. She goes to Desmond in his hospital bed to collect signatures. Alex brusquely orders his driver to be careful with Jane's money, which now fills the trunk of his car, before plying Jane with more lies. She is insatiably in love with him. As the coup de grace, he makes off with one of Jane's cars.

Another young man, Dennis, turns up by chance at Sandra's door, and she falls in love with him. Unfortunately, Doris is ready for another boy toy, snatches him, and quarrels bitterly with Sandra. Sandra naively supposes she deserves happiness. In a dream, she marries the poor young stranger instead of Chief Esiri, who looks on approvingly. In reality, Chief Esiri wants revenge for being jilted. Dennis goes to America, evidently on the money Sandra has amassed from the chief, and writes a nasty letter rejecting her. She is fired from her job and evicted from her duplex, allowed to leave with a single box of clothes. She takes a last look around and collapses.

Jane, semicomatose with shame, remorse, and anger, gets a phone call telling her where to find Alex. She goes to his hotel room, pulls a gun, and shoots him in the head. The "senior girls" theme song plays as she is led away in handcuffs.

The strands of the plot are braided together so that Jane and Sandra reach their catastrophes simultaneously. Since Aristotle, we seem to have only one essential metaphor for talking about plotting: a piece of rope, or it could be string or ribbon, which is "denoué," unknotted, at the denouement, difficulties unraveled; or the loose ends are tied up, in a pretty bow or a hangman's noose, an elegant firm containment. In this case it is a stout rope being laid, fibers twisted in parallel for strength.

The stories of Sandra and Jane are similar almost to the point of redundancy. Both women rise from streetwalking, taken up by good men who know what market they found the women in but who still love them and establish them in fashionable occupations, luxurious housing, and matrimony—redemption and respectability, all in one comfortable package. Both of them throw all this away. The obvious moral is that there is something wrong with women who prostitute themselves: they should not be trusted. But their naiveté is emphasized even more than their treachery. Sandra's role in the conversation where Doris and Thelma lay out their principles—money comes before love, women should rigorously pursue their own interests in a world dominated by men—is to register shock at the ideological scandal. Later she will disapprove of Doris's marriage to Daniel because she thinks a woman should look up to her husband. She is not a calculating creature; in fact, the poor thing cannot calculate at all. Her mistake is to suppose she is entitled to love, to romance, after years of selling herself in a quest for security.

Jane is more culpable. The resources typical of daytime television are used to emphasize that divorcing your devoted husband while he lies in a hospital bed with his legs amputated is wrong. Her infatuation with Alex is compounded of sexual desire, romantic love, and a dazzling, utterly blinding fantasy of wealth, glamour, and power. She is a dupe. Then she sounds the depths of guilt and sorrow. Shooting Alex in the head is not the Christian thing to do, but it is a sign of character. But what character? Is this the conclusion of an argument that women are wicked, without self-control, and dangerous, or the spectacle of an erring mortal, a woman who recovers her pride and courage to assert rough justice, to play out the last scene of her tragedy on her own terms? At the film's end Jane wields a gun, as Doris wielded a car at the opening. This framing seems to pose the question of whether women should be trusted with these powerful objects.

The film sets up these sharp psychosocial ambivalences but does not resolve them. The doubling of the plots, adjacent but separate, does not double the pity and fear. As viewers, our attention is dispersed as well as ambivalent, which detaches us a bit from emotional involvement, encouraging us to reflect on the systematic qualities of the world that produces such similar stories. Doris and Thelma, largely detached from plot lines, establish the film's terrain, articulating the rules of the game. They are players who have already won, and their ruthless principles are true enough that they will never lose. Doris and Thelma are the hot stereotype of the "senior girl," created for us to heap opprobrium on. They are also agents of an analytic demonstration of the way of the world.

And then, finally, there is the strand involving the tall beautiful prostitute Helen—formally the most radical element, because these episodes are attached to the film entirely on the grounds of thematic extension. As soon as she acquires any depth as a character, she slips away. An outlier, her vignettes never touch any of the other stories or characters in the film, in violation of the ordinary logic of film (or soap opera) construction, and for that matter they are discontinuous with one another. Nnebue might have hired four actors instead of one to play in these four episodes; that would have emphasized even more the episodes' function of expanding the social space the film surveys. This critical survey is at the center of the film's purposes.

Nnebue's formal strategies open up extensive social space, but the same unrelievedly grim things are going on everywhere. Glamor girls are treacherous, greedy, domineering, and self-centered. Some men are much better, but others are even worse. Conflict between age-grades is as merciless as conflict between the sexes. Sandra had tried to play things straight and got nowhere. Doris and Thelma show that being hard as nails is the way to survive in a predatory environment, where emotional violence is constant and apparently structural. The world of *Living in Bondage* seems saturated with meaning in comparison, opening out into emotional, familial, spiritual, and cultural dimensions. The comparison highlights how narrow, barren, and decultured the lives in *Glamour Girls* are. The secularity of *Glamour Girls*, with nothing visible beyond the arid desires of the players, makes the glamor garish and thin, and even the gender stereotyping loses its potency in this general spectacle of the lost. The irony of this spiritual reduction is latent, held off—apparently too far off for the later born-again Nnebue, who, a rumor has it, has destroyed the master tape of the film.

GLAMOUR GIRLS 2: THE ITALIAN CONNECTION

Glamour Girls 2 (1996, two years after the first part) is not a sequel in the normal Nollywood sense of a continuation of the same story, relying on our investment in characters and dramatic tension. It is a sequel because Nnebue has more to show us about the topic. If part 1 always stays in the same social dimension, a hot but narrow zone, part 2 plays across a wider range. Formally it is also innovative and exploratory, but in different ways.

It opens in front of the female hostel of the Federal Polytechnic in Lagos, with the familiar theme song about "senior girls" playing over the credits. It is a busy scene, girls coming and going from men's cars at night. These are junior senior girls, unsupervised and on the make. Nnebue told me, "at a lower level, we have some glamor girls at the university; those ones graduate to be the senior ones, but this is how they started." Later a whole genre of films would develop from this setting (see chapter 11). A girl who has just emerged from a car greets her friends: "Whoever says money doesn't buy happiness doesn't know where to shop for it." She takes ₦20,000 ($235)—several years' tuition—out of her bag and slaps it down. "This guy is sitting on oil money."

In daylight, Fred (Zach Orji) is waiting in his BMW outside the hostel for his wife, Jessica (Tina Amuziam). She greets her best friend Anita (Eucharia Anunobi), who is getting out of another vehicle. Anita has been missing for two weeks. "I was broke so I went hunting in Lagos." Jessica is leaving school, going to Italy, where her husband has gotten her admission to a university.

A Hausa businessman comes looking for the girl to whom he gave the ₦20,000. He meets her roommate, who says that she is out with her boyfriend, that she goes with any man, that she has no loyalty. The Alhaji promptly invites this new girl—disloyal herself—for lunch. Later he ushers her into his bedroom. He opens a bag from which a snake slithers, and he turns suddenly stern and dangerous. "This is business. That is twenty thousand naira. But you have to make love to this snake." This is a money ritual, of course, in a common variant form in which the ensorcelled, often drugged victim vomits money. Often, as in Willie Akuffo's early classic Ghanaian film *Diabolo* 1 (1991), the victim is a prostitute and the setting a hotel room. The Alhaji blows powder into her face and she collapses, screaming in horror as the snake disappears up her skirt. The camera pans across the façade of the campus hostel; she staggers up the stairs and dies in the arms of her frantic roommate.

And now Sandra appears, our Sandra from part 1, sadder and wiser though still elegantly dressed. As at the opening of the first part, she is down and out and has come to see Doris, now the proprietress of a huge fancy building. Every inch the well-dressed businesswoman, Doris is handing out passports and tickets to Italy to grateful young women, university graduates, whom Doris is glad to provide with employment. She exhorts them to work hard and sends them down the hall to Daniel, who will arrange their transportation to the airport.

Doris is cold with Sandra. She takes a cell phone call from her partner Maureen in Italy about the girls' arrival, at the same time juggling a call on her landline. Phones are the most fetishized objects in this film; cell phones were new and glamorous in Nigeria, and landlines were also hard to come by, requiring an arduous, expensive process that normally involved bribery. Doris makes a proud little speech to Sandra about having sponsored over twenty unemployed university graduates for jobs in Europe and America—"That's my little contribution to assist this country"—before berating Sandra for having insulted her, "her goddess" who had done everything for her. She orders Sandra out of her office.

A new character, Sophia (Blessing Eremi), comes to Doris's house to complain about problems in her relationship with her chief. Sophia then visits a "native doctor," surrounded by the accoutrements of his trade, visually in another universe from the rest of the film, who prepares a love potion for her. He tells her to wash her "private parts" with the potion and add it to the chief's favorite soup. Between extended and utterly mundane shots of her at the stove, she covers herself with a wrapper and squats over a bowl on her kitchen floor. There is nothing sexy about this, any more than the snake disappearing between the legs of the student was sexy. These two episodes are the only points where the supernatural enters the film. They both spring from a popular folkloric or urban-folkloric culture, and Nnebue respects the visual prudery that culture maintains even as it tells the wildest stories about sex. The plain domesticity of the kitchen scene is integral to its power: men fear women's witchcraft because there is no way a man can protect himself from the one who cooks for him.

The love potion works marvelously well. Sophia's chief arrives angry. He has set her up in the best-stocked boutique on fashionable Allen Avenue on the condition of absolute discretion, but she has boasted of everything he had done for her to her friends, and one of them has jealously told his wife. The theme of treachery between women is constant in this film. Sophia wants to marry him, move into his house, and become a cowife. This chief superficially resembles Sandra's Chief Esiri in part 1—the only character in that film with a Nigerian name. But Sophia's chief is played by Jide Kosoko, one of the most famous actors from the Yoruba traveling theater tradition, and he brings a much stronger cultural ambience with him, in which stories about polygamy are natural. He is quick to forgive Sophia when she kneels and apologizes. She plies him with wine, newly fashionable among the Nigerian elite. Obviously a sponsor is paying for product placement—the wine is repeatedly called "beautiful," Kosoko holds up his glass appreciatively, the camera zooms in on the label, and both the name of the wine—"Celebrity"—and the name of the importer are mentioned. Her fridge is crammed with bottles. This is a love potion, too.

Some months later Sandra gets out of a huge SUV and proudly slaps the $500 she has just made—in American dollars—on Doris's desk. They have apparently patched things up. Doris says before Sandra goes to Italy she will take her to a club where she will meet "the women of the new era, women who rule men, women who have power in this country."

Like the party Doris took Sandra to in part 1 or the millionaire's party where Andy was seduced, we watch this one for a long time as spectacle, a spectacle of clothes and bodies, the social presence of fancy people, tables covered with food and drink. The dialogue is turned down and the music turned up, the camera mostly held below the level of the faces so they are framed against the high ceiling of the hotel ballroom. After more than five minutes of this, Doris proposes a toast to Sophia, whose forty-fifth birthday celebration this is, and says a few words about their organization, Women of Substance International, a philanthropic organization of women who have made remarkable achievements in their careers. Sophia's chief goes public with their relationship, declaring she is his wife.

The Women of Substance International gather around a boardroom table, Doris at its head in business attire with a huge cross around her neck. One of them, Vera (Clarion Abiola), has a complaint against Doris's partner Maureen (Dolly Unachukwu). An American agency offered $150,000 for a black girl to have sex with a chimpanzee in a pornographic movie. Vera sent someone to do the job, naturally not telling her what was involved. (Everyone nods.) The girl became a walking corpse, and Maureen injected her to death as a mercy killing. Now Maureen wants to keep most of the money. Vera threatens to go to the police if she doesn't get 70 percent. Maureen counters with a litany of problems she has fixed for Vera in Italy: girls who had to be eliminated because they had written incriminating letters, or needed medical care and then secret burial. Doris takes control: "Let's resolve this, it's a small matter . . ."

Maureen and Doris drive to visit the woman (Buki Ajayi) who brought Maureen up when her parents died. It's a warm family scene—the only time in either part of *Glamour Girls* we see anything like this, glamor girls being defined in large part by the fact that they live their lives outside of families. As a way of thanking Mama for her past generosity, Maureen takes away Mama's daughter Laura (Thelma Nwosu), her adoptive sister, promising her a better life in Italy.

Doris and Maureen distribute passports to a party of girls including Laura and Sandra. Everything is perfectly respectable and businesslike. Doris gives another of her speeches telling the girls to behave and be good ambassadors. They pass through Murtala Muhammed Airport in Lagos.

And then a title, "Italy," over a shot of traffic at night. The street looks like Airport Road in Lagos. Nnebue's budget clearly did not include the expense of location shooting in Europe—all we will see of "Italy" are interior scenes furnished with Nigerian-looking furniture. There are no Italians (the four white men in the film have Australian accents). Italy was prominent in the Nigerian imagination because of newspaper accounts of large-scale human trafficking networks taking Nigerian women to northern Italy.

A couple of Nigerian prostitutes eagerly await Maureen's arrival and scream with pleasure when she appears, asking if the new girls are hot enough and strong enough. Up to this point, all the women in the film who prostitute themselves have had the refinement to mingle in high society and be taken up by wealthy men, but the girls already working in Italy have the look, the talk, and the body language of the street. Four of them dance lasciviously, the camera getting low down, lascivious itself.

Maureen assembles the new girls, collects their passports, and launches into a speech of the now-familiar kind, telling them they must work to survive and be grateful for the chance. Into this speech she drops the fact that their work will be prostitution. They are shocked, but Maureen's rhetoric flows on seamlessly: prostitution is no longer taboo, there is talk of legalizing it, Italy is feeling the same economic pressures as Nigeria, and so on. Sandra objects and demands to be taken back home, but Maureen requires $45,000 to buy her way out. Sandra makes speeches about how she has been tricked into becoming a slave to someone she hates. Later in private a woman who has been there for a while warns her not to try to escape: those women operate like a syndicate, they are dangerous, have a surveillance system, are in league with the police, will have you killed. "God willing in a year or two you can buy your way out and work for yourself."[5] We catch one last glimpse of Sandra, sandwiched unhappily between two white men in a hotel bed. When she asks for her money, they say they have already paid her manager, and she slumps with disgusted resignation.

The scandal is not prostitution itself—a thoroughly familiar phenomenon sometimes, as we've seen, viewed with understanding as a strategy an individual may adopt out of necessity or desire for advancement. But the exploitation of a woman's body by a third party, enslavement by a syndicate as opposed to individual entrepreneurialism, is unfamiliar and shocking. The element of duplicity is also shocking, though nothing is more common than treachery in this film or in the whole run of Nollywood films.

Innocent young Laura, Maureen's adoptive sister who had been sent off by their Mama with injunctions to remember the Lord, announces she would rather die than practice prostitution—a fierce virtuous speech, shot in close-up. Maureen tells her enforcer Bruce, enormous in a bowler hat, to teach her a lesson. Laura breaks a bottle over his head and he kills her. Maureen instructs him to "take this thing away." Maureen's heartlessness is over the top, and there is no attempt to make it psychologically plausible. The scene is designed to make viewers scream at the screen in outrage at her wickedness—an example of Larkin's "aesthetics of outrage," a melodramatic concoction meant to provoke a reaction even at the physiological level against a social wrong.

With this, Maureen, Sandra, Doris, and the Women of Substance International all fall away, never to be seen again, and we pick up the story of Fred, Jessica, and Anita, whom we met briefly in front of the campus hostel at the beginning of the film. Fred has brought Jessica to Italy, and now he explains why: he wants her to prostitute herself. His rhetoric is not corporate but sweet talk in the idiom of romantic partnership. It will be their secret; then they can go home and open a business. When she comes back with cash from her first night out, he tells her, "This is the beginning of the rest of our lives. By the grace of God all our dreams will come true," and offers to draw her a bath.

He gets a call from an agency representing an American film producer offering $150,000 if she will be in a movie having sex with a dog. She refuses indignantly, sure it would mean her death, but he gets the agency to raise the price to $350,000 and claims a doctor has assured him there would be no side effects. He translates $350,000 into naira—thirty million, a number he repeats—and she relents. On the film set, she looks at the bed and the dog on it and walks off, but Fred coaxes her into playing her part. (The sex act itself is not shown.) Later, unhappy that Fred is squandering the money on high living, she tells him to go back to Lagos, build a house, and set up a small-scale industry. She will stay in Italy to make more money.

In Lagos, Fred goes to the polytechnic to meet Anita, whom Jessica has asked after, and invites her to help him move into the new house. It's palatial. "Is this your house? . . . it's just like paradise," she says. She sashays around, looking elegant herself, elated at the luxury, liking how it makes her feel. He brings out a bottle of wine; again the label gets a close-up. Both of them are suave, commenting on the beautiful fixtures and furnishings—everything has been imported from Italy. She can twirl from sofa to sofa without spilling wine from her champagne flute onto the leather. He slips into something more comfortable and then she says she feels sticky. He has a Jacuzzi.[6] In a scene that became legendary and established her career, Eucharia Anunobi as Anita shows what a Jacuzzi is for. She simpers behind a lavish pile of soap suds, flashing her long legs; she invites Fred to sponge her back, flirtatiously telling him not to look, and then pulls him in. From tub to bed, the whole sequence is an exercise in the visual codes of international R-rated filmmaking, the camera coyly dropping to bare legs as towels drop. In Nigeria, this was unprecedented boldness—we are a long way from Sophia washing her private parts in the middle of her kitchen. While they are in bed, Jessica calls. Fred gives her a report on the setting up of their plastics factory. When he hangs up he asks Anita if she wanted to say hello to her friend and she giggles.

They work out at an upscale health club, smiling and smooching. At home, he gets a birthday card from Jessica. Anita has a better present for him: she's pregnant. He's delighted and says he'll marry her. They go shopping for baby things.

A friend calls Jessica to tell her Anita is now married to her husband and they are living in the same house. Fred, troubled, sits down for a talk with Anita. Jessica is coming home and he wants Anita to move into a house in town. She is indignant. "You're telling me you're not man enough to control your own house? Isn't it an African tradition that a man can marry as many wives as he can care for, and if there is more than one wife in the house, they learn to tolerate each other?" The appeal to African tradition echoes strangely in this mansion, so full of imported objects and so empty of people, so cut off from any hint of social life beyond the couple—a temple to absolutely private consumption, hidden behind its massive gate. The ways Fred and Anita spend money are profoundly foreign to most Nigerians: the health club, the imported apparatus of childcare in a culture where babies are carried on their mothers' backs and play with wooden spoons and other objects of daily life. But perhaps the assumption of polygamy does partly account for Anita's complete lack of apparent conflict as she moves in with her best friend's husband.

Jessica does not see it that way. She comes through the airport and storms into the house. She bitterly claims she twice saved Anita's life when she had stolen other women's men. When Fred tries the line about African tradition allowing him more than one wife, she replies, "Fuck you and your damn tradition. So what is traditional is for a man to induce his wife to sleep with a dog, take drugs, and prostitute for him?" She pulls out a gun and shoots down both of them, blood spurting. The "senior girls" theme song starts up one last time as she drives off into the dark.

This final bloody rough justice administered by an angry woman with a gun echoes the end of part 1, but Jane is handcuffed after shooting Alex while Jessica lets herself out through the mansion's big gate. Even more remarkably, Maureen and Doris vanish unpunished. While Jessica's disappearance into the Lagos night might conceivably be interpreted as a case of moral ambiguity, Maureen's continuing wicked existence would seem to require a part 3. Perhaps this injustice simply gets lost in the film's remarkably open formal structure, its general loosening of the laws of gravity as it navigates through a world awash in scandalousness.

Part 1 was garish; part 2 is exorbitant. The clearest instance of exorbitance is the notion that a mansion and plastics factory can be built in Lagos on the proceeds from one woman's prostitution in Italy. What is the exchange rate? This is a fantastic version of the way towns in Edo State from which the Nigerian prostitutes who work in northern Italy are heavily recruited were being transformed by their remittances. The prostitution included the filming of sex with a dog for an exorbitant price, a third of a million dollars.

Sex in Italy is unnatural by Nigerian standards: our other closest glimpse of a particular sex act is Sandra in bed with two white men, and the dispute at the Women of Substance International board meeting is about Italian business, the girl who was sent to have sex with a chimpanzee. An American agency is doing the recruiting, and the film crew is Australian; they serve an international market of white men who have racist and degrading fantasies about African women, linking them to animals. Unnatural acts seem a logical extension of foreign prostitution. The girl who had sex with the chimpanzee turned into a zombie; Jessica similarly assumes the dog would lead to her death. The other instance of sex with an animal in the film—the money ritual with the snake at the beginning—is the key to these fears and to the whole symbolic complex. The foreign, the bestial, and the occult are strongly associated, intertwined versions of the danger of exchanging sex in a market that has lost all social restraints and become an interface with the alien in its most absolute forms. Sexual commerce with the foreign/occult brings supernatural amounts of wealth but deadly consequences, hence it is always associated with treacherous exploitation by a third party. To reverse the symbolic logic: sexual exploitation gets figured as a money ritual or a displaced version of one.

Jessica is treacherously exploited by both her husband and her best friend, the betrayal by another woman emphasized as much as her pimping husband's perfidy. Apart from the Hausa businessman with his snake, all the other treachery and exploitation we see is carried out by women. Women of Substance International is modeled on the women's clubs that are ubiquitous in Nigeria; the powerful associations of market women are also a relevant model, and probably also the coven of witches. But the organization is not particularly demonized on a gendered basis. The Women of Substance are thoroughly integrated with the male elite and share the same business culture and hypocritical rhetoric of economic enterprise, personal responsibility, achievement, and philanthropy. Nnebue is a connoisseur of this hypocrisy and an analyst of the institutionalized evil beneath it. He had begun exploring this material in *Dirty Deal* and would continue it in *Rituals* (1997) (chapter 8).

The stereotype of Nollywood's thematics—"scripts that highlight rituals, violence, vulgarities and other lewd values sell well" (Alhaji Adegboyega Arulogun, quoted in Ayorinde 1999)—is an exact if unkind and incomplete description of Nnebue's material. He was catalyst rather than sole inventor of this thematics, and his sensationalism was more easily and frequently imitated than the more searching qualities of his work. The staying power of the themes is a function of how deeply rooted they are in the audience's anxieties and desires, and nothing focuses anxieties and desires like the figure of the glamor girl.

CHAPTER 4

Family Films

FRAMINGS

The melodramatic family film is the queen of Nollywood genres and holds sway over nearly all of them. In common Nigerian parlance, "family films" and "love films" are the main constituents of the encompassing generic category of "emotional films." "Family films" is perhaps used less often than other genre names because it is almost redundant—how many Nollywood films are *not* about families? Some, like *Glamour Girls*, but not many. When people describe a family film they tend to move straight to naming the actors in it or recounting the story. "Family" does not mean "G" for general audiences—there is such a rating in the NFVCB system but only a tiny fraction of films get it, and there is virtually no production of Nigerian films directed specifically at children of any age. The way the ratings are applied shows how strict the moral principles around child raising are, but the fact that televisions are always on in sitting rooms means that in practice children are constantly exposed to films rated for mature audiences. The term "family films" refers to subject matter, not intended audience, and when Nollywood makes films about families it goes looking for trouble.

The family is the horizon of life in Africa even more than in most other places. In precolonial Igbo society—the world of *Things Fall Apart*—the clan was virtually the only form of social organization. Achebe shows us no political, civil, military, or religious structures apart from or beyond the clan, which is a segmented lineage structure, an extended family. The family extends into the spiritual dimension: reincarnation is understood to happen within families, and Okonkwo feels a metaphysical terror at his son's conversion to Christianity since his own eventual expected immortality as an ancestral spirit depends on having descendants who sacrifice to the ancestors, thereby keeping them alive (Achebe 1994b, 153).

That was then (and it was in Igboland—other Nigerian cultures were not so exclusively clan based), and much has changed. But even Nigerian university admission forms ask a question (to which the answer can be crucial) about the student's state of origin, and this means where the family is rooted, not where the student was born or raised—it may be a place she has never seen. One of the basic themes of African literature and celluloid film is that love relationships formed between apparently autonomous individuals in modern settings (universities, cities, or abroad) run into problems when one lover's individualism turns out to be severely compromised by family membership. (Achebe's *No Longer at Ease* is an example.) The breakdown of the institutions of the modern state and economy has thrown people back on family resources. Making one's career in Africa normally involves manipulating all available networks, beginning with the family. Most Nigerian extended families include someone who has made it, at least relatively, and so is looked to for patronage. Certainly every family includes a more or less infinite number of poor relatives in a village. Class consciousness, or the lack thereof, is deeply informed by these facts.

This background is not usually in family films, but it is there behind them. In American movies or television shows, one may find a mother-in-law unhappy because her daughter-in-law has not produced a child. In Nollywood, the ruthless mother-in-law's unspoken, vastly more potent arsenal of authority includes the supreme social value of fertility; the old tradition of marriages being contracted between lineages rather than individuals, which gave families a nearly absolute right to be in their children's business; and the option of polygyny (not quite respectable in some circles but utterly normal and accepted across wide swaths of Nigerian society and therefore always a live possibility and a threat to a wife's position) or divorce (in some Nigerian cultures, a common and easy thing; in others, such as the Igbo, heavily stigmatized and rare). The family is normally framed in fairly narrow dimensions in family films, but the exigent relative from outside the nuclear family stands in for this powerful wider context.

The films tend to show more or less nuclear families. This reflects changes in the way life is lived (urbanization being the most important) and in how families are thought about: the mutually reinforcing ideologies of Christian companionate marriage, the limited household as a unit of capitalist accumulation and consumption, and the modern family as a foundation of the state and molder of citizens. Nuclear families are of central interest not because everyone lives in them but at least in part because many people do not, as

Birgit Meyer acutely observes: the masses are curious and suspicious about what more modern and prosperous people are doing behind the walls of their compounds, and the videos cater to this curiosity, just as they make visible the supernatural realm (Meyer 1999a, 2002a, 2003a, 2006b). Daniel Jordan Smith, in a study of Igbo marriages, discusses how couples in companionate modern marriages based on love try to present their extended families with the façade of a happy relationship in order to keep the families at bay. This creates an incentive to solve problems through companionate negotiations, but also to hide problems—Smith's particular subject is women's reluctance to discuss their husbands' infidelities with their husbands or with anyone else (Smith 2009). The films get inside this privacy, showing couples discussing things in bed or over breakfast, modeling such partnership. (A family sharing a meal around a table is itself an emblem of modernity: in the more customary practice no room or table is set aside for meals, and people are served in order of seniority, the man first.). The films are devoted to scandal mongering and revealing hidden secrets, sexual infidelities being their favorite topic.

Family films are set in a range of dimensions. Many fit the international pattern of family melodrama, located in a private realm antithetical to the public, where intimate emotional relationships are paramount. Daniel Ademinokan's *Modupe Temi/I Thank God for my Own* (2008) is a tour-de-force psychological drama with only two characters, a married couple alone in their home; the film's publicity stesses this framing because it is so unusual in its extreme contraction—"One man, one woman, one house"—suggesting claustrophobic terror or perhaps the ultimate elimination round of a reality television show.

But family films may also be framed as the first level of the social as opposed to the private, and so the genre may be set against "love films," which are rooted in the perspective of the lovers themselves, while the family film sets romantic coupling in a wider horizon and perspective. In family meetings, elders deliberate and a whole range of life issues get adjudicated. The family film may take a large step in the direction of the genre with the next wider ambit, the "community film."

Nigerian television's initial framing of the family was through the situation comedy or drama. Not all situation comedies had family settings: *Basi & Company* was set in a rooming house, and *Village Headmaster*'s horizon was dispersed over a village and was more or less explicitly nationalist in its framing. *The Masquerade*—the other great original classic—was more (though not entirely) centered on a single patriarchal household, dominated by the senior male Chief Zebrudaya (Chika Okpala), the most dynamic character as well as the most authoritative. It included not one but two comic servants, Clarus and

Gringory—major characters, the latter played by the show's creator and writer, James Iroha, who, though Igbo himself, made Gringory an Efik. The household was not defined as the intimate emotional space of the nuclear family but, again, as a figure for the national family.

WOMEN AND NOLLYWOOD

Soap operas—that is, serials set up around the continuing, dramatic emotional lives of a set of characters—came later. Although on Nigerian television there was never anything like the more or less exclusively feminine housewives' space of American daytime television, the advent of soap operas was to some extent associated with women. Lola Fani-Kayode was the first important director and producer, her serial *Mirror in the Sun* providing inspiration by its high quality, sophistication, and enormous popular success. Amaka Igwe is very much Fani-Kayode's successor and was quick and generous in acknowledging the debt.

Women are a distinct minority behind the camera in Nollywood, but according to producer/director Madu Chikwendu women directors are more likely than men to provide their own financing rather than working for the marketers, with consequent greater control; women also act as executive producers for their husbands and gain influence that way. A few of the most powerful players in the industry are women. They tend to be writers and producers who may also direct, and several are notable institution builders. Amaka Igwe was an expert businesswoman presiding over perhaps the largest Nigerian film and television production company and a radio station; she also undertook projects to record the history of Nollywood and, with her husband Charles Igwe, created BoBTV (Best of the Best TV), an annual market in Abuja for audio-visual production and a convention attended by high-ranking figures from the government. Gifted with an exceptionally strong and clear mind, she was the most quoted analyst of the industry and a deep thinker about its future. The producer , writer, and lawyer Peace Fiberisima Osigwe-Aniyam, from the same mold, created AMAA, the African Movie Academy Awards, the glitziest and most influential annual awards ceremony, which has acquired a significant international dimension. Helen Ukpabio, a preacher who wrote books about her early career as a witch, founded an evangelical empire that includes nearly seventy churches in Nigeria, Ghana, Cameroon, and South Africa, and Liberty Films, which produced some twenty Christian videos between 1998 and 2010 (Ukah 2011). She writes the films and hires big-name Nollywood directors and actors. The films are distributed both through her churches and through the Nollywood distribution system and are among the best-selling films (Okome 2007a). The writer and producer Emem Isong, whose films explore psychological extremity and sometimes exploit daring sexual material such as lesbianism (*Emotional Crack* (2003), directed by Lancelot Imasuen), emerged as the most successful producer in the doldrums that followed the crisis of 2007. Some leading Nigerian actresses (including Joke Silva, Stephanie Okereke Linus, Uche Jombo, and Omoni Oboli) have turned to directing, writing, and/or producing their own films. Most of the women mentioned in this paragraph run private film training academies.

As consumers, women dominate Nollywood. The industry agrees that women are the primary audience—80 percent of it, according to Charles Novia (2012, 33).[1] Specific Nollywood genres seem more or less gendered: it is perhaps too easy to identify sentimental weepies with women and action films with a more masculine viewership. Overall, women viewers appear to exert a pervasive influence. *Living in Bondage*'s steady interest in strong women characters may be motivated in part by the generic influence of soap operas and by a consciousness of women viewers, even though the dramatic framing around a man's choices, the problematic of chasing wealth, and the ideological framing, both Christian and Igbo, are all strongly patriarchal.

More specifically, women are thought to be the ones who make the decisions about which film to buy. Men may also watch them, in the face of a strong if gradually eroding tendency for men (especially Igbo men) to look down on the films their wives love. Many men claim they never watch Nollywood films, but questioning sometimes reveals vast knowledge acquired by hearing and seeing thousands of them out of the corners of their eyes as they pretend to be buried in their newspapers. More specifically still, market women have been seen as the center of the target audience. They are archetypes of the female popular demographic and they are the ones who can be counted upon to have some money, the price of a movie, tied up in their wrappers at the end of the week as they head home to their families.

VIOLATED 1

Amake Igwe's *Violated* (1996) was not aimed at market women—or at least, it did not want to be seen as aimed at them. It sold 175,000 copies, a record that stood for a long time, so many different kinds of people must have bought it. But the marketing campaign assaulted the high end of Nigerian society, trying to capture it for the new video industry. Amaka's husband Charles Igwe had left a job with Citibank to explore the possibilities of Nollywood. The Igwes were consciously experimenting, trying to shape the new, unformed market, aware of its enormous potential. The film was advertised on the NTA for thirty days to create general interest, but the opening was held at the MUSON Center, the most prestigious cultural venue in Lagos, and the first night was by invitation only—bait to excite the snobbery of Victoria Island high society. The unsettled class character of the new industry and of Nigerian society were on display. It was a bit as if a soap opera opened at Lincoln Center in New York. *Violated* features Joke Silva, the most illustrious stage actress of her generation, who channels Joan Collins for her part as the unbearable mother-in-law. The two central characters are played by the stars of Igwe's serial *Checkmate*, Ego Boyo (who also produced the film) and Richard Mofe-Damijo, beginning his long reign as Nollywood's leading man. Music plays continuously on the soundtrack (not music written for the film, but songs by Luther Vandross and Boyz II Men, as well as classical selections), marking it as soap opera-like rather than cinematic. The level of luxury represented—the mansion, the Mercedes stretch limo, the pleasure yacht—was unprecedented and effectively unsurpassable in Nigeria, but the filmmaking, while generally of high quality, is occasionally jerky, the soundtrack occasionally noisy, illustrating the contradiction discussed in chapter 2 between the objects of desire and the means of their representation.

The film's opening is mostly in Pidgin, out of the mouths of ordinary people, nurses and a driver. The heroine starts poor, and her friends from her days as a salesgirl will keep up a relativizing commentary in Pidgin on her bumpy ascent through romance into the social stratosphere ("Dis love ting tire person"). The film begins in the dark, in the rain, in distress and confusion. An indistinct, anguished woman abandons twin babies and watches as they are picked up and carried into a clinic, where another woman is giving birth to a premature baby that does not survive. A nurse tells her driver that the doctor says she won't be able to have any more children. One of the nurses arranges for her to be given one of the foundlings in place of the baby she has lost. Ten years later the woman, Mrs. Sumbo Olu-Peters (Mildred Iweka), hosts a lavish birthday party for her son, Junior.

We meet Peggy (Ego Boyo) drifting pensively through the aisles of the upscale department store where she works, framed against shelves of commodities. Her Prince Charming Tega (Richard Mofe-Damijo) arrives to announce she scored the best marks in her class and so has gotten a job at his mother's bank. He sweeps her off in his impressive SUV. But first, she hands her boss a resignation letter and tells her off, to the immense satisfaction of her coworkers (and of anyone watching the film who has ever had a boss). She is fulfilling their fantasies, and they will continue to cheer her on.

Tega is ideal: he takes Peggy to his fancy house, solemnly gives her flowers for making him proud, kisses her with tender respect, pours champagne in front of his giant television, and gets down on his knees to make a speech, holding a little box with a ring in it. But she shakes her head—they don't know each other well enough. He takes this in stride. In following scenes he sponsors her makeover from Peggy the shop girl to Peggy the banker and takes her for a cruise on the Lagos lagoon in his crewed yacht.

But everyone has baggage. Tega's ex-wife Tessie (Funke Adepegba) turns up in his house with a mountain of luggage and an unbearable British accent, refusing to recognize their divorce. Detecting his mother's hand in this, he goes to see her in her enormous mansion. She orders him to remarry Tessie: he can sow wild oats with his salesgirl if he likes, but he must produce an heir with Tessie. This is a dynastic marriage, cementing an alliance with Chief Oghene's family. Tega is his father's heir, but his mother is his guardian until he has a child. This is high melodrama. His mother slaps him and he struggles visibly with his emotions as he tries to break free of this maternal domination, finally walking off.

In a restaurant, Peggy is spotted by Mr. Amadi (Kunle Bamtefa), who seems to know her as a prostitute. Peggy walks out, upset, and won't explain anything to Tega. She won't respond to his marriage proposal either. He is getting angry, and their relationship gets rocky. Peggy is disturbed by nightmares, fragmentary images of a surreptitious entry and running through the dark. Peggy goes to Tega's house and finds Tessie in possession, but Tega orders Tessie out. Peggy in banker's clothes goes to a village and stands distraught amidst the rough cement-block masonry of an empty house. Later she falls into Tega's arms, crying as the theme song plays: "You can count on this love in the storms of your life." They go boating again. Under a palm tree she tells him she loves him but does not want him to lose his inheritance—banks, airlines—on her account. He says his mother will come around.

A nice moment, but Peggy still has not explained anything and his mother has not come around. She writes out a check to pay Peggy off. Peggy laughs at it. "Is he so cheap? I can't be bought." Tega recognizes the renewed strains in his relationship with Peggy as his mother's doing. He rushes into his mother's bedroom to disown her, pouring keys and checkbooks onto her bed. Peggy's roommates notice she is pregnant. She gets sacked from her job at Mama Tega's bank and comes crying to Tega—also found at low ebb, asleep on his couch, liquor on the table—to ask if the marriage offer still holds. He smokes and doesn't answer.

But we cut to a church spire and the roommates throwing rice as the couple comes out and poses for pictures. In this film the wedding is a fleeting moment, conveyed as quickly and elliptically as possible, not a culmination or conclusion. Tessie's father learns of the wedding and withdraws his immense wealth from Mama Tega's bank.

Meanwhile, we have been getting to know the family of Joe and Sumbo Olu-Peters and their Junior. They are well off and love their boy, who has a computer in his room. Joe is a model of support and consideration, though he is away a lot. Sumbo is unhappy when he refers to the fact that she cannot have any more children and is even more disturbed when a new boy who looks exactly like Junior moves into the neighborhood and befriends him. Joe thinks her dislike of the new boy is irrational and arranges for them to have dinner with his parents, who turn out to be Mr. Amadi (who accosted Peggy in the restaurant and then appeared as Mama Tega's bank manager) and his wife. Crude Mr. Amadi remarks that the boys look so much alike that if he didn't trust his wife, he'd think Joe was the father of his boy too.

Peggy delivers her baby and Tega, who is trying with his friend Sam to get his own business started, comes to work looking like a new father, or "like shit," as Sam puts it. His mother intrudes, having heard about the baby "that gold digger" says is his. Tega accuses her of trying to frustrate his new business and orders her out, shouting.

VIOLATED 2

As part 2 begins, Peggy is having nightmares and flashbacks of twin babies—as we divine, she was the agonized woman in the dark at the beginning of part 1. She goes back to the village and finds one of her long-lost children, a girl named Courage. She's been sending money to the poor woman who picked the babies up that night, but the woman doesn't know where the boy is. Peggy still won't tell Tega what is going on. Mr. Amadi, recognizing Peggy at the bank, tells Mama Tega he used to know "Amuchi" very well and is surprised a noble family would admit her as a daughter-in-law.

Mama Tega invites Tega and Peggy to dinner. This is a trap: she has also invited Tega's ex-wife and her father, Chief Oghene. Tessie acts proprietary and won't keep her hands off Tega. Chief Oghene asks offensively pointed questions about where Peggy is from. Then the Amadis arrive. They address Peggy as Amuchi. Peggy wanders around the mansion in distress. The signature camera movement in this film is a plunging tracking shot down open staircases. (Charles Igwe was the Nigerian representative of Steadicam.) The camera's freedom of movement gives baroque volume to the immense interior spaces of the house—for Peggy, a nightmarish manifestation of the power she is up against. The party scatters into this extended space. Amadi tells Peggy she should leave town. Tega is informed by his mother that Peggy was five months pregnant when she left the Amadis' house. Tega finds Amadi trying to sexually assault Peggy, throws him off, and leads her away by the hand.

At home, Tega demands the truth. She tells him she was sixteen when she lost her parents and went to live with Mrs. Amadi, a distant relative. She refused Mr. Amadi's sexual advances. The night Mrs. Amadi was taken to the hospital in labor, an armed robber came to the house and raped Peggy. She was too ashamed to tell anyone. Five months later, when her pregnancy showed, Mr. Amadi threw her out of the house. She did everything she could to survive short of prostitution but could not take care of the twins she bore, so she abandoned them. As she made some money she sent it to the old woman who picked up the children. The woman won't tell her what she did with the boy. Peggy was reluctant to marry Tega because of this shameful past. She kneels to him for forgiveness, but he rejects her: "You should have told me. It was my right to know. Just leave me alone." Tega asks his mother for money, saying he's leaving town. Mama Tega and Tessie drive Peggy out of his house.

The Olu-Peters marriage is wracked by parallel strains. Fed by Mrs. Amadi's insinuations, Sumbo suspects Joe is having an affair. He angrily denies it and says her lack of trust will destroy the marriage. It seems he has been aiding a widow whose son is dying of sickle-cell anemia, a murky situation, but the thematic parallel is clear: keeping secrets is bad for marriages.

Peggy, installed again with her shopgirl roommates, has a revelation and goes to see the Amadis. On her way in she meets their son and his friend Junior, whom she takes for his brother. Mr. Amadi's goatish smell made the pieces of the puzzle finally fall into place: it was he who raped her on the night his wife gave birth, under cover of a fake armed robbery. Peggy says she is looking for her children; if she doesn't find them, she will come back and kill Mr. Amadi. Mrs. Amadi believes the accusation.

Peggy locks herself in her room, crying, but opens the door for Tega, who ushers in her daughter Courage. He is pleased with himself, and she is grateful but obsessed with her missing son. Together they search for him, a long, fruitless search, Tega's patience fraying as he tries to keep up with her. In their absence, their neglected baby is hospitalized. By accident at the hospital Peggy encounters the nurse who sold her twin baby boy to Sumbo.

Peggy goes to confront Sumbo—a desperate encounter, both women fighting out of the most fundamental emotional need. Sumbo is angry, scared, and aggressive. She has a birth certificate. Peggy counters that she has the doctor and nurse ready to testify. Sumbo offers money, but Peggy just wants her son. Sumbo argues that he is her son: she's done everything for him; Peggy left him to die, but she nursed him back to life from pneumonia. "Why do you want us all to suffer, because you want to indulge your belated maternal instincts?" They are both crying. Peggy says she has suffered, doesn't want to spend the rest of her life suffering. Sumbo retorts, "You want to take him away from the only home he has ever had. He's all I have and all I can ever have. What will I tell Joe? You know the pain of losing a child. You lost him for eight years; don't make me lose him forever." Something changes inside Peggy and she turns to leave. "Please promise me you'll take good care of him as you've always done." They hold hands. Peggy says, "Better to tell your husband he's not your son." "That will be difficult." "It's safer. I almost lost the man I love by keeping secrets."

Outside, patient Tega leans on his car, smoking. Junior and Joe pull up in their Mercedes, and as Peggy comes out of the house, Junior runs towards it. He falls, spilling his school books. Peggy rushes to him, holds his arm, brushes him off, and lets him go. He runs to Sumbo, calling her Mommy, and they go into the house.

Tega asks Peggy what happened but she doesn't say much, keeping her feelings to herself. The theme song comes up: "You can count on this love to tide you over . . ." But they do not embrace; the scene is not played as a big romantic moment between them.

EMOTIONAL PRIORITIES

Violated is about maternal feelings: Peggy's traumatic past that had to be processed before she could move into a future with Tega, Sumbo's brittle desperation, Mama Tega's domination and Tega's struggle against it. It is about feelings generally: the take-away moral is that couples should communicate and not keep secrets, but the heart of the film, the matter around which its narrative procedures are designed, is psychological and deeply interior. Peggy must process her trauma. The discovery that Mr. Amadi was the rapist comes not through detective work or divine revelation but intuitively, through smell, and through reliving the rape in dreams. Peggy's feelings about her lost son pass from shame, guilt, and numb loss to full engagement, steely determination, and then renunciation. Hardly any words are attached to this process. Peggy should heed the lesson she teaches Sumbo and share her feelings with Tega, but she is not wrong to guard her privacy, to insist on the priority of getting her own emotions in order.

In this she resembles the heroines of a main line of classic British fiction—Elizabeth Bennet of Jane Austen's *Pride and Prejudice*, for instance, also a young lady of painfully humble circumstances who keeps her glamorous, infinitely wealthy suitor waiting while she quibbles with herself about the finer moral aspects of the relationship. There has been a shift from a late-eighteenth-century register of moral and sentimental discriminations to the late-twentieth-century therapeutic idiom popularized by figures like Oprah (on the introduction of this idiom into Africa, see Spronk 2009). Built into the audience's response is a perhaps impatient anxiety that the young woman will miss her chance. But the cultural work these fictions do is to make a claim for—to create and expand—an autonomous space within women, where purposes are found and decisions are made, a basis from which they come to terms with their patriarchal societies.

At the same time, this is a film about marital issues. However Peggy may feel, the film makes the marital issues more important than the maternal ones for the audience. Peggy's relationship with her daughter Courage, and the girl herself, are never more than sketched in perfunctorily, and—as Tega observes—Peggy neglects their new baby because of her depressed obsession with finding her lost son. The film is busy all the time, meanwhile, showing us the texture and shifting dynamic of the relationship between Peggy and Tega, and our overriding concern is that things work out between them. The story around Sumbo Olu-Peters is also told as a story about her marriage and the price that her secret exacts on her relationship with her husband.

Fertility issues are a central theme in Nollywood, but in *Violated* the ending illustrates the triumph of the psycho/emotional over the biological. Joe will doubtless accept Junior as his son even if told the truth about his paternity, and his marriage will be happier. The argument that cinches Peggy's renunciation is that emotionally Junior is truly Sumbo and Joe's child in every way that matters to him and to them, and it would be cruel to impose her merely biological right of possession. She has gotten what she needs, which is the psychological release that will allow her to be fully present to Tega and the children already in her house. The rapist Mr. Amadi gets his DNA into everyone's family—Junior is his son, Courage is his daughter—but the film hardly registers this fact. It presents him as a loser, fired from his job and abandoned by his disgusted wife as unfit for marriage.

Violated's sophisticated, writerly formal structure—Igwe began as a writer—makes it possible to put the romance and fertility themes into play at once. This film about keeping secrets makes extensive, intricate use of restricted narration. We gradually come to understand Peggy's secret, as we see her flashbacks and guess at the connection with the confusing opening. We know more than Tega but much less than Peggy. She herself does not understand the whole truth—that Amadi was the rapist. And so on.

As a director Igwe takes advantage of the sophistication of her actors, employing restraint, inwardness, and latency as central strategies. *Violated* is full of agitated emotionality, but the emotions are often connected to secrets and so express themselves as restlessness, irritability, brittleness, or frustrated anger. Interiority is not evenly distributed among the characters: Tessie and Mama Tega are unbearable because deliberately flat and overdrawn. The men are projections of a woman's ideal, but they are observed with nuance. Tega must repeatedly go off to work out his own issues in order to return with a renewed resilient commitment to the relationship.

Restraint, inwardness, latency—these are not typical Nollywood virtues, and neither is making psychological resolution the crucial level of meaning. Normally the objectives are tangible: the man, the house, the flesh-and-blood children. The emotionality of Nollywood is legendary, but it is normally straightforward in motivation and expression and has a strong performative aspect. When mothers register a catastrophe such as the death of a family member or Andy's madness, they display a paroxysm of grief, something like a possession, flinging their bodies about and falling to the floor, needing to be restrained as a masquerade is restrained by its attendants.

Violated is unusually sophisticated, then, but its commercial success shows that it spoke to a broad audience. Igwe's sophistication is that of transnational television rather than art-house cinema. Lila Abu-Lughod, writing about Egyptian soap opera audiences, remarks on how rural or urban working women ignore the psychosocial complexities of the more sophisticated programs to concentrate on basic family relationships (2002).

GENRE AND CULTURAL INFLUENCES

Violated's overlaying of maternal matters and romantic love illustrates features of the generic relationship in Nollywood between the family film and the love film. As an international form, the film romance has a specific point of cultural origin: ancient Greek "New Comedy." In this stage tradition, the plot is always nearly the same in its essentials. Boy meets girl, but there are obstacles of conventional kinds: the blocking figure, typically a "heavy father" or rival suitor, and, behind such figures, a powerful law or consideration (often status or money). The plays invariably end with a wedding feast, where society reunites, renewed, around the young couple. When this form reemerged in the Renaissance, there was a new emphasis on the romantic emotions of the lovers and on psychological obstacles within them.

It is hard to exaggerate the extent to which this particular plot form saturates world cinema. In Hollywood, the informality and individualism of American culture normally substitutes some version of sexual union or romantic commitment for the culminating formal wedding; the kinds of obstacles (many of them psychological) proliferate, and the romantic plot is normally coupled with a second line of action. The second line of action may predominate, and if there is a ticking bomb to be defused, say, we may think of the movie as an action film, but it will still end with an embrace, a coupling of some kind. In Bollywood, blockages of young love by families are a staple. The Hausa film culture in northern Nigeria, influenced by Bollywood, is devoted to telling stories of this kind (Larkin 1997, 2000, 2003; Adamu 2005, 2007a, 2007b, 2010).

The foreign influences Nollywood chose are, overwhelmingly, American—Hollywood and soap operas—with, behind them, the influence of European literature, widely disseminated through the educational system. Most Nollywood scriptwriters are university educated, and while English and other Western literature has receded from the curricula of Nigerian universities, students can equally well absorb the forms of Western drama from Soyinka or Achebe, who mastered them as deeply as any modern writers. But the massive, saturating influence is from American popular culture, which is under everyone's skin, absorbed through countless hours of exposure.

Nollywood's relationship to these influences is not at all passive. Nollywood has established itself as a regional power in the pattern Sinclair, Jacka, and Cunningham describe as obtaining in global television, where American imports have been largely replaced by local products and "each 'geolinguistic region' . . . is itself dominated by one or two centers of audiovisual production—Mexico and Brazil for Latin America, Hong Kong and Taiwan for the Chinese-speaking populations of Asia, Egypt for the Arab world, and India for the Indian populations of Africa and Asia" (Sinclair, Jacka, and Cunningham 1996, 7–8). This "middle range," located between the global and the local, was unforeseen in simple models of cultural imperialism. It is a hybrid cultural zone. They quote Jeremy Tunstall to the effect that "countries which are strong regional exporters of media tend themselves to be unusually heavy importers of American media" (Tunstall 1977, 62).

> This suggests a process of indigenization in which the US generic models, in establishing themselves as "international best practice," also invite domestic imitation. However, the substitute products become adapted to the local culture in the process, whether for market reasons, for the sake of diversity, or to diminish foreign influence, and new "hybrid" genres are created.
>
> The resulting situation is not the passive homogenization of world television which cultural imperialism theorists feared, but rather its heterogenization. (Sinclair, Jacka, and Cunningham 1996, 13–14)

The transnational evolution of literary forms provides another useful parallel. In his "Conjectures on World Literature," Franco Moretti tries to formulate some laws underlying this process. The first follows an argument of Frederic Jameson's: "When a culture starts moving towards the modern novel, it's *always* as a compromise between foreign forms and local materials. . . . second, the formal compromise is usually prepared by a massive wave of West European translations; third, the compromise itself is generally unstable . . . but fourth, in those rare instances when the impossible programme succeeds, we have genuine formal revolutions" (Moretti 2000, n9). Nollywood has accomplished such a genuine formal revolution, creating its own distinctive set of genres. Only rarely do these genres simply correspond to the transnational forms with which they might be confused.

"Love films" that closely correspond to the international norm have become a major Nollywood genre. But the striking and decisive turn Nollywood made early on was to displace romantic courtship from the center of its most pervasive formal structures. Even in films about couples, they tend to already be married. The romantic comedy tradition obviously structures the story of Peggy's relationship with Tega: his mother is the blocking figure with the usual personality and motivations, Peggy has a status problem, Tessie is the rival suitor, and so on. The most conspicuous difference is the ending: as noted, the wedding is not the culmination and happens in a flash halfway through the film. The other line of action—Peggy's unfinished business with her twins—determines the overall structure.

This displacement seems related to the generic influence of television serials over this particular film and over the whole relationship of Nollywood love films and family films. Soap operas include romantic couplings and weddings, but they do not stop there as romantic comedies do. Soap operas are designed to go on forever, the consequences of love unfolding past the wedding into pregnancy, child raising, adultery, and divorce—all the messy continuations of life. Soap operas address women at their ironing boards, selling them laundry products to clean up the endless aftermath of sexual attraction. Nollywood films have a similar strong tendency to move the goal post past the wedding to other issues. Nollywood's sense of time is elastic, allowing it to follow the mysteries of fertility and fate through generations, unburdened by Hollywood's adherence to a strict version of the Aristotelian unities of time, place, and persons.

Deep cultural motives push Nollywood past romance and towards the larger picture. Fertility is an absolute value in Nollywood as in Nigerian culture. Failure to bear children is such a social catastrophe that fertility issues tend to trump all others. In-laws almost inevitably intrude into this situation and generally are extremely important. Daniel Jordan Smith devotes an article to exploring "the dynamic tensions created as Igbo men and women adjust to the transition from the role of romantic lover that now often characterizes courtship to the roles of mother and father, embedded in webs of kinship, that characterize marriage" (Smith 2001c, 129). This is a common theme in the films.

African attitudes toward age are also a powerful underlying factor. Hollywood and American culture generally are famously obsessed with youth, but Africa is gerontocratic. It is good to be older. Power of all kinds comes with age, including spiritual power, wisdom, and social significance. People do not become full adults and full members of the community until they are married and have children: parenthood "is regarded as a sine qua non for the attainment of the full development of the complete person to which all aspire" (Fortes 1978, 121). That is when individuals are in the center of things, are most interesting and most themselves. Stephen F. Sprague, in an article describing Yoruba formal portrait photography, paraphrases Robert Farris Thompson on a principle of the aesthetics of Yoruba sculpture: "*Odo*, depiction midway between infancy and old age, at the prime of life, is seen in the strength of the pose and in the facial expression, both of which seem to imply the subject's maturity and wisdom" (Sprague 2002, 177). In Shakespeare's society choosing (or exercising the right to refuse) a marriage partner was the one great decision of a woman's life, taken at the moment of relative freedom when she was passing from her father's authority to a husband's. But in most southern Nigerian cultures women have more freedom to realize themselves after marriage when, for instance, as well as the indispensable task of creating a family, they are expected to have their own economic pursuits, independent of their husbands, and build their own social careers through membership in women's organizations.[2] *Living in Bondage* is the story of a young man trying to find his place in the world, according to Okey Ogunjiofor, but it does not revel in the freedom of youth. Andy is already married and in a rush to get further established, to acquire the trappings—embroidered robes, attaché case, and Mercedes—of successful middle age.

There is a danger of underestimating the role of love in Africa. Alexie Tcheuyap observes that in the tradition of non-Nigerian African celluloid filmmaking, both filmmakers and critics systematically downplayed romance and sex as themes (Tcheuyap 2011, chapter 6; cf. Pfaff 1996). Similarly, Lynn Thomas and Jennifer Cole point out that Africanist social scientists, while obsessed with kinship, generally showed very little interest in love as a topic until the AIDS epidemic forced attention to affective structures, and tended to repeat the idea that love did not exist in precolonial Africa, which is wrong (Thomas and Cole 2009). But there is a specific conception of romantic love with a European genealogy that was imported into Africa and became one of the attractions of modernity for many Africans. In Achebe's *No Longer at Ease*, until the protagonist Obi Okonkwo meets Clara on his way home from England where he had been studying English literature, "he had thought of love as another grossly overrated European invention" (Achebe 1994a, 80). African popular culture is often crudely disrespectful toward finer feelings and ready to see romantic values overridden by other considerations (in fact, Obi's friends take these positions), but it is also enthusiastic about the idea of romantic love—the Onitsha market literature, for example, offered lessons in how to go about it. Media anthropologists have been interested in how African young people use foreign models of romantic relationships to build a "modern" subjectivity and identity, often as part of a generational assertion against their elders (for example Fuglesang 1994; Larkin 1997; L. Fair 2009). In *Violated*, Tega plays Aaron Neville on his stereo to create a mood and the boating scenes look like an MTV video. This culture of romance is set against his mother's wishes. The process of importing and critically assimilating foreign romantic materials is a dynamic that has been going on for generations.

This is not a stable process, and the ratio of love films to other Nollywood genres is not stable. There have been two booms in love films, one around the time of *Violated* and another since about 2007, when variants also flourished. The genre of "royal films" (chapter 6) is almost uniformly built on the ancient conflict between erotic desire and differences in social status, the choice of a prince or princess meeting parental opposition. "Campus films" are about young people who naturally couple, but romance is often overshadowed by violent conflicts. Campus films rarely lead to a marriage (chapter 11). By 2010 the Ghanaian director Socrate Safo was pushing the boundaries of sexual explicitness with titles like *Love and Sex* and *Hot Fork*, sparking Nigerian responses.

The name most closely associated with love films is Emem Isong, who began writing and producing in 1996. She has always appealed to an audience of relatively affluent young people who, like her, are avid consumers of international romantic comedies and dramas. In the early days no one else was targeting this demographic. Since 2007 Isong, her kind of film, and this audience segment have been in the ascendant. Such films concentrate on relationships between couples in an apparently self-contained world of young urban professionals; in contrast to almost all earlier films, they are less embedded in already-constituted marriages, wider family structures, and inherited forms of Nigerian culture.

CULTURE AND CLASS

In 2010 I went to a "film forum" at Amaka Igwe's house—an informal open monthly gathering where she showed a film, followed by discussion. That night we watched a rough cut of Emem Isong's *Guilty Pleasures*—a story of yuppie lust and betrayal—and I complained about its deculturation. One of the characters is an international fashion photographer and playboy and the film is in his style, in his imagined world. Igwe agreed and contrasted the film with *Violated*, pointing to how Tega's problems with his overbearing mother reflected the matriarchal character of the Urhobo culture to which they belong, as Tega's name makes clear. (The Urhobo homeland is in the Niger Delta. Richard Mofe-Damijo, who plays Tega, is Urhobo.) I was a little surprised at this, since when *Violated* came out it was widely accused of being too "oyinbo"—foreign, white—and Okome and I had seconded this opinion in print (Haynes and Okome 1998, 120). The criticisms were directed at the trappings of lifestyle and accents, which represented the lives of only a miniscule proportion of Nigerians.

Violated does deploy the familiar "federal character" of Nigerian television: Tega's family, including the Oghene family into which he married, are Urhobo; "Amadi" is an Igbo name, as is "Amuchi," the name the Amadis know Peggy by; "Sumbo" and "Olu" are Yoruba. Everyone (except for Mama Tega, who lives in a world of over-the-top luxury, and Peggy's friends from her pre-Tega life) leads much the same lifestyle: upper middle class, urban, and modern, with large comfortable houses full of imported objects, nice cars, business suits, children who argue over whose father has a bigger computer. Everyone speaks English and only English at home. Ethnic culture is subsumed by and largely lost in this transethnic, cosmopolitan national class culture. One assumes the Amadis, the Olu-Peters, and Tega and Tessie had traditional marriage ceremonies in their villages of origin that would have looked different from one another and very different from the way the couples live day-to-day, the world in which they are bringing up their children—but the film shows us nothing of the kind. *Guilty Pleasures* is, as it were, the world of those children now grown up, for whom the cultures their parents emerged out of are so distant they don't bother to think of them.

Peggy's story has a strong class dimension: she is Cinderella, an outsider, an orphaned househelp who is abused, hits bottom, finds "helpers" who get her as far as the department store job, and then hits the jackpot with Tega. Her Pidginphone friends cheer her on, emphasizing her mobility. She cleans up well, or rather, there seems to be nothing to clean up—there are no class markers inside her that need changing. Her language and appearance fit into Tega's life perfectly. Then she hits a class obstacle: Mama Tega's feudalism, which is coupled with stigmatizing Peggy's sexuality. The latter objection dissolves when Mama Tega learns of the rape and chooses Peggy (and her relationship with her son) over her employee Amadi. The feudalist objection buckles when Tega shows himself willing to be an independent start-up capitalist, struggling and meritocratic. The prestige of old money and her talk of the "noble" house, the family name, and the dynastic alliance with the Oghenes are not designed to get traction with the audience. All those values are embodied in her preferred spoiled, jet-setting daughter-in-law, not in anything that looks like "tradition."

The film's wild inflation of living standards really just provides a pleasurable decor for a struggle based in essential family relationships, in the standard manner of international cinema and television. One cannot quite call them "universal" family relationships because a particular ideological construction of the companionate marriage is so central. In Nigeria this ideology is new enough and so far from universal that it needs to be propagandized for and may face external opposition as well as its own internally generated problems. Originally a foreign, bourgeois concept, the model has been so widely disseminated in Africa by Christianity and popular culture that it is no longer the exclusive property of a particular class.

The "get rich quick" films are tense with desire for commodities and animated by moral questions about money. This is not true of *Violated* or, generally, of its genre. Tega's money merely emphasizes the purity of Peggy's motives and his own; a couple of times she expresses a cautious, practical sense of the advantages of Tega's remaining on decent terms with his mother since there are baby things to be paid for, but she never seems to want anything for herself. Men with their money rituals, 419, and violent crime, women who are ruthlessly ambitious about money, to keep or to get it, willing to prostitute themselves or sacrifice the happiness of a child in an advantageous marriage, women who are defined as consumers of wealth as opposed to fertile producers (Garritano 2013, chapter 2)—all these familiar Nollywood types have their own genres and appear in family films as problems. But while family films revel in comfortable homes, their values are centered not on ambition but on the cohesion of the family unit and the suffering often required to maintain it.

THE "ISOKO MAFIA" AND MIDDLE-CLASS MARRIAGES

Violated won the prize for best screenplay at the 1997 THEMA (The Movie Awards) sponsored by *Fame* magazine, a red-carpet event whose establishment the year before was a sign of consolidation in the new industry. *Violated* was up against stiff competition. Although the occasion and its coverage were tinged by talk of how far the industry still had to go, partly provoked by the recent stinging refusal of the FESPACO film festival (the central institution of Pan-African cinema) to admit Nigerian films into competition because they were on video (Omozokpia 1997),[3] in retrospect this was a high-water mark: a number of the films of that year have attained classic status,[4] and together they demonstrate an eruption of creative energy, an exploratory sense for a broad range of material, a maturing of craft and theme, and serious investments.

A certain kind of film, glossy, sentimental, and set amidst the upper-middle class of Lagos, was unmistakably dominant. *Onome* (see below) and *Mortal Inheritance*, directed by Andy Amenechi, a former NTA director who became one of the stalwarts of Nollywood, swept the awards in the English-language category. *Mortal Inheritance*, even more than the others, addressed a social issue about which it aimed to enlighten the public, in this case sickle-cell anemia. It is built around a romance comedy plot—a cross-class and cross-ethnic marriage opposed by the parents, with strong emphasis on the familial aspect as well as the lovers' own perspectives. The film turns tragic when the heroine dies from her disease.

Courtship is rare in this kind of film. Most are about already married couples. These films share a talent for social and psychological observation that gives them much of their appeal and interest: Igwe's sense in *Violated* for the way men talk to one another when a frazzled new father is alone with his best friend, or Zeb Ejiro's in *Fatal Desire* (1995) for how adultery and divorce are felt and discussed by a certain class of people. In spite of the stylistic excesses of Ejiro's movie—horror film-style nightmares and hallucinations, an improbable climax—the final effect is somehow not sensationalistic but earnest, sober, and serious toward its material and ironic rather than polarizing in its handling of even the least forgivable characters.

These virtues survive even in films whose stories, in summary, are very melodramatic, like Chico Ejiro's *Dead End* (1997), which strongly resembles *Violated* thematically: it also involves the dark secret of a child's identity, the question of whether the child's psychology and affections are determined by genetic inheritance or nurture, the cost to relationships of having secrets, and marriages based on false premises. In this film, family pressures on a woman to be fertile drive her to desperation, and melodramatic elements crowd in: child stealing, infidelity, murder, suicide, extortion, and drug addiction. The film's loyalties and attention are all with deliberately modern lifestyles, and it loves the modern institutional vocabularies of psychology and the law, which regulate a world that finally makes sense and is decent. It mounts a full defense of modern attitudes toward relationships, including parenthood, showcasing the discussions in bed that are a central institution of companionate marriages.

The melodrama functions here as Peter Brooks argues it did at its moment of origin in the eighteenth-century bourgeois assault on feudalism. Melodrama is a postreligious medium for exposing the underlying moral order. It concerns itself with ordinary life, representing the surfaces of the banal and the everyday, but through its exaggerated expressions and other forms of heightening, it reveals the hidden forces that shape reality. The underlying order is moral, a Manichaean struggle between polarized good and evil, rather than religious or psychological in a deeply individualized manner (Brooks 1976, 2–20). As Larkin puts it, following Brooks, "By staging moral dramas in excessive terms that reveal the primal ethical forces underlying society, melodrama makes ethics public and dramatically concrete" (2008, 182). In her excellent application of Brooks's theory to Ghanaian video films, Birgit Meyer emphasizes that "Brooks does not argue that melodrama simply reveals an already existing underlying realm of meanings waiting to be uncovered. The point is that, as a distinctly modern aesthetic form, melodrama is involved in creating such a realm as part of a new, modern mind-set" (2004, 100).[5]

This group of films gives a sense of a conversation going on within a society, telling stories drawn from ambient life. Zeb Ejiro's *Fatal Desire* and Chico Ejiro's *Deadly Affair* (1995, produced by Opa Williams) both are subtitled "A True Life Story." The Opa Williams film *Dry Leaves* (1997) opens with a vignette of a pensive woman writing a letter addressed to "Dear Opa" and ends with her sealing an envelope and addressing it to the filmmaker. This film, like others, is punctuated by dates—"July 8, 1994," "Sept 10, 1994"—creating an effect of circumstantial realism and proximity.

As in the initial burst of Igbo-language filmmaking, themes and motifs got passed around from film to film, as did settings (the same borrowed houses of prosperous people) and even footage (recurrent establishing shots of the Lagos waterfront and the bridges to Ikoyi and Victoria Island), as a tight network of people, centered in Surulere, collaborated on one another's films. This was the moment of the so-called "Isoko Mafia" (Nwagbara 2004), who enjoyed a certain hegemony during the second half of the 1990s. The Isoko are a very small ethnic group from the Niger Delta, neighboring the Urhobo—the two languages are nearly the same. Zeb Ejiro, "the Sheikh," who has been mentioned repeatedly as the creator of the long-running serial *Ripples* and who produced, cowrote, and directed part of the Igbo film *Nneka, the Pretty Serpent*, from early on had a reputation as the most powerful star maker in Nollywood. He nurtured a network of his fellow Isokos to work behind the camera, beginning with his brother Chico, also a star maker, who became known as "Mr. Prolific" for his fast and furious working style and his staggering output of films.[6] Another major Isoko family dynasty, the Amatas, was founded by Pa Ifoghale Amata, an actor and playwright. His sons Zach, Fred, and Ruke and grandson Jeta are all film actors or directors or both. Zeb Ejiro also cultivated other Isokos such as the editor Lucky Ewata and the soundtrack composer Sammie Okposio. The producer/director/writer/actor Opa Williams, a close associate of Chico Ejiro's, later had an enormous effect on Nigerian popular culture as a producer of standup comedy. The stars that Zeb and Chico created are mostly Igbos, and their films generally do not display a strong Isoko/Urhobo ethnic character. (Zeb's *Domitilla*, set in Lagos, reads as Delta because of its rich Pidgin and body language, however; Opa Williams's *Dry Leaves* and *Onome* make more of a point of their Isoko/Urhobo culture.) Doubtless the "Isoko Mafia" calculated that a cosmopolitan, transethnic urban setting would attract a larger audience than films grounded in their small ethnic culture.

I have remarked elsewhere on the irony of the consolidation of a bourgeois[7] style and setting in these films at the moment the Nigerian middle class was collapsing (Haynes 2000, 78). Chico Ejiro's films illustrate how muffled the registration of the social and economic cataclysm was and the difficulties of the genre in coming to terms with that material. *Tears for Love* (1995) is about a man who loses his job—the essential story of the SAP era. He is a banker at the top of his profession, wrongfully accused of fraud. We follow him and his family as they spiral downward through drink, domestic abuse, unpaid bills, selling off of possessions, and a scramble for money to pay for a desperately needed operation. But through all this we remain—except for very brief moments—hermetically sealed in the world of the upper middle class. The job loss is not connected to any wider social horizon, and the emphasis is all on the strains put on the marriage and the moral compromises and failures of both husband and wife. He goes blind, she nearly prostitutes herself, both attempt suicide, but at the end all this is miraculously undone and he is restored to his career as a bank executive.

Chico Ejiro's *Shame* (1996) grows out of *Tears for Love*. It also begins with a man losing his job, but this time there is an extended, realistic, and memorable representation of the experience of unemployment and loss of class status as we watch the protagonist Daniel (Richard Mofe-Damijo) walking the streets in search of work and adjusting to his new status as a watchman. (For an extended reading of the film in relation to the SAP economic crisis, see Haynes 2002.) Again, there are concatenations of bad luck, possessions sold off, and urgent hospital bills. He experiences the casual injustices inflicted on the poor and the routine brutality of the police toward anyone who falls into their hands. He is suicidal when an old classmate sees him by chance and offers him a new life (shades of *Living in Bondage*), and he is so disillusioned that he agrees to become a drug courier. His "friend" immediately begins chasing his wife and when Daniel is caught and thrown in prison in England, he impregnates her (this happened in *Circle of Doom* and *Evil Passion*). The film ends with Daniel unexpectedly reappearing with the police, having made a deal with them, and his friend is then arrested. Daniel vehemently denounces his friend's treachery and—the heart of the matter—his wife's moral failings. This last is characteristic of Ejiro's other films, for example *Dead End*. When the strains of the women's misfortunes break them, they are exposed, humiliated, and generally made to pay heavily, while the man at the center of the film emerges as an exemplar, his bond with his son the ultimate good. The companionate marriage has become a crucial locus of meaning and emotion, but this has a downside. Social problems are misrecognized as marital ones, and women are subject to inequalities in the symbolic realm as well as others.

A cluster of social topics established themselves firmly in this set of films and in the broader film culture. *Mortal Inheritance* (produced by Zeb Ejiro) set the mark for high-minded social concern. Andy Amenechi and Bond Emeruwa, director and associate director and cowriters, spent three months researching sickle-cell anemia in preparation, and the film was taken up as an educational tool by those suffering from the disease and the community around them. The THEMA judges amply rewarded the film's seriousness, but it was not a great commercial success—the topic was inherently depressing. Other issues turned out to be sexier as plot elements.

Hard drugs had only recently appeared in Nigeria as it became a major transshipment point for cocaine and heroin and Nigerian "mules" became an important part of the international drug workforce. The movies picked up the topic immediately: it is mentioned a couple of times in *Living in Bondage* and is a significant element in *Circle of Doom*, in both cases associated with the get-rich-quick theme. In *Shame*, the emphasis is on the economic necessity that forces the protagonist into drug running and the resulting destruction of his family. Drug addiction becomes a sign of moral collapse in films like *Dead End* and was established as a way children from good families go bad in Isong's *Breaking Point*, Christyn Michaels's *Crossroad*, Tade Ogidan's *Out of Bounds*, and *Dry Leaves*, all released in 1997. The drug addiction theme had been pioneered by Lola Fani-Kayode's television serial *Mind Bending*. Drugs became an integral part of the crime film genre when it was established and of the films about Nigerians abroad discussed in chapter 10.

Hospital scenes are common (*Dry Leaves* has an unusual number), perhaps a sign of television influence. (As well as imported hospital-situated daytime soaps, the NTA ran the serial *Memorial Hospital*, which Chris Obi-Rapu was directing while he shot his Igbo video films.) Medical bills acutely focus the distress of SAP, making of it a matter of life and death in the context of lost access to modern institutions. The need to pay medical bills drives young men to crime (*Dust to Dust*), young women to prostitution (*Strange Ordeal*, *Domitilla*), and older women to sugar daddies (*Tears for Love*).

Women turning to prostitution out of necessity had been a familiar part of the social landscape since *Living in Bondage*. It is a common theme in this batch of films: Zeb Ejiro's *Fatal Desire* (which also takes on domestic violence), Chico Ejiro's *Flesh and Blood* (1995, which also features mental illness), Jimi Odumosu's *Strange Ordeal* (1996), and *Onome*, culminating in Zeb Ejiro's *Domitilla: The Story of a Prostitute* (1996, part 2 in 1998), the most heavily advertised film of its era and a disappointment to many because its social concern outweighed the sex. As usual, the virtuous heroine's sexuality is not exploited very explicitly, but her colleagues show their stuff—the audience is owed that much. Later, *The Prostitute* (2001, directed by Fred Amata) relaunched the subgenre.

Homelessness is another key motif of the SAP era, exigent landlords being nearly as frightening as hospital bills. Nnebue's *Died Wretched, Buried in a N.1.3 Million Casket* (1998) puts a family out on the street as the result of economic hardship compounded by other misfortunes and the callousness and misplaced values of the extended family. *Dead End*, *Rattlesnake*, *Owo Blow*, and *Onome* all have moving sequences of searching the streets of Lagos for lost children.

RATTLESNAKE, *OWO BLOW*, AND *ONOME*: MELODRAMA AND THE LIMITS OF THE FAMILY FILM

The family may disintegrate under strain, to the point that the story stops being a family film and turns into something else. This is true of two long, highly successful, and remarkably similar films, Amaka Igwe's *Rattlesnake* (1995)—her first film, in Igbo—and Tade Ogidan's *Owo Blow* (1996, 1998), in Yoruba. (Like Igwe, Ogidan started out in television, continues to do much of his work in that medium, and has a reputation for high-quality, professional work.) Both films begin with their protagonists as children in families that are destroyed by injustice. In *Rattlesnake* an evil uncle (Nkem Owoh) poisons the head of the family to get at his wife and his wealth; in *Owo Blow*, the father stands up against corruption and is consequently thrown in prison, where he dies. Both the boy protagonists take to the streets and turn to crime. As young men they are highly successful criminal gang leaders, intelligent, ambitious, glamorous, with strong social consciences—Robin Hood figures. As they mature they try to become respectable citizens, dressing well, creating legitimate businesses, marrying, starting families, and doing good works. But both are dragged back into one last crime by their gang associates and get shot.

The two films are not identical. Igwe's emotional intelligence is on display, and her camera seems to take a woman's erotic interest in the young men. Ogidan shows a fiercer, more topical anger at social injustice. The second part, *Owo Blow: The Revolt*, has two titles after the credits, which together delimit the film's liberalism, by turns sharply political and anodyne: "This film is dedicated to the struggling masses of this country and the gradually disappearing middle class," and "Show some kindness to someone today; it would make a positive difference tomorrow." (On this film's critical position towards the unfolding situation of the 1990s, see Adesokan 2011a. Adesokan also discusses Ogidan in Adesokan 2012.) Igwe's protagonist falls in with the wayward son of a corrupt politician who has turned to crime for kicks and as a reaction to the bad dynamics and moral example of his family; Ogidan's protagonist falls in with a boy made homeless when the Lagos slum neighborhood of Maroko was leveled to make room for luxury housing, one of the great scandals of its day.

Generically, the two films' strategies are the same. They begin as family films and then turn into crime films—specifically, criminal biopics tracing a gangster's life story. Both protagonists have unfinished family business on their minds throughout their films, and at the end family again becomes the horizon as they try to start their own. Igwe's film has more of the episodic, unpredictable quality that comes from following out a life story, as opposed to compressing the meaning of a whole mortal existence into the neat structure of an Aristotelian plot. From childhood her protagonist is in love with the sister of his best friend; he seems destined for her and in fact makes her pregnant, but then he falls in love with and marries someone else. Life is like that. Soap operas are also like that, with their endlessly unfurling stories. It is natural to make this association because of Ogidan and Igwe's work in television, but these films express a world view that goes beyond this single generic influence: it is visible in Tunde Kelani's *Ayo Ni Mo Fe* (1994), for example, a film that strongly resembles both *Rattlesnake* and *Owo Blow*.

Melodrama is a mode, beyond any one genre, informing a whole array of them—really all Nollywood genres, if we break the association between melodrama and women's pictures. But we also need melodrama as a generic term, or something like it—Nigerians use the term "drama," a catchall—to describe open-form films that do not have a strongly defined plot form, theme, set of characters, or location and so do not fit into the other generic categories. Because of the very strong cultural tendency to imagine people in relation to families, such films tend to start from the breakdown of the family, but they can wander far off, with no given destination. A dramatic procedure keeps them going, not a teleology towards an ideologically invested plot resolution. They embody a sense of life as a lurching through a series of extremities, each of which is a test of character and a revelation of something in the social order—a callous indifference or systematic cruelty in the whole system, a hidden vice or unsuspected strength in an individual. As Brooks argues, melodrama in this way reveals the deep structures of life through the revelation of moral drama.

Onome is an example of a film that does not seem to aim at conventional kinds of closure and achieves what it achieves as a result. It is a product of the "Isoko Mafia": Opa Williams produced it; the first part, *Onome . . . Another Love* (1996) was directed by Chico Ejiro and written by Williams and Joe Dudun (who worked on *Nneka, the Pretty Serpent*); Williams directed the second part, *Onome . . . Looking for Tega* (1997), written by Fred Amata.

The film's problematic inheres in its point of view. It centers on a young woman named Onome (Uche Osotule), but its point of view, as Okome points out, is not hers but that of a senior man (Olu Jacobs) whose Urhobo name "Dafe" implies wealth (Okome 2000, 154–56). She is a waitress in a restaurant, and as the film opens her quick thinking during an armed robbery saves his life. He is grateful, discovers the depths of her miserable poverty in Ajegunle, the enormous Lagos slum, and takes her under his wing, paying her mother's medical bills and sending her to university. She becomes his project and something of an obsession. She is beautiful and both her university boyfriend and Dafe's wife suspect he is the father when she becomes pregnant, but this is not true. He is a big man who might be expected to have patron/client relationships with poor people, especially other Urhobos in the big city. A highly melodramatic series of events at the end of the first part links her by kinship—she is in hospital with a rare, sexually transmitted disease that requires a blood transfusion of a type so rare only Dafe's jealous wife can supply it, and a chance meeting reveals that Onome is her relative. In the second part she is linked by kinship again, but disreputably: Tamuno, the husband of Dafe's daughter Jite, makes Onome pregnant while she is drunk, callously rejects her, but eventually reclaims his son by Onome when Jite does not provide him with a child. He brings the boy to live with him, to Jite's chagrin.

Dafe, and we with him, watch helplessly as Onome is buffeted and soiled by life. She is "othered" as a poor person, an object of curiosity and sympathy, but these motives sponsor sustained, sympathetic attention, and the film notes the appalling landscape around her. In desperation she resorts to prostitution, between bouts of victimization caused by her fertility—the two unwanted pregnancies. Romantic love never enters the picture. Presumably she feels something for her university boyfriend, but we only glimpse him. Tamuno is obsessed with her until she becomes pregnant, but she does not reciprocate.

Finally Dafe sits enthroned in his magnificent sitting room, wearing a chief's beads, surveying the wreckage of his family. He ordains a settlement: Jite, who has been a spoiled daughter and an absentee wife, jetting around as her poor-born husband makes his career, must return to her husband and accept his child by Onome. By Urhobo custom, this means Onome herself will have a recognized relationship with the family. This is, if you like, the conventional reintegration of a family with which New Comic plots always end, but the tone is far different. As Okome describes it,

> After castigating Tamuno, Jite, and Onome in turn for having disappointed him and betrayed his investments of affection and money, he tells them they are now responsible for their own lives. In effect he is disowning them, disclaiming

> his patriarchal responsibilities, and retreating into the smallest possible unit of the modern, urban family: the companionate marriage. As he withdraws from the family meeting, he takes his wife's hand, turns to the onlookers, and says to them with determination: "From now on, I will devote my time to my wife." He leads her upstairs, beginning an ostentatiously private conversation about a novel he has been reading. (2000, 163)

Dafe's emotions and his private attempt to address the social issue of poverty through extending his patriarchal auspices have reached their limits. We are also at the boundary of the genre of the family film. It has overstretched itself, recovering its shape formally in the last scene but at the cost of ideological collapse.

ORDINARY MOVIES AND BETRAYAL

By 1997 Nollywood was producing hundreds of films per year, and family films were the most common. I have been concentrating on the high end, in terms both of sophistication in filmmaking and of the social class of people represented, and I believe this high end is where the genre of family films took shape. But the domestic scene in absolute ordinariness was also there from the beginning, in Andy and Merit's plain sitting room. The money ritual genre and the other get-rich-quick films and investigations of the wickedness of the elite developed from one side of *Living in Bondage*; the family drama about strains in a marriage developed from another. The indefatigable Chico Ejiro, a key figure in establishing the more sophisticated family dramas, also pumped out films with humbler settings. Later, as film production moved out of Lagos to southeastern Nigeria, a new level of relaxed ordinariness came with the frequent use of villages and towns as locations, where housewives tie wrappers as they go about their housework and their men while away afternoons on benches outside.

The family film is the workaday Nollywood genre. A producer needs to supply only a few actors in their street clothes, something for them to sit on, and perhaps a bed. The genre takes full advantage of the smallness of the screens on which the films are watched. The stories are elemental, springing endlessly from fundamental human relationships and retaining their interest without the benefit of art or novelty. The baseline family film is so ordinary, so ubiquitous, and so apparently timeless it is hard to imagine that it was not always just there. The setting and cast of characters are a given, and it has a typical, well-defined plot form, bringing with it a strong expectation of closure: the nuclear family, usually meaning a marriage, is under threat, which it manages to resist or not. The principle threat is betrayal by a family member.

Betrayal by an intimate is the most common theme across the whole run of Nollywood films, although it is unevenly distributed across the genres. The family film, with its inherent emphasis on the closest relationships, is the most fertile ground for betrayal—fairly teeming with it. Betrayal can take various forms, the most common being sexual betrayal of a spouse. Erring husbands are most often to blame, with their home-wrecking outside women; but wives err too, and this is more scandalous and more serious. In real life, philandering men are so normal that conventional wisdom holds that wives must finally acquiesce if the man continues to be a responsible provider for the family, however much violence the infidelity does to the basis of marriages founded on love (D. Smith 2009). But a loose woman threatens the bloodline and the very existence of the family. Films vary in placing the stress on the internal betrayer or on the outside seducer or other external force, which, as we have seen, may be an acute money problem. The outside force threatening the family may be supernatural. The supernatural force may or may not be linked to an internal betrayal.

FORMS OF THE SUPERNATURAL IN FAMILY FILMS

The supernatural appears less often in the set of films with upper-class Lagos settings than in others. Igwe's psychologism and the social observation of the "Isoko Mafia" are secular. In the Richard Mofe-Damijo vehicle *Out of Bounds* (1997, directed by Tade Ogidan) he plays a preacher who works miracles, but the miracles are only mentioned in passing and only as career milestones in a middle-class professional occupation—the attention is all to his philandering and his wife's fertility issues. The supernatural may appear peripherally, on the boundary between the middle-class companionate marriages and the social landscape outside them, "other" but familiar, mostly walled off but not entirely excluded, along with extended families wanting money and mothers-in-law demanding offspring. Chico Ejiro's *Dead End*, for example, begins with a woman consulting a diviner, never seen again. He warns her not to go to extremes to solve her fertility problem, but she does not heed his advice, which turns out to have been correct: the modern doctor she sees is a fake and a criminal who sells children. But as already mentioned, the film is deliberately modern in its outlook, and in part 2 another diviner extorts sex from a woman who consults him, as if to warn us away from such people.

This class and cultural difference has to do with subgenre and intended audience rather than an impermeable segmentation in the industry. Igwe's material was always secular, but she was unusual in that respect; Zeb Ejiro, on the other hand, worked on the luridly supernatural *Nneka, the Pretty Serpent* before turning to secular family films.

The supernatural manifests itself in a number of distinct forms in Nollywood films, some of which will be discussed in later chapters. In the genre of family films, the forms that matter most are ghosts, sorcery, divination, possession by a spirit, apparitions of spirits or deities, and Pentecostal Christianity. These forms are different from one another, but *Living in Bondage*, for instance, includes all of them. (In the order of this list: Merit's ghost, the money ritual, the Cult Mother's research among the spirits, her possessed state as she speaks, the spirit who appears to Andy as a prostitute, and his final release at the hands of the pastor.)

Wole Soyinka, in a passage from the "Author's Note" to *Death and the King's Horseman* often taken as a fundamental statement about African metaphysics and psychology, described the universe of the Yoruba mind as containing the living, the dead, and the unborn in intimate coexistence (Soyinka 2003, 3). Ghosts are the obvious way to dramatize this conception of reality. Ghosts are the spiritual precipitate of melodrama, bearing testimony of hidden crimes, embodying guilt, blurring the boundary between extreme emotion and reality. In Nollywood they haunt families, not (as in the West) properties acquired on the housing market or decrepit old houses or castles into which the unsuspecting might stray. (There is an exception to every rule: *The House*, 2012.) Normally ghosts are of wronged mothers, sisters, or wives—men seldom come back in this way.

Blood Sister (2003), written and directed Tchidi Chikere, is a well-known example of a ghost-featuring film. Gloria (Omotola Jalade Ekeinde) and Esther (Genevieve Nnaji) are sisters, the former good and the latter inexplicably jealous and hateful. As an unemployed university graduate, Esther comes to stay with Gloria, who is living an unostentatiously prosperous life in Lagos with her husband Ken (Tony Umez) and two children. Esther poisons Gloria, takes over Ken, and abuses the children. Gloria's ghost watches helplessly as her children try to negotiate a dangerous city street—they cannot see her. Their teacher Tricia (Oge Okoye) comes to their rescue and becomes interested in Ken. Gloria's ghost appears in dreams to Esther, Ken, Tricia, and to her mother Ulumma (Patience Ozokwor), who sometimes takes care of the neglected children in the village and sometimes appears in Lagos to plead on their behalf and to register horror at Esther's abominable pregnancy by Ken. The baby is stillborn, apparently as the result of spiritual forces. Gloria appears to Esther in a dream and blinds her by staring into her eyes. Further apparitions drive Esther out of Ken's house and back to the village, where she confesses her crimes. The elders condemn her to banishment and she hangs herself. The film ends with Tricia installed in domestic bliss with Ken and the kids.

Tricia is the third woman in rapid succession to sit or recline, pregnant, on Ken's sofa. Ken is weak. He always knows the right thing to do but does not have the will to do it, being no match for Esther. But he is a steady provider and is good at being a companionate spouse; marriage with him is an unquestioned good, the prize of the women's brutal contest. The film oscillates between the village and Lagos. The sibling rivalry begins in the village, as early scenes demonstrate; later the village is a refuge, but one where the children go hungry and must hawk oranges on the street. There is nothing wrong with Lagos except that its anonymity, coupled with the privacy of the nuclear family, permits the kinds of wickedness we are shown. Finally the village elders deal with Esther, but the posthumous angel of the urban middle-class house had already driven Esther away. The ghost seeks revenge and as such is an agent of moral order, but the emphasis is on her emotional concern—for her children especially, but also for her weak husband and even for her chosen successor, Tricia, who will restore emotional order so the ghost can depart in peace.

Professional diviners—called *babalawo* in Yoruba, *dibia* in Igbo, *mallam* if Muslim, and called in English, with varying degrees of respect, native doctors, traditional healers, herbalists, fetish priests, juju priests, or witch doctors—are familiar presences in Nigerian society. They provide the only kind of medical care that is available and affordable for most of the population, and even when Western medicine or psychiatry are options, many people will turn to diviners for certain kinds of issues or when other approaches have failed. Along with divination they are likely to practice herbal medicine to cure illnesses and perhaps concoct love potions or poisons. Some also practice sorcery. In some cultural contexts they are valorized as figures of tradition, but they are often demonized by Christian and Muslim fundamentalists and looked down upon by the establishment that practices and administers Western-style medicine. In family films, characters consult diviners about fertility problems, mysterious physical or mental afflictions, or other manifestations of bad fortune. They locate the spiritual source of the problem and prescribe sacrifices to address it. Diviners may also address money problems and practice money rituals. See below for their role as sorcerers.

In Nigerian films, gaining access to the supernatural is common and easy and there are many channels through which to do it. In the Yoruba movie *Iya*

Ibeji Eleran Igbe/Mother of Twins, Seller of Bush Meat (1997), a woman has a wound that will not respond to medical treatment, and a hospital doctor quickly agrees with her husband that they should consult a traditional healer. The film includes a good babalawo, a bad one, one who is dubious and possibly a fake, a mallam, and a prophetess from an African syncretic Christian church. A Christian friend of the family also has a prophetic vision. Such freelance amateur divination shades off into prophetic dreams, which trouble the sleep of many characters.

The myriad forms of African sorcery and "witchcraft" are a classic topic of Africanist anthropology. (The scare quotes reflect the objection that the term "witchcraft" assimilates many different magical practices and demonizes them.) The cultures that have contributed to Nollywood have diverse beliefs about these matters. Witches are an enormous presence in Yoruba films, but when I carelessly used the term "witchcraft" in a conversation about the supernatural in early Igbo films with the screenwriter and director Chike Bryan he corrected me, pointing out that witchcraft is not an Igbo thing. The anthropologist John McCall has been heard to say that "Igbos don't believe in witches, but they do believe in making films about witches." Nollywood has standardized a few basic types of sorcery, assimilating and demonizing them into witchcraft. Native doctors may be paid to use sorcery against people, striking them dead or afflicting them, or be paid to create objects imbued with spiritual powers that can be used for protection or nefarious purposes. Nonprofessional witches use witchcraft against members of their community or, especially, against their own family.

Witchcraft accusations tend to arise in situations that breed bad emotions that cannot be openly expressed. Peter Geschiere describes witchcraft as "the dark side of kinship" (1997, 212). In families, overt hostility is frowned upon and inequalities can be harsh, intimate, daily, and immutable. Polygamous families are especially apt to generate jealousies and so are particularly fertile grounds for witchcraft accusations. So are extended families with part living comfortably in a city while the rest suffers in rural poverty (Bastian 1993). Stories about witchcraft provide a map of domestic tensions, a dramatization of emotional structures. In family films, the two great (and linked) themes are fertility issues and competition over a man. There are three main forms of conflict: between cowives; between wives and outside women; and between mothers-in-law and daughters-in-law. Divination reveals the mysteries of fertility and enables it; sorcery can destroy fertility, tying up wombs out of jealousy.

In the movies witchcraft is highly gendered. Men are liable to sacrifice family members through a cult or following the instructions of a sorcerer in order to augment their wealth and power but seldom practice witchcraft themselves within the context of the family. Women may belong to a coven of witches, an organization external to the family but normally requiring that they sacrifice kin members. Wives and mothers are seldom simply after money the way men are, but, as Garritano (2013) argues, the bad women of the video world are often associated with unbridled consumption and—as we have seen with *Nneka, the Pretty Serpent*—such women may be linked to occult powers. But witchcraft inside the family, arising out of its emotional structure—the form most relevant to the family film genre—is mostly women's work.

In family films, apparitions of or possession by spirits most often function to give lurid force to the figure of the outside, home-wrecking woman or to explain the behavior of a wayward husband. In *Nneka, the Pretty Serpent*, Nneka herself is a human being, dedicated from before conception to a river goddess, and is "married in the water" (Bastian 1997): she has a spirit husband who gives her supernatural powers (the ability to morph into the shape of an animal and the laser eye beams are both standard elements in Nollywood's representation of sorcery). As I've already argued, these powers overlay and second a natural force of personality and a powerful, threatening social identity. Her ascendency over her hapless man is the result of both natural and supernatural forces—she has put a spell on him, and it takes both his fiancée and a pastor to undo it.

In the Christian video *Highway to the Grave* (1999) by the evangelist filmmaker Helen Ukpabio, a queen of water spirits (who runs a hierarchical, bureaucratized court, doubtless a feudal dependency of Satan's kingdom) sends a marine spirit to take on flesh as a beautiful woman to seduce men. She does this in one episode after another, revealing her supernatural character to her victims after the fact. In response, they call in medicine men. The wife of her last victim brings in a pastor who deals with one of the medicine men, who has turned into a problem himself, and then with the marine spirit.

The most potent and widely worshipped water spirit in West Africa is Mami Wata, who appears in various guises in Nollywood films. (Many but by no means all of the spirits in family films are associated with water.) She is a beauty who lives under the sea and is associated with sudden vast riches—the wealth of transatlantic commerce. (Mami Wata is much studied as well as much worshipped. See especially Drewal 2008, Frank 1995, and, in relation to Nollywood, McCall 2012.) But she is jealous, and those she chooses to marry must abstain from sex and are therefore sterile. The protagonist of *Compromise* (1996), made wealthy by a river goddess, is beset by women attracted to his wealth and by family pressure to provide an heir. This thematic runs parallel to that of money rituals (we remember Andy, having sacrificed his wife, is threatened with the sacrifice of his genitals), but while money rituals prey on families, Mami Wata prevents families from forming.

Pentecostal Christianity offers a complete array of spiritual services: Bible-wielding pastors dispose of ghosts, divine spiritual problems through prayer, take the field against sorcerers, and cast out demons. Nigerians have not turned to Pentecostalism in such astonishing numbers because they have lost their belief in other spiritual forces but because they feel threatened by those other forces. Inside the genre of family films, Pentecostalism often provides the answer to the supernatural problem. Inside the genre of Christian videos, families are almost always involved since everyone has a family and it will be affected by any spiritual problem. Nnebue's *The Maid* (2004) is an example of a Christian family film on the classic theme: a good but already backsliding Christian family is infiltrated by an evil spirit that possesses the servant and brings the family to the brink of disaster, seducing the husband and inducting the children into witchcraft before being cast out by a pastor. Teco Benson's *Six Demons: The Final End-Time Warning* (2004) ends not with the apocalypse (despite its title) but with family melodrama: a havoc-inducing wife is revealed to be a demon, defeated by an old auntie from the village, a Christian seer all in white.

SOME REFLECTIONS ON THE SUPERNATURAL IN NOLLYWOOD

The supernatural is engrained in Nigerian film culture and has been one of its defining and distinguishing attributes. Christianity and Islam are rapidly displacing indigenous African religious beliefs, but common to those indigenous beliefs and to the world religions as they are practiced in Nigeria is the assumption that this world and the one beyond are deeply and constantly intertwined and that fate, suffering, and justice are linked to supernatural agency.

But the role of the supernatural may be exaggerated. As the philosopher Barry Hallen writes, "Narratives of African worldviews often claim that the distinction between the spiritual and the natural, the mystical and the mundane, is not as sharp as in the West. The African consciousness is said to be steeped in, suffused with, a suprasensory sensitivity." This view is routinely extended to two stereotyped narratives about the African worldview, which distort these elements "totally out of proportion to their real significance."

> One such narrative is the progeny of the poetic-symbolist school. It gives the impression that the African consciousness, at the proto-rational level to which

> it has evolved, is a maelstrom of ancestors, cults, demons, divinities, incantations, magic, masquerades, sorcerers, witches, and agencies of predestination over which the individual can never exert sufficient control. . . . That humanity is the victim of forces it cannot fully understand and certainly cannot overcome becomes in fact the defining characteristic of the African worldview.
>
> A second type of narrative treats the beliefs inherent in African cultural traditions as a set of rules that are embalmed in the social fabric. Behavior becomes semiconscious, rote, governed by a memory that is unintelligent. (Hallen 2000, 37–39)

Many educated Nigerians, some commenting from more or less official positions, object to Nollywood on precisely these grounds: that the spirit-ridden world the films show does not correspond at all to their lived experience and that this form of popular culture reinforces a backward mentality that impedes social progress.

Hallen's project is to explicate the rationality of everyday language—everyday Yoruba language—as a counterweight and corrective. He does not deny the reality or importance of the supernatural elements but argues "that paying excessive attention to them can divert attention from the rational texture of the everyday discourse that governs normal life. And when the role of the ordinary goes under-reported, the importance of extraordinary elements such as the spiritual or metaphysical, which in cross-cultural terms are comparatively exotic, becomes enhanced and inflated" (Hallen 2000, 40).

One way to put the spiritual element of Nollywood into proper perspective is simply to observe that so many films get along without it. In the early days of Nollywood, at least half of all films had no supernatural element; by 2013 it was perhaps three quarters or more. (These are extremely rough estimates, really just guesses.) The variation is significant in itself, complicating the argument that the supernatural element in the films springs directly from some eternal nature of the African mind. Clearly the variation is related to generic and commercial factors: at first films about money rituals sold wildly, but now people are tired of them.

Perhaps it is appropriate to point out that the top-grossing Hollywood films of the decade 2001–2011 were *Harry Potter and the Sorcerer's Stone*, *Spider-Man*, *Return of the King*, *Shrek 2*, *Revenge of the Sith*, *Pirates of the Caribbean: Dead Man's Chest*, *Spider-Man 3*, *The Dark Knight*, *Avatar*, *Toy Story 3*, and *Harry Potter and the Deathly Hallows 2*. Every one of them features the supernatural, superheroes, or the animist world of children's animation; none respect the ordinary laws of physics (figures from Box Office Mojo 2012). I would not want Nigerians to reach conclusions about my own mentality on this basis. It is dangerous to simply read off systems of "belief" from movies. John and Jean Comoroff, in "Millennial Capitalism," point out that a great wave of irrationality has recently rolled around the globe, lest we be tempted to condescend to the supposed backwardness of other cultures (Comaroff and Comaroff 2000).

My strategy in this book is to explore how Nollywood's supernatural elements are bound up with tensions produced by history and with the social in its most familiar forms, the quotidian, what Pierre Bourdieu calls "habitus" (Bourdieu 1977) and what Raymond Williams calls "structures of feeling" (Williams 1977)—and, above all, how they are bound up with genre and the perspectives that genres embody.

Indian cinema immediately produced the genre of the "mythological," telling stories of the gods and set in their divine dimension, but Nigerian film culture has produced no such thing.[8] Hubert Ogunde, the founder of the Yoruba traveling theater, produced various kinds of plays, most of them secular, but at the end of his life he made a series of hieratic celluloid films (*Aiye* (1979), *Jaiyesimi* (1980), *Aropin N' Tenia* (1982), and *Ayanmo* (1988)) in which he played a priest, Osetura, who protects his community from attack by witches. These films are saturated with the occult and have spiritual combat at their center, but even here what is at stake is the human village.

In Nigerian film culture the boundary between this world and the supernatural is highly permeable and the supernatural may play a determining role, but it appears only as brief intrusions into a reality framed as human and this-worldly. There are exceptions to every rule. Franca Brown's strange *Lies of Destiny* (1996, 1998) spends a fair amount of time located in the spirit realm from which people are reincarnated. Some Christian films are framed in another dimension, like *Final Account* (2001), whose point of view is out of this world, that of a man who has died and flashes back on his many sins, but even here the attention is all on his life in this world—we are looking down, not around at the dimension he now inhabits—and at the end he starts up out of his coffin at his funeral to beg his wife (not God) for forgiveness.

In general, the films do not leave the impression that Hallen is trying to head off, of Africans living in a maelstrom of the supernatural, lacking agency, mere playthings of unpredictable powerful forces. The supernatural is contained within films, within genres; it does not tear holes in them. When powerful Igbo masquerades come out into a village square they often have a rope tied around their waists with a minder tailing onto it to prevent the mask from plunging into the crowd or otherwise wreaking havoc, so that the terror accompanying the masquerade is kept at a pleasurable level. Film genres control the dangerous dramatic force of the occult in a somewhat similar fashion. Usually the logic of the supernatural is doubled by or tethered to another social, moral, emotional, allegorical, or dramatic logic, or to several logics at once. The creators of *Living in Bondage* pointed out, as noted, that Merit's ghost could be seen either as a real apparition or as Andy's hallucination, that when Andy talks to himself he could be addressing his spirit double or just "going mental," as Obi-Rapu put it—this notwithstanding the sense on the set that dangerous actual spiritual forces were in play.

The films show a world full of wickedness and danger. Humans with bad purposes amplify them using spiritual means; there are spirits abroad that mean us no good; fate can be strange and cruel. Living in a world rendered chaotic by such forces leads to anxiety and terror, which Nollywood expresses and exploits. But God is the answer, the blood of Jesus protects and washes clean; good people can also exercise spiritual power, find allies, and enlist the help of a diviner; the moral and emotional force of a good woman can dwell in her household even after her death. As we leave the family film for genres with a wider social ambit, we will see dark forces linked to vicious political power, but we will also see spirits of the land enforcing moral and social order. Nollywood genres mobilize various spiritual forces to guarantee the order proper to their settings. Order on the spiritual level is a fundamental underlying issue, but Nollywood tends to make moral logic the basis of its dramatic logic, to see moral choices as the most immanent human concern. If Nollywood is fundamentally this-worldly, the most important things in its world are marriages and families.

CHAPTER 5

Tunde Kelani, the Auteur

Tunde Kelani is the most celebrated Nigerian video film director and the one on whom the mantle of a film auteur fits most naturally. From early on he has packaged his films for sale as a set, a canon, and festivals around the world have had retrospectives of his work (Barbados in 2003; Rotterdam, Los Angeles, and New York in 2004; Sao Paulo in 2011). Since the mid-1990s he has been the regular subject of university theses. The circumstances of his filmmaking are difficult but give him an exceptional level of creative control and ensure the integrity of his artistic vision. The world of his films is always recognizably the same, though in each one that world is variegated and the films' collective horizon is very wide. His personal style is unmistakable, but he is deliberately immersed in his Yoruba culture.

By 2012 Kelani was referring to himself as "the other Nollywood," unable to refuse the Nollywood brand entirely though he has always maintained that he is not part of Nollywood itself. He is not part of the parallel Yoruba video film industry either, though his films are mostly in Yoruba. He sometimes takes a leading part in professional organizations and discussions of the future of the industry; his production company, Mainframe/Opolumero, rents equipment to other productions; he hires actors who have reputations based in Nollywood or (more often) the Yoruba industry; he is an inspiration, a benchmark, and a challenge to everyone in his profession; and after he has arranged screenings of his films wherever possible, they end up in the market for VCDs, where they are invariably pirated. But he refuses the conditions the Nollywood and Yoruba film industries impose, preferring to work at his own pace, slowly, carefully, and therefore more expensively than the market will allow. (His budgets

FIGURE 4. Tunde Kelani in his office.

are not huge: he estimates his average is $100,000 or $120,000, about twice that of Nollywood.) Over the years he has experimented with various forms of financing and distribution for his films.

Part of what led to the "other Nollywood" formulation is that Kelani is so often called upon to represent Nollywood to foreign audiences. Anne Delseth, a film festival programmer, once said to me that international film festival audiences pride themselves on their adventurousness but the one thing they find indigestible is Nollywood films, which spring from an entirely different conception of motion picture entertainment. Audiences do not know what to do with raw examples of African popular culture, and programmers are afraid to charge €10 for films with poor sound, inferior visual resolution, and under-rehearsed acting. As Nollywood has become too big to be ignored, festival programmers have almost uniformly turned to one of two solutions to the problem of how to represent it. One is to show one of the excellent documentaries that have been made about Nollywood (for example *This is Nollywood* (2007), *Welcome to Nollywood* (2007), or *Nollywood Babylon* (2008)) and perhaps have a panel of experts discuss the phenomenon before exposing the audience directly to an example of actual Nollywood filmmaking. The other is to bring in Kelani.[1]

Kelani's films meet international technical standards (at least once the prejudice against video has been overcome). He is fascinated by equipment, happy to discuss in detail every camera he has ever touched, and, from the days of celluloid filmmaking when he co-owned the production company Cinekraft, he has set the Nigerian standard for professional competence and depth of resources. He meets international artistic standards also, but his films are not tailored for international audiences. No other Nigerian director has such a wide, deep, conscious, organic relationship with his culture. Preserving Yoruba culture—which means making it flourish in the present—is at the heart of his motivation as a filmmaker.

Kelani was born in 1948 in Lagos. His father was a fervent supporter of the political leader Obafemi Awolowo, and when Awolowo, then premier of the Western Region, introduced free primary school education (an initiative parallel to his creation of the first television station), Kelani's father sent Tunde to live with his own father in Abeokuta in order to take advantage of this gate that was being thrown open on the path to modernity. Paradoxically, this is where Tunde encountered Yoruba culture in all its fullness and depth of tradition. His grandfather was the *balogun*—a high chief—of his community. The family was predominantly Muslim, but Christians were living in their compound too, and the indigenous Yoruba religious and cultural practices were still strong. *Egungun* ancestral masquerades and other performers would come to pay their respects and perform in their courtyard, and Tunde got to know them. As a child he read to his grandfather, who was not literate, by hurricane lantern—read him D. O. Fagunwa and other Yoruba writers, who have remained a crucial resource and point of reference in Kelani's career as a filmmaker. In his 2011 film *MAAMi* he recreates all this, shooting the scenes of the protagonist's boyhood in Kelani's grandfather's compound, in the room Kelani himself grew up in, in his very bed. (An emotional polarity is reversed, however: in *MAAMi*, the room and the boy's life are flooded with the presence of his mother, whereas Kelani suffered terribly from being torn away from his own mother when he was sent to Abeokuta.) In the film the courtyard has become a cramped place for the masquerades to perform because the graves of his grandparents take up much of the space. Kelani dates the first inklings of his future as a filmmaker to childhood impressions of shadows from the headlights of automobiles passing across the wall of this compound.

Abeokuta is a heartland of the dense intertwinings that have produced modern Yoruba culture. Like Ibadan, the city was founded early in the nineteenth century by refugees from the collapse of the Oyo Empire and the wars that attended its fall. Like Ibadan, it was a city of about 200,000 people before any white men saw it, not a city created by colonialism, as are most of the major cities on the African coast. But Abeokuta became the first great center of Christian missionary activity in the interior of what would become Nigeria, much of it carried out by Yoruba missionaries. It was primarily in Abeokuta that Yoruba became a written language (Peel 2000). By the middle of the nineteenth century, newspapers in Yoruba were published there. The parents of both Wole Soyinka and his first cousin Fela Anikulapo Ransome-Kuti were prominent members of the educated elite of Abeokuta, at once fervent modernizers (both fathers were headmasters of Christian, English-language schools) and ardent nationalists (Soyinka 1989).

Kelani went to Ibadan with his secondary school class to see the landmark production of Kola Ogunmola's *The Palm-Wine Drinkard*, an exemplary collaboration of an official institution, the University of Ibadan, and the popular culture of the Yoruba traveling theater. This production made a deep impression on Kelani, who still dreams of a film based on it. Always in love with cameras, Kelani apprenticed with a still photographer, trained as a cameraman with the NTA, and went to London for two years to study filmmaking at the London International Film School. During his years in television he saw a lot more of the traveling theater artists. The repetitiveness of work in television made him restless, so he quit the NTA to become an independent cameraman and the coproprietor of Cinekraft.

He worked on all kinds of productions: high-end television serials, documentaries, celluloid films in Pidgin and English. The celluloid era of Nigerian filmmaking was dominated by Yoruba films, and Kelani worked on many of the most important projects. The traveling theater artists sometimes hired foreign filmmakers: in these cases, Kelani worked in a subsidiary capacity, avidly learning whatever he could. Sometimes he worked with Nigerian professional film directors, including Ola Balogun (*Orun Mooru/Heaven is Hot*, 1982) and Bankole Belo (*Efunsetan Aniwura*, 1981). Sometimes he worked with traveling theater actors who set themselves up as directors despite having no relevant training. On these productions, Kelani's role went far beyond that normally played by a director of photography: he would break the scenes down and sometimes call the shots. "They came from a theatre tradition: they were in control of dialogue and what they wanted to say; I was left alone with the cinematographic part of it," he says.[2] He made the transition to being an independent producer with *Iwa*, directed by Lola Fani-Kayode. He took the film on the road with the Cinekraft mobile cinema unit.

So when the celluloid era ground to a halt and video filmmaking began, Kelani was ready to launch himself as a director. He was used to video technology and clearly understood that the future was in video. The Cinekraft partnership had fallen apart; the Ibadan shipping magnate (later politician and governor of Oyo State) Rasheed Ladoja paid for the video equipment with which Kelani established his new production company, Mainframe/Opolumero. With this equipment he did (and does) advertisements and other commercial work to raise money for his films. A seasoned collaborator, he was connected with a wide spectrum of creative people. In 1993 he approached Alhaji Kareem Adepoju, a leading traveling theater actor known by his stage name Baba Wande,[3] who came up with the germ of *Ti Oluwa Nile*/*The Earth is the Lord's*.[4] Kelani, Adepoju, and Dele Omisakin retreated to Abeokuta, where together they developed the story and the script. (In the credits, with his usual modesty, Kelani gives credit for the writing to Adepoju alone.)

TI OLUWA NILE 1

Ti Oluwa Nile begins with a metaphysical prologue. Kelani and Adepoju are both Muslims, but the ecumenical opening title is from Psalm 24 of the Bible, first in Yoruba, then English: "The Earth is the Lord's and the fullness thereof, the World and those that dwell therein." (The film's title translates "The Earth is the Lord's.") Kelani, who was responsible for the film's title, says he consulted an Ifa priest when he made the film and that the phrase "the land belongs to the gods" is in an Ifa verse.[5] The first images are of the moon and a gnome-like spirit of the land. The first humans we see are worshippers, women in white carrying oil lamps and calabashes containing sacrifices. They pray under the crescent moon to the usual accompaniment of electronic noises. The spirit eats: the sacrifice has been accepted, the transaction between realms completed.

In the light of day, Mr. Johnson, in jacket and tie, is looking for land on which to build a filling station complex with supermarket and garage. He thinks the property Sanya (Gbolagade Akinpelu) is showing him is too far from town, though Sanya claims the whole area is urbanizing.

In a compound, men are laying the mats for a meeting to select a new family head. There is an elderly candidate they think is not deserving, but Otun (Adepoju) arrives with another senior chief and announces that the king (called by his title, "*Kabiyesi*," "his majesty"; the generic Yoruba word for king is *oba*; *Otun* is also a title, not a name) advises them to choose the elder. They accept this advice. Otun demands "entertainment" and objects when they bring just ₦100. He has come with another elder, he argues, and then there's Kabiyesi. He fingers the additional money in close-up. The family members shake their heads as he walks off.

Mr. Johnson likes a second parcel of land; Sanya mutters to himself, "Does he mean to get me into trouble? It's the land of the gods." But then he just puts a price on it, ₦200,000, then 300,000 when Mr. Johnson is surprised it is so cheap.

Kabiyesi (Dele Odule), a young man in white shorts and tee shirt, is playing table tennis with a school-aged girl in the atrium of his modest palace. His entourage is around him, but this is a disconcertingly informal image of kingship. When Mr. Johnson and Sanya arrive on a courtesy call he assumes the sacred beaded crown of Yoruba royalty. An unseen *dundun* drum, the instrument of praise singers, accompanies his entrance. From the throne he explains, half in English, that he was called home from London to take the throne and he is glad to have people coming to start businesses. He hopes Johnson will employ some of the young people of the town. Otun is trailed out of the royal presence by the chief who accompanied him to the household meeting: Why didn't Otun tell Kabiyesi about the money? Otun peels a ₦20 note off of a large wad to keep him quiet.

The fundamental structures of the film are already in view. The sense of human life as framed by a metaphysical dimension populated by spirits of various kinds, kept in a harmonious relationship with human society by the respectful allocation to them of their due through the food of sacrifice and the reservation of sacred times and spaces, and the image of the human community as presided over by a legitimate king, a priest-king who regulates the relationship of the human community with the divine as well as overseeing the transactions of daily life, the center of authority to whom all conflicts will be rapidly referred—these are among the most fundamental elements of the Yoruba worldview, embodied in the thousand-year-old Yoruba political tradition. The Yoruba traveling theater tradition inherited and derived legitimacy from its representations of these conceptions; its films representing the human community as a simple bounded polity presided over by a king are sometimes called, after the king's title, "kabiyesi films." Three kinds of disturbances typically threaten the harmony of the community in such films: attacking witches (the threat featured in Ogunde's late films); land disputes (what this film is about); and chieftaincy disputes or competition for a throne (which will come in part 3 of *Ti Oluwa Nile*).

But from the beginning, the bulk of the Yoruba traveling theater repertoire consisted of plays about contemporary life, observed with comical or satirical realism. The Yoruba have been living in cities for a thousand years and their plays and movies are full of crowded social life, fast-talking, wised-up characters, and infinite voluble squabbling. Traditional rulers are familiar figures in the real world and everyone knows that the institutions of traditional rule have always been shot through with corruption and naked exploitation. Traditional rulers are charged with preserving tradition, certainly, but as custodians of the community's welfare they are also responsible for its development. In the selection of kings (a council of kingmakers selects the ruler from among a pool of candidates qualified by their lineage) Western education, a successful career abroad, and a forward-looking perspective that will hasten modernizing development are seen as important assets. There is nothing unusual about this film's kabiyesi. A story about sacred land being sold to build a gas station might seem to be bluntly opposing tradition and modernity, and Kelani was motivated by an urgent sense of the need for environmental and cultural preservation: "I chose to focus on environmental conservation," he wrote in an email. "Our remaining forests and rivers were protected by taboos, and in an era of cultural vacuum, they seem to be disappearing and giving way to housing estates and filling stations, the rivers polluted and dying everywhere." But the reality the film opens up is complex, densely packed, cross-grained, concrete, and familiar.

J. P. (Jide Oyegunle), a court bailiff, makes his way home from work, entering his flat through hanging laundry and a blur of arguments about money. Why is his young brother-in-law there, since J. P. has paid his school fees? The students rioted and were sent home. Sanya arrives and invites him into the deal with Mr. Johnson, without explaining what it is. The next day they meet Mr. Johnson in Lagos to collect a check, reassuring him about the validity of the documents granting title to the land. Sanya wants to bring in a powerful chief to avoid legal problems. In a restaurant, Otun is offered ₦50,000, wolfs down the chicken and drink with which the conspirators ply him, and veers from cynicism to blasphemy. The land is said to belong to both the gods and the ancestors, but "the gods are nothing but fiction. We are the gods. If you hear any strange sound we are behind it. The spot is perfect for a filling station. Any god that trespasses will choke on the fumes."

As expected, a complaint about workmen digging up the sacred land reaches the royal court. Otun professes indignation. When Kabiyesi reproves J. P. and Sanya, they walk out, preferring to take the case to a court of law. The court case turns on the history of the town's founding; called to testify as a senior chief, Otun lies on their behalf. "All land belongs to God and to fake historians," Otun declares at the victory party after the judge declares in Sanya's favor.[6] Kabiyesi is sorry to have lost the case but thinks the project will bring progress and employment for their youth. "The land was just lying there unproductive . . ."

Life goes on. Workmen work at the site. Sanya throws a birthday party for his wife to celebrate the change in their fortunes, spraying money as they dance to a live band. J. P. acquires an outside woman and lies to her and to his wife. Their lawyer (Yemi Shodimu) is robbed by armed robbers, in the broadest comic style of the Yoruba traveling theater.

The gods fight their own battles, in their own time. Sanya is stricken during a visit to the construction site. The spirits appear in double exposure in his hospital room; he froths at the mouth, convulsing slightly as he dies. As J. P. sprinkles earth into Sanya's grave he urges the dead man to return to revenge himself on whoever is responsible for his death.

Otun dreams of running from a white-robed figure along a river and wind-tossed trees; dragged by invisible ropes, he shouts silently to the beckoning figure. Banging at the door awakens him: it is J. P.'s son, announcing that his father screamed in his sleep and died.

Despite his professed atheism, Otun rushes to a diviner to find out what is going on. The babalawo consults Ifa, telling Otun J. P.'s death is the second in a series and there will surely be a third. It is about selling a piece of land. There is no way to avert the third death except to avoid burying the second corpse.

Otun begins scattering lies in all directions with resourceful desperation. A doctor tells him embalming the body will cost ₦50,000—exactly Otun's share of the land deal—plus storage at ₦800 a month for thirty years. "Bankruptcy!" He goes to the head morgue attendant (played by the comic actor Kayode Olaiya, using his stage name Aderupoko), lying about why he wants J. P.'s body released to him in secret at midnight. A whole teeming world of corruption is revealed as they negotiate: "We are a mafia here, I have bosses as well as subordinates." At night, they wrestle the stiff body into a van with comic difficulties.

Otun suggests to Kabiyesi it is the king who will die if J. P. is buried, so when J. P.'s furious family comes looking for justice, Kabiyesi at first is inclined to avoid burial in his domain. But he gets angry when he learns Otun has the corpse.

Otun dreams of Ifa's warning. Now there are two white-robed figures dragging him along. He wakes hysterical to the recurring eerie sounds.

At J. P.'s funeral, Otun stops the pallbearers and sits on the coffin. Otun is deadly serious, his life at stake, his face stony; everyone is utterly scandalized and J. P.'s daughter is vehemently outraged; but this moment of physical drama is handled with such mastery that the effect is hilarious. Someone channels the pandemonium by suggesting the case be taken to Kabiyesi, which it is, everyone prostrating to him on his throne. Kabiyesi rounds on Otun, who makes a full confession and sings a lament to the gathered people:

> I tried all tricks to no avail,
> I hatched fruitless plans.
> None learns of the day of his death
> And remains at ease.
> Otun has learned about the hidden
> And that is an ordeal.
> Doing good is the best always.
> Please pardon me, I pray.
> Your highness, have mercy.
> I plead please save me.

He throws himself at Kabiyesi's feet. The crowd is shaking their heads no, and Otun's fellow high chief has called for the traitor's death. But the king says, "Now you have gone all limp like a vegetable. Who'll see you now and not be moved with pity? Or do we just leave you to your fate? Also, we can't stop the bereaved from burying their dead. What is the way out?"

Otun rests his head on the king's slippers, in repose, childlike. The electronic sounds accompany a closing montage of the Ifa divination tray, a rainbow over the town, the sacred land, and the face of the spirit.

TI OLUWA NILE 2

The response to *Ti Oluwa Nile* was gratifying, and "commercial pressures," as Kelani puts it, led to the decision to create two more films as sequels. Part 1 had been conceived of as complete in itself—not as the first part of a serial ending with a cliffhanger but as a "dilemma tale," a common African oral story form that ends with a question for the audience to debate. Dilemma tales are rooted in the live, interactive nature of oral performances and also in the assumption that stories are supposed to have morals to be taken away, thought over, and discussed. Kelani passed out questionnaires at screenings of the film, asking the audience what Otun's fate should be. (When he told me this, Kelani mentioned the way Ogunde's actors would stop the action of a play and ask the audience what they should do.)

The situation at the end of part 1 is emotional and immediate: a human being's life hangs in the balance, a familiar person, now naked in his humanity—a deeply cynical, greedy human being, a congenital liar steeped in corruption, a traitor (as his fellow chief calls him). But he has confessed fully, baring his soul, prostrating himself to beg for mercy. A religious dimension is clearly present. As at moments in Nnebue's work, the vision is akin to that in European late medieval art, darkly comic as it surveys a broad world teeming with corruption but also dedicated to the cure of souls in their individual frailty and pathos. But here we do not feel the presence of a sky god; earth is generative mother and judge, pulling victims into her. In the scene of Sanya's burial in part 1, Kelani puts the camera inside the grave, framing J. P. at its rim.

Adepoju's genius as an actor allows glimpses of the child inside the hardened man Otun. And the scene might be read as a popular referendum on the character he plays (the character that Adepoju as Baba Wande habitually plays), the wily rogue—a figure that is central to Nigerian folk culture as well as popular culture (informing, for example, Nnebue's tall prostitute in *Glamour Girls*). He is hard to give up. Adepoju and Kelani share with their audience a wicked sense of humor, a connoisseur's appreciation for *wuruwuru* and *magomago* (various kinds of tricky business), a feeling of recognition and cultural ownership as Sanya, J. P., and Otun plunge ahead with this scandalous deal, assuming they will figure out how to bring it off later. The film is built on a moralizing but also complicit familiarity with a world where almost everyone is after money almost all the time, where social life is largely a matter of pressures to be exerted, resisted, or given into, and where influence is routinely used to threaten the innocent and silence those who would ask questions.

Part 1 ends with Kabiyesi on the hook as the one who must decide Otun's fate, but the way the scene is shot makes public opinion visible. In part 2, after due consultation with religious authorities, Otun is exiled and left to his fate, assumed to be death. What else could be done? Otun has gotten himself into trouble with metaphysical powers, and the human community must not get in the way. J. P.'s family exerts political pressure, and in any case an unburied corpse is an impossible scandal.

Part 2 is about Otun's exile. Adrift in the world, washed up on a shore, he has survived an attack by armed robbers on a vessel in which he was a passenger. He takes refuge in a ruin that, it happens, is where the gang has stashed their loot. The police raid the hideout and take him in. He is nearly wordless under questioning, remaining silent when asked his name. In the restaurant scene of part 1 in which he was brought into Sanya's conspiracy he had made a point of the fact that he was not wearing his chieftaincy beads and referred to himself by his proper name rather than his title: "Otun is at home;

it's Asinyanbi here with you." Now, stripped of his title, he seems to have lost his name, too. He stares at life, estranged, an outsider to everything, often lost in thought. The police throw him into a cell along with the armed robbers. He screams like a rat as the gang leader, still a source of broad comedy as he overplays the role of scary criminal, tortures him.

Released from prison, he is picked up on the road by Madame Akere (Golda John), a prosperous businesswoman, recently widowed, whose mother is pressuring her to remarry. His clothes are filthy and torn, his body language is humble, and he tells her that he does not know where he is going, that his is a troubled existence. She takes him home with her.

The story of his life in her household plays around the deep tension in Yoruba society between its social hierarchy and its sense of the absolute worth and dignity of each human being (Drewal, Pemberton, and Abiodun 1989, 16). He appeals to her (and to her mother, who is dying) as an emblem of pure suffering, redeemable humanity. Also, she likes him as a man—she will make all the sexual advances, laughing at his modest timidity. He grasps at the chance to recover any place in life, becoming her gardener. But his engrained arrogance begins to reassert itself immediately, and as he rises in the lady's favor he becomes tyrannical toward the other servants in the household until they frame him for trying to rape one of the maids. Madame Akere throws him out of the house.

He hears his family has given the title of otun to someone else. Other sequences provide more news from home: Kabiyesi summons Mr. Johnson to say he should complete his filling station project but at another location that was not fraudulently acquired; the mortuary headman Aderupoko is hauled before a corruption investigation and is fired.

Exiled again, the ex-Otun Asinyambi prepares to hang himself in a forest. But below the tree where he is perched with his rope, he sees an albino man being led along to be used in a money ritual. He intervenes, and in gratitude the albino takes him to a babalawo who performs rituals that he promises will free him from death and from the ghosts in his recurrent dreams. He asks for the *babalawo*'s help in reclaiming his title.

And so he reappears in the streets of his city, prostrating himself in front of a disconcerted Kabiyesi. The old otun and the new one insult one another, outraged. So part 2 ends at another dramatic climax, promising a sequel built around the venerable theme of a political struggle over a chieftaincy title.

Parts 1 and 3 are solidly rooted in the life of a community, but the period of exile is dreamlike and mysterious because based in the experience of an estranged man, a dead man walking, barely hanging onto his connections with this world, subject to random picaresque adventures. Adepoju underacts, allowing his face to be haunted, letting us do his wondering for him.

TI OLUWA NILE 3

Asinyambi returns as a hard, obstreperous character, dragging his doom behind him. His return is an embarrassment to the town. Kelani relishes embarrassing situations. The film opens with the most essential image of legitimacy, the king on his throne and the babalawo chanting Ifa verses: "the landowner is vindicated . . ." But the king is irritable—hadn't the babalawo predicted death for Otun?—and tells him to "stop that lousy incantation." Asinyambi's family is embarrassed, having reassigned not only his title but also his wife and clothing.

Asinyambi forms an alliance with Prince Adewale (Lere Paimo, another distinguished traveling theater actor). Adewale had been a candidate for the kingship but lost because, despite being a wealthy cocoa merchant, he is illiterate. They begin a campaign to overturn the election of Kabiyesi and install Adewale in his stead and to restore Asinyambi to his title as otun.

Kabiyesi's election is brought to a court of law for trial. Adewale's case is that he received more votes from the Ifa oracle, but Kabiyesi was given the crown anyway because he was literate. One of the kingmakers takes the stand to say there was no manipulation: the oracular votes were only one element in the decision, and because of Kabiyesi's generosity, enlightenment, and exposure to the wider world, as well as his literacy, the kingmakers had unanimously decided in his favor and Ifa supported this decision. "You should know the majority's wish is God's wish." He clearly is talking about democracy, and the political resonance of this speech could not be lost on anyone in 1995, two years after the Babangida regime annulled the election of M. K. O. Abiola as president. The speech is a cultural as well as political manifesto, with its model of a thoughtful blending of traditional and modern considerations.

The conflict is fought on several levels. Both Kabiyesi and Otun armor themselves spiritually, their heads anointed for protection. The faction sponsors rowdy street demonstrations. A line of beleaguered police separate the surging demonstrators from the opening ceremony for Mr. Johnson's filling station, where women dance, Mr. Johnson and Kabiyesi in his beaded crown make speeches, and masqueraders perform. In separate sequences, the head of the Efe masqueraders comes to Kabiyesi for permission to perform. He explains their function: the Efe masquerades precede the more serious—the deeply serious and powerful—Gelede masquerade (Drewal and Drewal 1983). The Efe masqueraders are jesters and satirists; it is their business to operate an intelligence service to know what is happening in their community and then to castigate misdeeds in their performances. We then see the Efe and Gelede masks perform, the songs accompanying them explicitly supporting Kabiyesi in his conflict and denouncing Asinyambi. Kabiyesi rises to join the dancing, this mass of moving bodies providing an image of legitimacy and vitality to balance the turbulent crowd stirred up by Adewale and Asinyambi.

Adewale and Asinyambi try to bribe the judge, but he denounces such behavior and rules in favor of Kabiyesi. Immediately after the judge delivers his verdict, the gods deliver theirs. Asinyambi is stricken in bed. Now in his recurring vision, the two figures in white dragging him remove the cloths from their faces.

The babalawo is with the king in council, reaffirming and reflecting on the order of things. Both men have been through a lot. Kabiyesi has survived the challenge to his legitimacy, but the relationship of the man and his role was strained, as we saw him in a private night of drunken self-pity and as the crowd denounced him by his proper name. The babalawo also had been framed repeatedly (as have all the other babalawos in the film) by little bits of dramatic material that showed him not as a revered oracle but as someone negotiating difficult social relationships.

The babalawo picks up the theme of ownership and stewardship of the land. From the beginning, the opposition of sacred land and filling station was tempered by Kabiyesi's commitment to progressive development. No one is against development. Even Adewale, in a campaign speech, promised what all politicians always promise: electricity, running water, tarred roads. The contrast between Adewale and Kabiyesi is not in stated objectives; it is between a corrupt, ignorant backwardness incapable of making real progress or safeguarding what is valuable in the tradition and an enlightened rule that can do both. The babalawo says, "Truly, the lord owns the land. But he has handed it over to Orunmila [the god of wisdom]. Our trees, forest, water, and land must be well taken care of because of our children coming behind." Kabiyesi replies, "Old one, our lack of organization, inability to do what is right, as well as our dishonesty and nonchalance are the bane of our society." "It is true, your highness, I can say there is almost no difference between the way Ifa has designed certain things and the things enlightened people do. But because of ignorance, our nonchalant attitude does affect us. [In English] We don't want to respect our culture. [In Yoruba] And any nation that fails to respect her culture will collapse totally."

Asinyambi's nightmare vision continues. Now he is in white, going to meet a water goddess, also in white, his image upside down. She is saying something but there is no sound. Asinyambi gags and dies.

The spirit of the land munches the food of sacrifice, an image repeated from the beginning of part 1, and the frame freezes. Kabiyesi dances with his people and the masquerades under the final credits.

DRAMATIC ORGANIZATION

The second and third parts of *Ti Oluwa Nile* are more loosely organized dramatically than the first, and this would seem to be related to Kelani's collaboration with Adepoju and, in general, with the Yoruba traveling theater traditions and procedures. (Not all of the actors in *Ti Oluwa Nile* are from the traveling theater, it should be noted; several of the guest stars in part 2—Golda John, Franca Brown, Ngozi Nwosu—are not even Yoruba.) Such collaborations have frequently been difficult, and from the time traveling theater artists began making films they have been accused of merely setting up a camera to film their stage plays, with no sense of the techniques of cinema. The advent of video increased the proportion of mere filmed theater, partly because the simplicity of video technology encouraged autodidacts to be their own directors and partly because the economic conditions of that moment enforced the lowest possible budgets. The original opposition between stage and film has broken down to a considerable degree—it has been decades since stage performances ceased, so the younger generation has performed exclusively for cameras.

But deeply rooted procedures remain that are antithetical to standard film practice. Traveling theater plays were an oral, improvised form. Plays would be developed by the troupe working together, improvising from a rough scenario. A script might be written down later, recording the fruits of this evolution, but each performance would be different, the differences being in part the result of a finely honed instinct for what was working with a particular audience. (On the process of creation and other aspects of this tradition, see Karin Barber's (2000) masterful book.) Films are made in an abbreviated form of the same process. Typically there is only a skeletal scenario, from which the actors will improvise. The situations are mostly stock, so the actors can take off immediately, knowing what to do—a singularly rapid and therefore economical way to make a film.

The characters are often beyond stock; many actors of the old school develop a persona by which they become known and play essentially the same character, often with the same name, in many films: so Kayode Olaiya keeps appearing as Aderupoko and Kareem Adepoju/Baba Wande is often cast as the kind of sly rogue he plays in *Ti Oluwa Nile*. Exploring the unique interior life of a new character is not what these actors do for a living, and they may feel that departing from their usual role would damage their brand. As Barber shows, stage acting, like other forms of African oral culture, is built on what she calls an "aesthetic of immediate impact": the play is conceived of less as an integrated, overall artistic architecture than as a series of moments where the immediate relationship of live performer and audience can be exploited to its maximum. Moreover, acting expresses personal force and vitality, a metaphysically undergirded cultural value that encourages actors to chew up the scenery (Barber 1987, 2000). All these factors make actors disinclined to fit themselves into the limited role imagined by a film director who is keeping a sense of the overall design in mind at all times.

As Akin Adesokan argues, Kelani has always managed to exert his authority as a filmmaker in all these respects (Adesokan 2011b, chapter 3). The scripts evolve out of a collaborative process, but once the film's form is set, he holds his actors to it. (The script of *Ti Oluwa Nile* was written in English; translation into Yoruba was left to the actors, but under Kelani's close supervision.) If there are sequences that depart from the templates of international filmmaking, it is not because the actors are running away with a scene but because Kelani is taking an exploratory interest in a situation, for instance the funeral service for J. P. inside the church in part 1, which the standard rigorous Western codes of dramatic relevance would not justify. Like other Yoruba film directors who work in a style Kelani helped to create, the vital presence of individuals in a scene is emphasized through cinematic means, through shot-reaction shot patterns that make personhood pop out vividly. The central Yoruba spiritual concept is *ase*, which is the life force, spiritual energy, the power to make things happen, the divine spark that is in all things (Drewal, Pemberton, and Abiodun 1989). This principle of animation informs the scenes Kelani films and his filmmaking too. Latent forces are always ready to erupt—comedy and humor, and heavier things as well.

Perhaps one can see traces of the socioeconomic organization of the traveling theater in the presence of Aderupoko (the morgue attendant) in each part of the film. When the traveling theater troupes traveled, plays were conceived of from the ground up around a stable set of actors and their specialties. When television and films became the predominant form, they exploited the possibility of massing star power from a number of troupes. The standing organizations became uneconomical and broke up, replaced by "caucuses," networks of actors who act in one another's films on a reciprocal basis, often without cash changing hands. An actor who is part of a successful production would expect to be called back for the sequels. Something would be found for him to do, whether his part was required by dramatic logic or not. Aderupoko turns up in part 3 as an *okada* (motorcycle taxi) driver; in his final incarnation, Asinyambi takes him on as a driver as he campaigns to recover his title.

The later parts of *Ti Oluwa Nile* are unusual for Kelani because he did not assert full control over these social and commercial structures. Yoruba (and Nollywood) filmmaking routinely produces sequels to successful films for commercial reasons, even if dramatic logic did not require so much space—the sequels are filled up with this and that. Kelani never did such a thing again.

THE KELANIAN

The sequences in which Aderupoko appears seem, in retrospect, quite Kelanian, however. In Kelani's next film, *Ayo Ni Mo Fe*, the scandalous state of mental health institutions is explored, as the corruption of the morgue is explored in part 2 when Aderupoko is hauled in for questioning by a committee of investigation and fired. Later the hospital director questions him again: What are the bodies used for? (Rituals, of course.) Are the supervisors involved? Yes, all of them. This scene of an indignant reformer questioning an incorrigible reprobate who represents a thoroughly corrupt social sector is reminiscent of Kelani's third film, *Koseegbe* (1995). Aderupoko is unrepentant, obstreperous, sarcastic, and very funny, pointing repeatedly to the hypocrisy of the powerful who ask him and his kind to do the dirty work—an irrepressible, Falstaffian perspective on the largest themes. (On the subversive laughter of the Yoruba popular theater see Barber 1987.) Part 3 returns to this material.

All of Kelani's films include musical and dance performances. Dancing is some of what fills up part 3; similarly, part 2 has two long party scenes. The first features live music—the same band of jokers who played at Sanya's wife's birthday party in part 1, wearing goofy costumes and singing satirical songs. Traveling theater performances always included substantial musical elements, having developed out of variety shows. Nightclub or party scenes were a way of integrating live music in popular contemporary styles with the dramatic action. Traditional forms of music were a natural part of plays with traditional themes. In celluloid films, the biggest musical stars could be hired: King Sunny Ade performs in *Orun Mooru*, for example.

Kelani's *MAAMi* includes a memorable nightclub performance by Yinka Davies as well as masquerades. *Abeni* (2006) also features nightclub performances. A dance competition is central to the plot of *Saworoide* (1999), and

Campus Queen (2004) and *Arugba* (2008) are built around music and dance performances. When I suggested to Kelani that the prominence of these performances was an inheritance from the traveling theater he said no, that the role of music and dance were far broader and more fundamental in African culture than that. He dated his personal sense of their centrality to his childhood experiences in his grandfather's compound in Abeokuta and spoke about the huge annual festival in honor of the *orisha* (goddess) Oshun in Oshogbo, in which he immersed himself as he made a 1996 documentary about it (*Oroki: Osun Osogbo Festival*).

The variety of materials we see in *Ti Oluwa Nile*, then, is essential to all Kelani's work. I mean both the specific materials and the variousness itself. At the heart of Kelani's conception of filmmaking is the premise that life is various, full of one thing and another at the same time, with contrary emotions, perspectives, and social realities bumping up against one another. My attempts to engage him in conversations about genre have never gone very well, and I finally came to suspect this was because he simply does not think in terms of genres as modes of representing one or another exclusive perspective on reality. In this sense, genre is uncongenial, even antithetical to his thinking. For this reason Kelani tends to disclaim responsibility for one of the films he directed, *Abeni*, which was a collaboration with Amzat Abdel Hakim (known as Laha), an actor and musician from the Republic of Benin. Kelani feels Laha is too full of his own love life as a "fine boy" and that his story, which is the basis of the film, is too exclusively about romance. Kelani has no use for what he sees as a narrow, self-centered way of being in the world and the kind of art that comes out of it. "It's boring!" he said. His films bear a strong family resemblance to one another—"A Mainframe film is a Mainframe film!"—and each one is a mixture. This does not mean that each of his films does not have a specific framing, location, shape, and flavor. Kelani quit his successful career in television because he could not stand the repetition involved in making television serials.

AYO NI MO FE

Kelani's next film was *Ayo Ni Mo Fe* (1994), which, like *Ti Oluwa Nile*, began as a collaboration with Adepoju. There is no king on his throne in this film; it is about private lives. Private life is, however, as in *Ti Oluwa Nile*, embedded in a thickly rendered social experience of an ambivalent modernity, a world of fuel scarcity, AIDS testing, and the American visa lottery. *Ayo Ni Mo Fe* is unusually decentered. In Kelani's other films, if traditional kingship and religion are not in sight, modern institutions tend to provide a setting and structure (in *Koseegbe*, the customs service; in *O Le Ku* (1997), *The Campus Queen*, and *Arugba*, a university; in *Thunderbolt/Magun*, the National Youth Service Corps in which all university graduates serve for a year and the school to which the protagonist is posted; in *MAAMi*, sports).

The plot is also unusually decentered. Ayo, the self-destructive protagonist, gets himself fired from his job and, caught irresponsibly between two girlfriends, loses both of them and ends up leading a street gang before his rehabilitation. (For a summary of the winding plot, see Haynes and Okome 1998.) The plot had meandered so much by the end of part 1 that the writer Wale Ogunyemi was called in to give shape to the second part (1995). The Yoruba film tradition is particularly fertile in producing stories that twist and turn remarkably. Yoruba films tend to rest more visibly on a metaphysical substructure of supernatural forces than do melodramas like *Onome*, *Rattlesnake*, or *Owo Blow*. Such forces make people their playthings; the most personal thing about us, our destiny, is shaped in a dimension beyond our ordinary knowledge. Ayo would seem to be living out his destiny, his *ori*, a spiritual matter. But there are no apparitions or guardian spirits; the complexity and mysteriousness of life and the universe are embedded in the structure of the story itself.

The film is not concerned to make clear choices about world view. Mental illness is central to an important subplot that explores the scandalous dysfunction of "traditional" methods of dealing with the mad, which are presented as fake, evil, and retrograde, and the film champions Western medicine. (It is dedicated to the great social reformer Tai Solarin "and all those dedicated to the cause of the mentally ill.") But then the story shows that having sex with a madwoman does actually, as a babalawo claims, cure barrenness (as does holding the issue of such a union on one's lap), while interrupting someone having such sexual relations brings a curse carried down through the generations. (Saheed Aderinto (2012) notices this contradiction and the fact that destiny is against Ayo and Junmoke [his first love] marrying, as they finally agree, though the conventions of romantic comedy would push them towards union.)

Ayo Ni Mo Fe introduced another of Kelani's abiding concerns: the young and their situations. *O Le Ku* also centers on a young man; in his later films, Kelani makes a young woman the central character (*Thunderbolt*, *The Narrow Path*, *Abeni*, *The Campus Queen*, *Arugba*). In all these films the young are faced with a choice of romantic partner, but romance is not the only or usually even the main concern. Kelani clearly likes and often admires his young heroes and heroines, but we are never entirely within their points of view. The attitude is rather the sympathetic amusement of an older observer, and the focus is less romantic than psychological and moral, with a strong dose of ribaldry, often at the expense of the heroine's dignity. (*Thunderbolt* carries this to a comic extreme.) The heroine's partner will have his own story and his own issues. *The Narrow Path* has black and white flashbacks associated with both the heroine Awero and her lover Odejimi. What she has to work out is not so much her feelings for Odejimi but an analytical understanding of gender relations and the discovery of her own capacity for leadership. In *The Campus Queen* and *Arugba*, again the heroine demonstrates leadership in a situation in the wider world that is not neatly coordinated with, or is more important than, the choice of partner. Kelani's interest in the young intersects his interest in social institutions to make education a recurrent theme.

AKINWUMI ISHOLA

Kelani's third film, *Koseegbe*, the story of a virtuous bureaucrat struggling against corruption, squarely addresses the central issue in contemporary Nigerian politics and social life. It also initiated Kelani's fruitful collaboration with the writer Akinwumi Ishola. No other Nigerian filmmaker has taken such a deep and consistent interest in literature. Kelani is particularly dedicated to Yoruba literature, including works in English by Yoruba writers, such as Faleti's novel *Magun* (from which *Thunderbolt* was made) and the Femi Osofisan story on which *MAAMi* is based.

It is a mark of his strength as an auteur and of his active engagement throughout the formation of the scripts that his work is so unified in spite of his absorbing the creative force of major writers. *Koseegbe* began as a stage play of the same name, and in spite of Kelani's reverence for the playwright it was clear to him that Ishola did not know how to write for film. Kelani was still in touch with the Hollywood director Bruce Beresford, whom he had gotten to know while working on the film Beresford shot in Nigeria, *Mister Johnson*, and he asked Beresford to send him the script of his then-current project, *Driving Miss Daisy*, to show to Ishola as an example. Ishola writes in longhand and Kelani types up Ishola's drafts himself, making changes as he goes along to structure them as film scripts, sometimes adding material of his own.

Ishola's friends have given him the nickname "Honest Man." *Koseegbe*'s probity is amply mixed with humor and a warm sense of human frailty, as its virtuous hero is shown to be at war not just with a cabal of corrupt powerful men who are used to having their way with the law but with, in effect, his whole society, which has relaxed standards. His family and even his own personality are not without faults that the wicked can catch hold of and use against him.

The film was immediately hailed for its high seriousness. Nigerian academics and other cultural authorities are given to pontificating about what Nollywood films ought to be—moral, public spirited, drawing on the wealth of traditional culture but pitched towards an enlightened modernity, as opposed to the shoddy commercially driven products Nollywood films are held to be. These pontifications are often rigorously utopian in their ethics and show no trace of understanding of how films actually get made or of the practical motivations of those making them. But Kelani's films, especially his collaborations with Ishola, actually embody this ideal and are universally cited as examples of doing so. I do not mean that Kelani's films are merely approved of by people acting in their official capacities; they are loved and highly valued by the public at large as the realization of a broadly based ideal, which no one else realizes as fully or as well, or with such transparent purity of motive. Kelani's films have not made him rich, but they have brought him fame and an unassailable place of honor.

This elevated position in contemporary film culture may be rather lonely, but Kelani is in a tradition of frank, earnest purpose.[7] Ladi Ladebo's celluloid films *Vendor* (1987) and *Eewo/Taboo* (1989) are perhaps the most immediate precursors. Karin Barber has described how Yoruba traveling theater artists liked to set themselves up as instructors, self-appointed mediators between modern institutions and their audience, which was in general a shade less educated than themselves (Barber 1987). This tradition lies behind the pedagogical scenes in *Ayo Ni Mo Fe* in which a lawyer reads the definition of rape to someone who needs to hear it and a doctor lectures parents on how to ensure their children avoid typhoid, or the speech by the matron of an orphanage in *MAAMi* about the abandonment and adoption of children. *Arugba* contains instructions on oral rehydration therapy by a health worker—a scene foreign viewers may find intrusive but which has roots that go back to the very beginning of film culture in Nigeria, the educational films (often on health issues) that the mobile vans of the Colonial Film Unit took around to neighborhoods and villages. The oral rehydration scene is in effect an inserted public service announcement on behalf of the Lagos State government, whose funding allowed the film to be completed; as part of the financial arrangement, Kelani showed *Arugba* in every Local Government Area[8] in the state with his own mobile cinema equipment.

Akinwumi Ishola often appears in the films he wrote for Kelani as the spokesperson for linkages between past and present, tradition and modernity. He is what an elder should be, white hair and beard framing a face full of wisdom, benevolence, and humor, sometimes cheerfully risking self-parody as he mediates between official and popular culture but potent with genuine gravity and authority, shifting easily to passion and asperity. In *O Le Ku* (1997) (based on his novel of the same name about life on the campus of the University of Ibadan in the 1960s), he appears briefly as what he is, a university professor. (He is retired from Obafemi Awolowo University. See also chapter 11.) In this scene, he epitomizes the project of the famous "School of History" at the University of Ibadan: "You must work hard, it's up to you. You've heard one professor from Oxford said Africans had no history?" (The name of Hugh Trevor-Roper, who made this notorious statement, is on the blackboard behind him). "Is that true? We know it is not true, but who will write our history for us? It is not safe to allow strangers to write our history for us." His students assent with spirit. At the opening of *Saworoide* he is a babalawo who forges a mystical bond between ruler and people and introduces the political allegory that structures the whole film and its sequel, *Agogo Eewo/Taboo Gong*, where he appears briefly again. In *Thunderbolt* (which he did not write) the intellectual climax is a lecture he gives as a professor at a gynecology conference: "The purpose of my paper is to encourage a more humble, a more academic, more research-oriented approach to African medical practice. Western medical profession itself, if it can drop its toga of pride, still has a lot to learn from the so-called African herbalist." In *The Campus Queen* he is lecturing again, telling students they must return to their culture, quoting Faulkner on how the past is not gone or even past, and denouncing the nation's leaders for their slavish imitation of the West even after independence. When a student points out he is dressed in a suit, he promises to stop wearing Western-style clothes. In a later lecture he is indeed wearing African clothing as he defines democracy and denounces Nigerian political parties for acting like gangs, not true parties. In *Efunsetan Aniwura* (2005), a project with which both Ishola and Kelani have a long, complicated history,[9] the historical drama about the powerful nineteenth-century Ibadan female chief is introduced and concluded by scenes in the present in which Ishola and an interlocutor discuss the history of Ibadan and Yorubaland. They are framed against Mapo Hall, where the Ibadan chiefs met, an iconic building whose pillared façade is a motif in the indigo *adire* cloth that Ibadan women dye. Kelani (who shot the film as well as directed it) surrounds their conversation with images of contemporary Ibadan, its streets crowded with minibuses, dwelling on the heroic sculptures and other landmarks that recall its history—a visual essay on the past in the present to accompany Ishola's informal lecture, overtly educational and commemorative, of a piece with the title at the end of the film that gives the names and dates of all the women who held Efunsetan Aniwura's title of Iyalode of Ibadan.

RECURRING ELEMENTS

The blending and coexistence of past and present, tradition and modernity, is a nearly constant theme in Kelani's work. The object is never to prove that one side is superior and could subsume the other but to reach a convivial consensus and reconciliation. The call in *Thunderbolt* for a synthesis between traditional and modern/Western medicine is perhaps the most programmatic example. The production of a culture that was at once modern and proudly Yoruba was the project of Kelani's father's hero, Obafemi Awolowo. In Kelani's films the relationship does not seem dialectical in a Hegelian sense where thesis and antithesis enter into a (single, irreversible) historical process to produce a new thing, a synthesis, displacing the prior forms. The traditional and the modern are expected to go on being poles, fountains of meaning that do not run dry or lose their difference from one another. Kelani is distressed by the general failure of modernity in Nigeria to produce the expected enlightenment, but he remains dedicated to that project. He is if anything even more distressed by the decay of Yoruba traditional life in all its forms, speaking bitterly of how masquerading and drumming traditions are dying because Christian and Muslim fundamentalists disapprove of them (see Klein 2007), for example, and the Yoruba language itself is fading out in the younger generation. He is committed to preserving what can be preserved and to recording the rest, so that it will continue to be a strong living force in the present.

The table of themes (table 1) illustrates some of the recurring elements in Kelani's films. It makes visible gradients in the focus and settings of the various films between the traditional and the modern and between the personal and the political. More importantly, it shows the tendency to mix them up. There is a general orientation towards the social. Structures of governance are usually in view. Institutions have a fundamental legitimacy of purpose about them but are beset by corruption, much of it presented rather genially as arising from normal human character—but still it must be earnestly combated. The other constant is that Yoruba culture is also always on display, in deeply rooted or contemporary forms or, most often, both.

The artful casting of Kelani's films reflects this mixing and a strategy of including iconic figures that bring their own resonances to the project, so that each film presents a broad united cultural front and a vision of the richness of Nigerian culture. In *Thunderbolt*, for example, the cast includes the rising

TABLE 1 Tunde Kelani, table of themes

	Ti Oluwa Nile 1–3 (1993–5)	*Ayo Ni Mo Fe* 1 & 2 (1994–5)	*Koseegbe* (1995)	*O Le Ku* 1 & 2 (1997)	*Saworoide* (1999)	*Thunderbolt / Magun* (2001)	*Agogo Eewo* (2002)	*The Campus Queen* (2004)	*Efunsetan Aniwura* (2005)	*The Narrow Path* (2007)	*Abeni* 1 & 2 (2006)	*Arugba* (2008)	*MAAMi* (2010)
traditional music and dance	x			x	x		x	x	x	x	x	x	x
modern music and dance	x	x	x	x		x		x			x	x	x
talking drums	x		x	x	x		x	x	x	x		x	x
masquerades	x									x		x	x
babalawo	x	x			x	x	x		x			x	
cloth	x		x	x	x		x	x	x	x		x	x
oba in council	x				x		x		x	x		x	
dispute over throne	x				x		x						
corrupt chiefs	x				x		x		x			x	
corrupt chiefs with wives	x	x			x		x					x	
broad comedy	x	x	x	x	x	x	x		x	x	x		x
selling communal property	x				x		x						
journalists			x		x		x	x					x
protest demonstrations	x				x		x	x	x	x			
schools and education		x	x	x		x		x		x	x	x	x
modern medical institutions	x	x				x					x		x
young heroine		x		x	x	x		x	x	x	x	x	
young hero		x		x	x				x		x	x	x
romantic choice		x		x		x		x		x	x	x	
tradition v. modernity	x					x				x		x	

young Nollywood star Uche Obi-Osotule, Ngozi Nwosu (Andy's second wife in *Living in Bondage*), two actors from the University of Ibadan, both of them now regrettably deceased (Joe Emordi and Larinde Akinyele, a favorite of Kelani's, who taught mass communications), and three important writers: Ishola, Wale Ogunyemi (who had written the screenplay for *Ayo Ni Mo Fe* 2), and Adebayo Faleti, an important television personality as well as writer and author of the novel *Magun*, on which *Thunderbolt* was based. The casting can be laced with irony or freighted with symbolism, as when Faleti is cast as a wise commentator in *Saworoide* and *Agogo Eewo*, or merely sly, as when Peter Fatomilola, a mainstay of the illustrious drama program at Obafemi Awolowo

University, puts in a cameo appearance as a grizzled palm wine vendor in *O Le Ku*, or when Peter Badejo, the greatest Nigerian dancer of his generation, is cast as the minister of sports in *MAAMi*.

Kelani exploits the capacity of cinema to be a total art form, incorporating many others, as a way of representing the fullness of his culture. The relationship with literature is fundamental, as we have seen. Yoruba verbal arts—proverbs, praise names, songs, Ifa verses, incantations, "deep" vocabulary and turns of phrase (see Barber 1991, 2000)—saturate the films.

Music and dance, as already suggested, are structural in Kelani's conception of cinema. Drums are iconic, especially talking drums (*dundun*), associated with kingship and praise singing, and *bata* drums, associated with Sango worship and masquerading. Both kinds of drums are also used in popular music. Talking drums sound under the Mainframe/Opolumero logo, and they provide nondiagetic linkages between sequences in *Koseegbe*. *Saworoide*, which ended up as a political allegory (see chapter 8), started out as a documentary film about a bata drummer who died while the film was still in the early planning stage. Dancing is a fundamental, and perhaps the most heavily symbolic, state of the human body and of the human community. The king joining his people in dance at the end of *Ti Oluwa Nile* is an example. *Arugba* gives mythic force to the relationship between the legendary king Sango and his bata drummer. In addition to dance's ritual and social forms and functions, staged dance and dance drama are contemporary art forms, and Kelani's films provides a survey, from the neotraditional idiom of the performance the protagonist goes to see in *O Le Kú* to the hip-hop numbers of the University of Lagos Creative Arts Department students featured in *The Campus Queen*.

"Cloth," in Nigerian parlance, means African clothing—the actual cloth may be imported Holland wax print, elaborately embroidered, or it may be locally handwoven or dyed according to local traditions. In any case, it is a powerful signifier of culture with its own rich symbolism, as deep as the language of the drums. The checked box on table 1 indicates Kelani is highlighting it, often with dazzling force. In the party scene in *Koseegbe* in which the hero is congratulated on his promotion and the campaigns to seduce and corrupt him begin, the glorious shining cloth worn by the guests expresses prosperity and well-being. Cloth can also indicate affiliation, as when family members or associations of friends dress in cloth of the same pattern to attend a wedding or funeral. In *Agogo Eewo* costumes color-code opposing groups of demonstrators.

The architecture of Yoruba towns and cities, much of it dating from the colonial era, may not be remarkable to a Nigerian audience, but it conveys a sense of well-worn habitation, an old, even ancient, style of urban life. With traditional settings, like those in *Efunsetan Aniwura*, comes an enveloping, concentrated cultural presence embodied in objects—cloth, woven mats, carved wood, calabashes, beaded crowns and staffs, and so on. All the elements of this material world are threatened—calabashes replaced with plastic buckets and jerry cans, dyed fabrics with used Western clothes, earth and stucco with barren concrete surfaces—but they are all still around, easily available. They just need to be assembled. Kelani went to the Benin Republic to shoot *The Narrow Path* because pristine traditional villages have become hard to find in Nigeria, but normally being pristine is not the point.

The traditional arts Kelani features, like drumming or *adire* dyeing, might perhaps suggest a way of thinking about the element of repetition in his own art. He also plays with a set of repeating elements. It is not a closed set—in fact novelty is valued—but the inherited elements are prized so highly that they are conserved over many years. The heritage reproduces itself and keeps on flowing out of its own resources, the individual work gaining identity and strength by rooting itself, being recognizable as playing with materials that have proven themselves essential. The art is in mobilizing these elements in shifting patterns and renewing them, responding to the moment.

AUDIENCES

Kelani enjoys his role as cultural ambassador to the world. It is part of what keeps him afloat as a filmmaker, though perhaps it is more important psychologically than financially—foreign money has never played a significant role in his revenue streams. First and foremost his purposes are oriented around being an artist of and for his own culture, an exhorter and custodian.

Underlying everything else is a commitment to, and a pleasure in, bringing his cinema to a popular audience. In 2011 I was with him in São Paulo, Brazil, for a film festival retrospective of his work. It was Black Consciousness Month in Brazil. The organizers had arranged for us to spend part of a day in a *favela* called Heliopolis, one of the largest slum neighborhoods and the best organized. Years of strenuous activism by its residents had created, among other things, a large community center containing schools and a cultural center with indoor and outdoor theaters. While we waited for the program to begin, Kelani contemplated the outdoor theater, which was like the idea of a theater reduced to its simplest geometries and realized in plain cement, painted a vivid tropical blue. It clearly inspired him, and he told stories. In Norway, somewhere near the Arctic Circle, his films had been screened in a theater made of ice at a festival of indigenous filmmaking. Because he made films in Yoruba, he counted as "indigenous," along with reindeer herders and Amazonian Indians, never mind that the Yoruba were far more populous and had been living in cities longer than Norwegians. (I was making this point about the vagaries of categorization; he was not bothered.) He had gotten involved with a project to teach poor kids in Haiti how to make films and made regular trips there to lead workshops until the 2010 earthquake put an end to everything. He invested in his own mobile cinema equipment and used it to screen his films in the Benin Republic during the period when he made *The Narrow Path* and *Abeni* there. Yoruba is spoken on both sides of the border that the British and French drew between what became Nigeria and Benin, and he had mounted a one-man campaign to restore the cultural and linguistic unity of the Yoruba now separated by official barriers and the languages of the colonizers. (This is a running theme in *Abeni*.) He used the mobile cinema equipment to show *Arugba* around Lagos State, an experiment in creating an alternative to Nollywood circuits of funding and distribution. But the Lagos State government seemed to have cooled in its support.

Inside the Heliopolis cultural center, in the larger theater where *MAAMi* was screened, he told the audience that bringing his work to them was the best and most important part of his trip to Brazil. He obviously meant it. I had seen him facing a much larger audience in the plush seats of Lincoln Center when he was being celebrated with a midcareer retrospective at the African Film Festival of New York (Haynes 2007c), and he was clearly thoroughly happy and slightly dazed then, but now he was more deeply moved. This was what it is all about for him: the assembling of a popular audience in solidarity, and the act—which had a performative aspect to it because it was not a routine, commercial experience in a theater taken for granted as part of the urban infrastructure—of bringing cinema to them, of bringing a piece of their own African culture back to them against the tides of history.

* Part 2 *

CHAPTER 6

The Cultural Epic: Representing the Past

INTO THE PAST AND TO THE EAST

The "cultural epic," also called the "traditional film," is a major, flourishing Nollywood genre, distinct and immediately recognizable because it is set in a particular landscape: a "traditional" past of thatched villages, spears, and sometimes fanciful costumes. Outside this genre, Nollywood has almost never represented the past, for strong practical reasons: Nollywood's low budgets and lack of physical infrastructure, the consequence of its economic structure, mean that films are not made in studios where period sets could be constructed, and there are no warehouses full of period props and costumes to be drawn upon. Though flashbacks are a standard device, Nollywood generally does not seem troubled by any sense of anachronism that would require a producer to come up with period automobiles for a scene that was supposed to take place thirty years in the past (Haynes 2007b).

Thatched villages are no longer easy to find near Lagos, where almost all early Nollywood films were shot, even when they were set in the Igbo southeast of Nigeria (usually called "the East"). But in the East, such villages can be found or constructed cheaply using local labor and unused land, and shooting on location in the Igbo heartland where most of the cultural epics are set makes a wealth of cultural resources, such as local performance troupes, more easily available. The sudden efflorescence of the cultural epic genre in the late 1990s coincided with, and helped to drive, a broader shift of film production to the East. Lagos is an expensive and congested place to make movies, and it is distracting—filmmakers often preferred to get out of town just to isolate the actors from the importunities of their lives and the temptation to run off to other jobs. The Igbo marketers who largely control the film business are based in Idumota Market in Lagos but were from and maintained close relations with the East. Onitsha—the great commercial center of Igboland on the banks of the Niger River—had always been a principle hub of the video film distribution system and increasingly played a major role in financing films as well.

The early cultural epics were mostly shot in villages around Enugu, which were exceptionally welcoming to film crews. Bond Emeruwa says the crews were sometimes fed for free and town criers would go around calling for extras. (On the relationship of film productions and villages at a later date, see McCall 2012). For a brief period Aba (another important video distribution hub) rivaled Enugu as a place for filmmaking, but Aba was rowdy and insecure, and getting anywhere could take hours, while Enugu—historically an administrative and mining center, not a commercial one—was calm and had good infrastructure. Costs were far lower than in Lagos. Enugu had the oldest and largest television broadcasting facilities in the East, and some major stars live there, including Pete Edochie and Nkem Owoh. Enugu boasts a number of tertiary education institutions, which provided extras to play young spear carriers and village maidens; it is also full of retired civil servants, many of whom were happy to be elders in the movies. The leading roles were mostly filled by Lagos-based actors and the deals were made in, and the money came from, Idumota or Onitsha, but for a while Enugu was the center of Nollywood movie production, with daily casting calls at the Presidential Hotel. Establishing shots of Lagos were often spliced into films that were shot in Enugu. According to Emeruwa, there were only a few nice houses in Enugu available to the filmmakers, so the houses themselves became stars, featured in one film after another. Sam Dede remembers waiting until midnight for another film production crew to vacate the house in which his production was meant to be shooting.

THE BATTLE OF MUSANGA AND *IGODO*

The genre of the cultural epic was launched with fanfare in 1996 by *The Battle of Musanga*, produced by Gab Onyi Okoye, known as "Gabosky." An opening title introduces the film's nature and subject:

> This is the true life story of what happened in 1863 when the first white missionary priest arrived Arochukwu and was kidnapped by the wild and primitive people of Musanga, who had a tradition of using a human head for the coronation of a new king. The Aros faced a bloody British reprisal and Ohafians had to come to their rescue . . .

The word "epic" was used extensively in the advertising campaign for the film, got picked up jocularly in the public's reaction to it, and became ensconced in the name of the genre. The film's budget was epic: Gabosky, who had made his money with a string of clothing boutiques and other businesses, claimed to have invested ₦10 million (above $100,000) in the film, far more than anyone had ever put into a video film before, as he liked to point out (Okoye 2004; Ayorinde (1997) gives a figure of ₦7 million). The other "big budget" films of 1996 had budgets of around ₦2 million. Gabosky did not spend his money on a constellation of big-name stars, but rather on a very large cast and on "cultural" display: costuming, traditional architecture, and generously proportioned performances by musicians, dancers, wrestlers, and masqueraders. Four different groups are credited with the lovely music of drums and flutes that runs the length of the film's soundtrack. The costumes of the British characters are implausible, but care was taken to make the Igbo costumes historically accurate, which meant that many of the women were bare breasted. This proved shocking and unacceptable to audiences: the missionaries had struggled to get women's breasts covered up, and Nigerian society seemed nearly unanimous in wanting to preserve this aspect of the colonial heritage. A frequently expressed sentiment was that it was wrong to expose African womanhood to lustful foreign eyes.

The epic budget rather stunned the industry. It took a few years before anyone else made a cultural epic. *King Jaja of Opobo* (1999, directed by Harry Agina) was another big-budget production (it had a cast of 1,500 and a crew of 44; *Official Site* 2000). It also strove for historical accuracy in representing the mid-nineteenth century. Frequent titles keep us precisely located in time and space as the film tells the story of one of the most famous men of that time, an Igbo who was enslaved and taken to Bonny, on the coast of what is now Rivers State, where he worked his way up to become head of one of the great "canoe houses" that controlled trade in the Niger Delta. He struggled with the British colonial authorities and left Bonny to create his own kingdom at Opobo. Local pride in the Rivers heritage helped raise the money for this monument to a hero, but the film did not do well commercially.

Other examples of films based on historical events, whose enthusiastic support by an ethnic, political, or religious community helps offset their large budgets and limited commercial appeal, include hagiographic Catholic films about the missionaries Mary Slessor and Father Tansi, the Nupe film *Manko* (2006), and Jeta Amata's international collaboration *The Amazing Grace* (2006) (not to be confused with the Hollywood film *Amazing Grace* that appeared at the same moment and had the same subject: the composition of the famous hymn by John Newton, a former slave ship captain turned abolitionist preacher).

Igodo: Land of the Living Dead, which appeared in 1999 while *King Jaja* was in production, is a very different kind of film, and its enormous popularity relaunched and largely redefined the cultural epic. This branch of the genre is legendary rather than historical; linked to a Nigerian literary culture in which Joseph Campbell's *The Hero with a Thousand Faces* is a familiar point of reference, it is stuffed with archetypes. A son of the thunder god Amadioha is persecuted as a child; when his parents are killed he flees into the forest and is raised by a wise hunter. As a young man, seven wicked elders conspire to put him to death through a false accusation. He grows more and more Christlike as he suffers his passion, warning as he dies that the sins of the fathers will be visited upon the children. His vengeful spirit inhabits a tree in the town and begins killing off the inhabitants, beginning with the seven wicked elders and their families. This tree can only be felled by a certain knife, to be found in the hills of Amadioha. (When the townsmen in desperation try cutting the tree with ordinary machetes, the tree bleeds and wounds appear on their king.) Seven heroes are appointed to bring back the knife, taking on the burden of self-sacrifice for the sake of their community. Instructed by a *dibia* (an Igbo diviner), they set out through the evil forest and the land of the dead. In the course of dangerous encounters with supernatural creatures, most of them die. At the cave of Amadioha's shrine, its guardian demands a human sacrifice and one of them volunteers. Igodo alone survives to bring the knife back to his town, which is renamed after him.

Igodo began as a project of Don Pedro Obaseki. Obaseki points to the inspiration of D. O. Fagunwa's *Forest of a Thousand Daemons* (translated from Yoruba by Wole Soyinka, 1982); others have remarked on *Igodo*'s resemblance to Wale Ogunyemi's famous dramatization of Fagunwa, *Langbodo* (1979). In Obaseki's conception, the film would express his own Edo (or Bini) culture. (Igodo is the name of the legendary first ogiso, or king, of what would become the Kingdom of Benin, the major regional power between Yorubaland and Igboland.) But when he finally found a producer—the young businessman Ojiofor Ezeanyaeche of OJ Productions, flushed with enthusiasm for the film industry after his success with the money ritual film *Blood Money*—OJ insisted on Igboizing the film. OJ brought in Kabat Essosa Egbon, who had been Obaseki's student in the University of Benin Theatre Arts Department, to work on the screenplay with him and brought in the veteran Andy Amenechi to codirect the film with Obaseki. The film was shot in locations all over southern Nigeria—around Enugu, Anambra, Oshogbo, and Abeokuta.

ACTORS

OJ also, following the normal line of thinking, wanted to protect his large investment in the film by casting the most familiar movie stars. But Obaseki insisted on his own casting ideas. Finally most of the major roles were given to actors with stage training and experience, like Nobert Young (who played the title role) and Sam Dede.

The Battle of Musanga brilliantly captures the lithe movements of mostly naked bodies at home in the natural world or in the dancing arena, but the most impressive examples of grace and agility are by bit players. *Igodo*, on the other hand, is an actor's movie. Its action sequences can be clunky and the actors sometimes seem to be posturing their way through their heroic quest, but the actors are charismatic, individually and collectively. The seven heroes are all fine bare-chested specimens of masculinity. (The epic might have begun as a more masculine genre than, say, the family film, but female viewers were given plenty to look at.) Sam Dede, who played one of the heroes, remembers the vibrant atmosphere on set as the actors pumped themselves and one another up into the legendary heroism of their parts. On film, they crowd the screen, sinking their teeth into their lines.

The genre also became a showcase for the authority of senior men. *Igodo* launched the late-blooming career of the preeminent example of a retired civil servant turned actor, Moses Osuji, whose flowing white beard and distinguished mien established him as the oracular face of tradition in more than a dozen subsequent films (Ejiogu 2005).

Igodo featured Pete Edochie as the dibia. More often he has been cast as a king (in Igbo, *eze*, *obi*, or *igwe*, the latter being a term of address, like the Yoruba *kabiyesi*, but in some places used as a substantive title; Nollywood has made "igwe" the standard term). Edochie is a subtle enough actor to play different roles in various genres, but always as a senior man: righteous king or tyrant, crime boss, a loving or (more often) stern father. He is the suave, sophisticated archvillain of Nnebue's *Rituals* (chapter 8). Edochie had played the role of Okonkwo in David Orere's 1986 thirteen-part television serial version of *Things Fall Apart*. Achebe's book—by far the most widely read novel in Nigeria and assigned in schools across Africa (Lindfors 2004)—had established Okonkwo as the central instance of Igbo masculinity, and Edochie filled the role with authority. His movie roles in the cultural epic genre have given him space to vary this archetypal representation of patriarchy. Edochie's enthroned igwes may project a lofty serenity, diplomacy, and benevolence, but normally they are stern with at least a touch of roughness, and Edochie brings a strong

FIGURE 5. *The Staff of Odo*, a cultural epic with Pete Edochie (left) as tyrannical igwe and Ramsey Nouah (center) as the true prince returning from slavery in Brazil.

physicality to the roles. He is mountainous, rocky, his anger like lava, his will radiating from him like waves of heat. The social order around him is held in shape by his will and force of personality as much as by custom. Not a lover, he is a progenitor and patriarch. Women are quick to cower in his presence, fearing a tongue lashing.

Only Olu Jacobs, who with his wife Joke Silva reigned as the royal couple of the Nigerian theater before Nollywood began, rivals Edochie in kingly roles. Audiences enjoy Jacobs's smooth authority and emotional range, and directors like to work with him because he is a tractable, consummate professional. But he is Yoruba, and some complain that he does not understand the nuances of Igbo kingship. Edochie on the other hand is himself an Igbo chief and is respected for his deep knowledge of his culture. He can exercise this authority on film sets with the same peremptory roughness he demonstrates on screen.

ACCURACY AND AUTHENTICITY

From *Igodo* on, one of the epic's main functions has been as a fantasy space for the individual personality. It invites identification with archetypal heroes, glamorizes physical prowess, and dramatizes personal assertion in the most extreme forms. This aspect of the genre is as important as the representation or evaluation of the historical past.

Some epic films work at historical and cultural accuracy, and some don't. I discussed this with the writer Joe Dudun (a specialist in the genre) and Bond Emeruwa in the courtyard of Emeruwa's Surulere office, a sea of mud at the time from a day of torrential rain. They both take research seriously. Dudun reads whatever he can in preparation for writing a screenplay and will spend weeks among the people whose history he is going to write about, absorbing the oral tradition, observing the customs, and seeking the collaboration of those who can perform the culture in one way or another. But when asked about the general level of commitment to accuracy in the genre, their answer was lengthy, deliberate, and withering: most productions are not bothered about accuracy at all. The film scholar Femi Shaka also notices the anachronism and lack of "historical accuracy and the principle of verisimilitude" in most Nollywood productions (2003). A blistering critique by Emmanuel S. Dandaura and the film director Obi Okoli of nine films concludes that from their "analysis of the language use, costumes and other cultural icons depicted in most of these films it is obvious that core Igbo values and some vital cultural practices have been so bastardized, grossly misrepresented, distorted and misapplied. Indeed, if the younger generation of Nigerians were to rely on these films to understand the Igbo world view in terms of their dress sense, religious practices, socio-political organisation and other routine cultural practices, that generation will most likely end up disoriented" (Dandaura and Okoli 2010, 73–74).

The lack of accuracy is regrettable. Nigeria has an endless variety of cultures, all of whose traditional forms are being rapidly eroded by urbanization, intolerant versions of the world religions, and Western education, and it would be good if more filmmakers shared Tunde Kelani's commitment to documenting his own culture. But lack of accuracy does not stop the epic from expressing social and psychological desires and pressures or from creating a usable past. Knowledge of the past is held in many different forms and locations; individual films may be complex, not entirely determined by one consciousness or purpose. A production might have a director in too much of a hurry to get on to his next job to worry about accuracy but still include a performance by a local dance troupe that is full of deeply rooted cultural elements, provoking the strongest reactions of identification and pride from those who can recognize them, who would then forgive everything else and claim the film as an authentic expression of their culture.

In one video store in Surulere where I go, the shopkeeper invariably presses every epic film she has into my hand, assuming this is what will interest the white man, and repeats, "This is a library film. You can put it in your library. It shows our culture." Epics are accepted and used in this way. For some middle class kids growing up in Nigerian cities, epics may be more powerful in shaping their imaginations of history than anything they learn in school or than occasional brief trips to their ancestral village, which they are apt to regard as "camping," amusing themselves with their electronic devices until the batteries run out, cultural and linguistic distance preventing them from absorbing much from the village elders. African parents in the diaspora—not just Nigerians—use Nollywood epics to demonstrate their roots to their children and non-African friends.[1]

The generalization of images of the past in the epics is in itself powerful, for better or for worse, even if motivated by carelessness, even as it erases local authenticities. As with the use of the English language and the homogenization of witchcraft and other discourses about the supernatural, the stereotyping of the past allows the films to travel across internal cultural and external national borders.

The fact that cultural epics are nearly all in English has deep consequences.[2] Reasons for shifting from Igbo-language filmmaking to English were discussed in chapter 3. This decision was not reconsidered with the advent of the epic, though the cultural stakes were higher and English was patently out of place in the traditional setting. The most prominent, proximate model for the epic genre was the television version of *Things Fall Apart*, which was in English—naturally enough, since it was addressed to a national audience and was based on an English-language novel.

In a paper addressing the debate about what language celluloid films about Yoruba culture should be made in, written in 1990 before the advent of Nollywood, Taiwo Oloruntoba-Oju evokes the value of the cultural continuities that come with filmmaking in indigenous languages:

> The setting and characters could be as rural, traditional or metaphysical as possible without setting off linguistic incongruities or tampering with the aesthetic apprehension of verisimilitude on the part of the audience. Such characters include witches, old folks and warriors, with the numerous, mostly

> untranslatable, incantations that go into the settling of conflicts. Maidens with their water-pots at river-sides or widows at gravesides turn words into songs smoothly, without straining credulity. The quality of festive songs and dances, which match the songs naturally, is equally enhanced. The drum medium is easily employed. The *gangan* (talking drum), the *bata*, *agogo* (castanets), etc., speak in languages that blend easily with the medium of expression and are easily understood. The list of aesthetically pleasing complements to the language used in these films is actually endless.
>
> The linguistic medium enhances audience receptivity even at the thematic level. It may be noted for instance that most of the titles of these films derive from well-known moral, cultural and metaphysical idioms. For instance, the term *aiye* as it occurs in the films *Aiye*, *Jaiyesimi*, *Opon Aiye* and the popular T.V. serial *Omo Araiyele*, etc., immediately sets off metaphysical apprehensions and even dread. It enhances immediate grasp of the thematic implications of the films and immersion in its metaphysical terrain. But in English the term *aiye* simply translates as "world" or "world people" which does not make sense (or make related sense) and would be laughable as the title of a film in our setting. (Oloruntoba-Oju 1990, 6–7)

The English-language cultural epics lose much of this immediate, spontaneous legitimacy and easy flow of meaning and affect. The scripts of cultural epics have seldom been based directly on literary works, but the films are all fully scripted, in English, and the scripts tend to have a strong literary or literary-dramatic character. Sometimes they seem full of careless inventions and inappropriate rhetoric, impediments to a realistic representation of the past.

HISTORY AS SUBJECT

Yoruba films with traditional settings clearly were a model and an inspiration for the cultural epic, but the epic was perceived as something separate and different. In Yoruba films about the past, as patented by Hubert Ogunde in his late celluloid films from *Aiye* (1979) to *Ayanmo* (1988), the classic situation is of a good polity presided over by a priest-king on his throne, beset by witches and then restored, through supernatural means, to peace and legitimacy. Such films are not necessarily set in the past, but they usually are. Because they are so archetypal in intent, historical time tends to be irrelevant. This is certainly not the only kind of Yoruba film about the past (see the earlier discussion of *Efunsetan* and Ogunleye 2014), but it tends to influence the others. Igbos do not believe in witches, so in cultural epics other supernatural forces are involved: deities who wreak havoc because of a violation of a taboo, as in *Igodo*, or evil deities served at shrines by sorcery-practicing dibias, who may in turn serve a tyrant, as in *The Battle of Musanga*. Perhaps emulation of the Yoruba example is at work when wizards duel in epics, as in *Ibuka: King of the Forest* (2000) and *Agbako: The Land of a Thousand Demons* (2000).

Entirely human and secular causes may disrupt the basic homeostatic model, notably the slave trade, strongly present as a theme in *The Battle of Musanga* and quickly establishing itself as a subgenre with Chico Ejiro's *Slave* (1999) and *Freedom* 1 and 2 (1999).[3] *The Battle of Musanga* also initiates, in the video tradition, the theme of the coming of Christian missionaries. Subsequent treatments of this topic will present it as a spiritual war between Christianity and indigenous spiritual forces, but *The Battle of Musanga*, in the manner of *Things Fall Apart*, does not. A final title warmly endorses the evangelization of Igboland, but the martyred priest has no supernatural backing, though both the bad Musangas and the good Ohafians wield effective juju powers.

The highly decentralized political character of precolonial Igboland, largely organized as it was in autonomous clan-based villages, perhaps influences the nature of the epic. The city-states and protracted nineteenth-century wars of Yorubaland provided structures for stories to become well known to many people, as the story of Efunsetan Aniwura is entwined with the city of Ibadan in Tunde Kelani's film. Rev. Samuel Johnson's *History of the Yorubas* (published in 1921, but written in 1897) is immensely important in this respect, a great repository of historical narratives that then reentered the oral tradition, becoming, for instance, the basis for several Yoruba traveling theater plays. The exemplary Igbo story, on the other hand, is Achebe's fiction about a fictional clan that could be any clan in any village. Arochukwu is the one historical place name occurring in multiple films, as its traders and the priests of the Arochukwu oracle Ibinukpabi (or Ibin Ukpabi), the "long juju" as the British called it, traveled widely in Igboland, serving as diviners, judges, and slavers. (They carried the condemned off with them to be sold, as seen in *Musanga*, which is set in Arochukwu; the name also appears in *Igodo* and *Ibuka*.) The broad historical patterns of external intrusions—slavery, colonialism, evangelization—are the most obvious common topics in Igbo history.

Therefore in general, while both the cultural epic and the Yoruba filmmaking tradition aim at conveying a horizon of the imagination, an expression of traditional culture and values whose original and clearest expression is in the past, the epic has a greater tendency to have as its subject historical change—changes in the way people live. In Yoruba films the object tends to be to continue tradition as a living force, not to seal it into a past whose difference is the point. The continuities between past and present are stronger for the Yoruba than they are for the Igbos in various ways—a stronger adhesion to the language, a greater tolerance for the persistence of indigenous religious practices, the existence of powerful intermediary cultural forms such as the traveling theater, a gentler experience of urbanization since the Yoruba, unlike the Igbos, already had very old cities.

IGWES

As representations of the Igbo past, the most surprising feature of the cultural epics is the complete occlusion of republicanism and village democracy as political forms (Haynes 2005a, 16–17; Haynes 2006; Dandaura and Okoli 2010; Olaoluwa 2014). In the movies, there is always an igwe surrounded by a council of elders. Kingship was not unknown among the Igbos, but generally the Igbos did not have kings and did not want them.[4] In *Things Fall Apart*, when the first white men come to Mbanta, "They asked who the king of the village was, but the villagers told them that there was no king. 'We have men of high title and the chief priests and the elders,' they said" (Achebe 1994b, 148). One of the first things Achebe shows us about Igbo society is direct democracy in action, the ten thousand freeborn clansmen of Umuofia meeting to debate a resolution to go to war (ibid., 10).[5]

The British, themselves saddled with an absurd monarchy and aristocracy, had trouble understanding a democratic African society; in any case they could not tolerate it, because of the inherently antidemocratic character of the colonial project and the practical necessity, given how few British colonizers there ever were in Nigeria, to institute a policy of "indirect rule" through pliable local chiefs. Since chiefs in the required sense did not exist in Igboland, the British invented them: the so-called "Warrant Chiefs" (Afigbo 1972). They were generally despised. Often they were drawn from what many Igbo considered the dregs of society, and they were hated not just for their collaboration with the colonizers but for their flagrant corruption. Under successive structures of colonial and postcolonial governance, "traditional rulers" were certified or invented in order to play a mediating role between local communities and higher levels of government (Jones 1970; Harneit-Sievers 1998; cf. Mamdani 1996). They have blossomed in number and social prominence since the 1970s (Harneit-Sievers 1998). Over time they became familiar elements of the political and social landscape and gradually lost some or most of their aura of illegitimacy. But hear Achebe, in his 1983 screed *The Trouble with Nigeria*:

> The bankrupt state of Igbo leadership is best illustrated in the alacrity with which they have jettisoned their traditional republicanism in favour of mushroom kingships. From having no kings in their recent past the Igbo swung around to set an all-time record of four hundred "kings" in Imo and four hundred in Anambra! And most of them are traders in their stall by day and monarchs at night; city dwellers five days a week and traditional village rulers on Saturdays and Sundays! They adopt "traditional" robes from every land, including, I am told, the ceremonial regalia of the Lord Mayor of London!
>
> The degree of travesty to which the Igbo man is apparently ready to reduce his institutions in his eagerness "to get up" can be truly amazing. (Achebe 1983)

Why have the igwes so completely displaced the memory of republicanism and village democracy in the movies?

I have never seen an epic that offers an image of village democracy beyond a bare glimpse of rule by a council of elders until an igwe can be installed. *Pestilence* (2004) begins in such an anomic, unhappy state, before a whole new set of institutions—chief priest, laws and customs, and an igwe—can be instituted. In *Kasalama: The Slave Merchant*, a dibia addresses the elders of a community, reproaching them for the delay in choosing a new igwe after the death of the old one: "Any community or a group of communities without an igwe is like a slave land." Monarchy is assumed to be a stronger, normative form.

The proximate example of Yoruba "kabiyesi films" must be a powerful factor, reinforced by other national political and cultural framings in which the Igbos needed an equivalent monarchical figure. The British imported into Nigeria the durbar of traditional rulers, a crucial form of political spectacle in colonial India. In the 1950s, following the same logic, after the Northern and Western Regions had set up their own "Houses of Chiefs" as upper legislative chambers on the Westminster model, the predominantly Igbo Eastern Region decided it had better have one too (Jones 1970; Harneit-Sievers 1998). The displays of ethnic identity within the Nigerian national identity at FESTAC continued the tradition (Apter 2005). Larkin points out that from colonial times, "For Northern rulers, having one's installation filmed became part of the symbolic repertoire of royal authority. . . . Filming, and the demand to be filmed, had become part of how elite status was constituted" (2008, 104–5). Coverage of traditional rulers remains a staple of Nigerian television programming.

Dramatic convenience and habit probably also enter into it. Monarchical decisions, even after consultation with a council, are more efficiently represented than the palavers of democracy or the diffused functioning of the segmented lineages of Igbo clans. The Hollywood model of action by a single hero may also be relevant. The emotional structures of the (more or less) nuclear family are easily projected onto a monarchical royal family, with a pleasant sense of inflation, enabling the whole usual set of romantic and family-melodramatic issues to be played out in this setting: jealousy among cowives and/or siblings (*Red Matchet*), and children whose romantic choices do not meet with parental approval (*Ola*) or are otherwise wayward or persecuted (*Amina*).

The folklorist Chukwuma Azuonye argues that

> royalty (in the sense of the majesty of the king as an embodiment of sovereign power) has remained one of the most highly cherished values in Igbo thought in a situation in which monarchy (in the sense of the monopoly of power by one man or one family) is viewed as anathema. It would, therefore, appear that the saying *Igbo enwe eze* is better translated as "The Igbo abhor monarchical power" [rather than as "The Igbo have no kings"]. (1995)

As Azuonye put it succinctly to me, the Igbos rejected monarchy because every Igbo man wants to be a king himself and therefore can't tolerate anyone else holding the position. (Cf. the title of Henderson's *The King in Every Man: Evolutionary Trends in Onitsha Igbo Society and Culture*, 1972.) For our purposes, this provides a beautifully efficient explanation based on the relation of, and the difference between, movies and real life.

Igbo titles were and are eagerly sought after: "It is the ambition of every free-born youth to rise to chieftainship, and in this democratic country the highest honours are open to every freeman equally," G. T. Basden observed in 1921 (Basden 1966, 255–56). Achebe's Okonkwo is obsessed with titles, and in *Living in Bondage* Andy Okeke naturally converts his new wealth into the social prestige of chieftaincy. Igbo titles signify distinguished status, but—unlike Yoruba or European feudal titles—they never entailed executive authority or parcellized sovereignty over a defined territory. There can be only one *otun* at a time (originally the general commanding the right flank of a Yoruba army), but there is no natural limit to the number of titles an Igbo community can confer. Basden continues: "In modern times the dignity of the chieftainship has been degraded and the tendency is to bring the whole system into disrepute, owing to the wholesale and indiscriminate sale of titles to any youth who can produce the stipulated fee" (1966, 256). So-called "money chiefs"—"men or women of means on whom chieftaincy titles or positions have been awarded for hard cash by cash-starved or avaricious eze"—seem to be a phenomenon that predated contact with the British (Azuonye 1995, 67–68). Bond Emeruwa waved a hand around his Surulere neighborhood, saying there were thirty chiefs on his street. They compete for prestige in a currency devalued by inflation. In precolonial republican Igboland, titles existed independently of a monarchy, but in imagination, in the movies, all the social and emotional desires invested in title taking can find expression in one collectively fantasized plenipotent figure on a throne.

No less remarkable than the somewhat invented quality of the figure of the igwe is the way it has traveled beyond the borders of Igboland. Senayon Olaoluwa and Adewole Adejayan describe how mostly Yoruba soccer fans in southwestern Nigeria christened Thierry Henry, a Frenchman of Antillean extraction then playing for a British team, with the title of "Igwe" (2011). In another essay Olaoluwa adds examples of how "igwe" has spread: it is the title of a Yoruba hit gospel song and the brand name of a top-of-the-line electricity generator; in South Africa, where many young professionals marinate themselves in Nigerian film culture, people wearing any style of Nigerian clothing will be hailed on the street with cries of "Igwe!" (Olaoluwa 2011). This is all Nollywood's doing. It has created probably the most widespread image of traditional African kingship for the whole continent.

THE SETTING

As the epic genre took shape with remarkable speed in 1999, a typical, nearly invariable setting emerged, codifying a representation of the past: a village of thatched dwellings, an igwe surrounded by his council in a palace decorated with animal skins (some productions use zebra-striped or leopard-spotted machine-made cloth), and a diviner with one eye outlined with white caolin and a shivering, rattling iron rod who shuttles between a shrine and the palace. The royal entourage—strapping guards, wives, and maidens—often wear matching outfits. Ordinary folk discuss events when they meet on paths or by the waterside where women fill water pots. Cultural troupes perform dances to mark important occasions.

There may be two rival villages (as in Zeb Ejiro's *Red Matchet*, 2000), or a village and another place from which missionaries come (*Festival of Fire*, 1999), or an Igbo village and a far-away northern Nigerian kingdom linked to it by accident (*Amina: Unity in Diversity*, 1999), or a village and the Brazil from which the enslaved prince of *The Staff of Odo* (2005) returns. Rarely, as in *Musanga* or Lancelot Imasuen's *Adesuwa* (2012), three or more centers compete for power. Budgetary reasons doubtless account for this general economy of scope. Still it is extraordinary the extent to which the horizon of these films is conceived of as nothing more or less than the village, imagined as a bounded entity riven by internal conflicts and/or in tension with an outside force. We are almost never sunk so deeply in the personal or the domestic, or in the lineage or some segment of it, that the ultimate (monarchical) political structure of the village is not visible. When family problems are played out in a royal family, the personal becomes the political, and often the throne is at stake.

The films look much the same, then, but beneath the surface the epic is quite unstable ideologically. Representations of the past perforce convey interpretations of it, and the films do not agree about how the traditional past is to be valued.

IDEOLOGY CRITIQUE: *THE BATTLE OF MUSANGA*

The Battle of Musanga maintains a balanced Achebean view of precolonial Igbo life: it follows directly from the television version of *Things Fall Apart*, ideologically as in other ways. (Yusuf Mohammed was director of photography on both projects, for example.) The film immediately calls attention to the least defensible aspects of Igbo tradition as practiced in Arochukwu: human sacrifice, the killing of twins because they are thought to be an abomination, slavery, the forced marriage of an orphaned girl to a drunkard. Nothing is done to heroize the missionary, but when he demands that such practices stop, he is saying the right things—the things the film's audience would feel their ancestors needed to hear. When he threatens that if they do not stop these practices the white man's army will come to enforce God's will, however, the film's audience probably shares the reaction of the missionary's audience, which grumbles and disperses, one of them angrily asking, "Who gave him authority to talk to us like that? He must be mad!" Other aspects of tradition—the drumming, singing, and dancing, the wrestling and masquerading—are presented at length and clearly cherished. The Arochukwu igwe and elders are genial, responsible, and thoughtful.

The story puts this ambivalently presented community between violent opposing forces when the "wild and primitive people of Musanga" kidnap the white missionary to use as a human sacrifice at their new king's coronation. The British colonial authorities, seen at their headquarters in Calabar, understand only that the missionary was kidnapped in Arochukwu and threaten to destroy it if the missionary is not released. The British are aware that, in general, their exploitative motives are clearly recognized and are a political problem. Like the Aro elders, they seem human and are attempting to be intelligent, though their actions have a crude character born of their ignorance of the situation.

The savage king of Musanga and his dreadlocked dibia jabber in an incomprehensible made-up language when they are not roaring in English. The point is that they are not Igbo; they are some reprehensible version of Africanness that has been split off and cast out for reprobation.

Their danger paralyzes the Aros until a hero arises: Izuogu (Alex Usifo-Omiagbo), a wealthy, public-spirited citizen who volunteers to undertake a dangerous journey to locate where the Musangas are holding the missionary and to enlist the military aid of the warlike and virtuous Ohafians. (The Musangas are fictional, but the film reflects the historical character of the Ohafians, the Aros, and the relationship between them, on which see McCall 2000, chapter 4.)

These schematic distinctions blur somewhat as the film goes on. When we first see the king and elders of the Ohafians, who will generously and out of principle agree to do all the fighting necessary to rescue the Aros, they are discussing their commitment to justice while eating the flesh of a man one of them has killed because he was attempting a rape. The old ways, even the good old ways, can have a shocking alterity, like those bare breasts. (This quality of *Musanga* has been almost entirely lost in later epic films.) The film culminates with a long scene of the coronation of the savage Musanga tyrant on his skull-adorned throne, preceded, at great length, by the very same kind of cultural displays we saw in Arochukwu: the dancers and masqueraders, the sweet-toned drums and piping flute. Culturally, there is no difference. And the tyrant himself gives an impeccably nationalist speech about the white man having come across the great sea to enslave and exploit and pollute the African race with his own ways, as prologue to the decapitation of the battered and miserable white missionary so his skull can be used as the king's footrest. One might assume that the speech is commendable by the audience's standards, but the action is not. Ohafian warriors attack, interrupting the ceremony and annihilating the Musanga.

Igodo does not have ideological issues obtruding from it in anything like the same way. (Don Pedro Obaseki told me the death in prison of the winner of the annulled 1993 presidential election, M. K. O. Abiola, inspired his story of heroic self-sacrifice, but most viewers probably do not make this connection.) The film's frame, however, asserts the necessity of understanding an underlying spiritual and cultural formation in order to rectify life in the present. *Igodo* opens with a crisis in the contemporary world—ambulances wail and flash, carrying off victims of a mysterious plague—that can only be resolved by summoning the now-ancient titular hero from the depths of the forest. His narrative of the legendary past forms the bulk of the film and suggests how to deal with the present emergency. (The film ends with a title indicating a sequel was intended, but it was never made, leaving the crisis in the present unresolved.) Epics often suggest, as Nollywood films in general do, that in the depths under the surface of our lives are luminous archetypes and symbols, crimes to be atoned for, spiritual forces that must be properly aligned and obeyed or disease and infertility will result.

IDEOLOGY CRITIQUE: IGWES AGAIN

A good igwe, as priest/king, presides over properly ordered human life and is a symbol of order in himself. In the framing story of *The Staff of Odo*, an old priestess describes the village from which she is exiled as a place of peace and harmony, with a king who ruled with fear of the gods and the ancestors, handling every case with utmost carefulness, always consulting the gods before passing any judgment and talking to the council of chiefs before enacting any law. As the historian Afigbo writes, there was an "absence of clear distinction, or even of an attempt to distinguish, between the political and the religious in the governmental process," and, even in the cases where Igbos had kings, the system was what he calls "Constitutional Village Monarchy," in which the king's power was strictly limited by consultation and the consent of the governed (Afigbo 1972, 16–17). Azuonye glosses the various names by which Igbo kings are called:

> By and large, the *eze* occupies, not the apex of a hierarchical social order (as is suggested by the title, *Igwe*, which implies "the one with the gods who dwell in the sky"), but the centre or heart of a closely woven social system (as suggested by the title, *Obi*, which implies "the one who occupies or represents the centre"), surrounded by an inner council of *nze* or minor *eze*, with the populace occupying the outer fringes of the circle but operating within the same egalitarian and republican order in which the possibility of movement into and out of the inner circles or the centre itself is never foreclosed. (1995, 68)

Most films are too preoccupied with the igwe and his royal family to show this constitutional reciprocity beyond the more or less token presence of a council of elders, but some do. Zeb Ejiro's *Red Matchet* 1 and 2, for example, balances the central story (the rivalry between the late igwe's sons for the throne and the mythic quest for a lion's head the heir must accomplish) with a considerable role for the elders who govern during the interregnum and the strongly felt presence of the villagers, who discuss current events, live thematically parallel situations, and perform extended "cultural" and political rituals such as going to the border of the village to greet the returning heir. *Kasalama* is another epic emphasizing ordinary people and, in particular, ordinary women. Sometimes political competition is presented as such a dirty business that there is no room for the higher values an igwe is supposed to represent, as in Chico Ejiro's *Odum* (1999).

The igwe is a sharply ambivalent figure, often figured as a tyrant. Azuonye finds in Igbo folk tales about kings two distinct types, tales of the ideal *eze* and tales of the deviant *eze*, the latter violating the constitutional relationships that should link him reciprocally to his people and restrain him from tyranny (1995). In the movies, tyrants quickly became stock figures; one might speak (though I have not heard anyone do so) of a tyrant subgenre of the epic, stemming from the old Igbo ambivalence or antipathy toward monarchy.[6] In Chico Ejiro's *Festival of Fire* (1999) and Lancelot Imasuen's *Ibuka: King of the Forest* (2000), ordinary people cower in fear when they hear their rulers coming. Surrounded by intimidating bodyguards, contemptuous of the populace, rapacious, capricious, gratuitously cruel, and driven by turbulent ambitions, it is easy to see in these tyrants a figure for Nigerian military rulers. The tyrant's untrammeled egotism allows no freedom for anyone else.

In *Musanga*, the king is the highest expression of a savage people; in other films, we identify with the community over whom he tyrannizes, and the film's story (as with the tales of the deviant *eze*) is dedicated to his overthrow. Sometimes the problem can be solved using indigenous resources: a hero arising from among the oppressed people, a good heir or dynastic rival for the throne, a good dibia serving a good deity to contend with the tyrant's bad dibia and bad deity, the gods themselves acting to enforce their taboos and morality.

SPIRITUAL FORCES

If indigenous resources will not do the job, the tyrant is probably a sign of a whole epoch of darkness, the required remedy being modernity or, more often, Christianity. The films in which Christianity is the answer overlap with the faith-based genre of Christian videos, where indigenous religious forms or even the whole traditional culture may be seen as Satanic. Films about brave Christians coming to a town or village and casting out the indigenous demons and their wicked cult adherents are common, whether the temporal setting is past or present. *Narrow Escape* (1998) and *The Beginning and the End* (2001) tell, in contemporary settings, the story familiar in cultural epics of sons of the soil who run away from tyrannical fathers, become priests, and return to free their communities from spiritual bondage.

But Christianity has less hegemony over the cultural epic than one might expect. Christian filmmakers for whom African tradition is the work of the devil do not need to bother to recreate it in the epic genre; it is easier and more important for them to deal with its extensive legacy in the present, dramatizing the urgent choices facing living souls. Besides, Christian videos typically have small budgets, insufficient for entry into the epic genre. Those who spend money on historical recreation tend to see something valuable in the past.

Individual epics may present polarized visions of the past, then, as something to be treasured, as a guide for the present, or as a nightmare from which to awaken. But the industry is not set up around an ideological conflict with antagonistic blocs of filmmakers or producers. People move fluidly back and forth among a set of recognized options. OJ Productions, which was a major player in establishing the genre, produced the good igwe films *Igodo* and *Egg of Life* (a remake of *Igodo* with female heroes) but also the tyrant films *Ibuka* and *Agbako: Land of a Thousand Demons* (in this case, the tyrant is a dibia, not an igwe).[7]

Overall, the genre presents the past as an ambivalent inheritance, to be owned and evaluated. So in *Agbako* the evil sorcerer Agbako is opposed by a good dibia before being finally overcome by a Christian missionary. Igbo traditional culture is figured as an arena in which opposing forces struggle, rather than as inherently good or bad, though the outcome of this film would suggest that Igbo society cannot save itself without the help of Christian grace. (The missionary priest is, as he discovers, a son of the soil, the illegitimate child of the late igwe.) Similarly ambiguous is *Festival of Fire*, which tells the story of a missionary sister coming to a village where twins are sacrificed. At length it is revealed that the chief priest who does the sacrificing is her twin, and he offers his own life in atonement as he realizes that killing twins is a mistake. He does not, however, convert to Christianity. His god Amadioha seems less evil than misunderstood, and in its political dimension the village passes from the rule of a good old king to the frightening ascendancy of his tyrannical son, as if it had no inherent nature. The sense that traditional culture contained good as well as evil spiritual forces and good as well as evil people is central to the genre of cultural epic, providing a basis for the normal morally polarized melodramatic conflicts that fill Nigerian films.

A crucial feature of this landscape is the strict enforcement of strict moral codes by indigenous spiritual forces, normally centered in a shrine with its priest or priestess. As Zeb Ejiro pointed out to me, such forces work immediately, causing malefactors to drop dead on the spot or suffer in other spectacular and visible ways, which makes them good for drama—better than a Christian system in which rewards and punishments may not be meted out until the (invisible) afterlife. In the violent anomie of contemporary Nigeria, this is an immensely attractive vision, with its supernaturally enforced limits on tyranny and outrageous behavior, whether public or secret. An old-fashioned, sometimes sentimental cultural nationalist argument about the dignity of the African past is part of the genre's inheritance, but the epic also addresses more pressing and immediate needs. Even people who consider themselves Christians can admire the efficacy of this moral coding and can think of it as part of their African cultural heritage, what makes them who they are. In Nigeria today it is impossible to make anti-Christian movies, but a certain resistance to Pentecostalism's rapid destruction of indigenous forms may express itself in images of a traditional world that was orderly, clean, stable, righteous, and noble, in marked contrast to the degraded modern present.

GENERIC INSTABILITY

The cultural epic was established during the dreadful days of the Abacha dictatorship and consolidated at the moment of transition to civilian democratic rule, which likely accounts for the initial prevalence of films involving governance and social morality. But because the genre is finally defined by its setting alone, it is inherently loose, permeable, and unstable. Many things can happen in the epic, and other genres can invest its landscape with their own forms and concerns. The nature of some genres, however, discourages them from crossing over. The money ritual theme is tied to its contemporary moment, for example, though the epic abounds in human sacrifice for other reasons. Vigilante and crime films (chapter 7) likewise cannot find the specific social and political conditions that give them their logic. Comedy enjoys its contemporary settings so much that it sees no need to go anywhere—moving into the past would sacrifice topical material with no compensating gain.

But romance found fertile ground in the epic landscape. Competition for the hand of a prince or princess appeared early as an archetypal/folkloric motif, as in the 1999 Cinderella film *Oganigwe*; the motif is sometimes invested with political meaning, as in *Ijele: Son of the Masquerade* (1999) (a bad princess seeking to establish herself as a priestess and the good, legitimate priestess are rivals for the hero), or *Ibuka* (where again the hero is chosen by fate or gods). The Yoruba celluloid films starring Adeyemi Afolayan (Ade Love)—*Ajani Ogun* (1976), *Ija Ominira* (1978), and *Kadara* (1980)—provided a model for a fuller flowering of romance in a traditional setting.

Rising Sun (2003) is unusual because it largely abandons the normal horizon of the village. The heroine (Genevieve Nnaji) is a widow traumatically victimized by social custom and her late husband's extended family (a social topic that has been the subject of films with modern settings, such as Tade Ogidan's *Saving Alero*, 2002). She goes mad and lives alone in an abandoned hut where a roaming hunter (Kenneth Okonkwo) finds and falls in love with her. The film is almost entirely devoted to emotional expression, which, while searching, often takes a highly rhetorical, literary form, with frank disregard for plausibility in manners of speaking. The emotional structures are anachronistic, and the costumes are fanciful. *Ola: The Morning Sun* (2004) mixes high-flown literary declarations of love ("Silver and gold have I none except my heart, my love, and my friendship") and epic bluster ("let him feel the wrath of the lion") with the verbal mannerisms, body language, and cattiness of an overprivileged princess and her girlfriend attendants. *Ola*'s costumes and jewelry are a fashion designer's fantasia on Igbo tradition (Nigeria has a flourishing fashion industry, which regularly employs traditional elements in its high-fashion designs); the bright chemical dyes of the costumes match the bright, synthetic music on the soundtrack. The soap opera (or the telenovela, which not infrequently has a historical setting) has brought the epic under its sway. The cultural epic seemed designed at first for family consumption and reflected the heavily patriarchal character of precolonial society, with women largely (though certainly not entirely) relegated to minor roles. As the romantic element predominates, however, it feminizes the genre and gives equal attention to women.

The subgenre about slavery often includes the romance element. Izu Ojukwu's *Sitanda* (2006), a high-profile example, is about enslaved lovers separated by bamboo slave pens; the hero also has to contend with the advances of the ruling princess, tyranny taking romantic form. In another sign of the privatization of the epic form, in this film's framing story in the modern world, the crisis to be solved through understanding an ancient curse involves not the whole community but a marriage on the rocks.

ROYAL FILMS

The igwe-centric, romantically inflected epic seems to have inspired the "royal film," a genre with contemporary settings, which I believe then in turn influenced the epic. The royal film is about domestic, often romantic, conflicts in the household of a traditional ruler. It is a subgenre of the family film. Unlike in the epic, we seldom see kings conducting public business. Oracles may still play a part and there may be talk of the community being affected by violated taboos or curses arising from individual behavior, as in epics, but such elements tend to be abstract and distant; in *The London Boy* (2004), for instance, it is not clear whether such threats are real. Sorcery and other eruptions of the supernatural into the domestic are not at home here. The plots regularly feature a prince or princess in love with a commoner. Such stories have been around in Nollywood since the beginning: Chris Obi-Rapu's *Taboo* (1993) is about a princess in love with an *osu* (an outcast in Igbo society); in *Violated*, part of Tega's mother's objection to Peggy is that her family is noble and she is a nobody.

The royal film became a brand with Andy Amenechi's *Royal Palace* in 2007.[8] An igwe (Olu Jacobs) declares he will divide his immense wealth and settle the succession on the child who cures him of his mysterious unhappiness. This sets off intense competition among his numerous wives and their children and the revelation of a previously unrecognized illegitimate child.

Another film from 2007 was as influential as *Royal Palace* in establishing the genre: *Princess Tyra*, a Nigerian-Ghanaian coproduction set in Ghana but directed by a Nigerian, Frank Rajah Arase. It stars Van Vicker, Jackie Appiah, and Yvonne Nelson, three of a cohort of young Ghanaian actors who crossed over to Nollywood, becoming some of the biggest stars of their generation. (The others in this group are Majid Michel and Nadia Buhari.) The film was heavily marketed in Nigeria. Princess Tyra and Prince Kay, both glamorous cosmopolitans with British-inflected accents, are betrothed to one another in a dynastic alliance formed amid scenes of astonishing luxury (ostriches and antelopes roam among expensive vehicles) and clouds of rhetoric about the beauty and spiritual character of Africa. But Prince Kay finds the protocols of palace life suffocating—the flower petals spread before his feet as he emerges from his luxury vehicle, the servant in her uniform of tie-dyed miniskirt, halter top, and head tie who kneels to wash his feet before he can leave his room. He falls for the foot-washing servant and makes her pregnant, preferring to marry her and spurn Tyra in the face of fierce opposition. Such a maelstrom of melodramatic elements is then unleashed—orphans, rape, a lost identical twin sister, leukemia, hired thugs, Canadian visas, and more—that at the end of part 3 the marriage has still not taken place.

We are naturally on the side of young love, and the films make us identify with the Cinderellas and the abused (sexually and otherwise) maids and bodyguards suffering abjectly in the palace and with the outsiders drawn into this strange world. Nollywood is on the side of love matches and companionate marriages, but the melodrama in royal films is not really being mobilized in concerted opposition to an old, oppressive social order. The plot type in which young love faces parental opposition because erotic desire has crossed a status boundary flourishes in societies with rigid status boundaries. But rigid status boundaries are not really Nigeria's problem, though in a few families marriages will be constrained by dynastic considerations, and there are certainly ethnic divisions enough to trouble conservative parents. (Stories about cross-ethnic romances are fairly common in family films.) The "reciprocal convergence of elites" is Jean-François Bayart's phrase (1993) for the process through which Africans who reach a certain level of success in any field—business, the military, academia, medicine, law—take traditional titles, while traditional rulers exercise political and economic power and now tend to get their titles in part because of educational qualifications, and business success is closely intertwined with government contracts and licenses. In principle different kinds of social capital are involved, but in practice there is a fairly unified if porous elite, set against the impoverished masses and struggling middle class.

The existence of the royal genre itself shows the enduring fascination of the trappings of this particular kind of power and authority. But in spite of parading archaic forms of social prerogative, the royal films are mostly not really about old money or traditional power. They represent the consolidation of a wealthy class of people who gained their fortunes under military rule and neoliberalism. The palaces are brand new and adorned with huge flat-screen televisions. Shopping and consumer commodities are strongly featured. The world of the royal films is reminiscent of Dubai and the other monarchical emporia of the Persian Gulf, which are a playground and secure investment opportunity for wealthy Nigerians and are linked to Nigeria by many commercial ties—a place for traders to shop for handbags and watches, or film producers to buy cameras.

Everyone living in Nigeria feels the arrogance of the powerful. Royal films like *Princess Tyra* are mostly about arrogance—not about legitimacy, which is central in the epics—and royalty provides an elaborate apparatus for expressing it and exploring it as theme. Nollywood is ambivalent when it comes to arrogance too, condemning it out of moral and sentimental principle but also constantly parading it as wish fulfillment.

Tyra herself is a study in arrogance. Her treatment of the humble foot-washing maiden causes Kay to remonstrate, "Do you address humans as animals, because you are royal?" When she goes shopping she orders the mall manager to clear it of everyone who is not a subject of her kingdom. He objects: "I have shoppers from all over the world; I might lose my customers." A shopper amid the shelves demands, "Who the hell is she anyway?" But she insists on her royal command. Two more of the central confrontations of the film happen in shopping malls; in these scenes, the limits of Tyra's royal pretensions are tested with increasing mockery and outright refusal.

Arrogant behavior in luxurious shopping malls also features in Arase's hit of the year before, *Beyonce, the President's Daughter* (2006, with a two-part sequel, *Return of Beyonce*), of which *Princess Tyra* is more or less a remake.[9] Chico Ejiro's *The President's Daughter* (2000) has a similar scene in which the spoiled main character enters a boutique and orders everyone out so she can shop in privacy. In these two cases political power rather than royal status encroaches on the free market, giving an extra piquancy to the power of money, and we have crossed the overlapping border of another genre, the political film (chapter 8).

CHAPTER 7

Crime, Vigilante, and Village Films: Violence and Insecurity

Armed robbery was not a new story in Nigeria. In the early 1980s the most theatrical and iconic part of the Buhari military regime's War Against Indiscipline, a harsh response to the squalid circus of the preceding civilian Second Republic, was the public execution by firing squad of armed robbers lashed to empty oil barrels on Lagos's Bar Beach. But the breakdown of law and order reached new, outrageous levels in the 1990s and only got worse as military rule ended.

Oracle, a 1998 OJ Production directed by Andy Amenechi, begins with a bus on a road, Christian music on the soundtrack. The music turns threatening; dangerous-looking men are scattered around the bus and an ominous car trails it. The bad guys start shooting passengers, ordering them off the bus and forcing them to the ground as they scream in fear. Police arrive and there is a hail of bullets, with casualties on both sides. As the credits roll, dollars drift down the screen.

Issakaba 2 (2001, directed by Lancelot Imasuen) likewise has a sequence before the credits with a bus on the road and the sound of clapping and praying. A man on board makes his way up the aisle, Bible in hand, preaching. But he is not really a preacher: he's an armed robber, with an accomplice on board. Pandemonium breaks out as he pulls a gun and collects the passengers' valuables, grinning at the terror he is causing. He gets off the bus and into the car that has been trailing them.

Time Up . . . No Place to Hide, another 2001 film from the prolific Imasuen, begins with a confrontation between a governor and a priest. The governor has appointed him to a government commission, but the priest continues to denounce political corruption so the governor suborns three marijuana-smoking thugs to assassinate him. The thugs don police uniforms, but their bullets bounce off the priest as he prays for the good of the state. Still in uniform, they hold up a luxury bus, shooting passengers and the armed guard such buses carry, saying they know someone on board is carrying ₦3 million.

Buses were especially tempting targets for armed robbers in the 1990s because the banking system worked so badly. (Neoliberal reforms in the following years led to a rapid improvement.) It took a week to transfer money from one bank to another across town, and transferring funds between Lagos and Onitsha and the other commercial centers of the East was, as a practical matter, hopeless. So the traders plying that route, the country's busiest, carried with them all the money they needed for their business. The naira, once worth more than the pound sterling, had fallen to more than a hundred to the dollar, rendering the largest denomination naira bills worth less than five dollars, so the traders' cash filled undisguisable Ghana-must-go bags. As Nollywood filmmaking moved to the East, its lifeblood was on those buses as producers or their boys carried their own Ghana-must-go bags from Idumota to film sets around Enugu or Aba. The bus passengers who were not traders or movie producers would be carrying considerable amounts of money too, if they had it, since in the not unlikely event of a road accident or gunshot wound they would be left to bleed to death unless they could pay cash upfront for medical treatment.

Ashes to Ashes 1 (2001, another OJ Production directed by Andy Amenechi) begins with the leader of a gang of armed robbers with a megaphone ordering the residents of a whole street to bring out their valuables. The gang is large and armed with automatic weapons, and they have taken undisputed control of the block. The residents lie cowering in the street, their VCRs and electric fans in front of them. Jonathan Gbemuotor's handheld camera captures their screaming terror in tight framings. A woman pulls her money out of her bra. The gang piles into a van and takes off as the police arrive, followed by another van with vigilantes hanging out of it. Under the credits the armed robbers and the police fight with automatic weapons.

As usual Nollywood was doing an excellent job of representing the fear in which people lived. The unrealistic element in these scenes from *Oracle* and *Ashes to Ashes* is that the police show up promptly and give battle. Normally they would not. Almost surely outgunned by the criminals, the police likely did not have radios or fuel for their vehicles. Probably their pitiful salaries had not been paid, discouraging them from risking their lives. People assumed that they collaborated with the armed robbers, or themselves moonlighted as armed robbers, or that the same big men who sponsored the gangs of armed robbers were paying off the police.

The state had lost its monopoly of violence, or had sold it off, or was renting it out—in any case, the government seemed incapable of doing anything about the situation and clearly did not care to try. Law and order were sovereign only in patches. Violent depredation held undisputed sway for long periods of time, anywhere. Criminals blockaded the most important highways for hours, invaded the most luxurious homes, hijacked the most expensive cars in broad daylight on the fanciest streets of Lagos. In 2001 Bola Ige, the serving attorney general and minister of justice of the federal government, was shot to death in his own bedroom—a crime that has never been solved.

Everyone lived in fear of violence and talked about it constantly. For many, it was a matter of personal experience; everyone heard eyewitness accounts as well as rumors; crime stories saturated the newspapers.

RITUALS AGAIN: POWER AND THE OCCULT

The newspapers regularly carried reports about bodies found with parts missing—eyes, genitals, breasts, internal organs—apparently removed for use in occult rituals. Much of the Nigerian press is frankly sensational in tabloid fashion, but even the most respectable broadsheets may report such matters and other accounts of witchcraft, like accused sorcerers disappearing or transforming into animals in the plain view of a crowd. In many cases, depositions at police stations are part of these reports. (On such stories and the role of the press, see Bastian 1993 2001.)

Nollywood was closely identified with money rituals from the beginning, but repetition eventually exhausted the commercial potential of the theme and ritual films had dwindled. The so-called "Otokoto" scandal of late 1996 (see below) brought the subject blazing back in a way that linked it with political power. Otokoto was followed by a series of other sensational, well-publicized stories that intertwined political power, the occult, and violence. The "Bakassi Boys" were vigilante groups that appeared in 1999 and spread through the eastern states of Abia, Imo, and Anambra, fighting crime with spiritual weapons as well as guns and machetes. In a famous incident in late 2000, before a crowd of 20,000 people in a traffic roundabout in Onitsha, they decapitated "Prophet Eddy" Okeke, a syncretic Christian preacher accused of ritualism, kidnapping, and every other dark misdeed. They played football with his head. University campuses were frequently closed down because of violent "campus cults." In 2004 a large contingent of police invaded a traditional shrine in Okija, Anambra State, finding scores of corpses and registers that showed many leading politicians patronized the shrine. Nollywood quickly picked up on all these scandals.

Owerri, the capital of Imo State, was a sleepy Igbo provincial city that had been invaded by young armed robbers and 419 fraudsters. On September 20, 1996, a gardener who worked at the Otokoto Hotel was found in possession of a freshly decapitated human head belonging to an eleven-year-old boy. He said he was delivering the head to a prominent local businessman who was the brother of a minister in the Abacha military government. The gardener soon died in police custody under mysterious circumstances. The police publicly exhumed the body of the headless boy on the hotel grounds, provoking a popular uprising. For two days, rioting and arson were directed—apparently with precision—against characters the crowd thought were suspicious. More human heads were reportedly uncovered in a church and a body was found in a 419 suspect's cupboard. According to the pathologist who examined it, it "was deliberately roasted and carefully preserved . . . [and] had some of its flesh sliced off" (from the official Imo State government *White Paper on the Report of the Judicial Commission of Inquiry into the Disturbances of 24–25 September 1996 in Owerri*, quoted in Enwerem 1997, 8).

The incident made headlines for months. Two trials sent a number of accused to the firing squad amid allegations of manipulations by big men, notably Chief Emmanuel Iwuanyanwu, a "moneybags" who owned newspapers, an airline, and sports teams and was a serious aspirant for the presidency of Nigeria (Ehirim 1997; Uwugiaren 1997). The government failed to act on recommendations of an official panel of inquiry, which named as among the remote causes of the riot the corruption of both the former military governor of the state and the chairman of the Imo council of traditional rulers, whose palace was damaged by the rioters. Instead of sanctioning the offending chairman, Abacha, who cultivated support among traditional rulers, gave orders to rebuild his palace (Agbaegbu 1999).

Sober academic analyses of these events discount the most sensational rumors. Daniel Jordan Smith, in his pair of articles on the Otokoto affair (2001a, 2001b), maintains that there was never any strong evidence linking the 419 men with the ritual killings; throughout "Ritual Killing" (2001b) he focuses on the phenomenon of the rumors surrounding Otokoto, including their distortions of verifiable fact as well as the social meaning they carried.

Stephen Ellis's investigation of the Okija shrine scandal is similarly anticlimactic. He finds the eighty-three corpses littering the grounds of the shrine, sixty-three of them headless, were not actually those of victims sacrificed on the spot for ritual purposes: they were the bodies of people who had sworn oaths at the shrine and had then dropped dead because they were foresworn, or otherwise died bad deaths and could not be properly buried. Their families, according to custom, had carried the bodies to the shrine for disposal. Still the registers kept by the shrine's secretary were hard and shocking evidence of the huge sums the shrine was charging and of the patronage of what seemed like nearly the whole political elite of the East. Ellis concludes shrines are a source of moral legitimacy in a political world where there is little or none—the word of a politician is worthless unless backed by an oath sworn at the shrine, whose violation would bring death (Ellis 2008).

These were seismic events in the Nigerian national imagination because they linked the elite, including the political elite, with dark occult practices. Such associations are frequent, even standard, across Africa, but normally at the level of rumor. *Radio troittoire*, "sidewalk radio," as it is known in the francophone countries, has flourished under tight dictatorial regimes in Togo, Cameroon, Congo, and other places. The Nigerian situation is different because the country is simply too large and its political structure too complex, with too many centers of power, to be subjected to such tight surveillance and regulation. Even in the darkest days of the Nigerian military dictatorships, the press made noise, and the law never became entirely irrelevant, no matter how often it was violated, because the livelihood of Nigeria's large and prestigious body of lawyers depended on it (a point made to me by the political scientist Jibrin Ibrahim). The Otokoto and Okija shrine scandals were remarkable because the newspapers picked up, aired, apparently endorsed, and amplified the popular understanding of these events, which was that the elite were implicated in money rituals and other deadly spiritual practices that lay behind their wealth and power (D. Smith 2001b). Solemnly official organs of government—the court system and commissions of inquiry—publically investigated these claims. The net effect of the incidents was to legitimize and extend the symbolic complex Nollywood had already patented.

TWO TYPES OF RITUALS

It is useful to distinguish between two kinds of rituals in which human beings are sacrificed so that others can gain power by consuming their spiritual substance. The kind familiar to us from *Living in Bondage* depends on an underlying belief, common in many places in Africa, that witches prey on their kin—witchcraft as "the dark side of kinship" (Geschiere 1997, 212). *Living in Bondage* linked money rituals to marital tensions and the idiom of family melodrama, shifting the framework from kinship to even more intimate emotional relationships.

In the other type of ritual, humans are sacrificed for the sake of political power. Money may or may not be involved. Such practices were associated historically with kingship and secret societies, and the victims were often slaves or other outsiders to the community. Human sacrifice accompanied the funerals and installations of obas in the Yoruba and Benin political traditions (Johnson 1921, 45–46; Peel 2000, 69–71). (An instance of ritual self-sacrifice in Oyo in 1946 formed the subject both of one of the most famous plays of the Yoruba traveling theater, Duro Ladipo's *Oba Koso*, and of Wole Soyinka's literary masterpiece *Death and the King's Horseman*.) Such practices may not have entirely ceased. In 1997 the oba of Ijebuland created a storm of controversy when he announced that while human sacrifice had been stopped, the accession to his throne still involved eating the heart of the previous oba and that he wished to put an end to this practice ("In Ijebu" 1997); in 2002 an eze-elect in Imo State went public with his refusal to carry on the tradition of gathering thirty-four human heads to accompany his predecessor to the other world ("No Human Heads" 2002).

But the magical use of body parts (most often consumed in a soup) is now primarily associated with ambitious big men, particularly politicians and businessmen, and their anonymous victims are snatched off the streets and highways. Ellis has written a fascinating account of how, in Liberia, the practice of human sacrifice by secret societies, theoretically at least for the religious benefit of the community and subject to various restraints, turned into a privatized market in body parts for the benefit of politicians and others looking for a shortcut in a general anarchic, murderous scramble for power (Ellis 2001, 220–80). In Nigeria today, more mutilated bodies turn up around elections because politicians look for magical insurance, and such rites are associated with armed robbers and with the criminals who practice 419. The problem seemed to increase in the 1990s. A perhaps unreliable official statistic put the number of victims of ritual murder between 1992 and 1996 at 6,000 (reported in *Frankfurter Allgemeine Zeitung* 2 February 1996, quoted in Harnischfeger 2006, n18). Enwerem claims that in spite of their ancient antecedents, money rituals are thought of by most people as a recent phenomenon (1997, 4).

Witchcraft is always political, as Geschiere says, because it is always about power inequalities and jealousy (1997, 69). But its political meaning is variable. Geschiere points to the dominant reading of witchcraft in the Anglo-American anthropological tradition as a conservative, leveling mechanism through which the threat of witchcraft attacks within traditional communities keeps their ambitious members in check, but he also points to another opposing body of literature that sees witchcraft as associated precisely with the accumulation of wealth and power (Geschiere 1997, 5, 16 and passim). Johannes Harnischfeger, discussing the situation among the Igbo, writes that the powerful let it be known that they have hired the most expensive and fearsome spiritualists as a way of intimidating those who might challenge them through spiritual or other means, and that they likewise have the resources to dominate the processes of witchfinding. So "it is therefore almost exclusively the local big men . . . who make use of witchcraft trials to terrorise their opponents" (Harnischfeger 2006, 62–63).

The Otokoto scandal focused the money ritual theme upwards, toward big men, and made it express a critique of power in Nigeria. If the flood of oil money had presented a crisis for traditional notions of wealth and work, it also lifted many if not all boats and sponsored a general albeit uneasy optimism. But the seemingly endless aftermath of Structural Adjustment brought catastrophic contraction for most people. The widespread fear that one's body parts will end up in a ritual soup consumed by a big man is itself understood as a form of class oppression and is taken as evidence that the nation has been taken over by evil characters employing evil forces to acquire and keep power, in the absence of any other form of legitimacy.

The betrayal of kin sacrifice creates anxiety in the most intimate spheres, then, but the trade in body parts is associated with a range of pathologies in public life and paranoid visions of a predatory secret order. It generates fears that especially haunt the anonymity of the city and the open road.

The distinction between the two kinds of rituals was attested to by a "native doctor" paraded at the Lagos State Police Command in 2013 as the head of a syndicate selling live human beings as well as body parts for ritual purposes. "Asked why he did not use any of his children since he has eight of them, he said that would reduce the potency of the ritual concoction, adding that its potency depended solely on strangers being used." Talkative and apparently cheerful, he provided a price list: about $250 for a whole live human being; $20 to $50 for a head "depending on the market price"; $25 for hands (Usman 2013).

In practice, however, Nollywood almost always mixes the two kinds of ritual sacrifice. Few films framed on the more public level can resist the melodramatic thrill of intimate betrayals of family members. In *Living in Bondage*, Andy's abduction of the prostitute Tina as a way out of the requirement to sacrifice his wife introduces the note of danger in the urban night that is a function of the body parts trade. (This is a danger especially for prostitutes and is featured in many films about them, including the most famous, Zeb Ejiro's *Domitilla: The Story of a Prostitute*, 1997.) The young millionaires dance to Oliver de Cocque's anthem, declaring themselves "the rulers of the world." They are actually just driving nice cars and buying chieftaincy titles from a village; they stand for a predatory elite, but we do not see the levers of power. In the wake of Otokoto, other films developed the political dimension.

BLOOD MONEY

Nollywood immediately responded to Otokoto with half a dozen or more films. In general, Nollywood's reaction was less political than the Owerri rioters had been. Nnebue's *Rituals* (1997) stayed the closest to the actual events and extended them farthest into the political dimension; it will be discussed in the next chapter, which is about "political films." Comic versions (!) are touched on in the chapter after that.

The most commercially successful of the films was *Blood Money: The Vulture Men* (1997), directed by Chico Ejiro. This was the first big hit from OJ Productions, demonstrating the producer Ojiofor Ezeanyaeche's impressive knack for turning headlines into films that moved a popular audience. *Blood Money* takes the Otokoto story in several directions. As Birgit Meyer notes, it transfers the setting from the provinces to the glass and steel offices and elaborate mansions of Lagos, because the money ritual theme is felt to belong not in the backward periphery of national life but in its modern political and economic center.[1] *Blood Money* also links the story to the international trade in body parts (Meyer 2003b, 2006b). Simultaneously, it pushes it back toward the kin betrayal type of ritual and, generally, toward Nollywood's familiar resources; in fact, *Blood Money* seems to be based more on *Living in Bondage* than on Otokoto.

Mike Mouka (Zack Orji) is a bank manager who, like Andy, gets himself in trouble by falling for a 419 financial deal and then reconnects with an old school friend, Chief Collins (Kanayo O. Kanayo, who played Chief Omego in *Living in Bondage*), now immensely wealthy and part of a secret cult called the Vultures. Initially shocked, Mike agrees to join the cult. He is asked whether he wants instant wealth or protection to deal in human body parts and chooses the former. For the instant wealth option, he has to produce a child for sacrifice. By an unfortunate coincidence, the child he abducts is Chief Collins's only son, making them enemies. The enchanted child is placed in a room that fills with money. Three years later the Great Vulture is hungry for Mike's blood, but

Mike is told he can buy time by sacrificing the one he loves the most. He offers his wife, from whom he is in fact estranged, but has no more luck than Andy in fooling the cult. Finally he sacrifices his mother, who, like Merit, comes back to haunt him. As part 1 ends, Mike is told he must bring seven human heads to lay his mother's ghost. In part 2 Mike sets about acquiring the seven heads while suffering from his mother's ghost, the anger of Chief Collins, and torture at the hands of the police. (Though the chief of the police is part of the cult, some officers are honest and are trying to root it out.) The resolution of all this is deferred until a part 3 that never appeared.

The Vultures offered Mike two distinct options, corresponding to the different kinds of ritual just described. His story revolves around kin sacrifice and a secret room, but elements from the other kind of ritual are mixed in: he has to sacrifice the one he loves most, but the victim in his secret room is a boy he hoped was anonymous; he becomes a serial killer stalking the city to accumulate the heads he needs, but he needs them to settle a debt to his mother.

The element the film picked up from Otokoto is the trade in human body parts, which features in sequences scattered through the film. As it opens, Chief Collins completes a shipment of body parts by arranging the murder of a woman checking into a hotel room, whose breast is cut off. The buyer, Farouk, appears to be Lebanese, which is symbolically loaded: the Lebanese came to West Africa to play an intermediate role in the colonial economies and continue to link the international and African national economies in a variety of businesses, from importing foodstuffs to running cinemas and exporting "blood" diamonds. It is not clear what Farouk's international buyers want with the body parts. Implied is both an ultimate big-man magic by undefined world powers and the international medical trade in kidneys and other organs, which is not an important business in Nigeria as it is in India, southern Africa (Comaroff and Comaroff 1999), and other places but which Nigerians interpret as a symbol of vampirish neoliberal globalization (McCall 2002).

"VILLAGE FILMS" AND GEOGRAPHIES OF ANXIETY

The anxieties and terrors embodied in this set of films are not localized: they are general and everywhere. We saw that in *Living in Bondage* the evil that was in the city was also in the village: Chief Omego and Andy both shuttle back and forth and so does the movie. The city—Lagos above all—is sign and symbol of anxiety. Onookome Okome, in an essay called "Writing the Anxious City," posits as a central Nollywood genre the "city film," which means, basically, films about Lagos (2003). But the films discussed in this chapter are mostly set in the villages, towns, and cities of Igboland. Obvious reasons for this include the opening up of the East as a location for shooting movies and the fact that the events of Otokoto, the Bakassi Boys, Prophet Eddy, and Okija shrine took place there. The special ideological and imaginative problems Lagos poses also matter. Elsewhere I have discussed some of them, working from Matthew Gandy's observation that Lagos has been in a real sense unimaginable: coming to grips with the actual whole, including the huge "informal" slums where most people live, was so difficult that historically the administrators and urban planners of the city did not even try (Haynes 2007b; Gandy 2005, 2006). The Lagos of *Living in Bondage* contains no one who is not Igbo and no sign of government or public institutions. Nollywood's representation of the full political, social, moral, and spiritual crisis of the 1990s required not just illustrations of the problem, which Lagos was exceptionally good at providing, but also a horizon in which some sort of solution or at least a way of going on with life was conceivable, and Lagos was bad at providing that.

Lagos has the character of the Nigerian state: an invention of the colonial era, a mesmerizing source of wealth but outside fundamental structures of social and political morality. Achebe describes the attitude with his usual clairvoyance in *No Longer at Ease*, as the protagonist, returned from studying abroad, is welcomed by the Umuofia Progressive Union, the home town organization of people from his village—his clansmen, essentially—living in Lagos: "In Nigeria the government was 'they.' It had nothing to do with you or me. It was an alien institution and people's business was to get as much from it as they could without getting into trouble" (Achebe 1994a, 37).[2]

The crucial moral and social arena is the village, at least for Nollywood's popular audience. The genre of "village films" (sometimes called "community films") is Nollywood's representation of that arena. This is a genre without a distinct inauguration, since the village scene was already so familiar from other media and so many different kinds of stories take place in this setting, from the anxious and frequently terrifying dramas surveyed in this chapter to the comedies discussed later on. The framing social level is above that of the family, though families, both nuclear and extended kinship structures, are usually prominent in it. The genre gives us an imaginable community, with locatable (if often problematic) sources of moral, spiritual, and social authority: elders, traditional rulers, shrines, churches, priests. But we are far from an image of the village as a bounded and inviolate projection of traditional authenticity. The villages we see are fully part of contemporary society. Daniel Jordan Smith reports that in the early 1990s, in the Igbo villages where he did research most adults (over 90 percent of the men) had lived in a city for at least a year (2001c).

The point of the village setting in these films is not to escape from the violence and corruption of the nation but to confront those things where they matter most, in the last redoubt of moral and spiritual legitimacy. The system of dual social morality sent sons of the soil to the centers of the new economy to "chop" (eat) their share of the national cake by any means necessary and bring home as much of it as possible, no questions asked, while crime in the villages was kept to low levels by the old rigorous morality and close-knit social memory of the clan: stealing a chicken would make one's descendants less marriageable for generations. But things were eroding in the villages, rapidly, and this was deeply shocking.

The Biafran War (1967–1970) ravaged Igboland, leaving it awash with guns and nihilistic, damaged, hopeless young men. The guns were all they had. The war also left gender roles in tatters. Often left to their own devices, women were raped in large numbers and many watched their children die of hunger. They demonstrated their toughness: female "attack traders" crossed and recrossed the battle lines to make a little money to feed their families. Others turned to prostitution.

For a while the armed robbers and prostitutes had the decency to practice their trades outside their villages, on the roads or further away. But by the 1990s, crime in the villages themselves was evidence of a distressingly complete social disintegration. And little or nothing seemed to stand in the way of the absolute hegemony of money as a social value in Igboland. The intelligence, restless mobility, and daring for which the Igbos are famous had made them the national champions of 419 and other criminal rackets like drug dealing. The newspapers editorialized about the "rough" money from these enterprises that was flowing into Igbo politics, exerting a powerful influence behind the scenes and sometimes showing itself with appalling directness. At Christmastime, when Igbos are expected to return to their villages for an annual display and sharing of wealth, it was new and frequently dubious money that reigned. University lecturers, too penurious to want to go home to be humiliated on these occasions, grumbled in their staff clubs about how little of this wealth sprang from socially productive activities. Urban dwellers expected to retire to the village but had to accept the fact that in some sense they could not go home again, that the community they knew and imagined was fatally damaged.[3] The whole filthy tide of Nigerian national life seemed to be flooding over Igbo villages.

SPIRITUAL CRISIS

The general sense of social disintegration and raw fear turned people towards religion, but here too the situation was fraught. The spiritual situation had always been complex. Merit in *Living in Bondage* could live and be exemplary in multiple sets of values and cosmologies simultaneously, but syncretism is generally the product of a history of conflict, and the latent tensions within it are easily activated. Adam Ashforth writes about the anxieties attendant on the situation in which almost every African lives, of negotiating among three radically different systems of belief: an indigenous African world view; the perspective of Christianity or Islam; and the scientific rationality of Western education (Ashforth 1998).

Last Burial (Will His Soul Rest in Peace?) 1–3 (2000, directed by Lancelot Imasuen) shows the multiple affiliations that are a normal and normally desirable feature of Nigerian social life coming into conflict. Ogbuefi (Clement Ohameze) appears to be an ideal Igbo man: a wealthy businessman, head of a devout Christian household with residences in Lagos and his village, who makes large donations to the Catholic Church (of which he is a knight) and to the igwe to support a community water project. Then he is revealed to be a member of a secret Brotherhood, the source of his wealth. Emissaries of the cult inform him of his impending death; afterwards, the Brotherhood insists on its own macabre funeral rites. But because he was a titled man, his *umunna* (extended patrilineage) and the igwe think he should be buried in his own compound with traditional rites including a masquerade and drums, while the church and his devoutly Christian widow Susan (Eucharia Anunobi) want him buried by the church in its cemetery.

Ogbuefi is alive for much of the film, maneuvering urgently. His real loyalties are to the church and to his nuclear family (he has sacrificed his own soul but not a family member for the sake of wealth). The point is made repeatedly that it was his free choice to join the cult, but that choice is not explored—this is not a psychomachia like *Living in Bondage*. It is a village film, and the drama is on the social level, with spiritual projections. There are multiple centers of power and dramatic interest: each of the three spiritual forces (Christian, traditional, cult) has a visible social constituency that holds meetings; the emotional center of the film is the widow Susan; two ordinary middle-aged villagers comment on developments throughout the film. All the elements of this society are accustomed to living with one another and negotiate easily, except for the cult. The cult was a hidden presence—Susan is shocked to discover her husband was a member. The cult's spokesperson is Ogbuefi's brother Nnado

(Sam Dede), who claims half of the umunna belong to one cult or another. He means to take over Susan with the rest of his brother's property. His confident, suave, intimate tone expresses the cult's power, but he seems to be the only cultist known to the community. The others come and go in a convoy of expensive vehicles, like politicians or military rulers. Their power is exercised not through visible political or social institutions but through spiritual means, and the struggle over the corpse becomes spiritual warfare, represented with the usual special effects. A famous dibia hired by the umunna is driven comically from the field. The decisive duel is between the supreme commander of the cult and the Catholic priest, seconded by Ogbuefi's young son (Chinedu Ikedieze), who had been fortified by the visitation of an angel in a dream.

Many Nigerians, especially but not only Pentecostals, conceive of contemporary life in terms of spiritual warfare, carried out on an individual level but also as a cultural, social, and political campaign. In the cities, people are used to living next to all kinds of things; again, it is in the villages, where the indigenous spiritual traditions are rooted and the social and physical space to be contested is limited and sharply defined, that the spiritual and cultural struggle takes its most impacted forms.

In this great spiritual and cultural conflict, Nollywood is generally on the side of Christianity. But—as we saw with the cultural epics—Nollywood's position is not unified or simple, and it does not generally take the radical Pentecostalite position that traditional culture is all to be shunned because it is tainted with Satanic influence. *Last Burial* is typical in its balance and nuance: just as Susan, representing the Christian nuclear family, has conflicts with her husband's extended lineage, but resolvable ones, indigenous spiritual practices are treated indulgently, as they generally were by Catholic and mainstream Protestant denominations in Nigeria before the advent of Pentecostalism. The funeral masquerade gets screen time as an enjoyable cultural spectacle, and the dibia's magic also provides an enjoyable spectacle, though finally his spiritual powers are not to be taken seriously. The cult is antithetical to Christianity but is split off, culturally, from tradition: the cultists wear dapper western suits, drive good cars, and worship an invented deity in what looks like an office space.

SHRINES

In real life, the classic form of the spiritual conflict in villages is the destruction of traditional shrines by Pentecostal Christians. Sometimes this happens with the assent of the community; sometimes it is a violent assault provoking bitter conflict. Shrines and the conflicts around them are central in many village films, as in many epics.

Arusi-Iyi/The Protector—The Destroyer (1999, a Sunny Collins production directed by Fred Amata) shuffles many of the elements of *Last Burial* and, as the title suggests, expresses similar complexity and ambivalence. Chief Danco (Kenneth Okonkwo), a wealthy cultist with houses in Lagos and his village, is warned by his cult priest that the spirit of his gateman Fred is incompatible with his own, so he fires Fred and refuses to pay his back wages. Beset by calamities and desperate for the money, Fred goes to the village shrine, Arusi-Iyi, for justice. (*Arusi* means "shrine" in Igbo.) In repose the deity takes the form of a mask, turning into a frightening dog when on the hunt. Danco refuses the summons to appear at the shrine. He prays to his cult god; his wife prays to Jesus; his mother tells an incidental story (which the film illustrates at some length) of a whole family wiped out for defying Arusi-Iyi. Danco is haunted by dreams and apparitions, his business is destroyed, and finally the dog leaps into his Land Cruiser. His wife gets him to a priest and he confesses his cult membership and calls on Jesus as he dies. Fred's father informs him that Fred was marked from birth to be a Catholic priest, but the father was unwilling to let his only son become celibate and end the lineage. Fred had promised to take Arusi-Iyi as his god in return for justice but now becomes a Christian. This problem is left for part 2 to sort out; part 1 ends with an explosive public confrontation as Danco's wife's attempt to bury her husband as a Christian is interrupted by Arusi-Iyi's masquerade—the bodies of those killed by the deity must be dumped unburied at the shrine—and by a phalanx of cultists.

Oracle, the influential 1998 film with which this chapter began, puts the threat to a shrine in a context that has nothing to do with Christianity. The armed robbers we see in action before the credits are also in the business of stealing masks from shrines. They go to see a Lebanese-looking international art dealer in a Lagos high-rise. This is an OJ Production carrying a trailer for the recently released *Blood Money*, and this scene closely parallels the international body parts theme of that film, though the theme of neocolonial cultural predation is left undeveloped.[4] If the international interest in Nigerian body parts was ambiguous, a diviner in *Oracle* later reveals that the dealer wanted the mask for spiritual purposes. As the dealer examines it, its power overwhelms him.

The robbers—they are brothers—find that to steal the mask of their village's shrine deity they need confederates with inside knowledge. Their uncle brings in Okimkpa (Pete Edochie), a complex figure who had declined to become chief priest of the deity. The mask is stolen, but the mask is only the face of a powerful and now angry deity. The conspirators briefly enjoy their new wealth in the village and in Lagos—this film, like all the others discussed so far, shuttles between the two locations. Then the deity takes them down, one by one. The story resembles *Ti Oluwa Nile* (even the scary electronic noises are the same), but while the supernatural agency of Kelani's film is abstract and might even be interpreted and felt as allegory, the deity of *Oracle* is a visible, active, powerful dramatic presence, a savage incarnation of savage justice, a terrifying immediate fact of life.

This is a fundamental aspect of shrines in Igbo life and so in the movies: they are not merely symbols of "tradition" in Christian or cultural nationalist discourses, portrayed as embodiments of good or evil; they are important, durable social facts. John McCall, commenting on the array of legal systems at work in Nigerian society, notes, "Arünsi [truth-seeking jujus] remain active in village life to this day. There is no need to speculate about a *resurgence* of precolonial practices to understand why, in the face of an evident failure of national law, indigenous legal rationalities come into play" (2004, 59). The Okija shrine scandal of 2004 was a spectacular public revelation of how true this is. The registers of visitors kept by the shrine's secretary had five thousand names in them, including several governors and other leading politicians.

Ellis explicates this scandal by tracing the historical role of shrines. Some of them, like Ibinukpabi, the "Long Juju" of Arochukwu, were the most important translocal institutions in Igboland in the precolonial period. During British colonialism

> In the absence of any official local authority that enjoyed the full respect of the population, shrines continued to exercise judicial and other functions semi-legally or even clandestinely. They performed many roles that the colonial system was unequipped to encompass, such as divination, communicating with spirits, and dealing with problems of premature death and infertility. (Ellis 2008, 449)

We might pause to notice the close coincidence of these roles with fundamental thematic concerns of Nollywood films and the parallels with Nollywood's relationship with more official kinds of culture and social structure. Ellis continues:

> It was the half-tolerance, half-suppression, of older systems of governance that made Indirect Rule so thoroughly ambiguous, the official organs of Indirect Rule being shadowed by institutions such as shrines whose actual powers often exceeded those they were officially deemed to have. (2008, 450)

The nationalist movement, originating among the western educated elite of Lagos and other cities, cultivated links with secret societies in the villages. Postcolonial governments co-opted the structures of indirect rule. Military rulers continued the old technique of linking with local centers of political influence by associating with shrines and other indigenous institutions, and after 1999 the governors and power brokers of the Third Republic did the same. Ellis employs a phrase of Ogbu Kalu's: "the more the formal ideologies and ethics of the Nigerian state are seen to be threadbare, the greater the tendency towards a 'villagization of the modern public sphere'" (2008, 461). The corollary of this exploitation of traditional spiritual legitimacy by corrupt politicians, however, is that the shrines have been discredited by association and are now tied in the popular imagination with the money rituals of big men. Famous 419 scammers patronized the Okija shrine, and its priests were accused of being 419 by police, Christian, and Okija Town Union officials.

Ellis concludes his analysis of the Okija shrine scandal in this way: "Rival clientelist networks, connected to the very top of the Nigerian state, were vying for control of Anambra State by using the Okija shrine, and perhaps other shrines too, as nodal points of their relationships. Exposing the shrine through the press was a clever ploy to uncover and embarrass a competing group" (2008, 459). So the whole event was just about ordinary politics, not really about cultural or spiritual politics, though cultural politics informed the commentary on it. The event was not a dramatic battle or revelation in a *kulturkampf* between "tradition" and "modernity" or Christianization. It illustrated permanent principles of Nigerian politics: the more you see, the less you understand; and you cannot be too paranoid about conspiracies. In a postscript, Ellis notes that nothing really changed as a result of the Okija shrine scandal: the implicated politicians carried on normally with their careers.

Nollywood's village film genre, then, was not only a moral and psychological reversion to village roots in times of stress; it also parallels processes of political transaction and ideology and allows the exploration of a crucial arena of social and religious conflict. From a distance, the conflict is polarized and abstract, but the genre localizes it in a dense, complex social fabric. As always in Nollywood, individual films, each following the binary logic of moralism and melodrama and asserting a principle of effective justice, must give us closure. But like the cultural epic, the village film genre is a discourse, not a position, its coherence more a matter of horizon and images than ideology, its strength finally lying in its ability to explore a complex situation. In keeping with the profoundest principle of African life, Nollywood is dedicated to negotiation and compromise, to guaranteeing the integrity of the community.

VIGILANTE FILMS

Vigilante films—a subgenre of village films—are closely associated with the rise and fall of their historical inspiration, the Bakassi Boys. In the late 1990s the commercial cities of eastern Nigeria were subject to brazen and systematic pillaging by large armed gangs of criminals. In one rampage, a gang of 120 men attacked a market, killing dozens and injuring hundreds. In another case, over thirty passengers on a bus were slaughtered. Women and children took to sleeping in churches for safety (Baker 2002). The police did nothing, their weakness, inefficiency, and corruption on full display. In Ariara market in Aba, after a particularly outrageous incident in 1998, a mob led by shoemakers spontaneously attacked the criminals in their headquarters, killing many of them. Out of this uprising a vigilante group was formed, the Bakassi Boys, which was immediately successful in killing or chasing away criminals in Aba and enjoyed immense popular support. They were popularly believed to be "armored" against harm by bullets or knives and equipped with truth-seeking divinatory charms—machetes and necklaces that would identify malefactors and force confessions.

The Bakassi Boys were invited into Anambra State by the governor at the behest of Onitsha traders, and into Enugu and Imo States. The Bakassi Boys instantly reduced the crime rate in Anambra to near zero and became heroes, or superheroes. They always had tense relations with the police and federal government, and alarm and disquiet began to erode their popularity. Their methods were ghastly: their signature was public amputations and beheadings in markets and traffic roundabouts, the bodies set on fire and left in the streets for days.[5] This littering of public spaces with charred, smoldering corpses was shocking to many people. And evidence mounted that the Bakassi Boys' claims that they delivered disciplined, righteous, inerrant justice were far from the truth. A blistering 2002 report written by Human Rights Watch (HRW) and a Nigerian NGO made the case against them, finding that the vigilantes were not turning captured criminals over to the police as they were supposed to do; that they commonly used torture to extract confessions; that they frequently killed innocent people and engaged in criminal activities; and that they were being used by politicians, including the Anambra governor, to intimidate and assassinate political opponents (Human Rights Watch 2002). The Bakassi Boys were officially disbanded in 2002 but continued to operate.

Nollywood was very close to the action. The main scenes of Bakassi Boys activity, Onitsha and Aba, are major film distribution and financing centers. By far the most popular and iconic vigilante film was the four-part *Issakaba*

FIGURE 6. Lancelot Imasuen's *Issakaba*, the most famous vigilante film

series (2001) ("Issakaba" is "Bakassi" backwards, more or less), which, like *Last Burial* the same year, was made from a story by Anambra native Chukwuka Emelionwu, coproduced by Emelionwu's Kas-Vid and Mosco, an Onitsha outfit, and directed by the ubiquitous Lancelot Imasuen. The series was far from being an entirely local, entirely Igbo production, however, and the films were an electrifying success all over the country (and in Ghana) because they captured a widespread emotional state. *Issakaba* is an example of Nollywood chasing headlines, dramatizing events while they were still going on. Nollywood avidly picked up and amplified the strong theatrical element in the Bakassi Boys' strategies of sowing terror among criminals and showing the populace they were now in control through their menacing swagger and spectacular public executions. The vigilantes' iconography—black clothes, red headbands, bulging muscles, brandished machetes and guns—passed into Nollywood's essential repertoire. The Anambra state government provided the vigilantes with vans, which became familiar elements in the urban landscape. The vigilantes hung out of them, bristling with weapons, as they weaved around the roads, zigzagging in wild minatory fashion like a masquerade plunging through a crowd. John McCall, an eyewitness, observes, "This very image is returned to again and again in the movies, accompanied by the *Issakaba* theme song. Thus, when the movies gained popularity, the valorizing anthem irresistibly sprang to mind whenever one saw the vigilante vans passing on the road" (2004, 61).

The vigilante films were built on the foundation the village films had created. The Bakassi Boys originated in major urban commercial centers and spread through high-level political negotiations, but the films revert to the familiar horizon of a village in crisis, beset by a powerful cabal and presided over by a troubled igwe or, in the case of *Okuzu Massacre: The Robbers Revenge* (2001), by an igwe who himself sponsors the criminals that terrorize his corpse-littered community. This film (directed by John Evah for Chico Ejiro's Grand Touch Pictures) is solidly rooted in the community, but political levels above the village are featured—at one point, the state governor is on the phone with a minister of the federal government about replacing the igwe.

In the *Issakaba* films the vigilantes are brought in to a series of villages. In the beginning of the first episode, *Issakaba: The Story of My Town*, the vigilante leader Ebube (Sam Dede) warns the igwe and assembled elders, in his proverb-inflected fashion, that the cleansing they ask for may cause tall trees to fall, and indeed by the end of the film the most prominent (and apparently public-spirited) chief is revealed to be the patron of the armed robbers who terrify the town, and the igwe's own son is implicated and sacrificed to bloody justice. The armed robbers have the backing of a powerful dibia with whom Ebube fights a culminating battle with spiritual weapons, but the main business of the film is revealing how far up into the town's political structure the corruption has spread.

Issakaba 2: Belong to Us and Have Peace (2001) shifts the focus from armed robbery—the Bakassi Boys' classic issue—to Nollywood's classic issue, money rituals. In this town, the chiefs are ritualists, and corpses are piling up with parts missing. The film is composed mostly of disconnected episodes in which Ebube reveals one secret crime after another. The crimes arise out of common situations: jealousy over business success, a quarrel over land. Things are not what they seem, but Ebube always senses when evil is about, the vigilantes' machetes glow red in the presence of criminals, and their cowrie-studded leather belt, when dropped over the necks of the guilty, forces instant confessions.

John McCall argues that while the *Issakaba* series undoubtedly heroizes the vigilantes and valorizes vigilantism, it also expresses nuanced ambivalence, in two different ways. One is the

> charismatic performance of Sam Dede as Ebube—the leader of Issakaba. Dede's embodiment of cool philosophical detachment in the face of danger and violence aligns him with classic action heroes, from Clint Eastwood's lone gunman to Richard Roundtree's unflappable Shaft. Like them, his reflections on the nature of his violent occupation also reveal a sense of its moral ambivalence. . . . If history has proven anything to Nigerians, it is that power, no matter who wields it, will eventually corrupt. Thus, when Dede's character warns, "the danger in hunting down evil is that you gradually become that which you seek to destroy," the sentiment resonates with Nigerians. (2004, 56–57)

The other form of ambivalence is built into the story of parts 3 and 4, in which Ebube's second-in-command becomes corrupt, taking bribes and, when he is ejected from Issakaba, starting his own gang with the aid of rituals-practicing chiefs who were targeted by our heroes. This new gang is a criminal imitation of the Bakassi Boys, designed to discredit them and sow confusion: "as a result," McCall explains, "the real Bakassi Boys are disbanded and dispersed. Corruption within their membership has undermined their cohesion and their reputation." McCall points out that all three sequels were made in 2001, but their release was staggered so that part 4 went on sale in late 2002, just after the release of the HRW report. The evolution of the movie series paralleled and anticipated the rise and fall of the vigilantes' reputation and public support (McCall 2004, 62).

Issakaba expresses ambivalence about vigilantism, but the Bakassi Boys pushed so many of Nollywood's buttons that it was more or less boxed into a positive portrayal. The films' image of the vigilantes is starkly different from that of the HRW report. The supernatural dimension is crucial—not so much the vigilantes' protective charms but the divinatory ones. The movies reinforce the Bakassi Boys' own claims: "confessions obtained by torture, as reported by HRW, are nowhere to be found in the movies. . . . Acceptance of the efficacy of these truth-seeking jujus is crucial to the claim that vigilantes can administer justice without recourse to due process of law" (McCall 2004, 58). The HRW report also points to their arbitrariness and corruption, their targeting of the most vulnerable, not the most powerful.

McCall sees that the *Issakaba* films and the HRW report both seek "moral clarity—a formula for action that can make justice possible" (2004, 56). While not contesting the report's accuracy, he exposes the naiveté of its call for a return to an official justice that never actually existed and had no prospect of coming into being. Consequently, endorsing the vigilantes felt like the only real option for citizens and for Nollywood, and the endorsement expresses a real political vision.

> While the failure of the Bakassi Boys is now evident, the movies still capture a profound longing for social transformation at a community level. In the movies, heroes step forth from their ordinary lives and take political reform into their own hands. This reform operates through highly localized insurrections—a village-by-village overthrow of corruption—implying that only a nation of communities that have exorcised their own demons and established trustworthy leadership can hope for effective reform at the highest levels. . . . The vigilante movies capture a shared vision of what Nigerians wish vigilantes could be, and in the case of *Issakaba* they also gesture at what they unfortunately appear to have become. While the cinematic version is romanticized and fanciful, from a Nigerian perspective it may be no more so than HRW's expectation that Nigeria's government can readily reform itself. (McCall 2004, 63–64)

PROPHET EDDY OKEKE AND *ASHES TO ASHES*

Ashes to Ashes 1, another OJ production (OJ himself claimed the story credit) directed by Andy Amenechi, is a slick culmination of the vigilante film genre. The action sequences are convincingly staged and powerfully captured by Jonathan Gbemuotor's kinetic camerawork, the special effects are stylish and original, and the sprawling narrative structure accommodates a compendium of motifs from vigilante and ritual films. It was produced in 2001, the great year of the vigilante film, but it already is clearly a late instance of the genre—evidence of the astonishing speed with which Nollywood can invent, consolidate, and then begin to recycle a new genre into its wider film culture. The vigilantes, here called "Mbassi Boys," look and act exactly like their counterparts in the *Issakaba* series, and in fact their doings would be incomprehensible without the other vigilante films: they appear out of nowhere, without explanation or insight into their organization or purposes. Unlike the *Issakaba* series, the film's point of view and dramatic center are not with the vigilantes or their leader, even though the vigilantes' interventions are crucial.

The film has two dramatic centers, one being a money-ritual-practicing Prophet (Justus Esiri). Most of the malefactors combated by the vigilantes are linked to him. He is clearly modeled on Prophet Eddy Okeke, the syncretic church leader accused of multifarious criminal activities and decapitated by the Bakassi Boys, his nefarious life and bloody death illustrated on posters sold in Nigerian markets.[6] The Prophet's church, which makes its adherents rich, resembles the popular "prosperity gospel" churches. He fingers a wand topped with a cross inside a circle. His syncretism is a demonic parody of Christian truth: he regularly cites Abraham's willingness to sacrifice Isaac before he orders new adherents to sacrifice their mothers or wives. In an apocalyptic scene he goes into the wilderness to pray: "I have performed signs and wonders as instructed." A "Book of Life and Death" descends from the heavens into his hands while a voice from above instructs him to study it. "Do not let the sacrifices stop. Go and be fishers of men."

The appearance of false prophets is one of the signs of the Last Days before the apocalypse predicted in Revelation, and in the apocalyptic state of Nigeria it is easy to believe, or to wish, that the end is near. Nnebue's *Endtime* (1999), a study of a Satanic wonder-working churchman, is another embodiment of this vision (Haynes 2007a). In *Last Prophet* (2001, directed by Lancelot Imasuen), another movie version of the Prophet Eddy story, he is also presented as a powerful sorcerer and false prophet, first glimpsed making a blind man see and performing a baptism; his signs and wonders (the phrase is used repeatedly) attract followers from other congregations, to whom he distributes wands like the one in *Ashes to Ashes*. Finally vigilantes force him to confess that his powers come from his wife, who was sent from the mermaid kingdom. (The world of marine spirits frequently serves as a manifestation of Satan's kingdom in Christian videos, for example Helen Ukpabio's *Highway to the Grave* (1999), though that link is not made explicit here.) In *Time Up . . . No Place to Hide* (also 2001) the Prophet Eddy figure Igbakigba is played, as in *Ashes to Ashes*, by Justus Esiri, but this time he holds a miniature sword, not the wand—he is not a syncretic prophet but the usual politically connected ritualist, opposed by a good priest.

Other representations of religious falsity may not spring from a Christian perspective at all. Prophet Eddy was accused of practicing 419, a secular form of fraud; such charges are aired against the Prophet Eddy figures in *Last Prophet* and *Ashes to Ashes*. *Issakaba* 2 began with an armed robber posing as a preacher on a bus; one of its central villains calls himself Man of God and dresses like a preacher from the Aladura syncretic sect to gain entrance to a compound to rob it. Everyone knows conmen abound in the mushrooming, high-profit business of opening new churches. The fake preacher is a familiar figure in Nollywood and may be the object of comical satire, or the agent of satire, as in the recklessly brilliant *Holygans* (1999), in which a pair of charlatans start a church as one of their projects. There are also films like *Out of Bounds* about merely human preachers who betray their calling and lose themselves in falsity, usually because of sexual temptations. The figure of the fake or false preacher may be invested by a whole blurry continuum of ideological positions, from the most fervent and orthodox Christian imagination to a disillusioned satirical resistance to the rapid Pentecostalization of Nigerian society.

The other dramatic center of *Ashes to Ashes*, besides the doings of the Prophet, is the sacrifice, at his behest, by the weak Osita (Francis Agu) of his beloved and virtuous wife Abigail (Chiega Alisigwe)—quite precisely and completely the story of *Living in Bondage*, dropped into this new genre. (Agu played Ichie Millions in *Living in Bondage*.) Abigail's apparitions are much more elaborate and articulate than Merit's—"I am as real as your conscience. . . . Turn your soul away from the dark and go to the light"—and in keeping with the canny extravagance of the style of *Ashes to Ashes*, the scenes between Osita and Abigail before and after her death are more laden with romantic imagery and gushing sentiment than the corresponding scenes in *Living in Bondage*.

Unlike in *Living in Bondage*, Pentecostal Christianity is not the answer: the vigilantes are. A good priest digs up, in the presence of an extended family, the fetishes that one of the Prophet's followers has used to blight the family's fortunes, but it takes the sudden upstaging appearance of the vigilantes to identify the culprit and force a confession. Osita, in angry despair, tries to shoot the Prophet but fails; again the vigilantes appear. Osita is taken away for punishment while the vigilante leader pursues the Prophet, who is laughing sardonically and appearing and disappearing at will, into the wilderness—the kind of spiritual battle with which the *Issakaba* films climax.

So part 1 ends, with a trailer for a second part subtitled *The Last Battle*. This title suggests something like a Christian apocalypse, but part 2 syncopates the defeat of the Prophet with the rise of a bad igwe with a bad dibia behind him, a familiar, recurring sort of problem to be resolved in the third part.

The narrative profusion and lack of closure as the film moves from part to part is related to the absence of an inherent spiritual hierarchy. The vigilantes do not fit into a Christian dualism. Their power suggests a polytheistic world, where what is effective is the personal force of a spiritual big man and the hard truths of a truth-divining machete. Perhaps the lack of closure is also related to the film's indistinctly defined location. We get glimpses of the urban landscape of Onitsha, not the familiar coherent village setting, and there is nothing like the close attention to the political context within the affected community that we get in *Last Prophet* or *Time Up*. *Ashes to Ashes* explodes the boundaries of the vigilante film; the vigilante theme becomes one among other patterns in the fabric.

This intermingling and incorporation is what happens in Nollywood when the original pressure that created a new genre or cycle of films subsides. The vigilante film was so closely tied to the Bakassi Boys that it declined sharply when the organization was suppressed in 2002, though its legacy was soon revived in films about the militants of the Niger Delta.[7]

CRIME FILMS

I have presented the vigilante films as growing out of the money ritual and village film genres, but they are also of course a species of crime film. The Nollywood crime film had precursors on celluloid, especially Eddie Ugbomah's crime thrillers such as *The Rise and Fall of Dr. Oyenusi* (1976). (The influence of American blaxploitation films on Ugbomah is regularly noted.) This was a criminal biopic, as were influential early examples of the crime genre on video like Amaka Igwe's *Rattlesnake* (1995–96) and Tade Ogidan's *Hostages* (1996) and *Owo Blow* (1996–98), all socially conscious melodramas that featured heroes who turned to a life of crime after being brutally treated by society in one way or another. Around the time of the vigilante films there was an efflorescence of crime films with various roots. *Bloody Mission* (2008, produced and directed by the martial artist Natty Bruce Idigbogu) is a karate film transposed to Lagos. Ralph Nwadike's *419 Connection: Deadly Rose* (2000) perhaps springs from the tradition set by the early Igbo get-rich-quick film *Circle of Doom*: it features complex rivalries among two well-armed gangs of fraudsters and a romance between the criminal mastermind Rose (Barbarah Odoh) and an undercover Interpol officer trying to break her ring. Chico Ejiro's *Outkast* (2001) looks like a continuation of *Glamour Girls* 2—it begins with a group of prostitutes in bright wigs arriving at the Lagos airport after being deported from Italy. The women follow Nnebuean trajectories, with the wrinkle that they also turn to armed robbery, the film exploiting to the hilt the imagery of women in revealing outfits with guns. The big man leading a criminal organization in an urban setting adorned with prostitutes and nefarious senior girls remains a Nollywood staple, as it has been from the beginning, pioneered by Nnebue's *Dirty Deal* and renewed by his 1997 *Rituals*. The ascendancy of political "godfathers" (as they are called) in the reestablished civilian regime, the inspiration of Francis Ford Coppola's *The Godfather*, and perhaps the name of the antihero of *Rituals*, Don Pedro, led to a spate of films with "Don" in the title, like *Dons of Abuja* (2004), while the continued devaluation of the naira turned millionaires into billionaires, resulting in titles like *Billionaires Club* (2003). The advent of the Nigerian action thriller is associated with the director Teco Benson and his *State of Emergency* (2000), *Formidable Force* (2002), *Accidental Discharge* (2003), *Blood Diamonds* (2004, shot in Sierra Leone), *Mission to Nowhere* (2008), and many more. Benson went to some trouble to cast Sam Dede, recently retired from the role of Ebube in the *Issakaba* films, in his big detective film *War Front* (2004).

Benson's action and detective films clearly imitate Hollywood, but the crime film generally is a case in which the Nigerian genre is shaped by strong forces that make it quite different from parallel international models. The most obvious of these forces is the effect of extremely low budgets on the representation of violence. Filming violence at the international standard is an art, and an expensive one, requiring not only the budget to smash or blow things up but also cranes, dollies, and multiple camera units, extensive coaching and choreography by highly trained professionals, stunt doubles with medical insurance, and so on. The international standard has been set by Hollywood and by Chinese films that draw on the resources of ancient martial arts traditions and the elaborate staged combats of the Peking Opera. Violence might appear to be the universal language: it is violent films, American and Chinese, that are the most easily exported around the globe and whose international profits fuel those powerful film industries. But violence is cultural, like everything else. American culture at its deepest levels undergirds Hollywood's representations of violence, from its original devotion in the silent era to galloping horses, gunslingers, rushing trains and automobiles, and Buster Keaton's sublime, balletic explorations of Newtonian physics in a world of runaway machinery and collapsing buildings to the current computer-generated apocalyptic mayhem.

Nollywood does not have the resources to do these things well, and when it does them badly the world's connoisseurs of cinematic violence are apt to judge it harshly. But we should be alive to the ways Nollywood's objectives—its meanings and purposes—are different. For many or most Nigerian cultures, the ultimate image of human power is a king sitting immobile on his throne. The king is immobile because he has others to commit violence on his behalf and, more fundamentally, because his most important powers are spiritual and are exercised on the spiritual level. So in Hubert Ogunde's celluloid films the priest-king Osetura, guardian of his community, maintains an unruffled calm as he deals with threatening witches; so the Yoruba traveling theater bequeathed to Nollywood the sorcerers' duel as an archetypal form of combat, which would evolve into Bible-wielding pastors countering the laser beams of demonic opponents. The shift to spiritual weapons deflates the physical aspect of a scene of confrontation and affects dramatic construction. The *Issakaba* films were so powerful partly because they yoked supernatural power with the iconography of violence, thuggery, and well-muscled heroism, but *Issakaba* 2, for example, is flat dramatically, not just because it is so episodic in structure but also because of the ease and immediacy with which, in each episode, Ebube's spiritual instincts and weapons allow him to detect evil and destroy it. Blood flows abundantly, but there is more posturing than fighting of the conventional kind. Like Osetura, Ebube has only to show up to guarantee the problem is solved. Only the culminating battle with a worthy opponent, a spiritual foe wielding spiritual weapons, generates dramatic tension.

Nigerian films typically do not make an art of creating dramatic tension. They are seldom built on the taut Hollywood model around a single dramatic action—a caper, or a ticking clock to be stopped. Nollywood crime films tend to favor the baggier form of the criminal biopic. *Rattlesnake* and *Owo Blow* (discussed in chapter 4) are examples of narrative sprawl. Izu Ojukwu's 2001 *Desperadoes: The Story of Derico* (Derico was a notorious armed robber operating around Onitsha) features a convincing bank robbery scene and a car chase, but by American standards it is loaded down with too many plot lines, all of them having to do with family: a heavily sentimentalized police official's daughter, sibling bonds, the mother back home. Family melodrama cracks open the crime film genre, as roots irresistibly break stone.

And the Hollywood staple of the detective film or police procedural has not found fertile ground in Nigeria. The intrepid American sociologist of literature Wendy Griswold, who undertook to read all the Nigerian novels ever published (she analyzed 476 of them, published up to 1997), observes that while Western crime novels often take the point of view of the police, Nigerian authors are loath to do so because of the disrepute and incompetence of the Nigerian police (Griswold 2000, 242). Teco Benson's action films (or Emeka Okpala's *Armed Forces*, 2000) show their American influence most strongly as they dwell on the professionalism and sexy weapons and gadgets of their lawmen; and *State of Emergency*, for example, moves through sleek, clean, empty urban spaces, startlingly unlike the cluttered Nigerian reality familiar from Nollywood films. (Chico Ejiro's *Blue Sea* (2001) is equally ambitious in its locations, featuring two robberies of a freighter anchored off Lagos and a waterborne chase scene.)

Moreover, Griswold continues, while Western crime fiction is largely about detective work, that is, the (ultimately successful) exercise of reason, this is not true of the Nigerian books, set in a world that seems not to be amenable to logical deduction. Griswold's whole discussion is haunted by the theme of rationality and its bafflement. "Crime novels and political novels do the same thing. They tell a story of rationality and its limitations. When told by men and women as committed to modern rationality as is the Nigerian educated elite, such a story is profoundly pessimistic because it describes a public sphere that is ultimately irrational" (Griswold 2000, 242).

Nollywood's culture is exceptionally rich in nonrational resources and tends to frame issues accordingly. The original Igbo-language Nollywood get-rich-quick films were full of criminal activity—*Living in Bondage* includes theft and murders by gunshot and poison, and the films that followed featured 419 fraud, drug dealing, and so forth. But they are generally framed as being about sin and social dysfunction rather than about crime. *Living in Bondage* is typical in the absence of detectives, police, or courts; resolution comes from the two great Nollywood matrices, the supernatural and the melodramatic.

CHAPTER 8

Political Films

The end of military rule in 1999 did not solve all of Nigeria's political problems, but it created a more open environment in which previously dangerous topics could be aired. Reporters covered the unearthing of millions of dollars looted from the national treasury by Abacha and his associates, and a Human Rights Violations Investigation Commission, created in 2000 to investigate abuses of authority over the previous decades, toured the country taking testimony. Its proceedings were broadcast and the nation paid close attention. Newspapers bulked up in order to provide more political coverage now that spoils were distributed through a broader process rather than being allocated behind closed doors by a small military elite.

Nollywood naturally moved into this new territory, making what people called "political films." Sometimes these were thinly disguised retellings of recent events, like *Stubborn Grasshopper: Loved Power, Died in Power* (2001), produced by Sam Onwuka and directed by Simisola Opeoluwa, the story of Abacha himself, or *Oil Village* (2001), also written and produced by Sam Onwuka, which recounted the "judicial execution" (as the British prime minister called it) by Abacha of Ken Saro-Wiwa, the writer and minority rights and environmental activist. Sometimes they recounted wild stories from the new political dispensation: Andy Amenechi's *The Last Vote* (2002) is transparently the story of Dr. Chimaroke Nnamani, made governor of Enugu State by a political godfather who then fell out with him over patronage issues. Purely fictional films felt free to explore the doings of high office holders. Filmmakers were no longer discreet about using military men or police officers as representative big men, doing the things big men do, like hiring university students as prostitutes (*Girls Hostel* (2001), *Claws of the Lion* (2005)). The new action thriller genre moved onto formerly forbidden ground. The jacket copy of Teco Benson's *State of Emergency* (2000) reads, "Anarchy has become the order of the day! Kill a civilian, it's a different ball game. But kill an Army Major, that means war." The jacket of *First Lady* (2002) features a lot of guns—three tough guys with automatic weapons, a military firing squad, police attacking demonstrators—and quotes a bit of dialogue: "Tell the president and the entire state how you executed the FIRST LADY to take over her position or I'll blow your fucking head up."

New film genres do not come out of nowhere. As we have seen, Nollywood had been exploring the workings of political power in a broader sense in a number of different ways. Several Nollywood genres broke through the boundary between their social concerns and the realm of "the political." That boundary is arbitrary as a matter of theory; in practice, it had been (erratically) policed by the State Security Services. It took only short steps to create "political films" out of existing resources. This chapter, therefore, recapitulates and extends themes and arguments of earlier chapters and discusses some films made before 1999. Because of this genre's multiple origins, it coheres less than other genres in its settings, plot types, and so on. What holds it together is its subject matter: the doings of politicians and other actors in the political domain. And political films are usually informed by Nollywood's typical moral preoccupations and tend to turn to Nollywood's typical melodramatic procedures for revealing the "moral occult" (Brooks 1976).

This whole book is meant in part as a rejoinder to the common criticism that Nollywood is merely commercial entertainment that avoids politics or serious social issues. Nollywood is routinely dismissed in this way by those approaching it from the perspective of African celluloid cinema from the rest of the continent, a mostly noncommercial cinema that generally has been created out of a high sense of social purpose and for the first decades of its existence was often framed by militant pronouncements. Ferid Boughadir, surveying the tendencies of African cinema in 1983, called the political tendency "the royal road" (122, 240–41).[1]

In Nigeria, Nollywood films have always been attacked for their lack of social and political utility from more politicized or at least cultural nationalist positions in the Nigerian universities, the media, government, and elsewhere. In a stern memo to film producers written in 1999, for example, the head of the censors board, Ademola James, complained in typical language that the films were dominated by the exploitation of "negative tendencies" in Nigerian culture including "occultism, cultism, fetishism, witchcraft, devilish spiritualism, uncontrolled tendency for sexual display, bloodiness, incest, violence, poisoning, etc. . . . From all indications, indulgence in the production of film with 'negatively based themes' is driven more by excessive commercialism or love of profit to the detriment of a sense of social responsibility and relevance." He goes on to recommend that filmmakers turn to other topics, including "politics," which "have been almost totally ignored" (James 1999).

In the 1990s the film industry's commercial orientation was in striking contrast to other sectors of Nigerian cultural production such as literary drama, which has always been dominated by politically radical figures like Wole Soyinka and Femi Osofisan,[2] or Nigerian popular music, which produced a number of oppositional voices of whom Fela Anikulapo Ransome-Kuti is the best known, or Nigerian print journalism (closely linked at the time with the literary community), which kept up a steady stream of outraged and distressed commentary on the state of the nation. A culture of opposition expressed itself through guerrilla print and broadcast media as well as through more conventional outlets, but this oppositional culture hardly communicated at all with the video film industry.

An exception that proves the rule and demonstrates the missed opportunities is *Babangida Must Go* (1993, also known as *Maradona*, a nickname for Babangida because his skills as a political dribbler matched those of the Argentine soccer star). A fierce agitprop film mixing news footage, chanted Yoruba poetry, and skits by Yoruba traveling theater actors, it was made during the insurrection that followed Babangida's annulment of the June 12, 1993, presidential election. Babangida had organized a seemingly endless "transition to democracy," inventing and lavishly funding two political parties to perform an elaborate charade of representative democracy, rigging and rerigging the process until no one could believe in it. But Babangida "dribbled himself into his own net," as people said—finally an election had to be held. It was won by the billionaire M. K. O. Abiola, but as votes were being reported Babangida decided to annul the whole election. This was too much: Lagos exploded in rioting, eventually put down by soldiers spraying bullets at random from their vehicles. Babangida's credibility was destroyed. He was replaced by a short-lived interim military regime and then by his henchman Sani Abacha.

Babangida Must Go was made and sold during the insurrection. It is an example of the political potential of "small media," the new generation of cheap, portable, uncontrollable technologies like photocopiers and audio cassettes that played such an important role in the Iranian revolution (Sreberny-Mohammadi and Mohammadi 1994). Video technology allowed *Babangida Must Go* to be made. The problem was circulating it after the insurrection ended, in the absence of a distribution alternative to the Idumota marketers. The filmmaker Gbenga Adewusi had to flee the country to escape from the State Security Services once military rule was reconsolidated; eventually, with the help of his father-in-law, a wealthy industrialist, he negotiated his return and resumed his career. (For a full study of this film, see Haynes 2003b.)

No one was interested in repeating his experiment. Nollywood is a risk-averse commercial enterprise. Most producers are so small that the banning of a single film might threaten their existence.[3] Commercial failure is also a dire prospect. These are the limits within which Nollywood has to address political matters, and they are real limitations of form, ideology, and cultural imagination, since Nollywood films need to be recognizable and compelling to a broad popular audience—immediately saleable, and believed to be so by the marketers, who like dependable profits and do not like trouble. But that connection to the audience, that coincidence of vision, is also the strength and importance of the films, their significant role in the Nigerian democracy.

TRADITIONAL RULERSHIP

Traditional rulership is central to several Nollywood genres, and as a theme and set of symbols it is too strong ever to go away or lose its potency. The artistic resources attached to it are too valuable to discard, recourse to traditional forms of legitimacy is an inevitably recurrent option in thinking about African politics, and the symbols of traditional rule are ingrained in popular consciousness, intertwined with the most fundamental structures of feeling.

Traditional forms of all kinds are far from merely allegorical: they are still very much facts of social life, as noted in previous chapters . But traditional rulership is also allegorical, providing a coded way of talking about national politics that was particularly important in the days of military rule. On the symbolic level traditional rulers have variable meanings, as in real life, where traditional rulers may be felt to be a last bulwark of legitimacy and cohesion but where they have also been in structural complicity with successive forms of predatory central government. On the level of political thought, the figure of the traditional ruler may be rich and fertile or a blockage. I suggested in chapter 6 that the uniform failure of the cultural epics to imagine a world without igwes, to remember or think past that figure to the prior model of Igbo village democracy, impairs the genre's ability to provide images of a culturally rooted civil society that would be useful in constructing a democratic future.

Historical narratives are the expression of a living present, whose strongest motivations are to be found in the fabric of everyday life. Big manism, whose lineage in Igbo society is derived from the republican but undemocratic patriarchal and gerontocratic aspects of the traditional polity, so dominates contemporary social, political, and economic life that it is not surprising to see its shadow cast back across history. A thick layer of local power brokers is in place everywhere. The sources of their legitimacy in "tradition" might not withstand scrutiny, but that is beside the point. They fill the landscape, and the thorough corruption of all aspects of life mean that supplicating for the aid of a big man, who probably wants to be addressed as a chief, is an absolutely familiar experience. I suspect, depressingly, that a century of this, since the British imposition of the warrant chiefs, has made anything else nearly unimaginable.

The Yoruba have a deeper investment in the figure of the king but also a stronger tradition of progressive handling of traditional culture. The history of Nigerian celluloid film offers several examples of liberal or radical allegories based on the *kabiyesi* genre, such as *Ija Ominira* (1979), made by Ola Balogun and Adeyemi Afolayan (Ade Love) from a novel by Adebayo Faleti, and Ladi Ladebo's *Vendor* (1987). And the Yoruba were more outraged politically by the 1990s: M. K. O. Abiola was Yoruba, and while the whole nation was incensed by the stealing of his 1993 election victory, the Yoruba questioned whether other parts of the country were not faint in sustaining the protest, particularly the Igbos, who in the political geometry of Nigeria have sometimes allied themselves with the reactionary north as a counterweight to their natural progressive allies and rivals in the west. It is no accident that *Babangida Must Go* is in Yoruba and emerged from Yoruba popular culture, not from English-language, Igbo-dominated Nollywood.

At the same time, on another level, the presence of old, resilient traditions both of kingship and of representing kingship, as in the traveling theater tradition, softened the Yoruba imaginative response, as compared to the Igbo. Other deep historical factors are probably in play. For many Igbo the experience of modernity often came in one great shock as they migrated from villages to cities. One form of life broke open into an utterly different, half-comprehended one, encouraging an apocalyptic vision in the Christian idiom of End Times or paranoid conspiracy theories involving evil cabals, the occult, and perhaps foreign powers. The get-rich-quick theme was bound up with this sense of dislocation and apocalyptic social change. Many Yoruba also moved from villages to cities, but the Yoruba have been living in their dense, boisterous cities for a millennium, with familiar venal chiefs jockeying around a king. Greed is understood as universal and timeless, and the community is stronger—not a village as a distant reference point but an urban neighborhood where people actually live.

KELANI'S *SAWOROIDE* AND *AGOGO EEWO*

So *Saworoide/Brass Bells* (1999) and *Agogo Eewo/Taboo Gong* (2002), films directly about politics made by Tunde Kelani in collaboration with Akinwumi Ishola, are biting films with hard edges—both end with bad rulers struck dead.[4] But they are also humorous and humane about the spectacle of roguery and end on the note of unity.

Saworoide's opening title declares, "This is the parable of the drum as the voice of the people. It is the story of the pact between an ancient community and the kings that ruled over it . . ." As the king of Jogbo dies, his voiced-over memories and a montage of traditional images inform us of the magical constitution of this polity. As prescribed through Ifa divination, the babalawo (played by Ishola) takes seeds out of a ritual pot, placing half inside the royal crown and the other half inside a drum; successive kings and drummers had a powder rubbed into incisions. A king who was illegitimate or sought excessive wealth would die of a splitting headache if he wore the crown when the drum was played. The new king is greedy and rejects the traditional incisions and oaths, and he has killed a couple with a rival claim to the throne, though their young son escapes to be raised in the forest under virtuous tutelage. As the logic of folk tale would have it, the boy grows up (now he is played by the young Kunle Afolayan) to fall in love with the king's (illegitimate) daughter; the young lovers' perils end when the sacred drum brings down the tyrant. The film ends before the young man is installed, but the proper inheritance of legitimate roles and the restoration of legitimate traditional forms are assumed as normative ideals, and the narrative gives them magical sanction.

But, in the manner of *Ti Oluwa Nile*, this story takes place in a multifaceted contemporary world where every element is problematic. The new king wants a shapelier, better-educated, more presentable wife, which leads to a running story about the jealousies of polygamous marriages. The king and his chiefs are eager to enter into corrupt relations with the foreign timber companies that control the main local industry, at the expense of farmers, the environment, and even the sacred forest. The king and chiefs demand that foreign bank accounts be opened for them. There is an array of countervailing forces aside from the providential redeemers already mentioned. The king is confronted by a television journalist demanding to know where he got the money for his fleet of Mercedes Benzes.[5] The next sequence features a moralizing old man (played by the writer and media personality Adebayo Faleti) who reclines on the palace steps, observing everything and warning that the corruption of those in power will have repercussions. A montage of demonstrations follows;

they turn into an armed rebellion led by the Youth League. They wreck logging equipment and finally steal the crown away from the king. In desperation the king turns to the colonel in charge of his security forces, who recovers the crown but claims it for himself. It is this military ruler, civilianizing himself for his coronation ceremony, who is killed by the sacred drum.

The film provides a complex allegory, then, which reveals the elements of contemporary Nigerian politics. Even as the film works with the symbols of kingship, it insists on the democratic aspects of the traditional constitution. The heir apparent does not dominate the end of the film; the triumph really belongs to the Youth League and the young drummer who has just inherited his sacred role. Abacha died between *Saworoide*'s writing and its release, relieving the filmmakers of serious anxiety—making a film in which a clear representation of Abacha collapses to general rejoicing was not a safe thing to do.[6]

In 2002 Kelani and Ishola produced a sequel to *Saworoide*, *Agogo Eewo/Taboo Gong*, set in the same multifarious, bubbling world. This film is obviously an allegory of the civilian presidency of Olusegun Obasanjo (1999–2007). The young prince of *Saworoide* decides to pursue his studies rather than taking the throne; the Obasanjo figure Adebosipo (Dejumo Lewis) is persuaded by a delegation of Jogbo chiefs to come out of retirement and rule. (Like Obasanjo, he has become a commercial farmer. Jogbo is a fictional town; both films were shot in the distinctive rocky urban landscape of Abeokuta, which happens also to be Obasanjo's hometown.) Adebosipo understands the chiefs want him as cover for their corruption (Babangida bankrolled Obasanjo's candidacy with the enormous wealth he had stolen, needing to ensure that he would not be prosecuted for his misdeeds in office), and he is beset by his grasping wife and other schemers. But he stands firm. As his conflict with the chiefs turns serious, he reinstitutes an old custom, parallel to the magical drum and crown of *Saworoide*: a gong that, when sounded, will cause corrupt chiefs to die. One of the chiefs employs a gang of youths to disrupt the ceremony, but other youth groups have also mobilized. In the resulting stand-off, the ceremony goes forward. The wicked chiefs confess or drop dead. The film was made in the midst of anxieties about possible violence before the 2004 election that gave Obasanjo a second term; Kelani meant the peaceful ending of the film as a model of conflict prevention (Haynes 2007c, 13).

Kelani says Adebosipo is Obasanjo as he wanted him to be, not as he actually was, and the film's strategy is the oldest in the world for circumspectly criticizing a ruler—blaming those around him rather than the ruler himself. The film is meant as advice to Obasanjo, but in the concluding voice-over Baba Opalaba (Faleti), who once again has been providing running commentary, addresses not the ruler but the citizenry, admonishing them to stay mobilized: "There you are. Mere sermons won't stop robbers. Only force can curb their activities. We sit down and dream, we lie down, yet no change. Only when we get up on our feet can our dream be realized. . . . Hence the youths that have just pruned the shoots of conspiracy. Don't throw away your machetes. As soon as new evils sprout cut them off promptly."

NNEBUE'S *RITUALS*

Of all the money ritual films based on the Otokoto incident (chapter 7), Kenneth Nnebue's *Rituals* (1997) responded most fully to the motivation of the rioters who pushed the original discovery of the boy's decapitated head into the headlines. The riot was itself a form of popular culture and popular politics, expressing a diagnosis of the rotten state of Nigerian society and taking direct measures against it. Peter Geschiere suggests that notions of the occult have lost none of their relevance to contemporary African politics because of a structural similarity between witchcraft and politics in the single-party or military state: both involve a cabal and depend on secretive, personal power struggles behind closed doors (Geschiere 1997, 5). In Nigeria this situation reached an apogee with the final paranoid dementia of Abacha, who almost never emerged from seclusion in the presidential palace, ruled through a tiny, venal clique, and surrounded himself with spiritualists. After his death, newspapers carried stories about secret recesses in the presidential mansion where human sacrifices were reportedly made. Given Nigeria's coup-plagued history and the clientelist organization of politics and the economy, imagining a secret cabal as the real source of power made sense. That a principal in the Otokoto affair was the brother of one of Abacha's ministers merely confirmed the widespread impression that the military president was the apex of a system with such a base, or at least that money rituals provided a perfect metaphor for the state of the nation.

Rituals is Nnebue's most developed social vision, employing to the fullest and giving a new coherence to the forms he had elaborated in earlier films to anatomize the ways power works in Nigerian society. The film begins with Richard, a cardiologist practicing in America, returning to Nigeria because his father is sick with what Richard knows to be a treatable medical condition. But his father belongs to a secret cult that believes a human sacrifice is required to save him. Richard argues to his father that by following the cult rather than his medical expertise, the family is abandoning its investment in his education. When Richard refuses, his brother Ben procures a human head to offer on the cult's altar. The father dies anyway, and Ben murders Richard to secure the inheritance. This prologue to the rest of the film shows Richard swallowed up by his family's superstition and greed, and along with him goes the promise of his generation: educational enlightenment coupled with genuine filial affection and a desire to remain rooted in his culture and community even as he opposes its darker side. The prologue creates the context for what follows and serves as an allegory of the whole wrecked project of national development.

We then meet the film's antihero, Don Pedro (Pete Edochie), who has come to persuade his old friend the minister of education to release a student cult member accused of beheading a fellow student for ritual purposes. Such cults infest Nigerian university campuses, and subsequent scenes illustrate their typical activities: violently controlling the sexual lives of female students, intimidating lecturers to get good grades, and murdering rival cult members (see chapter 11). Don Pedro is the patron of this cult. That we see him for the first time in the Ministry of Education demonstrates how far his influence extends into institutions that are supposed to represent enlightenment and modernity. (See the reading of this film in Okome 2003.) In the next scene Don Pedro's own cult, the Vampires, meets in a modern office building. The cult's influence over the police is the main point: a member arrives to the high thin wailing of a police escort's siren, and Don Pedro wins the release of Ben, imprisoned for Richard's murder, with a phone call promising a police official a carton of cash and a chieftaincy title.

We then follow Don Pedro to the "De Merit International 1997 Award Night" ceremony, this film's equivalent of the bank opening ceremony in Nnebue's *Dirty Deal* and the Women of Substance International extravaganza in *Glamour Girls* 2. In this case, the Nigerian national anthem is played as the camera pans the still crowd: what is at stake now is dominion over the nation itself. Once again the rhetoric of philanthropy unfurls in great clouds of hypocrisy. When it is time for Don Pedro's award, we learn that he has a PhD in political science from Oxford and is a businessman and captain of industry with many companies in petroleum, finance, and other sectors. He has over twenty traditional titles, and (like Chief Ogbu-Orie of *Dirty Deal*) he is hailed for his donation of crime-fighting equipment to the police. He is truly the prince of this world, master of things visible and invisible.

An extravagant party at his house follows, recorded at length. Don Pedro circulates among his guests with a huge cigar and an Igbo cane, knocking fists with other chiefs in the traditional salute. People dance to the live music of Bright Chimezie's band. Guests "spray" the band. In the midst of the party, Don Pedro orders his men to provide two heads for use in money rituals, one for an igwe, the other for a commissioner aspirant. His men seduce two young women into accompanying them downstairs into a secret room. Don Pedro comes down to find the women stripped to their underwear, handcuffed and screaming into their gags. He makes a sign for their heads to come off. The film cuts back to the party, where someone is spraying Bright Chimezie with a stack of bills. The party continues, with more spraying in different styles. Don Pedro sprays and is sprayed, money flying everywhere.

These two scenes of the awards night and the party present essential emblems of Abacha's Nigeria, capturing the style of the elite—sometimes stylish indeed, charismatic, and accomplished, throwing money about with careless abandon because its supply was unlimited. But underneath, in the foundation of the luxurious mansion, is cold-blooded murder. Nnebue illustrates the "reciprocal convergence of elites," the interlocking of business, political, traditional, and educational leaders (Bayart 1993). Don Pedro embodies all these different elites in his own person, as we have been informed; he also embodies their organization as a conspiracy, which is a matter of social collusion, bribery, and—at its dark heart—participation in human sacrifice.

Having made this point about the organization of the dominant class, the film turns to demonstrations of the mechanisms through which power is exercised. Mid-level employees of Don Pedro's organization discuss the shock waves from their operation that has left the Lagos neighborhood of Ikeja littered with corpses; they watch television reports of one of their operatives being caught with human heads in her car and are assured that the matter is being taken care of. Don Pedro helps a governor in political trouble by sacrificing a virgin, whose tongue is supposed to make the governor persuasive. Young women are sold into Don Pedro's network. The Vampires meet and decide to run one of their number, Desmond, for governor. As part of this campaign, Don Pedro has bribed a traditional ruler to give Desmond and the rest of them chieftaincy titles. Don Pedro visits the student cult and enlists them in the campaign. Standing in the sunroof of a vehicle following a "Vote Desmond for Governor" banner, Don Pedro and Desmond throw cash to a crowd—a perfect image of the politics sponsored by the Babangida and Abacha regimes.

But then, in a village meeting, the tide begins to turn. Someone says Desmond's campaign has given a million naira to each village, but does he have the character of somebody who can lead the people honestly? If they share this money, they will have sold their conscience. Another agrees: "The amount the campaign is giving out is more than the state's business; it's an investment, and he expects it will be returned with interest. The call to service has become a call to loot the national treasury. We will share the money and then cast our vote for the right candidate." An argument breaks out over whether to share the money cynically or to refuse it.

Desmond loses the election, in spite of an enormous bribe paid to the election officer. Stricken, Desmond calls in a reverend father and a district police officer to make his confession: he has killed his wife and mother and used them in money rituals. "I belong to seven secret cults but none of them could change the wish of God." Don Pedro is informed that Desmond has confessed and that people are trooping through his house to see the roasted bodies of his wife and mother. Looking defiant and strangely happy, he declares, "We must dance the war song to protect ourselves." "AND NOW THE STORY BEGINS . . . WATCH OUT," the final title reads. Nnebue wrote a sequel but never made the film.

Rituals is an unusual ritual film because it is full of instances where occult means fail, not because of a countervailing spiritual power but simply because they don't work: human sacrifice does not save Richard's father, the governor who employs Don Pedro is removed from power, one of the Vultures dies in an attempt to "armor" himself against physical harm, Desmond's psyche collapses under the weight of guilt. Don Pedro maintains an aura of power in spite of numerous failures on both the occult and the merely political planes: he does not succeed in releasing the student cult leader, and, most importantly, he fails to get Desmond elected.

Altogether, *Rituals* gives a clear assessment of the state of Nigerian politics: individual regimes of evil can fail, at least temporarily, because of internal weaknesses, public resistance, or individual acts of courage or despair, but there is no visible force capable of reforming the system. The fortunate tendency of criminal conspiracies to destroy themselves has always been a basic principle of Nollywood films, and a necessary principle given the incompetence of the police and courts. Don Pedro is uncowed at the end of the film, just as Babangida, the self-proclaimed "evil genius" of Nigerian politics, was pushed out of the presidency but remains immensely powerful. Abacha was not driven from power: he died in his bed. Ordinary people understand perfectly well what is going on and are full of disgust, but they are also corruptible and divided. Bola Ige, the assassinated minister of justice, called their attitude "siddon look": sit down and look on, watchfully biding one's time.

MELODRAMAS

Because Nigerian family melodramas usually practice the inflation and glamorization of lifestyles normal in commercial cinema and soap operas the world over, and because the number of Nigerians who actually live in such a manner is tiny and is in effect limited to those with close relations with the government, many Nigerian films have wandered into the political context even if no political implications were intended. The male protagonist in Nnebue's *True Confession* (1995) is a candidate for governor, for instance, but the film is not really about politics. Since 1999 there have been several movies, resembling royal films, about melodramatic situations in imaginary First Families: the jacket copy of *The President's Daughter* (2000) explains that the heroine was expelled from her foreign university and arrested for using cocaine. "Suddenly, all eyes are on the president. Will he pull the strings and get his daughter released, to avoid defeat at the elections, or will he allow justice to take its course and send his only child to prison?"

It is impossible and pointless to try to say precisely when the balance tips over and a film can be said to be political, but I submit that it has happened in *Dark Goddess* (1995), written and produced by Charles Owoyemi and directed by Andy Amenechi. This film grew out of the television serial *Fortunes*, with a clear inheritance from *Dallas* and *Dynasty*-style soap operas. Tokumbo Johnson, the glamorous, beautiful, and wicked "dark goddess," comes from an immensely wealthy family whose problems include illegitimacy, incest, blood cancer, and murderous disputes over inheritance and control of the family business empire. Tokumbo busily kills off various family members in her way.

This is, as far as I know, the first film to feature as a character the president of the country—a civilian, elected president, though the film was made during military rule. This president is visited by Fred Akin-Thomas, a billionaire power broker who, later in the film, marries Tokumbo. Fred tells the president that he has used his personal influence to get international bank assistance, now that they have a democracy in place. The president pleads for Fred's help in his reelection. Fred says Washington may reconsider its negative position on him if—through Fred—he does three things: first, appoint Washington's nominees as key ministers; second, ensure these nominees will take directives from Washington on policy matters; and third, increase Fred's personal allotment of oil from 125,000 to 500,000 barrels per day. "Who am I to say no?" the President replies.

The film chronicles various events in the life of a presidential candidate, Femi Gomez. Gomez is flogged by a dominatrix. When his personal secretary Raymond reveals that the dominatrix is actually a journalist, Gomez strangles her in a bubble bath. Later Raymond is seduced by a woman working for Tokumbo, who knows Raymond is planning to betray Gomez. Tokumbo proposes to help Raymond if he swears to worship the Dark Goddess—herself—all the days of his life. Gomez, drinking with his son, discusses his mad and draconian plans for governing. His son tells him Amnesty International will condemn him. Gomez threatens to kill his son if he reveals Gomez's stay in a Swiss sanatorium. When his brother Senator Barry, who has fallen for Tokumbo, comes to tell him that he himself will be running for president, Gomez shoots him.

In bed on the morning after their marriage, Tokumbo, unimpressed with everything, tells Fred she has business meetings worth $700 million for the next week and can't go to Spain for their honeymoon. She demands that Fred cut his ex-wife and son Jeff out of his will. Later Tokumbo tells the president she is as good a power broker as Fred and promises to be more effective than the Americans. She offers to destroy Gomez if the president will deposit $5 billion in her Swiss account and swear the oath to the Dark Goddess.

She summons Gomez and informs him he can never be president. "I want you to leave that in the hands of the masses to decide," he says, to which she replies, "Don't be naive, Gomez, a tiny but powerful cabal determines democracy in this part of the world." She blackmails him into holding a press conference to withdraw from the race. He then shoots his secretary Raymond for his treachery and kills himself after summoning from New York his daughter Amina, who will avenge him (an evident advertisement for a sequel).

Fred has a stroke after Tokumbo shows him a videotape of himself having sex with her mother, demanding that he pay her $12 billion out of his total fortune of $20 billion as damages or she will use the tape to destroy him in Washington. Fred lies on the floor of their mansion "like a cockroach." She shoots his son Jeff as the film ends.

This seems like, and in fact it is, a lurid, paranoid fantasy, but let us remember some things about 1995 in Nigeria. The scale of the fortunes mentioned in the film are only a slight exaggeration of what those at the center of power—Babangida, Abiola, Abacha—were acquiring, and power was wielded in ever more Machiavellian and deadly fashion. The position of first lady had been given unprecedented prominence by Maryam Babangida and then by Maryam Abacha; both were attractive, power- and money-hungry, arrogant women whose complicated sexual pasts were the subject of widespread rumors, including some involving the murder of inconvenient children from previous marriages.[7] The episode in which Tokumbo brings down Gomez prefigures the story of Dan Etete, a minister in Abacha's government who, a year or so after the film appeared, supposing his boss would like it if his pseudotransition to democracy were complete with some presidential candidates, announced that he would run. Furious, Abacha confronted him with evidence of his corruption—like Babangida, Abacha was said to keep such evidence on everyone—and demanded he give a press conference immediately to announce his withdrawal. Private oil allotments like Fred's were a standard feature of government. The demeaning treatment of the elected president by Fred, Tokumbo, and Washington is perhaps inspired by the perception of former civilian presidents Balewa and Shagari as errand-boys of the northern oligarchs, but it also prefigures the Third Republic in which talk of democracy, transparency, and Amnesty International is not entirely without meaning but real power is exercised through private influence on a breathtaking scale and responds to the exigencies of neocolonial powers. That the film's satire was directed at a future civilian government—the military is never mentioned—was doubtless a strategy to avoid the wrath of the regime.

Nigerian writers complain of the problem of keeping up with Nigerian reality while maintaining anything that looks like realism. The videos have perhaps been most adequate to the spectacle of Nigerian politics when at their most fantastic.

LOVED POWER, DIED IN POWER

Abacha had no real friends, so as soon as he was gone it was safe to attack him. Sam Onwuka's two-part *Stubborn Grasshopper: Loved Power, Died in Power* chronicles the Abacha dictatorship, beginning with the annulment of the 1993 election and ending with the dictator's death.[8] The second part shifts into the mode of family melodrama just described.

Names have been changed: Abacha becomes Alba, his wife Maryam becomes Sabina, M. K. O. Abiola becomes Chief Kash, Wole Soyinka becomes Professor Nobel, NADECO (the National Democratic Coalition) becomes WADECO, and Nigeria becomes the Republic of Wahala (*wahala* means "trouble" in Yoruba and Pidgin). Slight changes have been made in the story—the newspapers reported rumors that Abacha died in the arms of two Indian prostitutes, while the film has Alba with three Nigerians—but in general all the twists and turns of the history of the regime are represented faithfully and in detail, from the bloody suppression of the rioting in Lagos after the annulment to the forced resignation of the head of the interim national government, the violated understanding with Abiola, the assassinations of Kudirat Abiola and NADECO leaders, the arrests of Generals Diya and Yar'Adua, and so on. The film sticks close to the historical record; where certitude is impossible or has not yet been established, it follows common assumptions and speculations that must not be more extraordinary than the truth.

The film plods through the chronicle of events, in fact, with little internal drama or depth of characterization. There are satirical touches such as the scene where an elocution coach attempts to correct Alba/Abacha's notoriously bad English pronunciation (the dictator has the poor man hauled off after frustrating attempts to say "agriculture," "local government," and "country"), but the film is not predominantly satirical. It has a discernible point of view (surprisingly sympathetic to Ibrahim Babangida, surprisingly hard on Abiola, entirely positive towards NADECO though that was almost entirely a Yoruba organization and the film's personnel are mostly Igbo), but it seems intended to express a condemnation of military rule that would appeal to viewers from across the political spectrum. Designed like the hearings of the Human Rights Violations Investigation Commission to make the story public, it relies on people's memories and common experiences to ensure interest in the story.

There is an important shift in narrative strategy and even of genre between the two parts of the film. Part 1 has an elaborate apparatus for measuring public opinion. It begins with a political discussion, over a table full of bottles, between four friends: Chuks, an Igbo; Tunde, a Yoruba; Bala, an exaggerated version of a Hausaman; and Etim, from a southern minority group and by implication the stand-in for all the other Nigerians who are not part of the "big three" ethnicities. We watch television with them as the election results are announced and continue to look in on them throughout the film as they discuss and quarrel over the news and cope with problems like fuel scarcity and exorbitant prices. We similarly observe other conversations among anonymous people discussing the collapse of social services, unpaid salaries of civil servants, and so on, and women with microphones—apparently television reporters—interview people in the street for their reactions to political developments. All this demonstrates the immiseration, frustration, and anger of the general population, but it also shows how effective the ploys of the dictatorship were in sowing ethnic divisions and in buying time for itself through false promises. "WADECO" puts up a heroic resistance, but its leaders are killed or flee abroad; the first part ends with the assassination of Kash's activist wife (the historical Kudirat Abiola). Public opinion had reached the point of utter disgust but also of helpless impotence in the face of the regime's willingness to shed blood. The regime's collapse would come only with Abacha's death, caused at least in part by his debauchery.

Perhaps for this reason, part 2 drops the whole apparatus of soundings in public opinion and turns to family melodrama, based on widespread rumors about the Abacha family. Part 1 has just one scene with Alba's sons, in which he tells them they are free to grab whatever they want and they promise to take advantage of the situation. They become major characters in the second part, as does their mother Sabina. Rebuffed when she asks that an accused coup plotter be released, she confronts her husband in bed with two prostitutes. Meanwhile, one of her sons tells the other he should stop using the family name for business because in fact he is not the son of the dictator but of an emir connected with a coup plotter. Angry with his wife, Alba has the illegitimate son killed in a plane crash.

Alba's demise comes when a group of officers who have learned they are about to be sacked organize a party during which the dictator is lured by hired girls into a bedroom, prevented from taking the drugs he needs to stay alive, disconnected from his cell phone, and finally fed a poisoned apple. He twitches, foams at the mouth, and dies. We are not far from the world of *Dark Goddess* here, but again the point is that we are also very close to real history.

MELODRAMA AND IDEOLOGY

Melodrama, with its characteristic focus on individual emotional and moral choices rather than systemic issues, its polarization of good and evil characters, manipulation of emotional extremes, and preference for happy endings or at least closure, is a problematic tool with which to address political issues, as many critiques of Hollywood films have shown. Melodrama encourages emotional identification with individual characters, the argument runs, while creating a mystified and spectatorial relationship with social reality.

I am arguing, however, that the melodramatic mode is capable of an unusually strong grip on Nigerian politics because Nigeria's politics is so personal in its forms. The violation of the distinction between public and private wealth is the definition of corruption; personal relationships are essential in the patron-client structures that permeate politics and society on every level; and the immense personal power and fortunes amassed under military rule magnify individual desire, caprice, and vengeance as elements in national politics.

And if the ideological analysis contained in Nollywood films is underdeveloped, this reflects the almost entirely unideological character of contemporary Nigerian politics. The British set up a system in which national politics was an ethnically organized competition for spoils, and this remains the basic structure. Military rule was a ruthless kleptocracy. In the Third Republic the labor movement continues to decline, and the heroic stature of civil society groups faded after the dictators departed. Insurrectionary protests against a hike in fuel prices in January 2012 turned into an "Occupy Nigeria" movement and showed the depths of public outrage, the power of the desire (fueled by the international media, as in the Arab Spring) to live in a "normal" country, and the fragility of the whole structure of governance. But then things settled down again into the usual party politics. A report on the dominant Nigerian political party by the American embassy, made public in 2011 by Wikileaks, outraged Nigerian pride but its truth was generally accepted.

> The People's Democratic Party (PDP) cannot be viewed as a political party within the common western understanding. Like velveeta cheese, the labeling claims it is a party, but upon further inspection, it lacks key ingredients most political parties share. . . . Even the party's mission statement and directive principles lack an ideological basis upon which to form party policy. The PDP remains an agglomeration of interest groups formed around persons of prominence and power which are loosely tied together by a desire to remain in office and maintain access to the "national cake" or resources of the state. (American Embassy Abuja 2007)

Politics as a struggle between clear ideological alternatives was also inhibited in Nigeria by another historical legacy, the British colonial policy of indirect rule that allied the central government with traditional rulers, an alliance renewed under subsequent nationalist and postcolonial political regimes. (Ellis was quoted on this subject in the last chapter; see also Mamdani 1996 and Piot 2010.) This alliance required the state to swallow the contradiction between its own modernizing ideology and the utterly different beliefs, including occult spiritual ones, that legitimated the power of its royal partners.

All this is not to say there are no differences among politicians. Just as the moral character and purposes of the igwe or oba of a community really matters, governors, for example, can have a conspicuous effect on infrastructures. This came home to me in 2010, a decade into civilian rule, as I drove from Lagos to Ilorin: the roads in Lagos State had improved dramatically; those in Oyo were such a disaster that we had to take a long detour, since what should have been one of the nation's principal highways was impassable; at the border of Kwara State, things suddenly improved again. The governors of Lagos and Kwara were not above corruption: Lagos governor Bola Ahmed Tinubu (who initiated the reforms celebrated in the preface during his tenure from 1999 to 2007) has amassed a breathtaking fortune in real estate; Kwara's Bukola Saraki was arrested (but not convicted) on corruption charges in 2012. But there was something to their governments besides corruption.

Good or at least tolerable government can be driven ideologically by traditional, modernizing nationalist, or neoliberal values, or any combination thereof, so that terms like "liberal" and "conservative" have little clear relevance. Politicians often have résumés that span several cultural and ideological formations, like *Rituals*'s Don Pedro. Bukola Saraki is heir to the values and impressive political skills of the Northern elite: his father, also an important politician, was waziri of the Ilorin Emirate, and the son holds high traditional titles. Father and son both have medical degrees from the United Kingdom; the father was the chairman and the son a director of a major bank. Tinubu is descended from Madame Tinubu, the famous nineteenth-century trader and politician; his mother was also an important businesswoman and head of the national organization of market women and men. Tinubu has taken very high traditional titles. A former Mobil Oil executive, his transformation of the infrastructure of Lagos is intended to make Lagos a center of capitalist globalization rather than a backwater of kleptocracy.

This blended progressive ideological repertoire is shadowed by its evil twin, the old alliance of predatory central government with predatory local traditional rulers. So Nollywood's standard representation of political conflict features an evil cabal of reciprocally converged elites opposed by a coalition of the virtuous, allying traditional and religious figures and perhaps also labor unions, student groups, and journalists.

PARANOID STYLES, CLASS, DESPAIR, AND MORALISM

Nigerians have earned their paranoia. The vision of national life as dominated by a corrupt conspiracy has been a staple of Nigerian literature from the brutal and fanciful allegories of Wole Soyinka on down. In her survey of Nigerian novels, Wendy Griswold reports that at first she did not distinguish between crime novels and political novels, since both genres were always about corruption (2000, 122, 240–41).

Griswold presents a grim picture. "[T]he novels show all institutions—government, private, educational, medical . . .—to be similarly indifferent to the public welfare. Officials and organizations are sometimes the core of the problem, sometimes merely useless, but they never inspire trust. Protagonists must step outside of institutions to get what they want" (Griswold 2000, 253). The western novels on which Nigerian crime and political novels are to some degree based begin and end with a state of order, but the Nigerian fictions, while depicting a Manichaean battle between order and chaos, typically end in chaos and, in the case of the political novels, may not have an image of order as a point of departure (ibid., 239, 247–48). "If vigilantism and annihilation are the alternatives presented in the crime novel, the political novels are altogether bleaker in outlook, for they present no viable alternatives whatsoever. When the public and the private have been merged [through corruption], the damage cannot be undone; no basis exists for order to emerge from disorder; no social precipitate can organize the chaotic Nigerian mixture. This is the starkly pessimistic picture" (ibid., 256).

The writers' despair over the irrationality of Nigerian public life is, as Griswold understands, the mark of a particular class fraction, and she has a section called "The Glamour of Impotence" about the masochistic satisfaction the authors sometimes take in their alienation. The Surulere-based independent film producers are generally nearly as educated as the novelists Griswold studied (she deals with all novelists, not just the literary elite), but they are less self-consciously intellectual and less tied to literary culture. The educational level of video distributors is decidedly lower, as the producers like to complain, and, on average, so is that of the audience.

Partly as a consequence of these class differences, on the whole the mood and position of Nollywood is different from those of the novels. (Biodun Jeyifo (1984, 127) similarly contrasts the anomie of Nigerian literary drama with the traveling theater's nomic disposition.) Griswold remarks that the most common scene in Nigerian novels is the traffic jam, as the symbol of everything that has gone wrong with the country (2000, 120). While Nollywood is certainly not blind to what has gone wrong with the country, I do not recall ever having seen a "go-slow" in a film, while evocations of the romance of automobiles and even of Lagos traffic, especially on the freeways or at night, are ubiquitous. The films show a greater (though uneven) faith in institutions. Barber (1987) writes that African popular artists like to set themselves up as instructors in modernity for their slightly less educated audiences; this is in Nollywood's DNA, along with the wholesome nation building of NTA television serials like *The Village Headmaster*. For every thoroughly pessimistic film there is one that celebrates the rationality and beneficence of, for instance, modern medicine, and there are probably a dozen that resolve their conflicts satisfactorily through the agency of a diviner or a Christian pastor.

Nollywood, like other film industries, sees itself as a dream factory, and the more public character of film production and consumption encourages expressions of faith in society and discourages the private despair that seems to provide much of the novelists' motivation. In Nollywood criminals are invariably brought to book by the police or otherwise made to pay for their misdeeds. In the memo quoted earlier, the NFVCB head assumes this narrative closure, which indeed is listed among the censors' formal criteria, and complains only that the films tend to dwell on the period of the enjoyment of ill-gotten gains and may not punish the malefactors severely enough.

> Even though countervailing "positive forces" at times in the form of divine intervention based on religion or eventual enforcement of the law of the land invariably triumph over the "evil forces," the resolution usually takes too long to unfold and the retribution or "pay-back" meted out to the "villains" of the stories many a time falls short of expectations. (James 1999, 1)

Optimism is officially mandated in the semipublic form of the films; no one would bother to interfere with the private despair of writers.

But the decisive element in the contrast between novels and videos is the moralism of popular consciousness, not official pressure. This moralism is derived from many sources, including the lesson that concludes folktales, Christian or Muslim homilies, the ethics of school textbooks or village and family councils, and the conventions of television melodramas. The demand that the bad should be punished and the good rewarded is ferocious and felt in the bone. No one can pretend that this ethical imperative controls national politics, but it seizes on whatever it can, the way crowds in the street will beat thieves to death when they can catch them, venting their frustration at the general mess of their country. Typically political films do not encourage optimism about the chances of truly reforming society as a whole, but individuals and local situations are dealt with rigorously and severely, and this provides at least temporary emotional satisfaction. Despairing vigilantism of the individual may be the mark of Nigerian crime fiction, but the films celebrate vigilantes because, as McCall argues, they bear the hopes of a grassroots politics (2004).

IS NOLLYWOOD PROGRESSIVE?

One should not expect a simple answer. The films spring from the Nigerian situation and express it in many ways. They are knowing about their society, sometimes angry, sometimes complicit; as I have said before, Nollywood is a discourse, not a position. Many Nigerian commentators complain that the unremitting spectacle of bloody violence, occult practices, unrestrained passions, glamorous wealth, and ubiquitous corruption, which film producers produce because they calculate that it will sell, has helped to degrade the social fabric, encourage backward thinking, and create a generation of absolute cynics.

Hyginus Ekwuazi's survey of Nigerian students found they do not associate Nollywood with social change. Strong majorities think the films show that acts have consequences but do not show the society they want to have or the way to get there (Ekwuazi 2008a). The screenwriter and director Chike Bryan told me the genre of political films peaked and waned in the early 2000s not because of censorship or the preferences of filmmakers but because the public stopped buying political films. They found them "dry," he said. Nigerians have a remarkable capacity to put up with their situation. Outrage burns out. Corruption is so much a fact of daily life that people get tired of paying to see it on film. They go back to coping with their lives, watching their favorite stars in torrid love triangles for entertainment. "Siddon look" is what one does when watching a film.

Moreover, Karin Barber suggests, in Nigerian popular culture moral outrage tends not to stay focused on politics as a narrowly defined dimension because in this perspective the state and formal politics do not occupy a privileged position; the Yoruba traveling theater seldom directly addressed political matters more because of

> deep assumptions about the nature of power, action, and character rather than from mere fear of censorship or lack of interest in current affairs. . . . the theater practitioners did not feel that the really fundamental moral and social issues of life were concentrated in the actions of the state. . . . Deficiencies in the state were seen as a manifestation—almost a by-product—of a more general, shared moral condition, and it was to this condition that the lessons of the plays were directed. Social regeneration would come from general human moral activity and from people's responsibility for the well-being of themselves and their families or communities. . . . It is not so much that one [political or social] level *signifies* another as that all levels are equivalent in being governed by a single, common morality. . . . The theater's populist insistence that everyone is at bottom ruled by the same moral exigencies may not spell "subversion" or "resistance"—but it is profoundly leveling all the same. Politics, then, is a subcategory of ordinary morality. (2000, 302, 304)

Politics as an unprivileged extension of a broader morality explains both why political films emerged from so many different generic sources simultaneously and why the political genre tends to subside back into the broader film culture. This leveling morality speaks truth to power, if it perhaps does not encourage political organization, and it can take vehement forms like the "aesthetics of moral outrage" Larkin describes, which is designed to provoke an emotional, even bodily reaction against injustice (2008, chapter 6). Certain political topics and incidents will stir up this outrage, as did the prolonged national crisis of governance. It matters that Nollywood has developed the capacity to express an outraged direct response to politics through this genre it has created. We cannot dismiss the passionate earnestness and the direct address to the audience as citizens expressed by, for example, the jacket copy of Lancelot Imasuen's *Dying for the Nation* (2001):

> It is now crystal clear that the operators of politics do not uphold their campaign promises and avowals. . . . But then you as you are can bring about a quantum and monumental turn around of the structurally, politically, religiously, socially, economically and morally bankrupt, ailing and sick Nation. How does what you do now contribute to the growth and sustenance of the nation's building elements and components? . . . Dying for the Nation. . . . brave it up now!

CHAPTER 9

Comedies

THE NEW MILLENNIUM: RISE OF THE MARKETERS

Fundamental shifts occurred in the Nollywood film industry around 2000 and shortly afterward. The most visible was the migration from VHS cassettes to video compact discs as the basic medium for Nollywood films. This transition was driven by the enormous quantities of cheap used DVD players being imported into Alaba International Market on the southwestern edge of Lagos, an important hub of the international trade in used electronic goods (Miller 2012). Alaba electronics marketers moved into the movie business as agents and rivals of Idumota Market on Lagos Island, the original center of film financing and distribution. Alaba businessmen form consortia to finance some of the most expensive Nollywood films, but for the most part they act as distributors for films financed and organized from Idumota.

Onitsha marketers also increased in number and importance. The numerical increase is partly explained by the apprenticeship system. Young men are apprenticed by their families to a marketer, normally for seven years, at the end of which their master provides a sum of money with which they set up their own businesses. So new generations of marketers are constantly spawned whether the industry needs them or not. Possibly an absolute majority of all Nollywood marketers are former apprentices, or former apprentices of the former apprentices, of one Onitsha marketer, Osita Okeke (called Ossy Affason after the name of his company), now a benevolent, humorous elderly gentleman, who began distributing phonograph records in the 1950s. Until recently nearly the whole film business in Onitsha was gathered in one building, 51 Iweka Road, a big structure of tiny concrete cubicles, each occupied by a marketer. When the authorities evicted the marketers from this building they settled in a strip of shops visible from the main east-west highway across southern Nigeria just before it crosses the Niger River. As this road enters Onitsha, the traffic takes on the character of the city: it snarls in gratuitous eruptions of eddying chaos, wedges of vehicles plowing aggressively up the wrong side of the divided highway amidst an incessant hurtling, clamorous jockeying for position.

Across the long bridge, Asaba is much calmer. Asaba is also an Igbo city, but the Igbos west of the river have a strong sense of a separate identity, speaking a distinct dialect and shaped by a history of living under the shadow of the Kingdom of Benin. "They are a completely different people," the receptionist in my Asaba hotel said of his rowdy cousins across the river, clearly finding comfort in the distinction. When in 1991 the old Bendel State was divided into Edo and Delta States, Asaba became the capital of Delta. The administration of Governor James Ibori (1999–2007) was astonishingly corrupt (a colorful saga ended with Ibori's arrest in Dubai on an Interpol warrant and his incarceration in a British prison), but while in office, his state flush with oil money, Ibori laid out an ambitious infrastructure for the new capital. Those profiting handsomely from the state government built pleasant neighborhoods of villas, and Onitsha traders built palaces where they could enjoy the low-key liveliness of Asaba, away from the tumult of the city where their money came from.

By 2005, Asaba had become an important location for film productions. By 2013, something like half of all Nollywood films were being shot in and around the city. Many films are still made in Enugu, but Asaba is cheaper, quieter, less crowded, and somewhat less beset by kidnappers targeting Nollywood stars. The Onitsha marketers who fund many of the films can easily keep an eye on productions. A number of Idumota marketers, who were from the East originally anyway, moved their families and main offices to Asaba or Onitsha while maintaining a presence in Lagos. Directors like the "clean frames" Asaba offers, free of the clutter of Lagos streets, and outlying villages offer convenient rural locations. It is easy in Asaba to create images of the Nigeria most Nigerians dream of living in: clean, orderly, low pressure, prosperous, with comfortable houses set amidst refreshing greenery and small cheerful commercial centers with convenient parking.

The eastward shift in the center of gravity of Nollywood increased the power and influence of the marketers. In 2001 they decreed a two-month moratorium on movie production, supposedly so that the industry would have time to reflect and reorganize itself. It was clear they simply wanted time to sell off the backlog created by the overproduction of films; they continued to make profits through the break while the rest of the industry went hungry. In 2003 they dealt decisively with an attempt by independent producers, the Filmmakers Cooperative of Nigeria, to set up a parallel distribution market in Surulere. They tried to demonstrate their new muscle again in 2004 with the blacklisting of some of the biggest Nollywood stars. They sometimes cited bad behavior on the set, but the main motivation was to control the fees the actors were demanding. This did not work, as the actors had the nature of the movie business on their side: their faces sell films, so they are indispensable.

Evolving technologies aided this shift in power. Video cameras became so good that it was possible to think anyone could operate them and that the art of lighting was largely unnecessary. In the early 1990s there were just a couple of editing and postproduction studios, located in Surulere. A decade later, it was cheap to buy a powerful computer and easy to run the software to do such work. Marketers would apprentice someone, perhaps a nephew, to a Lagos editor and then set him up to work independently in Onitsha. They could do without the expertise and the social and professional networks of Lagos. As the apprenticeship system continued to generate marketers, there began to be truly a lot of them, many of whom felt demystified about the processes of filmmaking and were eager to try their hands.

The result was a sharp increase in the already astounding numbers of films being produced, reaching a climax in 2007. Quality decreased because budgets shrank, each film being expected to sell badly in the context of the glut; because the pace of filmmaking accelerated to a frantic extreme; and because filmmaking was deprofessionalized as the marketers called the shots. Production crashed immediately afterwards as the result both of a crisis of unsustainable overproduction (Jedlowski 2013) and of the conflicts over the NFVCB's new framework for film distribution (discussed in chapter 2).[1]

The established independent filmmakers were of course unhappy as power shifted away from them. They and their films got lost in the flood, and turning any kind of profit was difficult. Their denunciations of interlopers and the general quality of films after 2000 strangely echoed the complaints of the celluloid filmmakers when video films first appeared a decade earlier. The independent producers had never liked dealing with Idumota (see, for example, Novia 2012), but they were accustomed to some deference for their creative talent. From early on there had been complaints about marketers killing films they did not like, imposing casting decisions, and occasionally offering unwanted story ideas, but for the most part they were not involved in the creative process. The great exception was Nnebue, and then, to some extent, Ojiofor Ezeanyaeche (OJ). When he first became involved with Nollywood, OJ was very young—in his mid-twenties—and he loved the movies and hanging out with movie people. According to a couple of sources, at this point he could not read or write (Novia 2012, 21). (He learned and—like Nnebue—eventually took some university-level courses.) In 1999 OJ gave himself the story credit for *Igodo*, which many understood as a gesture to impress his friends rather than as a claim to take seriously. He would go on to try directing, with ample help from an assistant director, another thing marketers were doing (or claiming to do) for the boasting rights. In the new millennium, other marketers grew more assertive about using their own story ideas and about acquiring or creating screenplays through their own networks.

Nollywood is essentially one dispersed system, without internal barriers. Important marketers normally have offices in Idumota, Alaba, and Onitsha, any of which may be the main one. The most common single model for a Nollywood film would begin with a deal made in Idumota between a marketer and a producer; a Surulere-based director and Lagos stars would be signed on; and the actual production would happen in Asaba or Enugu, drawing on actors and technicians based there.

But at the poles, one can construct quite different models of Lagos and Asaba films—people talk, in fact, of "Asaba films" as a distinct product line, the low end of the market. Bond Emeruwa estimates that at the end of the 1990s there were about sixty working movie directors who had experience in television and a television-derived sense of dramatic structure. Most of these directors were and are based in Lagos, and they formed the Nollywood establishment. Their screenwriters and actors are likely to be university graduates, quite possibly with training in a theater arts department and experience performing literary drama. The big stars are likely to make frequent television appearances, and they may earn much of their incomes as brand ambassadors for telecoms companies or breweries (see the postscript). A few producers try to get financing through corporate product placement. Producers will create a trailer and get it shown on television, probably in exchange for the rights to broadcast an old film. Their publicity repertoire may also include a premiere in the fanciest venue possible and paying for favorable coverage in newspapers, in the many celebrity gossip and fashion magazines, and in the influential blogs. The movie may be entered in the proliferating film festivals and awards competitions. Profits from VCD sales will be supplemented by sales for terrestrial and satellite television broadcast and Internet distribution. The producer may travel to New York (perhaps also Washington and Houston) to sell North American rights to distributors there. In these ways the average budget of $60,000 to $85,000 is recouped and, with luck, a profit is turned.

In the case of the paradigmatic Asaba film, none of this may be true.

FIGURE 7. On the set of an Amaco production near Asaba, with Nollywood stars Mercy Johnson and Chiwetalu Agu

An average budget is $20,000. An Onitsha marketer puts up the money and the film is shot across the river in Asaba, on a compressed schedule. It then immediately goes into the Onitsha VCD marketing system, sales driven primarily by the faces of the stars on the jacket, word of mouth, and the recommendations of vendors, many of whom are street hawkers working traffic jams. On location in Asaba, no one knows the name of the film they are working on except the producer: titles are carefully guarded secrets because catchy ones will be pirated and slapped onto another film before the one being shot can get to market. The actress Precious Kalu told me that sometimes people will stop her on the street and tell her they have seen her in such and such a film. Thus provided with the title, she goes to the market to look for it. But mostly she never sees the films she has acted in or learns their names. There is just the flow of work, for her, and a flow of entertainment for consumers.

The Asaba and Onitsha-based industry people I have talked with[2] admit that almost no one there has professional training, but they point out that they work incessantly and their immense on-the-job experience can at least sometimes produce results as good as that coming from more credentialed professionals. This is true. But in spite of the skillfulness and talent of individuals, this mode of filmmaking, based in apprenticeship rather than professional training, tends to have natural limits. Its practitioners work predominantly from imitation of existing examples rather than from first principles, hence the extremely repetitive quality, even by Nollywood standards, of Asaba films. The most notorious hallmark of Asaba films is the habit of extending them into multiple parts—commonly four, frequently up to six—forcing customers to pay several times for what might have been one movie. The scripts are not substantial enough to sustain such a long form, so the films are shamelessly padded with, for instance, long takes of cars being parked and people getting out of them. A producer who envisions sale to broadcast television or Internet streaming would hesitate to create such an unwieldy package.

COMEDY, NEW AND OLD

This period of structural transformation in the industry around the turn of the millennium was fertile in the creation of new genres, like those surveyed in the last chapters. Shortly after 2000 comedy films began to be spoken of as a new thing, though comedy was certainly not new in Nigeria. What people meant was that comedy suddenly became hot commercially and so began to be thought of as a major film genre among the others. Why at this moment? Nkem Owoh ("Osuofia"), the greatest Nollywood comic actor, had come into his own. He was joined by John Okafor ("Mr. Ibu") and by Chinedu Ikedieze ("Aki") and Osita Iheme ("Pawpaw"). The last two made a sensational entrance with their 2003 film *Aki na Ukwa*. Iheme and Ikedieze were in their twenties, but both are dwarves and appeared to be about ten years old. In their early films—they have appeared together many times—they played mischievous or strong-willed children. Later they took on adult roles—in *Boys from Holland* (2006), as we shall see in the next chapter, one is a drug dealer and the other a film producer. Their size is ironically ignored as they deal with women and threaten physical violence. Audiences enjoy their confidence and effrontery. But it was as children that they first made their mark, and children identify with them. Kids also love the clownish John Okafor. For the first time, Nigerian children found something in Nollywood they felt was for them. They pestered their parents to buy comedies.

And then it turned out there was a whole full roster of comedians who could carry a movie and sell it: Sam Loco Efe, Patience Ozokwor, Charles Awurum, Charles Inojie, Chiwetalu Agu, Amaechi Muonagor, Okay Bakassi, and more. A lot of them, including Owoh, Okafor, Iheme, and Ikedieze, are, coincidentally, from Enugu, giving a certain regional flavor to the recent efflorescence of comedy.

But the Nigerian comic tradition could not be wider, deeper, or older. In the Igbo masquerading tradition, as in others, young men perform comically for fun and entertainment—at Christmastime, they are out in every village and town soliciting money. Before the more serious masks come out during festivals, younger masqueraders perform satirical skits that chronicle the life of the community and target enemies of the community's values and well-being: thieves, adulterous women and shrews, the power hungry and hypocrites.[3] Carved masks from all over Nigeria demonstrate a rich tradition of stereotyping "strangers"—other Nigerian ethnicities, or white men and their local agents. All this flows into film comedy. Comedy was integral to the Yoruba traveling theater and to the forms it grew out of: *alarinjo* masquerading, concert party, vaudeville, variety shows, blackface minstrelsy, British Christmas pantomimes. The foundational television serials—*Village Headmaster*, *Masquerade*, *Basi & Company*—were situation comedies.

Comedy shadowed Nollywood from its inception. The history of Nollywood as it is usually told begins with the urgently serious *Living in Bondage* and proceeds through other dark and melodramatic genres that had little room for comic relief. But since comedy can be the most minimal of genres, requiring nothing but a funny man and a camera, it quickly leaked into the cheap new medium. Yoruba traveling theater actors like Baba Sala (Moses Olaiya Adejumo) and Big Abass (Ade Ajiboye) crossed over onto video immediately. Before *Living in Bondage*, Mike Oriehedima and others in Onitsha made short slapstick comedies in Igbo that were dubbed onto hand-lettered VHS cassettes and sold to traders, some of whom, like Ossy Affason, would end up in the movie business.

THE ROGUE

Antic roguery has always been central to the Nigerian comic tradition. In my first essay on Nigerian films, I described the character of Baba Sala in the following way:

> In *Agba Man* Baba Sala is a businessman who spends his time chasing girls and jealously trying to prevent his son and daughter from having romantic relationships. As usual Baba Sala is both miser and lecher; all his relationships with women are based on hard-nosed negotiations over how much sexual favors

> will cost. . . . [H]e keeps up an endless comic patter, but in an atmosphere of slapstick farce and fabliau-style intrigue, the cruelest forms of comedy. . . . (Haynes 1995, 110–11)

To a remarkable degree, this description fits the personae of other major Nigerian comedians, including Nkem Owoh and John Okafor. Roguery is not restricted to comedy, either, as shown by Baba Wande's part in *Ti Oluwa Nile* and Nnebue's antiheroes in *Dirty Deal* and *Rituals*. The rogue has deep cultural underpinnings, overlapping with the trickster figure. Trickster tales are a central form of folklore, such as the Igbo stories of the wily tortoise. The tricky Eshu is one of the most important gods of the Yoruba pantheon, crucial to human beings because of his role as intermediary with the divine—he must be invoked at the start of sacrifices and divinations. In one of the best-known stories about him, he walks through a town wearing a hat that is red on one side and black on the other. A fight breaks out between people who claim the stranger was wearing a black hat and those who say red; the god walks away laughing as men kill each other in his wake. The trickster is funny, but not in a comforting, lovable fashion. He embodies a fundamental but unsettling metaphysical apprehension and functions heuristically as a practical satirist.

PIDGIN

Comic fooling in indigenous languages and with strong local roots popped up on video immediately and will doubtless prove to be the most indestructible kernel of Nigerian film culture. On Nollywood's transethnic national level, comedy is inextricably linked with Pidgin.

Pidgin is pregnant with laughter to the point that in Nigerian discussions of its potential as a literary language people sometimes say it won't do for serious subjects because the reader will perpetually crack up at its pungent expressions. But Pidgin has seen pain; born in the slave trade, it is the tongue of "suffaheads." It is associated with "gisting"—with getting to the gist, the heart of a matter, the truth underneath pretentions and fancy words.

Pidgin began as and remains a contact language, spoken wherever Nigerian ethnicities meet. (Or, rather, where southern Nigerian ethnicities meet. Among northerners, Hausa serves as the lingua franca.) It is common, not exotic; it serves for everyday commerce and as the medium through which lower-level government functionaries communicate with the public, the language of police stations and army bases, of the drivers, mechanics, and food vendors gathered beside the national roads. Profoundly unofficial, it thrives in the nodes of the nation state. Pidgin's association with the lower classes and various kinds of inferiority make some Nigerians feel the same kind of shame towards it that some African Americans feel towards Ebonics (which is historically related to Pidgin). But it is also engrained in the elite on the deepest emotional and social levels. It is the language of sex and of frank discussions of relationships, tending to threaten the atmosphere of romantic courtship. Universities, another multiethnic node of the state and national culture, are awash in it—senior staff clubs as well as student hostels. Masters use it with servants but also with their most intimate friends at the most intimate moments. For that matter, it is a sign of intimacy with servants, of the incomplete process of class formation.

Pidgin is a strong example of what Mihkail Bakhtin calls "dialogism": the language is hybrid, always suggesting an opposition between cultures and social classes and associated with a critical point of view that is lower, more basic, pungent, humorous, and probably more truthful than official, respectable language (Bakhtin 1981). This perspective is associated with the grotesque and with what Bahktin calls the "lower bodily stratum"—the basic bodily functions of feeding, sex, and defecation, a world of bellies and buttocks, of hunger and drunkenness (Bakhtin 1968).

CLASS TENSION AND GENERIC LOCATION

Pidgin is integral, then, to a constitutive tension of Nigerian comedy: the opposition between the popular and the elite. A film like the Sam Loco Efe vehicle *The Prof and Den-Gun* (2007) has little on its mind besides playing "Grammar" (proper English) and Pidgin off one another, as a verbose and pretentious retired academic father and his son (who for some reason speaks Pidgin exclusively) chase the same gold digger. The Pidginphone Nigerian sense of humor is so strong it is tempting to say it is everywhere, but it is not. Besides films like those examined in the last chapters that respond to acute anxiety and crisis, no laughing matters, many others—family melodramas, love stories, and tales of ambition—construct an image of middle-class or elite life that excludes the popular. But even these environments may be infiltrated by comic servants, perhaps a gateman who will not shut up and, like Eshu, maintains confusion at the threshold.

The tension between the popular and the elite is aligned with the other fundamental opposed pairs of African life: the rural and the urban, the traditional and the modern. But the alignment is very rough. Pidgin is, after all, fundamentally a response to modernity, created at the moment of first contact with Europeans and the beginning of Africa's insertion into the modern world economy and, like African popular culture in general, continuing to serve as a creative mediator between the foreign and the deeply African, the old and the new. Comedy feeds on topicality, the ephemera of the moment, but nothing seems more eternal, more worn to comfortable, threadbare familiarity, than jokes about sons of the soil returning to the village in this year's imported fashions.

Nigerian comedy's social center of gravity, then, is low, but like Pidgin (and unlike most other Nollywood genres) it is not identified with a particular location. Movement between locations, however, a comedy of displacement, is a fundamental theme and plot type: the tension between linguistic and cultural registers turns into narrative as a character finds him or herself in an unfamiliar environment and reacts comically. The most common form of this is a village bumpkin, often himself roguish, coming to the city, clowning around, and encountering a more sophisticated set of tricksters, as in Nkem Owoh's *Okada Man* (2002). Connor Ryan has discussed three Yoruba comedies built on this model (2013). Kehinde Soaga's early *Lagos Na Wah!!* (1994) imported much of the Igbo cast of the Enugu-based classic television serial *Masquerade* to Lagos, where their characters encounter others played by an equally famous set of Yoruba comedians, the Awada Kerikeri Group. The principle that organizes the resulting extensive fooling is not ethnic—no culture "owns" Lagos and the transethnic medium of the film is prominently announced by the subtitle, "A Pidgin Comedy"—but rather the distinction between those who know the ropes of the city and those who do not (Oha 2001). In later chapters I discuss examples of comic heroes plunged into environments of even greater sophistication and unfamiliarity: Europe in a couple of Okafor comedies and Owoh's *Osuofia in London* 1 (2003) and a university campus in Funke Akindele's *Jenifa* (2008).

The displacement can also run from city to village. In *Ikuku* (1995, 1996), discussed below, two sons of the soil have become thoroughly alienated from their roots, and both are accompanied by even more foreign wives—a theme taken up in another Owoh film, *Osuofia in London* 2 (2004), which also works the related hoary theme of the "been-to," the Nigerian who exploits the prestige of having been abroad by pretending ignorance of his native culture.[4]

PLOTTING

While a number of other Nollywood genres and the European genre of comedy are associated with a regular plot form, the Nigerian genre of comedy is not. The boy-meets-girl plot of European comedy was at first (in Greece and Rome) the vehicle for plays that actually centered on tricky servants and an array of ridiculous social types, before the plot form was overlaid (in the Renaissance) with romantic emotion. Other comic traditions of farce, miming, satire, and so on have attached themselves to this great vehicle. As I argued in chapter 4, this plot has a relatively weak hold on the Nigerian imagination. Roguery and Pidgin both discourage the association of comedy with romance.

In fact, Nigerian comedy is rather weakly related to plot at all. Comedies often have a minimal, episodic structure; the scene is the main unit, each one an independent comic set-up. Comedy, especially if in Pidgin, tends to be the last refuge of improvisation in Nollywood filmmaking.[5] Individual comedians cultivate their own distinctive repertoires of verbal patter and physical gesture: Charles Awurum's gaping vacancy as John Okafor's straight man, the extraordinary mimicry and wriggling pelvis of Kingsley Ogbonna ("Dauda") (see the brilliant *Holygans*, 1999), Chiwetalu Agu's habit of cracking everyone up at the end of a scene with a bit of ribaldry. The comedy genre lost some of its commercial edge by around 2011 because so many films did not bother to develop an interesting plot structure, complacently relying on the funny man in front of the camera. He was left to goof around without much to do, trusting to his verbal flow, bits of slapstick, and sparks struck off at random between actors. The audience got tired of the shtick. Above all, Nollywood comedy is a great stream of talk. Often this talk enjoys going nowhere in particular. "Broken English" splinters, diverts, and fumbles with words. Nollywood comedy is characteristically a comedy of aggravation, of quarrelsomeness, a torrent of abuse and an exchange of virtuosic insults that can be provoked by anything or nothing at all.

The synopses of many Nigerian comedies might cause them to be mistaken for another genre, and often the synopses would suggest they are anything but funny. Funke Akindele's *Jenifa* tells the story, grim enough in summary, of a village girl who goes to university, suffers repeated humiliations, prostitutes herself, flunks out, and becomes HIV positive (see chapter 11). But the audience is kept in stiches through most of it. Even money rituals can be treated comically. The success of *Living in Bondage* provoked *Devil's Money* (1994) by the venerable comedian Afolabi Afolayan ("Jagua"), who came from the Yoruba traveling theater tradition but, based to the north of Yorubaland, worked in Pidgin. Jagua sacrifices a little boy for village-style wealth: he holds forth at a palm wine bar and has toughs beat up people he doesn't like. The spate of films in response to the Otokoto horror led Baba Sala to dust off *Obee Gbona/ Hot Soup*, an old play turned into a film in 1997. Baba Sala makes comic attempts to perform money rituals sacrificing both of his wives and a stranger who turns out to be his son, but, because the babalawo recognizes the virtue of his first wife and Baba Sala's low-grasping nature, Baba Sala himself ends up with the calabash on his head, in need of rescue from the small crowd of sensible family and friends. The money ritual is just another unremarkable avenue for his greed to take. In Owoh's *Okada Man* the ritual theme is a passing bit, the mechanism for the protagonist, a village loser, to enter his new life as a motorcycle taxi driver in the city. He is kidnapped outside his village, but the ritualist to whom he is delivered divines that, if sacrificed, his body would produce only counterfeit money so he is dumped, disoriented, on the streets of Enugu.

Comic parodies of other genres are not uncommon: *Ibu in Campus* (2011) will sell because of the inherent incongruity of dropping John Okafor's village idiot into the campus film genre, where he will bumble around the fixtures of this particular generic landscape. More often, comedies share the same territory with another genre without parodying or otherwise relying on it, as Okafor's comedies set in Europe parallel the plot form and thematic material of other films about life in the diaspora. The generic parallels arise because genres form in reaction to common social tensions, creating fictions around them, revealing the fault lines in the social structure as iron filings align themselves around a magnetic field. The laughter of comedies lands like blows, or a salve, or an exhilarated tingling, on the same sensitive spots that in other genres release anxiety, floods of tears, or violence. And comedies are subject to the same demand for narrative and moral closure as other genres and so borrow from the same limited repertoire of conclusions.

For example, the early Aki and Pawpaw movie *Charge and Bail* (2003) begins with a classic village film conflict: an overbearing, physically imposing, and politically connected older brother claims land being farmed by his younger brother, assaulting him so that he ends up in the hospital with unpayable bills. He and his tearful wife are helpless, leaving their young boys to deal with the situation. The children begin childishly, knocking a bucket of water off the head of their cousin, the oppressor's son, and farting in his face. Earlier, defending the family's honor, they had scared off a young man negotiating with their sister by telling him she carried a sexually transmitted disease; now they are willing to take a cut of her profits to help with the hospital bills. They systematically explore the power structure of the village as they desperately seek succor. In repeated scenes, the assembled elders decline to help, laughing with condescending incredulity at the suggestion that they should part with any of their money. A Catholic priest, resplendent in white vestments, has a similar reaction, though expressed with smarmy hypocrisy. The boys are supposed to understand that power and money are a one-way street, flowing from the lower to the higher and certainly not in the other direction. Suspecting their uncle is the one stealing cassava from their field, they set a trap and catch him, netting some complicit elders too. The uncle is brought to justice in the police station, where our resourceful heroes produce a typed contract: they will drop charges if he agrees to pay the hospital bills and never enters the land again. The uncle is revealed to be illiterate—a final humiliation—but affixes his thumbprint as his nephews triumphantly lecture him.

We have seen these problems before—treachery from within the family, a village dominated by a corrupt elite—but here they are reduced to ordinariness and so made manageable, given the wholesome premise that the secular state apparatus will ally itself with energetic citizens to overcome local structures of oppression. Nollywood had been casting dark suspicion on this premise, as we have seen, but it dies hard, desperate faith in it being reinforced by the obligatory moralism of African storytelling.

NKEM OWOH

Nkem Owoh started in television in Enugu, working in various capacities—actor, writer, production manager, script editor—on landmark serials including *Things Fall Apart*, *New Masquerade*, and *Basi & Company*. A protégé of Chris Obi-Rapu's, he was part of Nollywood from the beginning, translating the English subtitles for *Living in Bondage*. The next year, in *Taboo*, Owoh played a town drunk. Marcus staggers about gesticulating, sometimes complaining of being lost. But he knows and speaks the truth about everyone: whose father took land by force, which elder's children are in shamefully low occupations, who takes bribes and has affairs, who has tried and failed to assassinate the igwe. Much of this he says in order to be bribed into silence with money or drink, openly offering to sell his political support and boasting of his power to throw the town into confusion. He clearly takes pleasure in insulting people and invites the audience into vicariously sharing the pleasures of shedding inhibition and revealing the dark side of society. The part had originally been conceived of as a small one, but Owoh nearly ran away with the film.

Owoh's next big part was a serious one, as Odinaka in Amaka Igwe's *Rattlesnake*, another Igbo-language film (chapter 4). Odinaka is the wicked usurping uncle who kills his brother and takes over his wife, driving the young protagonist out of his house and into a life of crime. Odinaka is selfish, harsh, and domineering—elements incorporated into Owoh's comic persona.

IKUKU

In 1995 Owoh wrote, produced, directed, and starred in *Ikuku/Hurricane*. (Zeb Ejiro directed the second part, 1996.) This was the first important Nollywood comedy and perhaps the last important film of the initial phase of Igbo-language filmmaking. A village is being wrecked by a high wind because the high priest of the oracle Ikuku has died and not been replaced. A diviner (Chiwetalu Agu) determines the new priest must come from a certain family and excludes one of the two known males, Osuofia (Owoh), the town drunk, a part closely modeled on the Marcus of *Taboo*. A boy who will turn out to be Osuofia's illegitimate son is having visions of the deity, but until this is made known it is assumed the new priest must be Dr. Raymond (Zach Orji), a nuclear physicist who returned to Lagos from abroad at the government's invitation. He relocates to the village under protest and is comically unsuited to be a "fetish priest," as he calls it: he expects the oracle to have files and a bank account and puts on latex gloves to handle kola nuts. His wife, who has an African American accent, is even more lost in this environment, her curiosity leading to repeated violations of taboos: she sits on a sacred stool and it sticks to her, and so on.

Meanwhile other village institutions are also in crisis. The diviner is disgraced because the hurricane continues to blow in spite of his divinations and because his wife, proprietress of a beer parlor, is sexually wayward and a harridan. The igwe's son and heir has returned from New York as alienated from the village as Dr. Raymond, though rather than straight-laced and speaking fancy English, this young man's style is hip-hop. When his wife can't cope and disappears from the village, he disappears after her.

As in the much unhappier films surveyed in chapter 7, then, there is a metaphysical crisis of legitimacy linked to profound historical changes. But here the problem is cast in terms of culture and inheritance, not politics. Evil is not loosed in the land, only garden-variety corruption and foolish human nature. *Ikuku* is an example of self-confident cultural negotiation (Haynes and Okome 1998). The riddles are worked out in part 2, but part 1 already ends in celebration. The masquerades come out for the new yam festival, and the igwe dances joyfully with his people massed behind him.

Owoh will always be branded with the name "Osuofia," after his character in this film. He got so many offers to play town drunks in the following years that he started refusing the parts. Owoh is a fine actor with considerable range; in *The Master*, another major role (see Larkin 2008, 189–92, 213–14), he plays a quiet, humble family man forced by circumstances into a life of

419 criminal fraudulence. But he is strongly associated with the persona of Osuofia, whether or not he carries that name in a film. *Osuofia in London* softens the character, but he is still often not a nice guy. A typical comic rogue, he is self-centered, greedy, and scheming. He is domineering as well as irresponsible; characteristically, he is both at once. In *Ikuku*, as the town drunk he has made himself null socially, but his father took a title for him and he repeatedly (but unsuccessfully) stands on this status, trying for instance to make the waitress in a Lagos restaurant bend down as she serves him so he can look down her dress. In two scenes he takes an intrusive interest in young village women's sexuality, clearly prurient as he moralizes and warns them against lustful young men.

Osuofia is, above all, a talker, exceptionally voluble even in this voluble tradition, words streaming forcefully out of his collected mien. He plays with language and uses it as a weapon, jabbing, probing, overwhelming, a master of the novel insult—again, he is both irresponsible and domineering. Owoh is also capable of brilliant physical comedy, as in his mimicry of how the British walk in *Osuofia in London* or his exuberant dancing in the music video made to accompany that film, in which, like the igwe at the conclusion of part 1 of *Ikuku*, he leads a crowd as the village champion, the one who has conquered the land of the white man. Subversive decolonizer (Okome 2013), he also plays to the hilt the role of "been-to," exploiting the prestige of his foreign trophies, bowler hat, and white wife. Owoh frequently plays around the distinction between high and low culture, between affected "Grammar" and Pidgin, and he plays both sides. He exploits the browbeating made possible by cultural superiority—in the minor film *Made in Cambridge* (2007) he is an academic lording it over a rural campus until it revolts against him. But he is most himself as an actor when he is playing both sides at once. He loves the pretentions of a hick and very local tyrannies—claiming dominance, but in the context of a hierarchy in which he is low or marginal.

In 2004, in the wake of *Osuofia in London*, Owoh was reported to be making around a million naira ($7,000) per film—almost as much as Richard Mofe-Damijo, the highest-paid actor of the time, the heartthrob of *Violated*, a suave and classy cosmopolitan with extravagantly clear diction. A decade later, the reigning actresses were a similarly contrasting pair—two faces embodying the two directions in which Nollywood faces. Genevieve Nnaji is a beauty fit for international fashion magazines, who carries on her slender shoulders the hope of Nollywood crossing over into Hollywood; Funke Akindele is the sturdy, boisterous village champion, rooted in broad farce.

VILLAGE COMEDIES

De Prof (2006, directed by Charles Inojie) and *The Last Messiah* (2007, directed by Moses Ebere) are both built around Nkem Owoh. They are not particularly famous films, but precisely their typical, unpretentious, workaday quality, the maturity of their themes and points of view, and the genial sense that they are utterly at home in their skins are evidence of Nollywood's depth and strength as a cultural form. These are village films, and they seem to emanate directly from the village (in fact they are produced close by, out of the Enugu regional filmmaking infrastructure), but they are far from being a naïve folk art: the craft of the actors is polished and there is a quiet professionalism about the filmmaking. Undistracted by the flashy side of Nollywood, this kind of film is committed to the real life of the majority of the population, who live in villages or remember them intimately and feel villages are where Nigeria's heart and soul still are, who hardly bother to dream of escape to an urban mansion.

Like *Ikuku* and *Charge and Bail*, both films play around the themes discussed in chapter 7. Perhaps village films turned to comedy partly because the national mood shifted a bit after the end of military rule—none of the fundamental, structural problems were solved, but some things got better and people seized any chance to cheer up. More important is the shift in generic perspective itself. This is what genres are: a way of looking at the world, so the same world looks different when cast in another set of terms. The resilience that kept people going through the worst of times finds generic expression in these comedies. This laughing resilience allows the village to deal with, absorb, and even love Owoh's hard character. The comedian plays the problem, not the solution.

THE LAST MESSIAH: SHRINES AGAIN

The Last Messiah, like *Ikuku*, turns around the question of who will succeed to the priesthood of a village deity. The deity is immediately established as righteous and effective, striking down a man who has come to the shrine seeking to kill someone else under false pretenses. The priest, Uzondu (Fabian Adibe), is principled and unselfish, serving the community and the goddess, not himself. Owoh plays the priest's stuttering nephew Omaliko, whom we first see in the city quarreling violently with his wife and failing to support his family. He returns to the village, where he observes that his uncle is failing to turn a profit on the many big men in their big cars who come to the shrine. In part 2, Omaliko has the priest of a neighboring shrine (who agrees with him that "oracle business is a real gold mine") strike his uncle down (he survives, bedridden) and instruct him in the priestly arts so he can take over the shrine. The film's theme song expresses the changes Omaliko introduces:

> New management: you notice
> no payment, no service.
> In this life, nothing stays the same;
> tradition must change.
> Our village juju don incorporate.

Omaliko acquires a corporate advisor who sets herself up as secretary to the shrine. The jokes are similar to the ones in *Ikuku* when the oblivious nuclear physicist Raymond becomes the shrine priest, but there's a much sharper edge: the Okija shrine scandal of a couple of years earlier is invoked by the ledger in which she writes the names and addresses of clients and by the huge sums of money demanded for services, along with the whole theme of the shrine being hijacked for personal profit.[6] The secretary drives off a woman whose child is having convulsions because the mother cannot pay the extravagant consultation fee.

By part 3, the jokes about modernization have receded and we just watch how the shrine operates, the plot opening up into tangential stories. Omaliko is always browbeating people into paying up. He is comically persistent and his verbal assaults are studded with amusing insults, but mostly Owoh is not playing for laughs. The humor comes from the display of a whole range of human motives and the character people reveal when under pressure. Sometimes the shrine functions as it is supposed to, settling disputes, though Omaliko demands an unconscionable amount of money for the service. The centerpiece is a celebration Omaliko organizes for his mentor, the priest who struck down his uncle. The elders have reservations, but they are given drink until they are tipsy and say, why not? The full panoply of traditional culture is then brought out for display, including masquerades, and the big men who patronize the shrine get out of their big cars and dance their way to the high table. They are more or less bad, as far as we know them as individuals; the whole spectacle makes visible the mercenary society that has built up around the shrine. As in such scenes in Nnebue's films, all this is observed with silent mordant irony—"siddon look"—under the shadow of the predictable final revenge of the goddess through her revived true priest Uzondu. The film shows but does not waste time over this cleansing resolution: we know the gods fight their own battles, when they choose, and from the film's comic perspective it is inconceivable that the spirit presiding over the community would not defeat the attempt at greedy privatization and restore the common good.

DE PROF: ARRESTED DEVELOPMENT

If the village is felt to be the locus of spiritual and moral legitimacy, threatened and restored, thinking about the village is also based on the development agenda that is the unquestionable aspiration for nearly every African community: all villages wants roads, clinics, schools, electricity, and pipe-borne water.

The opening image of *De Prof* gives us the village as scene of development. The elders in their red caps are gathered in a roughly finished room; outside, we glimpse signs of recent earthmoving. Bona (Owoh) is running for local government chairman. This is the village democracy we hardly saw in the cultural epic: the red-capped elders are rooted in deep political traditions that feed into the structure of the modern state, as an old sense of community values and welfare feeds into the ideology of development. Bona introduces his younger brother Daniel (Clem Ohameze), who has just returned and wants to support the community. Daniel promises free education at all levels and pipe-borne water; everything he says is sound and reasonable, and the elders rise to their feet singing and dance out of the building. Where Daniel's money comes from is mysterious—someone will suggest money rituals, but Bona dismisses the idea and Daniel seems utterly virtuous. His largesse might stand in for several sources of development capital, such as subventions from the oil revenues of the federal government or remittances from abroad. It doesn't matter. The point is what goes wrong with the processes of development on the local level, and the film will show us much of what needs to be said on the issue.

First we are made to understand the nature of Bona, the elder brother and local politician through whom the project will pass, since Daniel lives in the city and now, he tells Bona as they leave the meeting in his SUV, he is tired and wants to go to his hotel. Bona is a conniving trickster, domineering and irresponsible like Nigerian politicians, a practitioner of politics as it is, which means "chopping" money meant for the public good. He sits with his friend Ekwedike (Amechi Muonagor) to discuss the situation. Exhilarated by the prospect of his brother's money, he's thinking of aiming higher than the local government chairmanship—perhaps the senatorial or gubernatorial, which will make him unimpeachable, not even chargeable or acquittable. The big official words are merrily thrown up in the air; having been told to count houses, he tries on the titles of chief census officer or chief demographic officer. Ekwedike petitions to be made his assistant. Conspiratorially, they plan to use the project to put something away for a rainy day.

Then, through Bona, we are made to see the community as a morass of irresponsibility and wickedness. "I know these people in the village better than you do," Bona tells his brother the idealist. Bona circulates through the village with a file folder and his sidekick to register families for the promised free education and pipe-borne water. Or, rather, he is looking for reasons to not register them, to hold down costs and (apparently) settle old scores. At the first house, they are appalled at the number of children who spill out for inspection, like circus clowns out of a tiny car: thirteen, living in two rooms. The father, besides his children engendered in the village, had lived in Cameroon and Kano and sired five children in each place by local women. He has brought them all home to take advantage of the free education. Bona argues that people like him, making "very very free with your manhood, flogging it up and down," would make the project unworkably expensive. Next an old man stops him, demanding to know why his house has not been registered. Bona dismisses him for not meeting the basic requirements of Igbo citizenship (building his own house—the man has inherited his brother's—and having children[7]) and then claims he is a ritualist, lost in the occult and guilty of dark deeds. Bona nimbly shifts the logic of his exclusions, exploiting the peremptory power of the bureaucrat with the file folder to claim that the citizen attempting to register always somehow fails to qualify. He stretches his fake reasonableness to absurd conclusions: the old man can have piped water if he builds a house in less than a week; lacking children, he may enroll in primary school himself. Bona tells the next man who accosts him that his house can't be counted because it is really a shrine, whose spiritual forces would burst the water pipes; he also accuses the man of being the father of an armed robber who cannot be let near the public good. The truth of these accusations, embedded in a fine stream of vituperation, is not clear, but enough of the shots seem to go home to inhibit romanticizing the village and its politics.

The elders revolt against Bona's obstructive antics and demand Daniel himself become chairman. The brothers fight bitterly. Daniel tries to buy his way out of the relationship by repaying Bona for having supported his education years ago. With this money in hand, Bona and Ekwedike go to the city, where they fall into the hands of 419 fraudsters who have created a fake government office in which a fake commissioner takes their money in return for a contract to collect bridge tolls. Bona is arrested when he tries to collect them. The village trickster has been tricked in town.

Daniel bails him out but Bona is not grateful. He stops sulking when Daniel announces he will step aside in the chairmanship election and support Bona with a huge sum of money, adding an offer to train his children. Daniel tells him to buy a fat white cow to be slaughtered in a reconciliation ceremony to let everyone know there is peace in the family. Bona is now on the best of terms with his brother, but the reconciliation, for Bona, does not extend beyond that tightest of circles: he refuses to reunite with his wife, leaves his own children to be raised by Daniel, and as the film ends is obstreperously lecturing and insulting his uncle and another elder who sits drinking with them.

The final reconciliation is bought at a high price. Daniel's decision to step aside so Bona can become local government chairman clearly sacrifices the public good for the sake of family unity. It is as if Daniel and Bona are colluding to turn this village film into a family film. We have seen that family drama infiltrates and exerts its hegemony over other genres treating public matters—epics, political films, crime films. In *De Prof*, the horizon remains that of the village film: till the very end the uncle and elders keep pointing to Bona's failures to live up to the values of the community, and Bona is glad to keep demonstrating his lack of respect for them. He will always be a problem, a bad citizen, an aging prodigal. Daniel's gestures of reconciliation do not bring the sentimental satisfactions of a normal family drama. Bona does not end up literally in the arms of his family. He is not that kind of person. But the family is right to close around him, so the film seems to say, with its unemotional lucid realism. Family comes first, the deepest underlying commitment, the bond of brothers more profound than emotional reward or the public good. Admittedly, this makes political change more difficult, and this is the film's final, sober, complicit step in the demonstration of how corruption continues to block development.

* Part 3 *

CHAPTER 10

The Nollywood Diaspora: Nigerians Abroad

The prodigious spread of Nollywood films around the world has been accompanied by the spread of Nollywood filmmaking around the world, as Nigerian actors and directors have traveled abroad to make movies and Nigerian expatriate communities have sought to express themselves in this essential form of modern Nigerian culture.[1] Perhaps twenty million Nigerians live abroad; they are a prominent element within Nigerian society, providing both practical succor and inspiration to those at home. The films set abroad are an extension of Nollywood in their direct derivation from fundamental conceptions and practices of Nigerian filmmaking and in their representation of life overseas, a crucial field of the Nigerian imagination. These films clearly constitute a genre (though it does not have a generally accepted name), with a typical setting, formal features, story arc, and moral and psychological themes.

The genre took off following the phenomenal success of Kingsley Ogoro's *Osuofia in London* in 2003 and Tade Ogidan's *Dangerous Twins* the next year. Other front-line Nollywood directors, including Lancelot Imasuen, Zeb Ejiro, and Chico Ejiro, along with too many of the major stars to mention, went abroad to shoot soon thereafter. In the same period, large-scale initiatives brought delegations of Nollywood filmmakers and actors to their fans in Britain and the United States, including the Filmmakers Association of Nigeria, USA, a project intended to organize the American market and encourage crossover projects; the NFVCB-sponsored Road Show in London; and the inauguration of the Nollywood Foundation's series of annual conventions in Los

Angeles, beginning in 2005, designed to build long-term connections between Nollywood and Hollywood. Two coproductions came of this networking: *30 Days* (2006), written and directed by the US-based Mildred Okwo, a film set entirely in Nigeria but reflecting an expatriate sensibility in various ways, including a central character who is visiting home from the United States, where he lives; and Imasuen's *Close Enemies* (2009), a Nollywood-style film shot in Hollywood with Hollywood equipment and support, financed by a US-based Nigerian producer.

Africans in Europe, North America, and elsewhere were at first supplied with Nollywood films in the most informal ways: travelers bringing them from home in suitcases and petty traders stocking African grocery stores and hair braiding salons. Then African (not necessarily Nigerian) distributors set up larger-scale systems for duplicating and selling films through video stores or (later) websites. The films were essentially all pirated; gradually, producers in Nigeria claimed some proceeds from such sales. The sale of discs is supplemented by irregular theatrical screenings and, since about 2012, has been eclipsed by Internet streaming and cable or satellite television broadcasting. These are at least potentially a more dependable source of income for producers. From Nollywood's perspective, foreign sales originally produced a mixture of interest, pride, and annoyance at the piracy, but no money, and so were essentially irrelevant, even as films set abroad established themselves as saleable commodities in the Nigerian market. After 2010, however, as the result of the shifts in the industry described in chapter 12 and the postscript, expatriate audiences became integral to the business calculations of "New Nollywood" filmmakers, who therefore have a structural reason to cater to them. Chineze Anyaene's *Ijé, the Journey* (2010), set in Los Angeles, broke box office records in the new Nigerian multiplex cinemas, but within a few years the novelty of the transatlantic theme had worn off and there was a perceptible danger of Nigerians at home feeling saturated by such films. The genre's history, then, has been shaped by typical Nollywood patterns of shifting and marginal economics, structural disjunctions, and flogging of successful models. But the commercial connection between Nollywood and the Nigerian diaspora will grow, and the social and emotional connection between Nigeria and its diaspora that Nollywood provides is deep and strong. Nollywood provides a way to share news and stories, to stay in touch, to maintain cohesion, to follow the dangerous fates of the emigrant bearers of their society's hopes and desperation, to understand the historical drama of the second great dispersion of Africans from the continent.

COLLABORATION

The desire to make films about Nigerians abroad has been apparent since *Glamour Girls 2: The Italian Connection* (1994). Soon a system was set up to actually shoot films overseas. The basic elements are one or more stars brought from Nollywood to add glamour and to make the film saleable in Nigeria and an expatriate host community that provides contributions in kind (actors, props, settings, hospitality) and funding by local African-owned businesses in return for having the businesses featured on screen.[2] These contributions allow the film to be made within a Nollywood-style low budget. The low budget is a strict necessity as the film will have to make its money back in the market for Nigerian films, although the producer may bank on a bonus from the host community, which can be expected to buy a number of copies of the film in hard currency and pay to attend screenings. The story often originates with an expatriate. Because of the circumstances of production, individuals may perform more functions in the filmmaking process than is normal in Nollywood: for *Man on a Mission* (2008), for instance, Romanus Ike Eze is the main actor, director, producer, story and screenplay writer, unit production manager, music editor, and rerecording mixer.

Within this structure of collaboration between the Lagos-based industry and expatriate communities, the impetus and resources for, and point of view of, a particular film are located somewhere along a spectrum. At one end are films like *Boys from Holland* (2006) and *Dubai Runs* (2007), both directed by MacCollins Chidebe, in which (as in *Glamour Girls* 2) the foreign location is a perfunctorily realized projection of the Nigerian imagination. The establishing shots of Dubai and Holland, including an aerial shot obviously outside a Nollywood budget, must have been acquired from a commercial film library; the rest of the sets are palpably Nigerian. The Yoruba-language film *Omo Eniyan* (2006) is indubitably shot partly in London but has only a sketchy interest in London as a source of wealth: the film's point of view is solidly rooted with the protagonists' families back home in Lagos.

On the other end of the spectrum are films like *Missing in America* (2004), written, produced, and directed by long-time New York resident Sola Osofisan, where the point of view is that of settled expatriates. Except for a few brief scenes the whole film was shot in the United States, and much of it has the character of a somewhat irritable letter home on the subject of all the mistakes and misapprehensions Nigerians suffer from when they try to come to America, burdening their expatriate connections in the process. Nevertheless, in spite of its cool gray wintry tones and slick New York imagery, *Missing in America* is clearly recognizable as a Nollywood film (see below).

The social and aesthetic integrity of Nollywood is spectacularly demonstrated in this genre of films. Tenaciously based in Nigerian popular culture, the diaspora films tend not to interact with the film cultures of their host countries to produce a hybrid Nollywood-British or Nollywood-German or Nollywood-Brazilian aesthetic, though certainly the Nollywood aesthetic itself has been heavily influenced by transnational media forms since its inception. The purpose of Imasuen's Hollywood-Nollywood coproduction *Close Enemies* was explicitly to take Nollywood to the next level of professional expertise; it did not aim at producing a culturally hybrid art form, and its themes of an infertile marriage and betrayal are quintessentially Nollywood.

Aesthetic and cultural boundaries may blur in the growing number of films like *Ijé* that began as the director's project at a foreign film school.[3] But even here, the situation is dramatically different from that of African filmmakers who go to Europe for training and remain there, depending on (and tailoring their art to) foreign funding and audiences.[4] There are Nigerian filmmakers abroad who are not at all part of Nollywood (including Biyi Bandele, Andrew Dosunmu, Andy Amadi Okoroafor, Nelson Aduaka, and Vigil Chime), but the ones considered here were always oriented towards careers in Nollywood or in some future version of Nollywood that they will help to create, and their films do not resemble the exilic and diasporic art-house cinema described by Hamid Naficy (2001).

The credits of Nollywood diaspora films sometimes show that technical personnel have been picked up where the film is made, but this seldom means a difference in the style and quality of filmmaking. (An exception, in this as in other respects, is *This America* (2005).) Invariably, some local foreigners are cast as actors, but they mostly seem to be nonprofessionals recruited out of the Nigerian expatriate communities' social networks. If they do have training as actors, their professional formation is overwhelmed by the Nollywood style of direction. Their performances are generally worse than those of the locally recruited nonprofessional Nigerians, since the Nigerians are steeped in the Nollywood aesthetic and therefore have an instinct for what to do. (Honorable exceptions include Simone McIntyre in *The London Boy* (2004).) The Nigerian expatriates who scout and manage the locations or provide costumes are all equally attuned to the Nollywood style.

The one film in my sample of movies made up to 2010 that does seem to cross over into another film culture is *Crazy Like a Fox* (2008), written, directed, and produced by Tony Abulu, who has lived in New York for many years. *Crazy Like a Fox* might be thought of as part of a trilogy of Abulu's films with transatlantic themes. *Back to Africa* (1997), the story of a beautiful African American looking for her African roots and the Nigerian father who abandoned her, is patently designed to appeal to an African American audience. *American Dream* (2006) is about a Nigerian's desperate attempts to get an American visa to visit a beautiful Americanized Nigerian with whom he has fallen in love; this film's concerns and much of its humor would resonate best with Nigerian viewers, like the extended hilarious scene in which the director himself plays an American consular official facing a series of applicants embodying familiar Nigerian ethnic stereotypes. *Crazy Like a Fox* is set entirely in New York, in a multicultural, upscale Harlem, and is shaped by the genre of black American erotica. Instead of an imported Nigerian movie star to headline the production we have Angel "Lola Luv" Fershgenet, an African American of Ethiopian descent who is a pinup model and figure in the hip-hop world. The crew is non-Nigerian, and while the credits include extras and secondary producers with Nigerian names and the script is discernibly Nigerian in its perspective on life in America, the film features only one African character (played by Karibi Fubara), a Nigerian who speaks Americanized English and has little of Nigeria clinging to him. "Tell me about Africa," commands his employer as she seduces him, but she and the film settle for an extremely perfunctory answer. The film is all about New York, apparently made for an African American audience, with a bit of exotic spice.

THE GENRE

Like other genres based on a setting, the diaspora film cuts across other genres: it includes comedies (*Osuofia in London*), tragedies (*Dangerous Twins*), and romances (*The London Boy*). It frequently incorporates or is continuous with themes and genres of films that stay at home in Nigeria but touch on the foreign. Crime films often involve drug dealing with an international connection (*Columbia Connection*, 2004) or 419 fraud practiced on foreigners picked up at the airport (*Dollars from Germany*, 2004). As already noted, the "been-to," the African recently returned from living abroad, is a familiar figure. OJ's *South Connection* (2004) is a concatenation of several of the themes having to do with the foreign that have been central in the Nollywood imagination, with the (then) novel twist that South Africa is the foreign source of exorbitant wealth for those with the stomach to do anything to get it. The film is always located in Nigeria, but it depicts the ardent desire of three ambitious young men to go abroad and the splashy return of the two survivors.

TABLE 2 Nollywood diaspora, table of themes

	Anchor Baby (Canada/USA)	*Black Night in South America* 1 & 2	*Boys from Holland*	*The Broken Pitcher* (USA)	*Coming to South Africa* 1 & 2	*Crazy Like a Fox* (USA)	*Crossing Paths* 1& 2 (USA)	*Dangerous Twins* 1–3 (UK)	*Dapo Junior* (Netherlands)
crisis driving Nigerian abroad		x							
visa and ticket problems	x							x	
airport sequence	x				x			x	
alienation/hardship sequence	x	x			x				
contact with African community		x		x	x				
advertising African businesses		x		x	x				x
discussion of cultural differences		x			x	x		x	x
crisis: money, courage, morality		x		x	x	x		x	
drug dealing		x	x		x			x	
prostitution		x							
other criminal activities						x	x	x	x
tourism sequence						x		x	x
shopping sequence		x			x	x		x	
romance with foreigner		x		x		x		x	x
romance with Nigerian			x				x	x	x
exploitation/racism	x	x				x			x
need to send money home		x						x	x
illegitimate demands from home									
betrayal by Nigerian intimates		x		x			x	x	
betrayal by foreign intimates	x	x				x			x
betrayal of foreign intimates		x						x	
arrest/imprisonment/deportation	x	x	x			x		x	x
establishment of life abroad				x	x		x		
return to Nigeria	x	x	x					x	
death								x	
direct cautionary advice	x				x				
Christianity				x			x		
non-Christian occult forces				x					
marital issues	x	x		x				x	

x			x							x									x		x			x			x		*Dubai Runs* 1 & 2
			x	x	x		x						x					x			x			x	x		x	x	*Europe by Road* 1 & 2
x			x	x	x		x	x		x		x	x	x				x	x		x	x	x	x	x	x			*Goodbye New York* 1 & 2
			x		x							x				x	x					x	x	x	x				*Home & Abroad* (Germany)
x			x			x	x		x				x		x			x	x			x				x			*Ijé, the Journey* (USA)
	x		x			x			x	x		x		x	x	x	x			x		x	x	x	x	x	x	x	*The London Boy* 1 & 2
					x		x			x	x	x					x	x		x	x		x	x	x	x	x	x	*London Forever*
								x					x		x	x	x			x		x	x	x	x	x		x	*Man on a Mission* (China)
			x		x			x		x	x			x		x					x	x	x	x	x		x	x	*Missing in America*
					x		x	x							x	x	x					x		x	x				*Mr Ibu in London*
										x				x		x	x							x		x			*A Night in the Philippines* 1 & 2
				x			x			x				x				x							x		x		*Omo Eniyan* (UK)
					x				x						x		x	x				x	x			x			*Osuofia in London* 1 & 2
x				x	x		x						x	x		x	x	x			x								*The Other Side of Life* (USA)
				x		x	x		x				x		x						x	x	x		x				*This America*
x		x			x		x	x		x	x	x		x	x				x	x	x		x	x	x	x			*Western Union* 1 & 2 (Germany)

Table 2 will I hope do much of the work of establishing the regularities of this genre. Themes are not counted on the table unless they are strongly present: hardship is talked about but not actually shown in *The Other Side of Life* (2003), for example. Some films show up in only a few rows because they concentrate so heavily on a couple of themes. Other films have narrative premises that set them apart from the standard story of a Nigerian struggling to live and make money abroad, obviating some of the typical themes and motifs, though others come roaring in.

The diaspora films follow the normal Nollywood pattern of repeating winning formulas, intensified by circumstantial factors: when a director or actor is abroad, he or she is apt to take advantage of the situation to work on several projects. So for example *The London Boy* and *Fateful Love* (both 2004) grew out of *Osuofia in London*. But—again, this is typical of Nollywood—actual remakes are unusual, and I do not attribute the remarkable similarities among my examples to imitation of some particular original, in spite of the inspiration provided by *Osuofia in London* and *Dangerous Twins*. Those two films are in fact atypical in their narrative framing. The similarities come rather from the persistence and extension of essential thematic complexes of Nollywood culture, a flexible cultural form that works in all sorts of environments. The films each seem independent and integral conceptions, with different things on their minds, from patriarchal anxieties about women's independent trading (*Dubai Runs*) to the spiritual direction of the Christian family (*The Broken Pitcher*, 2008), scary, devouring females (*Crazy like a Fox*), the triumph of romance over revenge (*Crossing Paths*, 2008), the Nigerian personality (*Home & Abroad*, 2004), or the question of whether a Netherlands-based drug dealer has sufficient cultural capital to marry a Nollywood star (*Boys from Holland*—he does).

REPRESENTING THE FOREIGN

The range of foreign settings is impressive: the United Kingdom and the United States, inevitably; Germany and the Netherlands, not surprisingly; but also South Africa, Dubai, China, the Philippines, and Brazil.[5] However, the films generally show a lack of interest in the foreign as such. The far-flung locations are not responsible for the important differences among the films, any of which could easily have been shifted to another continent (except for *This America*, which is centrally about the relationship of Nigerian immigrants to African Americans). There is little interest in the exotic for its own sake; the camera seldom wanders about foreign landscapes with a curious eye. In general, when representing the foreign Nollywood exhibits limited intentions as well as means. The Germans in *Dollars from Germany*, for example, are played by Nigerians of Lebanese extraction, with Nigerian accents. The lightness of their complexions is supposed to be an adequate signifier.

The films' establishing shots tend, as in Nollywood films generally, to be stereotypical rather than exploratory, moving us quickly to the interior scenes where nearly all the action and the talking take place. *London Forever* repeats, almost obsessively, the same iconic shots of Big Ben and red double-decker buses. *Goodbye New York* (2004) is careless about the image of New York it builds up out of library footage, including beaches and marinas that look suspiciously Californian. But in this film the very lack of integration between the establishing shots and the lived experience of the characters takes on ironic meaning: aerial footage of the solid, noble, sunlit spectacle of Lower Manhattan stands against the lives of the Nigerians whom we watch loafing and fretting through unemployment, tending bar, shoplifting, pimping and working as prostitutes, mumbling to one another in dim rooms. Shots of an American flag carried in a parade are spliced into scenes of rape and murder.

For obvious reasons the United States, Britain, and a generalized continental Europe loom large in the Nigerian imagination. Nollywood tends to be impatient with other kinds of foreignness. Naira, dollars, pounds, and euros are the only currencies mentioned, even when the films are set in Brazil or China. The police in Brazil (*Black Night in South America*, 2007) and in South Africa (*Coming to South Africa*, 2004) read suspects their Miranda rights as they arrest them, as in American police dramas. American culture overshadows everything: in *Mr Ibu in London* (2004), Ibu never shakes the idea that somehow getting to London involves going through the United States, and when deported back to Lagos, he flaunts American hip-hop style to advertise that he is a "been-to."

The films' narrative premises impose tunnel vision. Except in comedies, where the opportunity to travel abroad tends to tumble into the laps of the central characters, protagonists mostly leave Nigeria because of a more or less desperate need to make money. Sometimes we see the crisis that spurs them on; sometimes the films editorialize about the lack of opportunities in Nigeria through opening titles (*Black Night in South America*), voice-over narration (*Europe by Road*, 2007), or a montage sequence (*Man on a Mission*). In other cases, casual mention of the desire for a better life, greener pastures, or the golden fleece allude to what the audience understands perfectly well.[6] Wider and softer motives—curiosity about foreign cultures, love of adventure, a rebellious desire to wander, in short, the desire to travel for its own sake—almost never come up except in the comedies, and the harsh realities of life abroad for those without work permits, which is the situation of most of the protagonists, force them to pay undivided attention to the struggle to survive, get established, and if possible send some money home.

THE NARRATIVE ARC AND SET PIECES

Air travel itself reduces the journey to a few unremarkable hours, and the high cost of getting a permit to shoot in Murtala Muhammed Airport in Lagos (a tenth the average budget of a Nigerian film) and the daunting process of applying for permissions abroad often make the transition almost invisible apart from some standard library shots of planes taking off and landing and people coming out of terminals.[7] Characters are simply dumped into the foreign environment, a new city, where they have to make or keep social relationships in order to obtain food, shelter, and employment. The only movie I have seen that emphasizes the journey itself, *Europe by Road*, a harrowing tale of crossing the Sahara to Morocco and embarking on a disastrous sea voyage to Spain, was—paradoxically—clearly all filmed in Nigeria. Of necessity this film has no establishing shots of foreign cities, but its blinkered vision corresponds to the experience of the travelers, often moving at night, confined to the smugglers' route and safe houses, too miserable and terrified to think of anything but survival. They do not have the luxury of being tourists.

Most of the films have what I call an alienation/hardship sequence: the protagonists trudge disconsolately, carrying their bags, through the streets of the foreign city, unable to find a foothold and growing desperate. They rarely have contact with poor people in the host country. Coming mostly from the Nigerian middle class—poor Nigerians generally cannot even think of airfare and visas unless they are supplied by the organizers of a prostitution or drug-smuggling ring—they will collapse of hunger or cold on a shopping avenue or respectable suburban street, their clothes still immaculate, rather than find their way to a slum where accommodation is cheaper and the informal economy might offer work. *Man on a Mission* is unusual in offering us a brief glimpse of working-class life, but the emphasis is still on the gleaming tall buildings of the new China. *Dark Night in South America*'s São Paulo looks impeccably first world. We see no *favelas* or, for that matter, any Brazilians who are not of overwhelmingly European extraction. Such systematic erasures seem intended to keep the protagonists in visual relation to the desired life while emphasizing how difficult it is to attain.

Eventually the protagonists get established in the foreign land and are free to look around and enjoy themselves. What I call the tourist sequence places the protagonists in iconic foreign landscapes at a moment when they have "arrived." (Carmela Garritano calls such sequences moments of "cosmopolitan spectacle" (2013, chapter 4); see also Haynes 2003a.) These sequences are distinctive: plot movement is suspended, dialogue largely ceases, and the soundtrack music rises as the protagonists enter in their own flesh the world of travelogues and travel advertising. The images are as stereotyped as the establishing shots, to which they are related. The tourist sequences are formally similar to the hardship/alienation sequences, but the emotional polarity of the relationship between the figure in the foreground and the background is reversed from alienation and suffering to ecstatic identification and a sense of triumph.[8]

The tourist sequence often blends into a shopping sequence, in which the traveler is seen in the landscape of consumerism rather than tourism, giddily celebrating disposable income. Such scenes of "enjoying" are also common in films set in Nigeria; here there is an extra relish from being at a center rather than on the periphery of global consumer culture.

Usually there is a new lover on the protagonist's arm in both these kinds of sequences, so both blend into another familiar type, the romance sequence. *A Night in the Philippines* (2006), about a couple on a prenuptial honeymoon and worldwide shopping spree, invests heavily in all three types. The lover often represents relief from terrible loneliness and the promise of a new home. If the lover is foreign, the relationship takes on additional meanings: a successful relationship with the host country, a cultural and emotional adventure, the (perhaps ambivalent) prestige of consorting with someone with lighter skin. In the films that are most completely domesticated abroad and are most oriented toward expatriate audiences (*Crazy Like a Fox*, *Crossing Paths*, *The Other Side of Life*), romantic sequences take the place of tourist sequences.

MAKING CONTACT

To return to the narrative arc of these films: what the protagonists do, in their initial isolated desperation, is try to make contact with the African expatriate community. If they do not already have an address, they look for a neighborhood where Africans live, stopping black people on the street and asking if they are Nigerian and, if so, whether they will help. Someone eventually will, and from this point on the film will be principally set in the African immigrant community. Scenes will be shot in that community's shops and restaurants, sponsors of the film. The circumstances of filmmaking reinforce both the social horizon of the diasporic community that supports the film and the interests of the Nigerian audience at home to create a remarkably Afrocentric world. The official marrying a couple in the town hall and the doctor in an emergency room are apt to be Africans (*This America*). African American and Black British characters are often played by actors with Nigerian accents; actors that sound American or British may have Nigerian names. *Crossing Paths* carries this Afrocentrism to the limit. A collaboration by Nigerian and (mostly) Ghanaian US residents, it is set in an unnamed but clearly American space of McMansions and suburban offices (the credits reveal it to be a Washington suburb) that is populated almost exclusively by Africans. This fact is taken for granted: Africa and African identity are never mentioned, and no one talks of immigrating, traveling, or telephoning the continent.

The help the protagonists receive from the expatriate African community often comes with strings attached. In any case it is soon made clear that for an African immigrant without a work permit, the options are mainly selling drugs (for men) or prostitution (for women).[9] Sometimes they take menial jobs under exploitative conditions but are too ambitious to stay in them (*Man on a Mission, The Other Side of Life*), or the need to send money home is too great (*Goodbye New York, London Forever*), or both (*Western Union*), so they choose the faster track. This is a moment of crisis, discussed and dramatized at some length. The protagonists are shocked and dismayed at their options, having come from respectable backgrounds and never imagining that life would turn out like this.

CRISIS AND TRIALS

In spite of the foreign locations, we are on terrain that is familiar from, and central to, the general Nollywood tradition. If one is not especially interested in foreign cultures or landscapes for their own sakes, the social, moral, and psychological experience of landing in New York, London, or Hamburg is not terribly different from moving to Lagos from elsewhere in Nigeria. There is the same overwhelming first impression and the immediate need to find shelter and employment, which is bound up with the necessity to find a social network. Then one discovers that social networks follow different and treacherous rules in the intensely individualized and brutally competitive urban environment. Existing relationships are stressed to the breaking point. The protagonists move between extremes of hardship and glamor and suffer tests of endurance and moral limits. All this is shown in *Glamour Girls* 1, for example. Most of these issues are also in play if one is shaken out of one's familiar place in Lagos through loss of employment (as in *Shame*, which has memorable alienation/hardship sequences of walking the streets of Lagos looking for work) or through simple dissatisfaction with one's position, as in *Living in Bondage*. The scenes in which protagonists try to make contact with the African community abroad are genetically related to the frequently imitated scene in *Living in Bondage* where Andy runs into his old friend Paul by accident, which leads to questions about what he is willing to do for money and his introduction to the cabal that practices money rituals.

It is striking, given the importance of the supernatural and Pentecostal Christianity in other genres, that they are nearly absent from these films except for *The Broken Pitcher*, a collaboration between a church in Texas and the best known of Nigerian Christian video producers, Mike Bamiloye's Mount Zion Productions (Oha 2000; Ogunleye 2003a). Christianity figures to some extent in *Western Union*, *Crossing Paths*, and *London Forever*, and Muslim faith and culture are important in *Omo Eniyan*, but none of them contains anything like supernatural forces or spiritual combat.

So the central theme of psychological and moral trial as the protagonists come under extreme pressure in the foreign environment is usually put in predominantly secular terms. In the discourse on personality at these moments one can sometimes discern values and religious beliefs, common to the Igbo, Yoruba, and other cultures shaping Nollywood, that stress individual destiny, individual spiritual force, and individual dynamism and achievement as social values. These cultures are famous for sending people forth to realize and prove themselves and so are among the most far-flung cultures in the world. The two Igbo protagonists in *Coming to South Africa*, stranded and desperate, are lectured by an Igbo settled there as he offers them a way into drug dealing: "Every man has his own potential. You guys can make it on your own. . . . Are you willing to do whatever it takes to make money? If that's the case, I'll assist you." These values are not overtly ethnicized or traditionalized, however—there is no talk of an *ikenga* or *chi* or *ase*.[10] The idiom of the talk of realizing one's potential is more or less that of the self-help books that now crowd the shelves, racks, and tables at the front of Nigerian bookshops, a gauntlet one has to run to get to anything else, except that many of those books have a religious orientation that is remarkably absent in the films.

Sometimes there is a discourse of freedom, as in *Black Night in South America*: "This is not Africa. You're abroad: you've got the freedom to do whatever you want, however you want. The choice is yours." But this sense of freedom is always framed very tightly as a question of what one is willing to do for money and how much money one wants to have. In this example, a woman is counseling her sister to go into prostitution.

In their loneliness and isolation, the protagonists seldom find solace in making contact with home. Contact with home tends rather to remind them of the harsh necessity to make good in their situations on their own. *The London Boy* has poignant scenes of the protagonist calling Nigeria; he is understandably inarticulate in conveying the reality of London life to his family and is constantly confronted with urgent pleas for money that he cannot meet. The central character of *Western Union*, complaining to a friend about the pressures on him to send money home, is told: "You are right, this is why you are in Europe; you must live up to expectation. What they need from you is a constant flow of cash. This is Europe; you must make use of the only opportunity you have. . . . Get rich, or die trying."

Sometimes the protagonists honorably decide life abroad simply is not worth it, like the heroine of *Missing in America* who, in spite of what everyone assumes, came to New York to find her missing husband, not for a new life as an immigrant. In her final voice-over, she says, "It takes a special hunger to live in America as an illegal alien. I'm not hungry enough to live here like that. I'll go home where I have friends and family to help me raise my baby. America is a dream. For some it becomes a beautiful reality. For others, that dream is just a nightmare."

Europe by Road and *Coming to South Africa* develop the theme of struggling to get ahead in a social and moral void through a contrastive pairing of Nigerian friends who have come abroad together, one of them stronger, harder, more determined, readier to do anything than the other. In the latter film they both turn to drug dealing, but one pulls out while the stronger one stays in. It is not always clear where the first's weakness stops and his virtue begins, but the plot rewards him with a (white) woman, a job, and freedom after his brush with drug dealing, while the stronger one gets twenty-five years in prison.

The normal way of narrativizing the meaning of the moral crisis is by showing the consequent strain on kin, marital, or romantic relationships. This is, of course, the standard Nollywood procedure. Betrayal by intimates is the most prevalent of all Nollywood themes. What is special about diaspora films is that the protagonists are largely shorn of intimate relationships by virtue of their situation. But if they are married, there will be adultery (*Broken Pitcher*, *Dangerous Twins*, *Dubai Runs*, *Black Night in South America*, *Goodbye New York*). If they come looking for a missing spouse (*Missing in America*) or relative (*Black Night, Dangerous Twins*), they will find treachery. Some are betrayed by their families in Nigeria, who squander their remittances (*London Forever*, *Western Union*). A foreign lover or spouse may suddenly prove to be treacherous (*Dapo Junior*, *The Broken Pitcher*, *Crazy Like a Fox*, *Ijé*, and *Osuofia in London*, though in the last case she later redeems herself). As often, the Nigerian betrays a good foreign woman because of inordinate greed (*Man on a Mission*, *Western Union*, *Black Night*, *Dangerous Twins*). Betrayals of Nigerian lovers are routine.

It is worth stressing the extent to which these betrayals happen within the Nigerian community. The principal reason for this is the fact, already suggested, that the films are not very much interested in anything beyond the (extended) Nigerian community.[11] Racism appears surprisingly little in these films, though it is fairly often alluded to in passing as a structuring element in life abroad and is sometimes demonstrated by harsh police officers (a recurring theme in *This America*) or by those with depraved sexual interests in black bodies (*Black Night*, *Goodbye New York*). On the other hand, the films include a number of spontaneously generous white people, who are often betrayed or offended (*Home & Abroad*) for their pains. Only *Dapo Junior* puts white racism at the narrative and emotional center (Haynes 2003a). *Goodbye New York* is awash in bad feelings about being an African in the United States, concentrated in the relationship between a Nigerian and the African American girlfriend off of whom he lives. She makes him do things—fix her coffee, rub her feet—that affront his African masculinity, and he responds with a stream of insults and threats in Igbo, pretending all the while they are endearments. It is not at all clear that he has the moral upper hand.

This America, by the collaborative team of Oliver Mbamara, Bethels Agomuoh, and Felix Nnorom, is more deeply and systematically about the relationship of Nigerian immigrants and the African American community. The establishing shots are brilliant, but the film is never tempted to indulge in tourism, shopping, or romance sequences. Nigerian cousins, one settled in Brooklyn, the other newly arrived, both marry African American women in order to get green cards, and in both cases the relationship goes very wrong. Of all the films in this sample, this one is the least structured by Nollywood conventions, though it is rooted in an immigrant community in the standard way and Agomuoh is closely involved with Nollywood as the owner of the first Internet site selling Nigerian films. But *This America* is different from the others in many respects and so serves as an important reminder of the openness of the situation of the Nigerian diaspora and its potential to exert an influence on Nollywood filmmaking. One of its unusual features is that while the others normally contain a very brief and superficial discussion of cultural differences or make them an occasion for simple comedy, *This America* dwells on the subject from beginning to end. (The film is based on an unpublished book by Mbamara about the cultural situation faced by African immigrants.) Sometimes the situation is played for laughs—the newly arrived cousin cannot satisfy his simplest needs when he shops for food because what he calls "groundnuts" and "minerals," Americans call "peanuts" and "sodas." Because attention is evenly divided between the cousin who has adapted and the one who doubts he wants to adapt, there is no clear right and wrong as questions arise, such as whether a woman should be able to buy a man a drink. The African American society the cousins are faced with is not malevolent toward them, but they are shocked and endangered as they encounter its dysfunctions: gun violence, alcoholism, drug addiction, and what they see as carelessness about child raising and women's sexuality and fertility. The film simply watches and counts the costs of adapting to this utterly unromanticized environment.

THE NIGERIAN PERSONALITY: COMEDIES

Osuofia in London, *Mr Ibu in London*, and *Home & Abroad* spend most of their time watching comic Nigerians, entertaining masses of low motives and ignorance, goofing around and making fools of themselves in Europe—failing to understand indoor plumbing, waving at themselves in security cameras, and botching relationships with foreign women—but somehow nevertheless remaining the heroes of their stories and objects of affectionate, resigned identification for the audience. Irresponsibility is one of the essential elements in the images of the Nigerian national character that Nigerians have created for themselves, developed through countless newspaper editorials as well as through the rich panoply of tricksters and rogues in folklore and comedies. Nkem Owoh's Osuofia is a "bush" man, a villager, whose long-lost brother has died in England, leaving him an enormous fortune. John Okafor's Ibu is a poor, unsophisticated, and foolish security guard working at the Lagos port, who falls asleep in a shipping container and wakes up by the Thames. *Home & Abroad* is about two professional comics (one played by Okafor, the other by Victor Oswuagwu) who are invited to Germany to collect an award and perform. They bring on themselves the hardship/alienation sequence and the need to find Africans in the street because they miss their flight, get distracted by drink and a German lady on their arrival, fail to telephone the promoters who brought them, and do not show up at the awards ceremony. Similarly, Ibu doubles his hardship/alienation experience because he forgets the address of the first Nigerian who has taken him in off the street and needs to be rescued again by a second chance meeting with another Nigerian. Osuofia has to leave England in a hurry, pursued; in the other films, the protagonists are deported as manifestly unfit for life in Europe.

Europe is there as a reality to be faced and played with, but the relationships that matter are, as usual, largely with Nigerians. Osuofia's experience in London is shaped by his late brother and a Nigerian lawyer who conspires with his brother's British fianceé against him. (The lawyer feels his facade of assimilation slipping away in Osuofia's maddening presence). In *Home & Abroad*, the comics' fecklessness, childish greed, irresponsibility, quarrelsomeness, endless wheedling, geniality, humor, liveliness, and sheer force of personality are contrasted not with German rationality but with the rationality of the Nigerian promoters, who are based in Germany and operate according to European standards. They have invested ten thousand euros and their reputations on the awards ceremony, to which they had invited the Nigerian ambassador, and they are understandably furious when the comics do not bother to show up. The Nigerian community in Berlin (apparently deeply involved in the production of the film) is also represented by Lady Suru, whose African grocery store is heavily advertised. In the film, she is presented as an ambivalent figure at the center of an expatriate community prone to rumor, gullibility, and erratic swings between generosity, hypocrisy, and anger. In *Mr Ibu in London*, the key figure representing the film's point of view is Michael, a Nigerian who takes Ibu in for an extended stay and shows him the sights. Michael is motivated partly by sentimental reasons (Ibu embodies home), partly because he enjoys Ibu's comic reactions to London landmarks, and partly, doubtless, because Ibu's reactions make him feel superior, measuring how far he has come himself. But when Ibu makes unwanted sexual advances toward Michael's British wife, he is not amused.

All three films lavish attention on the theme of the "been-to." *Osuofia in London 2* is about the hero's triumphant return to his village. In *Home & Abroad*, before their departure for Europe the comics use the prestige of being "international" men, with passports and visas, to face down landlords and a police officer and to demand the admiration of their families. Their families keep at this game in scenes intercut with the men's German misadventures. The general Nigerian population in the film seems uncertain what a visa is, exactly, but is willing to be impressed. Similarly, in *Mr Ibu in London*, on his return Ibu finds an admiring audience for his implausible lies. The mood is gently satirical—not the kind of satire that is expected to change anything or carry a real message.

THE NIGERIAN PERSONALITY: *DANGEROUS TWINS*

The contrast and interplay between this familiar image of the irresponsible side of the Nigerian personality and the rationality of Nigerians who are used to operating in a foreign environment are at the center of Tade Ogidan's *Dangerous Twins*, the longest (it is in three parts) and richest of the films made abroad, which begins as comedy but quickly turns very dark indeed. Taiye, who lives in London, comes back to Lagos to see his identical twin, Kehinde. They are so much alike even their wives cannot tell them apart (Ramsey Nouah plays both parts). Taiye tells his brother he has not been able to impregnate his English wife Judy (Danielle Mobarak) and asks Kehinde to switch places with him to do the job. In London, Judy is taken aback but pleased by Kehinde's ardent lovemaking and extravagant presents, both so unlike the husband she is used to, and Kehinde makes his brother's business thrive by playing fast and loose with the rules. In Lagos, Taiye is too uptight to touch his brother's wife Shola (Stella Damasus Aboderin), who finds that this coldness outweighs the fact that Taiye likes to be a family man at home with the kids, while the husband she is used to was always out chasing other women. Taiye is shocked at the way his brother's business runs and sets out to reform it, firing workers who do not really work, getting rid of equipment he considers unnecessary, and refusing to pay bribes. (Akin Adesokan (2009a, 410) compares these austerity measures, imported from London, with the Structural Adjustment Program of the 1980s.) Morale suffers and, since Taiye's innovations are so at odds with the local culture, the business declines disastrously. In London, Kehinde succeeds in impregnating Judy, flies her around the world on expensive vacations, and, after the child is born, lies to his brother in order to prolong his new life. In Lagos, Taiye is vexed nearly to madness: he swelters in the dark when the electricity goes off since he refuses on principle to buy a generator, irritated at the neighbors' celebratory noise and furious that no one will listen to his brilliant business ideas. When his home is invaded by armed robbers, he escapes over the wall to call the police, who do nothing since their vehicle is grounded by lack of fuel and the power outage means they cannot phone their men on patrol. The robbers kill Kehinde's children and make off with all the family's money, leaving Shola hysterical.

This is all in part 1, which ends with a fine balance: Kehinde has stolen Taiye's life, and Taiye has destroyed Kehinde's. Taiye is rationality and morality, which do not reign in Nigeria—trusting law enforcement gets children killed. But Taiye has forgotten or refuses to know how to live there, a sexual and social failure and therefore an economic failure and a disaster to the family. In the later parts, he becomes a drug courier to return to England to reclaim the wife he loves, now a man of unshakable purpose, willing to get his hands dirty. Kehinde is full of the life force, sexy and fun, but also deeply irresponsible. In the later parts he completes his betrayal of his brother and goes on to betray Judy and various other women. Finally he is beyond unforgivable—a shell of a man, a compulsive liar and womanizer, a trickster who begins to be tricked over and over, condemned to endless systematic punishment.

If Taiye seemed in danger of losing touch with his society, the greater danger turns out to be Kehinde running off the rails into a moral, emotional, and social abyss. There is a danger in overestimating Taiye's alienation, in any case; he, like the Nigerian businessmen in *Home & Abroad*, may stand for rationality, but we should not simply identify rationality with foreign influence and the opposite with Nigerianness. The point is that Taiye and Kehinde are twins, both Nigerian, representing opposite sides of the national character. The film is ambivalent toward both sides and is extraordinarily inventive in turning this ambivalence into narrative.

WHAT THREATENS

The fact that Kehinde is seen as the greater problem reflects the thematic pattern that emerges from these films as a whole. The assimilation of Nigerians abroad to their foreign host cultures does not appear as a major threat. Nollywood films are not based on the discourses of authenticity and nationalism associated with celluloid cinema and with so much other officially sponsored cultural production in Africa (Meyer 1999a, 2003a, 2010a; Larkin 2008; Garritano 2008, 2013). African popular culture is comfortable with creolization and foreign trappings used as markers of African success and so is apt to react with pride to the sight of a Nigerian living a foreign lifestyle, at least as long as the Nigerian is sending money home. Diasporic communities have a sophisticated, lived experience of these issues. Still, it is remarkable how little the inevitable conflicts of assimilation are dramatized. One would think stories about children deserting the values of their parents would be ubiquitous, but there are only two examples in my batch of films: *The Broken Pitcher* briefly turns its attention to a teenage daughter who has begun meeting men in motels and asserts an American independent right to do so, and *The London Boy* is about the conflicts between the claims of a Nigerian couple's romantic love, situated in London, and the claims on each of them by their families back home. The film conducts a lively debate on the matter without coming anywhere near taking a position. The assimilation theme comes up most frequently in the form of shifting gender roles, either in a relationship with a foreign woman (*London Boy* again) or in a Nigerian marriage where the woman does better than her husband in the foreign economy and he is reduced to domestic labor in the home (*Black Night in South America*, *Goodbye New York*). Other films refer to missing persons, reflecting a concern that Nigerians abroad may get lost to their families, but cultural assimilation is not usually a prominent part of these stories.

The films are more worried about two other threats. One is simply the human carnage involved in the dangerous transition to life abroad. If there is one thing the movies agree on, it is that Nigerians need to be advised that acquiring wealth abroad is not as easy as they imagine. *Europe by Road* has the character of films made to discourage drug use or unsafe sex, luridly demonstrating the dangers of risky behavior to young people who might be tempted. The theme is sometimes directly expressed at the end of a film through a voice-over, a title, or a scene such as the one that ends *Goodbye New York* in which the protagonist, now back in Nigeria with nothing except very bad memories, advises a circle of young female relatives not to make the same mistake she made. But they do not seem to listen. The frequently sobering fortunes of the films' protagonists are balanced by the visible existence of a Nigerian community abroad, full of people who have made it.

The other threat is from within: that greed, fear, a social vacuum, and apparent necessity will lead to moral transgressions with devastating consequences. As I have been arguing, this is the central thematic of the Nollywood tradition as a whole. What the diaspora films see in the foreign is not primarily an occasion for adventure travel but the dangers of a moral holiday during which the thoroughly investigated dark impulses of the national personality can flourish. The moral logic of the diaspora films is Nollywood's, with the same need to punish transgression and the same ambivalence about wealth. In the denouements, the protagonists are suitably chastened if their strength has expressed itself in unprincipled ways, or they are allowed to go home if life abroad has roughed them up too badly, or they settle into a successful life abroad if they have passed their tests.

CHAPTER 11

Campus Films

DEMOGRAPHICS AND SEGMENTATION

The Nigerian film industry has always been segmented along linguistic and ethnic lines, but the usual commercial strategy has been to aim at the broadest possible audience in terms of age and class—the heterogeneous urban masses that Karin Barber identified as the social matrix of the African "popular arts" (1987). But Nollywood marketers came to recognize, perhaps inspired by the 2006 national census, that a new younger generation had appeared, with money to spend and with distinct tastes and interests. Often they are better educated than the traditional Nollywood audience.

"Campus films"—set on Nigerian university campuses and focusing on student life—came to target that generation and established themselves as a full-fledged, recognized genre. I'm not aware of another film culture in which films of this type are so important relative to other genres. This is all the more remarkable because relatively few Nigerians have access to higher education. Perhaps that fact accounts for some of the fascination. As the genre was consolidated, its point of view shifted from a popular one, external and tending to project sometimes lurid fantasies onto campuses, to a point of view more nearly of, by, and for people with direct personal experience of higher education.

Most of the actors, directors, and scriptwriters in Nollywood have had or are currently engaged in some kind of higher education. (This is not true of the marketers.) Many of the founding figures of Nollywood were university graduates,[1] and the educational level has risen as enrollments in tertiary institutions tripled between 1999 and 2013 to well over a million. (Nigeria now has 128 universities.) Graduates have trouble finding regular formal-sector employment so they have little to lose by trying their luck in the movies, and the growing prestige of Nollywood encourages them.

The mismatch between education and employment possibilities—the dominant theme in discussions of African higher education—is spectacularly illustrated by the case of the film industry. It's impossible to make a living from stage theater in Nigeria, while Nollywood figures among the major national sources of employment, but the universities continue to educate students in theater, not film.[2] Theater arts programs have had the unfortunate effect on Nollywood of fostering a stagey form of acting and an inappropriate literary/dramatic form of screenwriting (Haynes 2013). Many university graduates working in Nollywood studied something besides theater arts, as students often end up in programs that bear little relation to their interests or talents. Nkem Owoh appeared on television while earning an engineering degree from the University of Ilorin. Tonto Dikeh acted in a hundred films before finishing up her degree in petroleum engineering at Rivers State University of Science and Technology. Funke Akindele's law degree seems irrelevant to her acting career, though she put her familiarity with the University of Lagos campus to artistic use in *Jenifa*. The educational level of people in the industry is significant as a matter of social position more than professional training.

Universities occupy a prominent place in Nigerian society and the Nigerian social imagination in spite of the severe battering they took during the SAP era, the decline in the quality of the education they offer, the breaking of the pre-SAP ironclad assumption that a university education would lead to dramatic and secure upward social mobility, and the dismal statistics on postgraduate unemployment, illustrated by endless anecdotes of humiliation and despair. University education—or more exactly, the university experience and credentials—is still desired and aspired to. The struggle to obtain the places that are available for only a fraction of qualified candidates creates a sense of value in itself. Most careers near the commanding heights of the Nigerian economy—banking, telecommunications, petroleum engineering, management, and so on—depend on degrees; universities are still gateways to the elite and to foreign professional education and careers. As Yann Lebeau argues, African universities have shown themselves to be resilient and complex institutions, performing an array of social functions (2008). Campus films don't pay much attention to education as such, but they compellingly dramatize social aspects of the university experience.

ORIGINS OF THE GENRE

Nollywood has always been interested in universities and students. Kenneth Nnebue's *Living in Bondage* and both parts of *Glamour Girls* associate prostitution with students and unemployed graduates. The primary meaning of campuses for Nollywood is that they are full of young women, whose bodies are the main visual interest of the campus film genre. Titles often point straight to this feature: *Beautiful Faces* (2004), *Hottest Babes* (2008), *Naked Girls* (2009), and so on. These young women are in a state of great freedom and volatility—a period of dramatic career, romantic, and moral choices, undertaken when they are under less adult supervision than almost any other segment of the youth population. As university students they are socially privileged, though they may also be in desperate material need, which may lead them to prostitution.[3] In *Glamour Girls* and in general, undergraduate women are seen as continuous with—as a junior, cadet version of—"senior girls," independent, uncontrolled career women. Their sexuality, freedom, and privilege are fascinating for the popular audience.

Nnebue shared that popular fascination. Nnebue had left school after primary education, but as a grown man, after he had been given a chieftaincy title, in the same years when he was the most powerful businessman and among the most important creative forces in the nascent video film industry, he enrolled in the University of Lagos English Department to study—an example of the prestige of higher education. His films, crucial as they are in establishing frames through which universities were and are represented (as noted in chapter 8, his *Rituals* also includes campus scenes depicting a campus cult), are not at home on campus: they only pass through there and are not yet full-fledged examples of the genre of campus films. Many other films do the same thing, passing through a campus location because school is an episode in a character's life (as in *Fugitive*, 2001), or showing it in a flashback to, say, the beginning of a relationship. The early Yoruba family melodrama *Ami-Orun/Birthmark* (1995) is set largely on campus but from the perspective of a canteen worker whose long-lost student daughter will not recognize her.

I believe the first real campus film is Tunde Kelani's *O Le Ku* (1997).[4] Kelani has shown a steady interest in the young in general and in university students in particular throughout his work. The protagonist of *Ayo Ni Mo Fe*, rescued from a life of poverty and crime, flies off at the end of the film for overseas postgraduate education. Student militants play a major role in *Saworoide* and *Agogo Eewo*. *Thunderbolt* is about a woman doing her National Youth Service immediately after graduation. *The Campus Queen* is a campus film; *Arugbá* has so many other things on its mind that it is not fully in the genre, though the central characters are students and are often seen on campus.

Kelani's films are wholly at home in the university setting, though their point of view is not restricted to it. This is largely due to Professor Akinwumi Ishola, who wrote the screenplays for *Saworoide*, *Agogo Eewo*, *The Campus Queen*, and *O Le Ku*, which was adapted from his 1974 novel. No other campus films have such range and depth of perspective, reflecting the mature perspective of a senior faculty member with an acute sense of the social meaning and purposes of the institution. In *O Le Ku*, the cultural brokerage function of the university is clear from the opening. The film starts with a scene of students reporting on their lecturer's fanciful derivations of English words from the Yoruba, a whimsical tribute to the project of anti- or postcolonial production of Afrocentric academic knowledge in which the University of Ibadan, where the film is set, has played such a distinguished part. The point of view then immediately shifts off campus and into a deeply Yoruba world. The whole film seizes on the University of Ibadan on behalf of Yoruba society, Yorubizing the campus. But this has nothing to do with interethnic conflicts on campus. Shot in 1997, at the nadir of the University's fortunes and of the nation's descent into the hell of military dictatorship, *O Le Ku* is that rare thing, a Nigerian film set in the recent historical past. It recaptures the glory days of the 1970s, the period of Ishola's novel: Sir Shina Peters is performing his juju music on campus, the womanizing is innocent (by later standards), the campus cult is the Pyrates (called by their alternative name, the Seadogs), which was founded by Wole Soyinka and his friends as a lighthearted social organization devoted to nonconformity, chivalry, and rejecting colonial culture.[5] The atmosphere on campus is carefree and optimistic.

By *The Campus Queen* (2004), the vision has darkened. The film opens with a student selling her body. One of the student organizations we see maintains virtuous principles, but its rival is a criminal conspiracy, exploitative and murderous. The heroine is threatened with rape early on and is tortured and nearly killed at the end as she plays a dangerous game with a military governor and investigative journalism. But she prevails. The whole institution is in view: student government as well as competing cults, faculty, and administrators. Even the nonacademic university staff and the informal-sector workers providing transportation and food to the community play significant roles—few Nollywood filmmakers or scriptwriters would think to include them. The musical and dance performances in the film are a spectacular example of cultural brokerage, combining the energies of student performers from the University of Lagos Creative Arts Department with Kelani's technical virtuosity and Ishola's eclectic and multicultural sense of dramatic structure. The structural position of the stage numbers perhaps owes something to the opening glees of the Yoruba traveling theater. Formally, they are inspired by Yoruba dance traditions as developed on university and arts council stages, and perhaps by Bollywood too; on another level, Brecht is an influence, perhaps mediated by the work of Femi Osofisan and other Nigerian literary playwrights. Stylistically, American hip-hop is essential to the student contribution, and Kelani's multiple camera units produce images that swirl and jump as in a music video.

As usual, the work of Kelani and Ishola stands apart from Nollywood proper even as it shares the essential themes and motifs of this genre. Kelani and Ishola's clarity, scope, and depth of vision tend to get lost as the genre is appropriated by a point of view that is essentially that of students and former students. Attention becomes focused on a narrower range of hot topics, expressed with a realism based on direct experience.

CAMPUSES

A new strong sense of the autonomy of the campus signals this evolution. Phrases like "on this campus" echo through the dialogue: "I hope you're aware of the fact that no one dare double cross me on this campus!" (*Jenifa*, 2008); "Will you let that girl rubbish your reputation before the whole campus?" (*Dangerous Angels*, 2010); "You're about to recognize the greatest force on this campus" (*The Cat*, 2004); "She'll have me to deal with in this school" (*Girls Cot*, 2006); "I go show dat girl for this school" (*Life Incidence*, 2007); "But let me assure you of one thing, you will never go out with another girl on this campus until I graduate" (*Black Bra*, 2005); "It is obvious that you and your lesbian friend do not know who I am around this shithole you girls call a school" (*One More Man*, 2007). Such phrases point to the campus as a bounded social space in which power is exercised and reputations are made or broken—a strongly felt boundary that would not matter to the parents of students or to others looking at the campus from outside.

Sometimes this distinctive sense of space is coupled with a distinctive sense of time to form what Mikhail Bakhtin called a "chronotope" (1981). In this genre, time is a conveyor belt that relentlessly carries new generations of students onto campus and then flushes them out again. *Dangerous Angels* shows an especially acute sense of this quality of student time: cult members discuss the influx of fresh "jambites" (so called after the Joint Admissions and Matriculation Board exam they passed) to be recruited or sexually exploited; in various conversations, length of time on campus implies the accumulation of power through the organization of networks and knowledge of how things work. But then the villainous Foxy (Tonto Dikeh) thinks the power of the cult leader Conrad (Nonso Diobi) is waning fast because he is about to graduate. (Something similar is said in *Final Hour* 1, 2007.) Campus careers have a built-in expiration date.[6]

Many aspects of the visual representation of university life are common and standardized, but not how the physical space of the campus looks. Nigerian university campuses are among the purest expressions of the sense of space imported by British colonialism, which set all its institutions apart in splendid isolation, with wide green spaces designed to keep at a distance both the "natives" and the mosquitoes that carried their diseases. Such colonial spaces were in extreme contrast to the spaces of the "native" urban areas. In the postindependence era, the conception of universities as utopian spaces, carefully landscaped and potently symbolic, settings and figures for new social and intellectual lives, only increased. *O Le Ku* is shot so that the iconic buildings of the University of Ibadan campus have lost none of their power to signify a distinguished pedigree, a prestigious present, and a great future that would rub off on anyone privileged to sojourn there. Campuses still contrast sharply with how most Nigerians live.

Before the Rain (2008) glamorizes the wide-open landscape and stylish architecture of Nnamdi Azikiwe University, Awka. The campus seems an antechamber to spaces found in Abuja but few other places in the country, spaces symbolic more of sleek privatized wealth and power than of enlightenment and nation building. But *Dangerous Angels* (featuring some of the same actors and also directed by Ikechukwu Onyeka, who is something of a specialist in the campus film genre) does not glamorize Lagos State University. Sequences are shot in front of ordinary classrooms and in ordinary hallways, the walls covered with the detritus of years of announcements; in one sequence, the protagonist Amanda (Ini Edo) is framed in front of a staff toilet. In *Before the War* (2007) the campus buildings are quite depressing; they look like any other badly maintained government structures, the paint peeling off of them, surrounded by trash-strewn bare earth and crowds of idlers. Only close inspection reveals that the bystanders are all young and many are holding books.

Of all the campus films I have seen, *Before the War* has the grimiest setting and also the most vivid representation of violence, fear, and brutal domination as being primary experiences of campus life. But the film does not seem to intend to connect setting and experience. It is perhaps an example of inadvertent realism (Haynes 2007b), revealing things about which the film is not apparently making any particular point. Campus films are almost all set primarily in student hostels or rented student accommodations, and in some cases we get only the merest glimpses of anything else on campus. But in no film have I seen anything like the squalor in which many actual Nigerian students have had to live: blocked toilets, no running water, epileptic power supply, extreme overcrowding, bags of *garri* (cassava meal) from home the only meager source of nourishment. These conditions have improved markedly on most campuses since the 1990s, and many private hostels of a better standard have been built off campus. Still, showing the realities of student life in a more documentary fashion would work to explain the moral choices the characters make, the overall atmosphere of desperation, cynicism, corruption, and the scandalous failures of the official systems that produce parallel systems of power (Lebeau 1999).

STYLES OF PERSONAL ASSERTION

The films agree on the kinds of behavior to be carefully and repeatedly modeled, notably the suave lines used to pick up someone of the opposite gender and the language and body language of fierce confrontation. Fashions of clothing and speech are also central concerns and must ring true for a young audience.[7] In *Jenifa*, the protagonist's village background has given her stylistic deficits that need to be quickly overcome when she arrives on campus. The early sequences of the film (and much of the rest) consist of women students looking at one another and making fashion judgments, and we follow in detail the process of tutoring and investments through which the clownish village champion Suliat is transformed into the formidable campus personality Jenifa (Funke Akindele). In *Before the Rain*, the good Anita (Chika Ike) and the bad Mercy (Tonto Dikeh), who have grown up together wearing the clean modest tee shirts and severe head ties of humble virtue, trade up to weaves and baseline student style as soon as they reach campus. (The same thing happens in *Hottest Babes*.) They become steadily more fashionable as the film goes on, in contrasting styles, one hip-hop and the other elegant bourgeois. Mercy tells Anita's mother that Anita has been taking money from men to support her lifestyle, which is false but plausible given how she looks. Anita is on her way to a good marriage to a young man from a wealthy, powerful, and virtuous family—the reward for her integrity is social mobility, which the campus trains her for. The fashion gaze (Haynes 1992, chapter 3), a form of attention linked to the fashion process as a mechanism for enabling and controlling social mobility, provides much of the texture and interest of campus films. When fashions are discussed, the emphasis is usually not on designer names, foreign origins, or cost—the categories of consumerism—but on the enhancement of personal force that comes through fashionable appearance, an empowering of individual vitality that affects social standing and may suggest a spiritual dimension.

Demonstrating strength of personality—specifically, the ability to stand up to pressure and the threat of violence in antagonistic confrontations—is at the heart of the genre. The bounded character of the campus means rivals must clash and go on clashing until the power struggle is settled. The face-off is a common element in other Nollywood genres, whether between rival girlfriends or wives, crime bosses, sorcerers, or kings—a noisy collision of egos, opponents contemptuously sizing up one another, spitting venom, artfully and indefatigably singing the praises of their own strength and insulting the other's, accompanied by a whole body language of bridling, intimidating physical aggression. No genre invests in the face-off more heavily than the campus films. Almost without exception they amplify and formalize personal conflicts by expanding them into confrontations between rival cliques, with a typical dramatic structure: symmetrical groups of three or four friends meet in hostel rooms to "gist," plot, and react to events; the cliques face off in public spaces on campus, the leaders leading but sidekicks taking their choreographed turns to insult and threaten; physical violence erupts in the dark or brazenly in the light of day before terrified bystanders. These scenes sometimes ascend to a warlike rhetoric laden with imagery and proverbs, a rhetoric shared with the cultural epic and descended from literary dramas and, ultimately, the Igbo oral tradition: "step aside, before the guardian cloud descends on you with a storm" (*The Cat*). "Are you threatening me? You are playing with the tiger," says the evil dean to the virtuous student in *One More Man*, just before they both slip into abusing one another in Igbo.

The bad characters live for these moments. The good, no matter how independent and solitary by nature (like Amanda in *Dangerous Angels*), also must have or learn the arts of aggressive self-defense and must assemble their own clique or be able to call on one. The bad female cliques normally also function as prostitution rings. Male cliques are normally campus cults, and, almost as regularly, the female ones are too.

CAMPUS CULTS

While powerful secret societies have a long, deep, and widespread history in southern Nigeria, campus cults (also known as confraternities) have been tightly linked in the Nigerian imagination (and apparently in fact) with military rule, mimicking its brutal tactics and its opaque, cabalized structures of organization, thriving in its atmosphere, and patronized and sometimes used as a tool by military rulers (Bastian 2001; Ajayi, Ekundayo, and Osalusi 2010). Campus cultism peaked, at the end of military rule, with the spectacular invasion of the campus of Obafemi Awolowo University by a small army of cultists in July 1999. Six students were killed. Arrests were made, though in typical fashion no one was ever brought to trial. But President Obasanjo decreed that university vice chancellors were responsible for bringing cultism under control, and in the following years there were campaigns to eradicate cultism, sometimes by offering amnesty and rehabilitation to cult members. On some campuses where the cults did not have very deep roots, they were effectively suppressed; on others, they remained a powerful force.

Campus films almost always feature cults (see table 3).[8] *The Faculty* is the only one of the films I have seen that bothers to explain what the cults are all about, as opposed to assuming their existence as a ubiquitous feature of student life. It is also the only one where we see a concerted political campaign to rid a campus of cultism: central to its story (in part 1) is a student government election pitting a cultist against a candidate who makes speeches arguing that the cults' reign of terror should be replaced with freedom and real democracy. In other films, cultism is denounced, bad cultists get their just deserts, and sometimes a particular cult is rolled up by the authorities as the film ends, but few films try to imagine a world in which cults will no longer exist.

In the films, the cults have largely lost their association with the occult. Misty Bastian wrote in 2001, working from press reports, that discussions of cults "invariably" lead to rumors about initiations that are said to have an occult component and are often believed to give magical powers such as invulnerability to weapons and increased sexual prowess (Bastian 2001). Nnebue's *Rituals* makes the connection between student cults and "ritualists," but in the campus genre proper it has almost disappeared. Passing minor instances of the supernatural well up out of the general Nollywood culture: student prostitutes victimized by ritualists in *Jenifa*, a dream vision and magical powder that turns girls into lesbians in *Before the War*. *The Faculty* is the only film in which the supernatural plays an important role; not coincidentally, it is also the only Christian film, assimilating student cultism to a Satanic conspiracy. Even in this case, the supernatural and Christian elements dominate only the later parts of the film when it has moved off campus and out of the campus film genre. It is remarkable how little Christianity figures in the campus films given the conspicuous role played on campuses by Christian organizations (Obadare 2007) and the participation of Pentecostal groups in the campaigns to eradicate cultism (Eguavoen 2008).

TABLE 3 Campus films, table of themes

	Before the Rain 1 & 2 (2008)	*Before the War* 1 & 2 (2007)	*Black Bra* (2005)	*The Campus Queen* (2004)	*The Cat* 1 & 2 (2004)	*Dangerous Angels* 1 & 2 (2010)	*The Faculty* 1–3 (2007)
hostels as primary settings	x		x	x	x	x	x
male cults			x	x	x	x	x
female cults	x	x	x			x	
prostitution		x		x		x	
lesbianism		x				x	
off-campus crime		x			x	x	x
scenes of coercion	x	x	x	x	x	x	x
verbal confrontations	x	x	x	x	x	x	x
physical confrontations	x	x	x	x	x	x	x
rape or attempted rape			x	x	x	x	x
murder	x		x	x	x		x
male competition over female				x	x		
female competition over male	x					x	x
female main character	x			x		x	
romance	x	x	x	x		x	
scenes of lectures, studying, or exams			x	x	x	x	
cheating							
coercion or bribing of lecturers						x	x
lecturers: virtuous or neutral	x		x	x	x		x
lecturers: corrupt	x					x	x
university authorities: virtuous or neutral				x	x		x
university authorities: corrupt				x		x	
external authorities: virtuous or neutral	x			x			
external authorities: corrupt		x		x		x	
poor parents	x						x
wealthy parents	x			x		x	x
strong class tension	x						x
final expulsion, arrest, or death			x	x	x	x	x
graduation							
marriage	x						
betrayal of intimates	x						
the occult or supernatural		x					x

Girls Cot (2006)	*Girls Hostel* (2001)	*Hottest Babes* 1 & 2/*Super Babes* 1 & 2 (2008)	*Jenifa* (2008)	*Life Incidence / A Day to Destiny* (2007)	*Naked Girls* 1 & 2 (2009)	*Nigerian Girls* 1 & 2 (2009)	*O Le Ku* 1 & 2 (1997)	*One More Man* (2007)	*Rush Hour* 1 & 2/*Final Hour* 1 & 2 (2007)	*7 Kilometers* (2007)
	x	x	x		x		x	x		
x		x	x	x	x		x	x		x
								x		
x	x	x	x							
x	x									
x			x							x
x		x	x	x	x		x	x		x
x	x	x	x	x	x	x	x	x		x
x	x	x	x	x	x	x	x	x		x
	x	x			x		x	x		x
	x	x		x	x			x		x
		x		x						
	x			x		x	x	x		
x	x	x	x	x						x
		x		x		x	x	x		x
			x	x	x	x	x	x		
			x	x						
x	x	x		x						
		x		x		x	x			
x	x	x	x	x				x		
	x	x	x	x	x			x		
		x			x			x		x
	x		x				x			x
	x	x	x				x	x		
x	x			x		x		x		x
x		x	x			x				
x	x	x	x		x			x		
				x		x	x			
		x		x		x	x			x
x		x								
		x	x							

The genre's relative lack of interest in the supernatural must be related to a general decline of the occult element in Nollywood films after about 2005. (The occult is generally missing in diaspora films, as related in chapter 10.) It may also support my argument that representation of campus life shifted away from projections of the popular imagination to one based in lived experience. Eguavoen suggests there is no hard evidence of occult practices in campus cults and that such stories "seem rather to originate from the media than be based on students' experience" (2008, 17).

So the social space of the campus is desacralized and presented as largely unstructured by religious institutions and spiritual forces. Cultists are not armed with juju powers, but neither are they opposed by champions of a spiritual order—pastors, shrine deities, or vigilantes. The campus is also presented as de-ethnicized (not always true in real life) and inherently lacks any deep sense of locality. Kinship disappears on campus, except for tangential stories about parents (see below) and a few stray siblings.[9] Romances are common, but the institution of marriage seldom appears even in prospect. Sexuality is everywhere but fertility hardly exists at all. The space of the campus is remarkably abstract, devoid of most of the important structures of Nigerian society and also of the symbolic and thematic structures central to other Nigerian film genres. Even legally, campuses are autonomous, outside normal jurisdictions: the police cannot come there unless they are invited by vice chancellors (Lebeau 1999; Ojo 1995). The authorities on campus are weak. Lebeau suggests the authorities' abdication of control of campuses encouraged the rise of the cults. It is not even a matter of an informal sector supplementing the formal one; the cults sometimes influence or control official matters such as admissions and allocation of student housing (Lebeau 1999), and the films often show lecturers, deans, and vice chancellors working in collusion with, patronizing, or being intimidated by cults. On the ideological level, the higher meanings of university education are still present in campus films, but the plots show the cults dominating the ground. As with the African state, whose fatal disconnection from rooted social structures and values has opened it to corruption and pure power politics, the abstracted modern social space of the campus provides a clear field of play for raw power—force of personality, money, and violence—all embodied in the cults.

Some features of how campus cults operate shape what Raymond Williams would call the genre's "structure of feeling"—the collection of specific emotions, moods, perceptions, and ideas evoked and brought into relation by a concrete historical situation in all its material, cultural, and psychological dimensions (Williams 1977). One is the peculiar nature of recruitment to campus cults. Students do not choose to join cults: the cults choose to join the students, secretly vetting them and deliberating on their admission. Once the cult has decided to initiate a student, the student has very little choice but to agree (Elegbeleye 2005). *Final Hour* details this process. Many stories circulate in the real world of students having to flee from a campus because they have refused to join a cult that responds by threatening violence. One would expect, and one does find, movies about students facing temptation and making moral choices. What the cults introduce into the genre are frequent situations in which students are facing not temptation but coercion. The campus world is governed by forces that flaunt their power visibly, displaying their ill-gotten bling and insisting on their social supremacy, but that also operate in unpredictable, opaque fashion, without negotiation or compromise. No one is safe from them, and no one gets to choose his or her relationship with them. This is terrifying.

The main activity and purpose of campus cults is sexual coercion. Most conflicts between rival cults are said to arise from quarrels over women (Eguavoen 2008; Ajayi, Ekundayo, and Osalusi, 2010). *The Cat* is all about sexual coercion: repeatedly the cult leader Brown (Jim Iyke, who also played a rapist in *Last Girl Standing* (2004)) picks out female students and has his henchmen bring them to him. If they refuse his brutally delivered proposition, he rapes them while his henchmen hold them down. The coercive quality of cults reaches the most intimate levels of the self. Many films turn around a romantic couple resisting the demand by a cult leader that one of them submit sexually. Lecturers are also notorious for coercing students to have sex with them. This is represented often enough, but mostly the coercion and terror in campus films comes from other students.

This emphasis on coercion and terror closes off more positive possible ideological interpretations of cultism. Eguavoen describes persistent ideological splits in Nigerian discourses on student cultism, which are not entirely negative: cults are seen as settling conflicts as well as causing them and therefore as forming part of the system of regulating security on campus; the cults are thought to have fallen away from their original character as principled, honorable, idealistic, and admirable, as exemplified by Soyinka's Pyrates, but people remember that original character (Eguavoen 2008, 6–7). Campus cults partially resemble other kinds of groups of violent, armed young men that figure prominently in the Nigerian landscape: vigilantes like the Bakassi Boys, militants carrying out military operations in the Niger Delta, ethnic militias like the Yoruba O'oduwa People's Congress, religious groups like the *hisbah* in northern Nigeria. Like the campus cults, these groups have all clearly arisen as the result of gross failures and abuses of the Nigerian state and ruling elites and as such receive considerable sympathy from the public as well as from social scientists (for instance, Harnischfeger 2003; Ifeka 2006; Nolte 2004; Pratten 2008; D. Smith 2004). As we have seen, Nollywood has sometimes been sympathetic to such groups.

But campus films very seldom make any case for cultism. (A partial exception to this rule is *Black Bra*; see below.) *Naked Girls* ends with a title, "Say no to cultism," echoing the billboards prominently displayed in universities, and the films generally could serve as propaganda in the anticultism campaigns. They do not want to risk ambiguity. Redeemable people are shown to join cults for understandable reasons, but this is presented as a regrettable mistake. Cultists may prevent particular injustices, for instance by scaring off a lecturer trying to coerce a student into sex, but cults are never associated with the general cause of social justice. Cultism is regularly linked to corrupt authorities. The films generally reach the same conclusion as Misty Bastian:

> Equipped by their college cult education, not for continued modernization or the development of civil society in Nigeria, but to shore up the nation's kleptocratic elite, some young men are moving into what we might call postgraduate violence. What they have learned is pertinent to the Nigerian version of modernity that stresses the importance of (para)militarized power and terror and contributes to the material and spiritual insecurity . . . of everyday life in contemporary Nigeria. In a haze of hyper-masculinity and without much sense of any future worth considering, ex-cultists leave the campus but not the cult behind, and it is not only the universities but Nigerian society as a whole that suffers for it. (2001, 81)

In spite of this ideological disapproval, the films are so heavily invested in cults as a subject that their attitude is somewhat complicated. Cultists and student prostitutes are powerfully attractive figures because they have the things more or less all students desire: expensive clothes, cars, cellphones, perhaps nice off-campus housing. They also embody glamor, social prominence, and the ability to intimidate rather than be intimidated. In *The Faculty*, the glamorous and ambitious Shakira tells Dave he is not a convincing match for her because, unlike the men on campus with balls (as she puts it) and real drive, he does not belong to a fraternity. Cult leader, thug for hire, prostitute: they are the ones who are already players in the adult world of power. To get into that game means playing subordinate, dangerous, and degrading roles, but the students may take contracts for sex or crimes and then cheat their clients or work their own angles.

Their nerve and strong stomachs get them fast money, guns, and sexy clothes, which then allow them to dominate the campus.

Many students doubtless entertain fantasy images of themselves in these forms. There is so little else going on in *The Cat* besides Jim Iyke's character in his sociopathic tough guy pose, spitting out his words, ranting narcissistically, and having any woman he wants, that the producers must count on his fascinating appeal. In *Jenifa*, the taking of English names points to the fact that campus identities can be deliberately constructed personae; identification with Funke Akindele's Jenifa must underlie the actress's project of marketing a line of clothes associated with the character.

In both *Final Hour* and the almost identical *Dangerous Angels*, Nonso Diobi plays the male lead who is simultaneously a final-year student, a sincere romantic lover, and a cult leader. This last aspect of his personality is lost sight of for a long stretch of *Dangerous Angels* but can be invoked when needed. *Life Incidence* and *7 Kilometers* have similar characters. In the former film, the violent side of Nedu (Mike Ezuronye) establishes his manliness (in contrast to his romantic rival). He is easily redeemed in part because, as he explains, he only entered into the cult life to defend himself: because of his intelligence, a cult forced him to take exams for them, so he joined another one. It is understood in the real world that the only way to deal with a campus cult is to join, hire, or otherwise bring into play another cult. Self-defense takes forms that mirror the oppression: one needs a gangster side of one's personality that can face off with and finally face down the cult leader and a social network that includes muscle that can be called upon when necessary. This may be partly responsible for some films' apparent lack of integration in characterization and dramatic design.

Sometimes when the protagonists lack fierce sides to them, benevolent rescuing cults may spring out of nowhere to their aid, as in *One More Man*: the female lead is reduced to weeping catatonia at the climax as a female cult steps in on her behalf, while the male hero is unconscious and held hostage. In other cases, as in *Before the Rain*, *Dangerous Angels*, and the male hero of *One More Man*, the protagonist is revealed to have been working behind the scenes with steady, cool perseverance, in league with strong legitimate authorities of a kind that may be hard to find in real life.

FEMALE CULTS

In most journalistic and academic accounts of student cultism, the cults are assumed to be male: Bastian, for instance, discusses cults as exclusively and extremely masculine (2001). But in campus films there are as many female cults as male ones, and women are as aggressive as the men are. A standard plot form involves a love triangle in which two powerful women compete over a man, at least one of the women being a cult leader (*Beautiful Faces*, *Before the Rain*, *Dangerous Angels*, *Life Incidence*, *One More Man*, *Rush Hour* (2007), and its continuation *Final Hour*). The man may be a cult leader himself, but the women are stronger. Female sexual aggression coexists with male rape and coercion, setting up a formidable cross fire on campus.

Cults do not need to be present for women to be sexual aggressors, as demonstrated by *Nigerian Girls* (2009). Displays of cliquishness, sexual and social competition, and personal power are central to the films. Cultism, lesbianism, and prostitution networks are optional embellishments of the fundamental social structure, which is the female clique, and of the fundamental, scandalous social reality, which is women controlling not only their own sexuality but other people's. In *Before the War*, the same lesbian cultists who interrupt heterosexual unions on campus work off campus as prostitutes—in a scene with a senator, they drug and rob him. The apparent contradiction is grounded in the films' general notion of dangerous female sexual pathology.

Anecdotal evidence suggests female, bisexual cults are a real presence on campuses. But in their survey of gay-themed Nigerian films Lindsey Green-Simms and Unoma Azuah report that *Beautiful Faces* (2004), which seems to be the first campus film to include lesbian cultists and the love triangle of male and female cult leaders competing for a girl, emphasized the lesbian aspect against director Kabat Esosa Egbon's wishes because the producer, Kas-Vid, wanted to profit from the interest in lesbianism created by the popular *Emotional Crack* (2003) (Green-Simms and Azuah 2012). It is easy to read the representation of lesbian female cults as the projection of (predominantly male) fantasies or nightmares and to trace it back through the "Aristos" genre and the chicks-with-guns imagery of *Outkast* (2001) to the "Women of Substance International" cabal in *Glamour Girls*, and so back to the archetypal covens of witches. Is the embattled male psyche doing the projecting located off campus or on? Both, doubtless—in some cases at least the genre seems to express the anxieties of male students in the face of real as well as imagined situations, frequently outnumbered in the classroom as they are and disconcerted by the autonomy and power of the women they desire but must also fear.

In another essay Green-Simms argues that while *Beautiful Faces*

> grapples with the growing violence and corruption in Nigeria as well as with the many challenges and difficulties students face, it does so by channeling

> concern for students' educational opportunities into anxiety about women's sexual transgressions. In this way, I suggest that *Beautiful Faces* is typical of many Nollywood films that simultaneously challenge corrupt and wizened government institutions while also reproducing their normative and violent hetero-patriarchal position. (2012a, 60)

True, but the demonized transgressive figures share many characteristics with their virtuous adversaries. In spite of the fact that the screenwriters and directors of campus films are almost all men, these female characters are powerful and empowering role models—tough, independent, willful, self-confident to the point of arrogance, sexually self-directed, capable, and stylish. The parts are often played by, and written for, a set of actresses who have largely defined the genre, including Tonto Dikeh, Mercy Johnson, and Ini Edo. Celebrity gossip in the press creates the impression that some of these women's behavior in real life bears a strong resemblance to that of their campus film characters.

Black Bra demonstrates the genre's capacity to stake out a strong feminist position amid the swirl of stereotypes and projections. It begins with a cult initiation scene, women gyrating around bonfires at night. The cult leader's speech is full of the rhetoric of feminism: "Say no to all forms of male domination, oppression, and victimization on this campus!" This position is fairly radical in the context of Nigerian gender politics, and in combination with the cult imagery it suggests that the Black Bras will be demonized. But a brief story that follows the opening sequence, about a date rape and the cult's effective retaliation against the rapist, makes the abusive male behavior the women are organized against seem very real and their response seem appropriate and satisfying.

The main story is about Irene (Oge Okoye), a member of the cult, who is besieged by a serial seducer, Frank (Nonso Diobi). His pride and determination are enflamed by her stiff, contemptuous resistance. Finally his perseverance wins her heart. The cult warns her against him but wisely decides not to stand in the way of heterosexual love. It turns out Frank was only trying to score, cynically, and Irene turns out to be a hen-pecking nightmare in the pseudomarital relationship she demands. When Frank tries to resume his philandering, the Black Bras systematically thwart him through their formidable apparatus of surveillance and intimidation, and when he dumps Irene, they impose "the mark of Cain," ostracizing him. Violence is in their repertoire, but mostly their technique is to embarrass him as he makes his moves. His social and sexual career is destroyed. The male friends to whom he goes for counsel tell him that he has no choice but to make it up with Irene and that her fierce anger springs from deep emotion. The other men have no problem living in a world run by the Black Bras, abandoning Frank so they can go to a party the women throw. Frank seems to be developing real feelings for Irene, but she demands that if he wants to make amends, he must strip naked in front of the campus for a whole day. This he won't do, instead bringing in friends with guns. In a shootout, Irene and the leader of the Black Bras are killed. Later two members of the cult gun down Frank. A title informs us that all the Black Bras were expelled from campus and handed over to the police for prosecution.

In spite of this conventional anticult ending, Irene and the Black Bras seem to have the best of it. Irene has character flaws and the intemperance of youth costs her a potential love relationship and then her life, but she is a passionate woman wronged and scorned. The women's cult clearly exists for strong reasons. Their organization is the obverse of the social formation that supports men's sexual boasting and is based on women's social powers of silent observation, gossip, and gender solidarity. Much of the film creates amusement at their effectiveness and Frank's discomfort and frustration. The film's marketer must have been pleased with its title, suggesting a racy exploitation of undergraduate female sexuality, but the semiotics of these black bras tend elsewhere: they are sports bras that do not reveal breasts but restrain and protect them, suggesting athleticism and a team. Sometimes they are worn openly, flaunted as a badge of membership and a warning; sometimes outer garments are opened to reveal them, like a superhero assuming his or her powerful alter ego.

PARENTS AND SOCIAL CLASSES

I have been stressing the felt autonomy of the campus, but of course this autonomy is far from complete, and there are social and marketing reasons for showing the universities' linkages with the wider society. There are two normal ways of dramatizing this relationship.

One is to show the students' social origins through stories about their families. Some films efface this dimension almost entirely, but others emphasize it to incorporate the point of view of families that have sent or aspire to send a child to university, thereby giving a stake in the genre to a wider potential popular audience.

Poor and rural or at least modest and struggling parents evoke the role of universities as agents of social mobility. All three of the major female characters in *Before the Rain* are shown to have such backgrounds, which come into play again late in the film as they go home or are visited on campus by their parents. The normative virtues of these humble backgrounds are assumed more than developed, but the stories linking the girls to the families that are sacrificing to keep them on campus are clearly there to impose a moral burden on the students. This perspective is built into the whole fabric of the film, which is set up as a series of moral tests that the students pass or fail, as if their families were watching over their shoulders. Two of the three characters fail, flagrantly: they lie about their origins, claiming to be from wealthy and powerful families, and convert their educational capital into momentary social capital by throwing their parents' hard-earned money around campus rather than using it to pay their fees. (One of them literally throws money around campus, scattering it as other students scramble to pick it up, while, in intercut shots, her mother collapses from grief at having sold off her land). They smoke cigarettes, a reliable sign in these films of having taken the road to perdition.

In *Jenifa*, the protagonist's parents have little moral force in themselves: they are foolish, quarrelsome, somewhat greedy, frightened and credulous when faced with Lagos and the university. But they and their village remain a point of reference. Jenifa gets into her clique on campus through a social connection from the village and returns home to rebuild her life when expelled from the university; her campus rival turns up there to taunt her; and the film ends in a tearful scene in her family home after she is diagnosed as being HIV positive.

In *Hottest Babes* and its continuation *Super Babes* (2008), the protagonist's illiterate mother opposes her aspirations for a university education because of its daunting costs and frightening unfamiliarity and pushes her into an arranged marriage with an older man, who agrees to pay for her to go to university. But then the struggle to pay the bills ruins the husband's business and the mother is subjected to a predatory visit by her landlord, who has learned her daughter is at university and assumes she must have money. The mother may be narrow-minded, but social mobility does impose strains, costs, and risks. Once on campus, continuing money problems lead the hitherto virtuous protagonist into prostitution, and she spirals downwards to murder and bigamy. At the predictable catastrophe, her older husband and mother are strong moral and emotional presences.

Parents are not always poor. In *Girls Hostel*, the protagonist's father is a successful pastor and his wife a suitably well dressed and imposing matron. They represent a powerful, rigid Christian norm from which the daughter willfully strays, and at the end the film takes their point of view as they pray over her deathbed. In *Dangerous Angels*, the protagonist is the daughter of a powerful politician and her antagonist the daughter of a corrupt politician who was exposed and ruined by the protagonist's father. In *Girls Cot*, the protagonist is coy about the fact that her father is the nation's vice president. (Everyone finds it incongruous that she should attend a national university rather than going abroad.) She enlists her roommates and uses her connections to the political elite to create a criminal enterprise encompassing prostitution, extortion, forgery, and robbery. Finally it is revealed that she is the vice president's illegitimate and unrecognized daughter; her activities have been motivated in part by a promise made to her wronged mother on her deathbed to get revenge. Here the campus film meets family drama at its point of intersection with the political film.

Not infrequently, through a convenient conflation, powerful parents extend their influence to the power structure on the campus. The male love interest in *Before the Rain* is revealed to be the son of the head of a commission investigating corruption on campus. In *The Faculty*, the father of the ambitious antihero is head of a secret cult active on campus called "The Faculty." In *College War*, the campus cult leader's power comes from the fact that he is the son of an influential friend of the vice chancellor as well as from the gun he is toting. The wicked father of the wicked female antagonist in *One More Man* is also, as dean, the controlling official presence on campus, and he is moreover the patron and ultimate "capone"[10] of a campus cult. That children of university faculty and administrators are involved in crime on campus, that campus cults have patrons among the most powerful member of society, and that campus cults are hard to eradicate because when their leaders are arrested they frequently turn out to be the sons of governors or police commissioners are assumed facts in all discussions of student cultism. "There are people outside beating the drum for them to dance," Nnebue told me. So it is natural that in campus films wealthy parents are often tied to an immoral wider social order, and the conflicts between students on campus are a proxy war or allegory for a general struggle over the soul of the society.

In the first decade of the new millennium, across Nollywood's genres the representation of the contemporary socioeconomic situation shifted as Nigeria passed from the vertiginous SAP/military era to a more stabilized if grotesquely unequal, violent, and pervasively corrupt neoliberal order under civilian rule. The money ritual, that central symbol for predation and vicious social ambition, has disappeared altogether in the campus films, and while emergencies continue to tip young women into prostitution, which was a common symbol of the distressed downward plunge of the SAP years, generally we now see tensions and mobility between more firmly defined classes. The solidification of class privileges in nuclear families is expressed most clearly in the genre of the royal film (chapter 6), with its standard conflict between an arrogant family of high rank and the romantic choices of its children. In campus films, families of consolidated wealth and power send spoiled children to universities where they interact with those who managed to get there as part of the traditional function of universities as organs of meritocratic social mobility. The children of privilege may act obnoxiously, asserting their right to dominate the campus—*Girls Cot*, for instance, begins with harsh, taunting expressions of superiority. Sometimes the children of privilege fall in love with poor people and, as in royal films, their wealthy parents act obnoxiously, as in *College War* and *Nigerian Girls* (in the latter case, the wealthy daughter is also obnoxious).

CRIMINAL ASSOCIATIONS

The second main connection with the wider society that limits the autonomy of the campus, besides stories about parents, springs from the fact that the desired goods on campus—the clothes, cars, cellphones, restaurant meals, hotel pool parties—have to be financed from outside campus, and if wealthy parents are not picking up the bills this means prostitution for the women and crime for the men: armed robbery, kidnapping, assassination—rarely drug dealing, for some reason, though outside of the movies this is understood to be a major illicit activity on campus. These immoral sexual and criminal connections open up vistas, or at least repeated glimpses, of a very rough world off campus waiting to buy the bodies and sponsor the criminality of the young.

Good students are ambitious for a better life but accept delayed gratification. They trust in institutions and work hard. The bad ones want immediate gratification and understand the campus as a field for launching careers based on using what they have: the capacity for sex or violence. The women may fall into prostitution out of desperation, victimization, moral weakness, feckless temptation, or peer pressure. But mostly they turn to it out of ambition, greed, self-possessed maneuvering, free and often aggressive pleasure—the dangerous sexuality of a junior glamor girl.

They turn to these activities even when they come from wealthy families and have no practical necessity for doing so, as for instance in *Nigerian Girls*. (In *Girls Cot*, only the final revelation of illegitimacy makes it clear why the vice president's daughter has become a criminal; up to that point the question is never posed, whether out of dramatic carelessness or because generic conventions make such behavior unremarkable.) Universities are not for laundering a family's social reputation, turning ill-gotten money into social and cultural capital. They are places where those who will inherit power in the wider society—power frequently understood to spring from more or less criminal enterprises—demonstrate they have the skills and personality to manage that power in the rough and tumble of Nigerian society. The antagonist of *The Faculty* is determined to become president of the nation one day and so feels he must become president of the student government through any means necessary, including bribery, violence, and murder. He sees joining a cult as an indispensible step in his career. Without exception, films show campus cults as having strong internal hierarchies, with a leader of uncontested authority. Often the leader's authority rests at least partly on family wealth and powerful social origins. Poor students may join cults as a fast track out of their poverty, but they are apt to become foot soldiers in a social structure mirroring the larger society.

THE BORDERS OF THE GENRE

The solidification and familiarity of the campus film genre permits liberties to be taken. It allows marketers to slap inaccurate or misleading titles on films, which nevertheless indicate the genre. *Naked Girls* has no naked girls—it is about guys in cults, moralistically denouncing cultism while reveling in martial arts displays and gun violence and unfurling a melodramatic plot about brotherhood. *One More Man* shows that the genre provides such a firm containing structure that a particular film can have a radically unstable dramatic form, passing through a dizzying succession of other genres: this film shifts from cult film to romance and then to action film, intercut with the melodramatic tears of the heroine and the melodramatic transgressive confrontation of evil father and evil daughter, and finally, in its last moments, to the rhetoric of police and buddy films. It even has some shots of female cultists making their way single file among bush-covered hills in the vicinity of their exceptionally rural campus, shots that recall the imagery of the cultural epic, as if to prove that there is no Nollywood genre that cannot manage to touch all the other Nollywood genres.

When films stray off campus for any length of time, they tend also to depart from the genre's characteristic set of themes. As a genre, campus films are unusually tight and repetitive, and I have been arguing that they often spring from and appeal to an unusually distinct demographic segment. But in the normal way of Nollywood, this genre becomes material for the wider film culture, which likes to mix genres and elide generic boundaries.

The sturdy popular comic tradition continues to have its say. Chico Ejiro's *Computer Girls* (2002) is about a prostitution ring masquerading as a computer school, with Eucharia Anunobi-Ekwu giving hilarious mock lectures.

Made in Cambridge (2007) stars Nkem Owoh as an academic who has returned to Nigeria after decades in England. Shopworn comedy plays on the mutual incomprehension and hostility between the values and norms of contemporary Nigerian society and, on one side, traditional village ways, and on the other, the pompous "long grammar" and supposedly civilized lifestyle of an overbearing "been-to." Such cultural oppositions seldom feature in campus films, though the fate of a romantic relationship formed on a university campus when the couple returns to the very different culture and society of their villages of origin has been a staple theme of African novels and celluloid films. *Sherikoko* pairs a subdued John Okafor with Funke Akindele (the star of *Jenifa*) as his extremely "bush" but domineering wife. *Sherikoko* 2 reprises *Jenifa*'s situations: running by accident into old friends who now look slick, live in a fancy house, and have FALA ("foreign accents locally acquired") American accents and mannerisms, she is persuaded to join them as a "student" of "management technology." This means they are prostitutes and pay others to take courses for them.

Campus films may drag anchor and end up somewhere else. *The Faculty*'s transformation from campus film to Christian film as the protagonist moves into off-campus housing has already been mentioned. *7 Kilometers*, which always divided its attention between the student heroine's romance with her cult capone boyfriend and the gubernatorial campaign of her father, abandons the campus in its second part, turning to themes of marriage and—even more unusual in the campus film genre—pregnancy, as well as continuing its observations of the ways of Nigerian politicians. In *Girls Cot* the protagonist, threatened by campus cultists, moves with her roommates into a mansion and begins operating on a much more ambitious level. There is a touch of *Ocean's Eleven* in *Girls Cot*'s all-star cast, the luxurious settings, the assemblage of a team with complementary criminal talents, and the attention to the unfolding of their capers. When the capone of a campus cult tries to force himself onto one of the team she tricks him into coming to the mansion, where the inspector general of police (once the boyfriend/client of one of the girls, now blackmailed by them through their impressive intelligence-gathering capabilities) threatens the capone with his infinitely greater power. The girls then degrade the capone at some length, making him strip and kneel in the cultists' own standard ritual of humiliation. This episode might be taken as an allegory of the film's movement from the structure of power on campus to the structure of power at the national political level. Like *Girls Cot*, other films such as *Jenifa*, *Girls Hostel*, and *Super Babes* veer sharply towards the style and motifs of Nollywood melodrama as they end. Parental figures reemerge, weeping. *Life Incidence* (with its continuation, *A Day to Destiny*, 2007) fully embodies the campus genre—no film takes examinations more seriously—but the hero's three-year disappearance, which would be routine in Nollywood's general film culture, is inconceivable in the tight chronological frame of the campus film, and the final focus on the choice of a life partner and a wedding also indicate that we have passed off campus into wider fields.

CULTURAL EROSION

Actors go on being cast in campus films until (and sometimes well after) they are too old to be plausible as students—evidence of the power of the genre. But finally, like their characters, they have to graduate, often to movies that might be seen as continuations of the world of campus films. The cultists pass on into crime films or set up as senior girls. The actors who played the more virtuous characters in campus films may play similar roles in the glossy movies produced in remarkable quantity by the Royal Arts Academy, founded in 2010 by the producer Emem Isong and her partners. (Regular Royal Arts actors—Uche Jombo, Ini Edo, Tonto Dikeh—starred in many campus films.) The ascendancy of Isong and her kind of film, which has captured a whole vast swath of the Nollywood imagination with stories of the love lives of young urban professionals, was touched on in chapter 4. Youthful love (or lust) and youthful ambition, in various forms and combinations, fill a vast movie landscape that often is not neatly demarcated in generic terms. Familiar elements of several genres swirl around in what is simply called "drama" (*White Castle*, 2011, is an example.) The dominant Internet distributor of Nollywood films, iROKOtv, favors such films and carries them by the hundreds, as does the dominant satellite broadcaster Africa Magic.

The world of these films tends to be decultured in the manner of campus films. Again basic elements of Nigerian society and of Nollywood film culture are largely or entirely absent: family (a modern nuclear family may appear, but nothing beyond it), traditional social structures, ethnic culture, and a spiritual dimension. Some resemble campus films in conceiving of society as nothing but a field of play for personal ambition and conflicts between cabals—an anomic vision, more like *Glamour Girls* than like *Living in Bondage* and other early Igbo-language "get rich quick" films where ambition faced strongly rooted moral and social judgments. Yuppie love films, on the other hand, often seem to assume an underlying stable, normative order to a degree that requires ignoring much of the Nigerian national reality. They seal themselves off in an elite lifestyle with strong foreign influences, a world as apparently autonomous as that on campus. They are comfortable with a Nigerian identity and may

FIGURE 8. *Guilty Pleasures* (2009) is produced by Emem Isong and Desmond Elliot, partners in the Royal Arts Academy; *Love My Way* (2008) is directed by Ikechukwu Onyeka and stars Genevieve Nnaji, Jim Iyke, and Tonto Dikeh, all veterans of many campus films.

express pride in it, but at the same time the characters and the films they are in often seem simply to want to escape to a "normal" life as represented in foreign films and television. All vestiges of rooted Nigerian culture may be shed in this flight. Once while I was talking with the director Kunle Afolayan he gestured toward the Tyler Perry movie playing on a nearby television and remarked that many Nigerian filmmakers aspired to imitate exactly that kind of thing.

The imitation is not just of accents and lifestyles. The narrative structures of these films and of campus films are closer to Hollywood than are those of the most distinctive Nollywood genres. Campus and yuppie[11] films do not have the dispersed narrative interest or the wider social focus of village, family, political, or epic films. The Hollywood model exercises a direct and pervasive influence over the yuppie films, which are less clearly shaped by Nigerian society and its particular history, culture, aspirations, and anxieties than are campus films and the other Nollywood genres. The narrative structure of campus films may be influenced by special factors—the strongly bounded space of the campus and the tight framing of campus time—but, along with their emphasis on a central individual's purposes, the result is nearly indistinguishable from the Aristotelian unities of time, place, and person as redacted in Hollywood filmmaking. Both yuppie and campus films resemble a whole range of current Nigerian "glocalized" cultural products aimed at young audiences—hip-hop, music videos, standup comedy, televised reality and game shows—that have a strong local flavor even as they are closely modeled on American forms.

This kind of hybridity has always been essential to the African popular arts, which have been produced through a dynamic process of combining indigenous, traditional cultural elements with imported modern ones (Barber 1987). This process of mixing will tend to dilute progressively the indigenous contribution if the traditional culture in the hinterland is not strong and healthy enough to be generative, and these days traditional culture is in trouble. African culture has always expressed itself mostly in perishable materials: cloth, carved wood, buildings made of wood, mud, and clay—above all, in dance, music, and the spoken word, fleeting gestures and sounds in the air. "When an old person dies in Africa, it is like a library burning," the Malian writer and diplomat Hampâté Bâ said, in one of the most-quoted formulations about African culture. Traditional culture disappears quickly if it is not carefully transmitted and constantly renewed, and the social structures of renewal are crumbling as the younger generation largely abandons them, their lives and minds filled with Western education, urban life, and what's on their phones. Across the continent, the silent loss of traditional cultural forms amounts to one of the greatest cultural catastrophes in the history of the human race.

Tunde Kelani is committed to preserving Yoruba culture (chapter 5), and its erosion is a recurrent theme in his conversation. He tried to make a documentary about a *bata* drummer who died before filming could begin. The sons of the masters of this sacred music now play *fuji*, a recent syncretic form, and Kelani predicts they will soon turn to hip-hop. "We are on our last set of drummers in Yorubaland, unfortunately. Part of my work is to document as much as possible because I don't think we can win." He is bitter about how "a whole generation has been brainwashed into demonizing Yoruba culture" by Pentecostalism, and associates the alarming erosion of the Yoruba language itself with the fact that English is, as Adejunmobi puts it, "the language of success" (2002). "It started with the elite and then politicians, and it's now crossed even to traders in the market. They have noticed that the English language is used to loot in Nigeria. They have passively accepted their own fate, but they are determined that their children will join the looters. They communicate in English with their children, so the children become like another people."

Charles Piot argues that Africa has fundamentally reoriented itself: the era of hybridity is over, replaced by a wholesale abandonment of the past and the embrace of a radically different future. He cites several overlapping factors: Pentecostalism's demand for "a complete break with the past" (as Pentecostals often put it); an ardent desire to emigrate from Africa, a desire so widespread it sometimes seems nearly universal; and the sharp decline of the political configuration that linked state power with indirect rule by local chiefs, with its policy of endorsing traditional beliefs and practices that support chiefly rule, and its replacement, as the state has retreated if not failed outright, by neoliberal economics and nongovernmental organizations (Piot 2010).

Piot's main example is Togo; I believe the situation in Nigeria is less extreme, though the same forces are at work there too. Nigeria has a self-confidence born of its gigantic size. Nollywood itself is an enormous demonstration of commitment to Nigerian reality on every level. Nigerians could watch American films—in fact they are cheaper—but they prefer Nigerian ones. Though most Nigerians would agree that the Nigerian state is largely a disaster, the Nigerian nation remains essential as the framing reality of Nollywood. Piot's argument does have purchase on the many Nollywood films that have turned their backs on African culture and record the pursuit of individual desires measured in imported consumer goods or imagine living somewhere clear of the mess of Nigerian quotidian reality, but while such films have been flourishing, they represent only one of Nollywood's motives.

History does not move in straight lines. In my conversations with Kelani about cultural erosion, both of us oscillate between hope and despair. He says,

"Sometimes I give up and say it's too late, it's a losing battle. But again, something happens, and you think ah no, this can't die. There is too much Yoruba blood in them. Somehow they are going to come back to it." Even the parents who have decultured their children may regret it and hire tutors to teach them Yoruba. African music provides many examples of what looked like slavish imitation of a foreign model followed by a return to roots. Hip-hop arrives in African countries in English or French and then gets reworked in African languages and styles (Charry 2012). The Ghanaian film industry, originally almost entirely in English, was energized at a crucial moment by a burst of filmmaking in Twi. Kids growing up in African cities still learn the local dances of their families' villages and work them into the mix on urban dance floors (Carwile 2014). Such examples could be multiplied endlessly; they encourage one to wait and have faith, to enjoy the creative energies of the present even if the processes of erosion are not forgotten.

When video filmmaking was born, some saw a heroic assertion of Nigerian culture against a flood of imports, created under conditions that a rational person would consider impossible. Others saw a commercially driven betrayal of Nigerian culture, a thin version of a rich heritage expressed in derivative Western forms (a thoughtful example is Ogundele 2000). The cultural epic may be taken as a powerful medium for keeping Africans grounded in their past traditions or as an ersatz, careless fantasy that obscures as much as it reveals. And so on. I'm not trying to settle such debates about the ultimate cultural meaning of Nollywood. I see Nollywood as being on both sides of the question, as participating with mixed motives in the history of its time. What I have been arguing for all along is the vitality of Nollywood as a cultural response and, more specifically, for an understanding of Nollywood's genres as having been shaped by profound social values and purposes. This may be less obviously true of some films, but their very escapism captures an important motive in the contemporary Nigerian imagination.

CHAPTER 12

New Nollywood and Kunle Afolayan

In 2010 the phrase "New Nollywood" began buzzing in Lagos and other places where people talk about Nollywood (Vourlias 2010; Leu 2011; Ekunno 2011). It's the banner under which independent producer/directors are trying to "take Nollywood to the next level" by making better films with bigger budgets, films that can meet the aesthetic and technical challenges of being projected on big screens in cinemas rather than being released immediately as VCDs or DVDs for home consumption. Their commercial strategy depends on the multiplex cinemas that have been opening in Nigerian cities since 2004 and on African diasporic audiences.

Nollywood emerged out of the economic catastrophe of structural adjustment and the associated grim social and political turmoil. New Nollywood is premised on a new economic buoyancy, for some people at least—the middle class and a consumer economy have reemerged—and on an improved security situation, at least in some places, that encourages a revival of cinema going. Like the original Nollywood, New Nollywood is a response to deep, unsettling shifts in the audiovisual environment provoked by technological and other forces. By 2007 Nollywood was in a crisis of overproduction as a result of the proliferation of "Asaba films," as described in chapter 9. (Some 2,700 films were said to have been released in Nigeria that year, something more than half of them in Hausa or Yoruba.) The market was so saturated it was difficult for any film to turn a decent profit.

Meanwhile, new technologies have created new competition for VCD sales and eroded markets. Nollywood films are constantly broadcast on television in Nigeria and elsewhere in Africa, which reduces the incentive to buy them.

The South African-owned M-Net's "Africa Magic" is the biggest player in Nigeria and across the continent, with eight satellite channels (one each showing English-language Nollywood, Yoruba, and Hausa films; the others are more or less dependent on Nigerian content). M-Net will not publicly discuss how much it pays for the rights to broadcast films, but filmmakers complain bitterly: they say they were getting a mere $700 per film until about 2010, when payments increased somewhat. "Combo" DVDs from China that compress twenty or even forty films onto a single disc sell in Nigeria for the same price as a single Nollywood film; when pirated Nollywood films began appearing on such discs, they created grotesquely unequal competition for new releases. The markets for Nigerian DVDs in the United States and the United Kingdom have been severely eroded by Internet streaming (Jedlowski 2013). iROKO Partners had this Internet market nearly to itself for a year or more after it began in 2010, but then competitors appeared.[1] By 2012 iROKOtv had some 4,000 Nollywood titles. At that time the company claimed it paid $3,000 for the rights to stream a movie for three years, but people around the industry said actual payments were usually far less. The business model, at least at first, was to acquire titles in bulk, aiming at films that had already had their run in the VCD market and not bothering with filmmakers who want more money for a superior film. So, as with television broadcasting of films in Nigeria, the result was that the environment was flooded with second-rate free films, while the money from these sources did not compensate producers for lost revenues from depressed sales of VCDs or DVDs.

The National Film and Video Censors Board's 2007 "New Framework" for film distribution (discussed in chapter 2) temporarily disorganized the industry and depressed production. In this void, piracy rates escalated sharply: in 2013, pirated films were estimated to outnumber legitimate ones in the market by five or ten to one. The marketers, who themselves do much or most of the pirating, have real money, which buys them political protection from a government that has never been serious about tackling the piracy issue. Politicians now go to them for funds at election time and so will not do anything to interfere with their activities.

Filmmaking did not rebound to precrisis levels until 2011. (The bad relations between marketers and the NFVCB meant that it was harder than ever to come by reliable statistics about the industry.) Budgets also returned to about where they were, averaging ₦10 million (about $65,000). But profits were way down, and Nollywood was glum. People complained that the general run of films was uninspired.

Nigeria is full of contradictions and disjunctions, like the remarkable contrast between this crisis in the industry itself and Nollywood's cultural impact, which continued to expand and deepen as it settled into its hegemony over Nigeria and diffused around the globe. The situation is parallel to that of print media globally: people are as interested as ever in consuming journalism but want to do it for free online, so newspapers fold or retrench in the absence of a viable business model. The satellite and Internet channels contentedly digested the glut of Nollywood films from 2007 during the lull in production, the way a python slowly digests a goat before hunting again.

So the pioneers of New Nollywood had stronger reasons than ever to want an alternative to the old Nollywood. There was nothing new about independent Nollywood producer/directors trying to escape from the Nollywood market as it has existed, with its structural requirement that production be geared to working cheaply and quickly and its domination by marketers perceived as unwilling or unable to create structures that would realize the potential of a single film or of the film industry. Independent producer/directors have been restlessly experimenting with alternatives since the beginning. And public screenings of films are also not novel: premiering films in the fanciest venues possible and carrying them around for screening before likely audiences have always been common practices, inherited from the days of Nigerian celluloid filmmaking.

What was new were the theaters. All the cinemas in southern Nigeria closed during the SAP era. The new theaters are multiplexes located in upscale shopping malls in affluent neighborhoods of Lagos and other major cities. Ticket prices are very high by Nigerian standards (about $10; more for 3D), restricting the clientele to the elite. The locations themselves would discourage most of the population. The multiplexes show American movies and only gradually allowed in Nigerian ones.

New Nollywood filmmakers aim to open their films in these theaters, perhaps after a gala premiere somewhere else, and try to move from the circuit of the multiplexes to the Odeon cinemas in London or vice versa. From 2006 the Odeon chain cultivated an African diasporic audience with a series of glitzy premieres of Nollywood films (Jedlowski 2013). Filmmakers also try to arrange screenings before diasporic audiences in the United States and elsewhere on an ad hoc basis. In the United States there is no such dependable theatrical venue as the Odeon cinemas, but on the other hand the market for DVD distribution of Nollywood films is better organized. US distributors pay a reliable $5,000 to $10,000 for North American rights, according to Emem Isong in a conversation in 2012—a paltry amount but still a significant percentage of the budget of an average film. The British market for DVDs remains in the hands of pirates and normally returns nothing to filmmakers. New Nollywood films are sometimes shown in international film festivals—not a source of income, but the prestige helps in publicity.

Once all these options have been exploited, the films finally come onto the Nigerian DVD/VCD market, where usually they are quickly pirated. The long delay before the films become available to a mass Nigerian audience is something of a tease—people may have been hearing about the film for two or three years. The pirates are ready to pounce. The films' broadcast and streaming rights are sold somewhere along the line.

The filmmakers composing New Nollywood are a diverse lot. Tunde Kelani provides a model—he has been achieving their objectives all along, using different means. The director Lancelot Imasuen and the writer/producer Emem Isong are as central in the old Nollywood as anyone can be but are also pursuing New Nollywood strategies, and, at the same moment that they are inserting themselves into elite and transnational circuits, they are also establishing hyperlocal markets for films in their native languages, Bini and Ibibio. Their restless, creative experimentation in the face of harsh conditions is exemplary of the Nollywood spirit. Jeta Amata, scion of the Amata dynasty of Nollywood actors and directors, not only turned to theatrical screenings as a central strategy but led a return to making films on 35mm celluloid with *The Amazing Grace* (2006), a Nigerian-British coproduction, followed by *Black Gold* (2011), a Nigerian-American coproduction studded with Hollywood stars, including Mickey Rourke, Tom Sizemore, Vivica Fox, and Hakeem Kae-Kazim. Mahmood Ali-Balogun—a veteran filmmaker who has spent much of his career making documentaries and advertisements—also shot his 2010 feature *Tango with Me* on 35mm. Chineze Anyaene's *Ije, the Journey* (2010) and Lucky Ejim's *The Tenant* (2009), both on 35mm, were made by Nigerians who studied filmmaking in North America, where the films are largely set. Stephanie Okereke Linus began as a model and Nollywood actress, went to study directing at the New York Film Academy, and entered New Nollywood with *Through the Glass* (2007), shot in Los Angeles with a mixed cast of Americans and Nigerians. Obi Emelonye, a Nigerian living in London, made *The Mirror Boy* (2011) in England and Gambia with Nollywood stars and then *Last Flight to Abuja* (2012), featuring the British and Hollywood actor Hakeem Kae-Kazim and Ali Nuhu, the biggest star of Hausa films.

"New Nollywood" names an aspiration and a strategy, then, rather than a school of filmmaking or an artistic movement. The economic and demographic basis of the strategy does, however, create some commonalities (explored below). As the name implies, New Nollywood is an extension of Nollywood, built on the film culture and on the audience Nollywood created.

A PRECARIOUS BASIS

New Nollywood was launched on a precarious basis. (Moradewun Adejunmobi (2012) has also made this point.) In 2011 there were only nine multiplexes in this nation of 170 million, and only twenty Nigerian films were screened in them (Vourlias 2012b). The multiplexes slowly increased the number of Nigerian films they showed but—as the filmmakers bitterly complained—they were given only two slots per day, often at inconvenient times, while foreign films got more. The filmmakers were even more bitter about the money. The first week's take was split fifty-fifty, the management afterwards taking progressively larger shares up to 65 percent. The filmmakers had to pay 20 percent in taxes on their share, plus 10 percent to the distribution company they were required to use as an intermediary. Funke Akindele's *Return of Jenifa* (2011) broke all Nigerian box office records, but (rumor has it) of the ₦40 million take, Akindele ended up with only ₦5 million ($33,000). The cinema operators argued that their revenue split with Nigerian filmmakers was more generous than the one for Hollywood films, so that they were sacrificing money to support the national industry.

There simply were not enough screens, and the return for the few films that got onto them was too small for New Nollywood to grow beyond very modest dimensions. Ali-Balogun says he spent ₦80 million ($530,000) making *Tango with Me* (or ₦100 million, if savings from "good will" were figured into the budget) and claims the film made ₦30 million from screenings (some around the industry disbelieve this, calculating that such a return is impossible—as usual in Nollywood, it is hard to come by reliable figures). Even with a ₦30 million subvention he got from the telecoms company MTN while the film was in production, he would have fallen far short of recovering his investment had a deal with the London Odeon chain not come through. This is not a game for the fainthearted. New Nollywood films typically take years to make their money back, if they make it back at all.

The New Nollywood audience is also precariously narrow. The commercial premise of New Nollywood films is that they will—they must—appeal to the people who can afford the luxury of a ten dollar ticket in a country where 70 percent of the population lives on less than two dollars a day. Outside the Abuja Silverbird theater in 2012, two stretch limos with Silverbird vanity plates were on display, a black Mercedes and a white Hummer. The films should also appeal to Nigerian diasporic audiences, whose tastes overlap with Nigerian domestic audiences but are also somewhat distinct (better educated, more cosmopolitan, more concerned with the specific issues that come with transnational lives). Nollywood has always sought glamour, and there have been concerted efforts to appeal to an elite audience since *Violated* in 1996. But this was in the context of the industry's general firm rootedness in a broad popular audience.

An unprecedented segmentation of the Nollywood audience preceded and extends beyond the New Nollywood phenomenon. The campus films illustrate the new prominence of a new generation, relatively affluent and with different tastes and cultural orientation than their parents—but these films come from the usual marketers, not from New Nollywood independents, and are cranked out on the usual low budgets. Emem Isong and the Royal Arts Academy, with their romantic comedies and dramas appealing to a similar demographic, also flourish within the standard Nollywood framework, though they overlap with New Nollywood.

New Nollywood films are often self-conscious about their cultural situation, inheriting the sense of mission and responsibility that usually have come with African celluloid filmmaking. Because of their international dimension, the films tend to be aware of representing Nigeria to the world and may be actively trying to market some notion of African culture as part of their appeal to both foreigners and diasporic Nigerians. But—as the cinema owner Kene Mkparu pointed out to me—the kind of English spoken in *Tango with Me*, for example, would be incomprehensible to the audience in an Onitsha video parlor. Nigerian popular culture is marvelously broad and elastic in its social dimensions, but stretched too far, it does finally snap.

KUNLE AFOLAYAN

Kunle Afolayan is the leading director associated with New Nollywood, his prominence solidly based on superior talent and charisma. The shifting kaleidoscope of his career does not illustrate determined inevitabilities in the future of Nollywood, but it does illuminate the increasingly complex structure of opportunities and dangers to be negotiated. His situation and the evolution of his strategies are inscribed in his films.

When Afolayan made his entrance as a filmmaker he already had an extraordinarily rich heritage and training, none of it related to Nollywood. He is the son of Adeyemi "Ade Love" Afolayan, a Yoruba traveling theater actor who became

FIGURE 9. Kunle Afolayan directing *Phone Swap*. Photo courtesy of Kunle Afolayan.

one of the biggest stars of the Yoruba celluloid films, directing several himself. He discouraged Kunle from an acting career, however, involving him in the handling of money from his films and pushing him toward a career in banking that Kunle pursued for seven years. When Kunle wanted to act, Tunde Kelani—who had worked as director of photography on several films with Ade Love—cast him (appropriately) as the young prince in *Saworoide* and its sequel *Agogo Eewo*. When Kunle decided to become a director, he studied digital filmmaking at the New York Film Academy for a year, giving him a level of sophisticated training rare among Nollywood directors. His films have been made slowly and deliberately, with a careful attention to craft permitted by relatively large budgets. All this is very much in the manner of his mentor Tunde Kelani.

IRAPADA

Afolayan's first film, *Irapada/Redemption* (2007), is in Yoruba and springs from the Yoruba traveling theater tradition as it evolved through various media. Dewunmi (played by Afolayan) is a successful young building contractor living in northern Nigeria. His mother comes from their Yoruba village because she has been having ominous prophetic dreams and warns him to perform a traditional redemption rite against the impending misfortune. He refuses because he does not believe in such things. When she leaves, hurt and disappointed, her vehicle crashes and she is killed. Dewunmi's life falls apart in every dimension: his business is destroyed when he is betrayed in a major building project, and his marriage suffers because he won't tell his wife what is going on. He returns to the village for his mother's burial and discovers she was not his real mother—another shock. His real mother died, neglected, as she passed through the village on a truck with her baby, and he was taken in by foster parents. With the help of a diviner, Dewunmi begins a double quest: to perform the redemption rite and to find his biological father. Cross editing links these quests with his wife's difficulties in childbirth far away in Kaduna, implying that only the twin spiritual and emotional resolutions, as he finds his father and his father prays on his behalf, can save his wife from a Caesarean section or perhaps losing the baby.

Irapada is full of classic melodramatic elements: floods of tears, twists of fate, painful misunderstandings, secrets kept too long with the consequent need to beg for forgiveness, and lost parents and children. Its narrative form, punctuated by visions and ranging across generations, is clearly rooted in African soil. The spiritual framework, in which the mysteries of fate can be discerned through dreams and divination and problems in the spiritual realm can be addressed through ritual sacrifices, is ubiquitous in Nigerian film culture and particularly prominent in Yoruba films. Ecumenicalism of the kind the film shows is deeply rooted in African culture, though now under assault by fundamentalist versions of Christianity and Islam; the Yoruba are exceptionally ecumenical, it being common to find Christians, Muslims, and adherents of indigenous religious practices in the same families. Afolayan's films radiate the broad-mindedness, warmth, humanism, and moralism that are so characteristic of Yoruba culture.

Dewunmi at first rejects the diviner with asperity, possibly because he is a Christian, more probably because he is a modern, educated man. In any case, he learns his lesson. Later, as he is performing the sacrifice under the babalawo's direction, his Hausa friend Shehu offers Muslim prayers in Dewunmi's wife's hospital room, into which her Igbo friend Amaka brings her Christian pastors.

These friendships are central to the film. Nothing is more fundamental in the Nigerian national imagination than the stereotyped trio of the Hausa, the Igbo, and the Yoruba. *Irapada* has an Awolowist, Wazobian[2] politics that is integral to its structure rather than something preached or joked about. The strongest, least threatened, apparently unbreakable relationships in the film are the friendships across ethnic lines, and the Hausa and Igbo friends of the Yoruba couple fall in love with one another as they minister to their troubled friends. Code-switching is constant; a couple of scenes play around strong linguistic barriers, as if to draw attention to the problem that is normally overcome without apparent effort. The scene shifts back and forth from Yoruba southwestern Nigeria to Kaduna, the former political capital of the Hausa and Muslim-dominated North, looking lovely and green after the rains, with little or no hint of the communal violence that had torn Kaduna apart shortly before the film was made. (Perhaps the Hausa businessman's treachery and violence toward a Yoruba contractor—Dewunmi—can be read as such a hint.)

The film is designed, in the earnest and straightforward manner of the Yoruba popular arts, to illustrate basic human lessons: be humble in the face of fate; trust your friends; listen to your mother; don't let masculine pride keep you from discussing things with your wife—a point so important it is central to Dewunmi's father's story as well as his own.

THE FIGURINE

The Figurine/Araromire (2009), in English and Pidgin with bits of Yoruba, is a bigger, slicker, more cosmopolitan and ambitious movie: Afolayan's breakout film. In the manner of Tunde Kelani, Afolayan puts a wide ambit of Nigerian culture on display and makes resonant casting decisions. He features stars with backgrounds and personae as different as Ramsey Nouah (the reigning Nollywood male lead) and Jide Kosoko (a mainstay of Yoruba filmmaking who not infrequently crosses over into English productions); the avant-garde jazz musician Lagbaja provides the voice-over narration; and a small but iconic role, like those Kelani likes to give the writers Akinwumi Ishola and Adebayo Faleti, is played by Muraina Oyelami, a distinguished painter and academic who, as a founding member of both the Oshogbo Art School and Duro Ladipo's theater company, is a walking synecdoche for the modern arts in Nigeria. Oyelami's paintings and posters are a crucial visual presence in the film, and the Obafemi Awolowo University museum of archaeology and modern art is a recurrent point of reference. Afolayan expresses his own generation's urban African culture in the edgy fashion designs, interior decorating, architecture, and soundtrack music. The film sets itself outside and beyond the glitzy, self-contained culture of Nollywood, which habitually showcases what money can buy but often without much taste or sophistication. *The Figurine* can be seen as a return to the tradition of celluloid films like Baba Sala's *Mosebolatan* (directed by Afolayan's father and shot by Tunde Kelani) and *Orun Mooru* (also shot by Kelani, directed by Ola Balogun), which featured a performance by the juju music star King Sunny Ade and Suzanne Wenger's sculptures in the Grove of Osun in Oshogbo. Large budgets (Afolayan spent $350,000 on *The Figurine*, financed through personal savings and bank loans) are required for this kind of cultural engagement and ambition, of course, but so is an engaged and ambitious imagination.

A sepia prologue to the film, set in 1908, tells us the "old folktale" of the goddess Araromire, whose priest carves a figurine of her when she wants to come to Earth in the community of the same name. She brings her worshippers seven years of good fortune—flourishing children, bumper crops—followed by seven years of plague, misery, and death. The villagers revolt against a deity who would kill her own priest and burn down her shrine.

The main story (whose opening is dated 2001) turns on a love triangle. Sola (Afolayan) and Femi (Ramsey Nouah) are both in love with Mona (Omoni Oboli). When the film begins, the three have just graduated from university as archaeology majors and are beginning their obligatory year in the National Youth Service Corps. Mona was the star student, like a daughter to their professor (Oyelami). Sola is a genially corrupt slacker and womanizer, who gets the girl, while bespectacled, asthmatic Femi longs for her. On a hike, Femi and Sola discover an abandoned shrine with the figurine of Araromire in it, and Sola carries it off with him. That night, Mona informs Femi that she is pregnant by Sola and they are getting married.

Seven years later, they have all prospered spectacularly. Femi returns from abroad, now handsome, dapper, and speaking British-inflected English, and glides into a high-level position in finance. He resumes his friendship with Sola, who has become wealthy in business, and Mona, who is expecting their second child. Femi's younger sister Lara (Tosin Sibo) is living with them, helping out pregnant Mona while Mona helps Lara with her thesis—in archaeology, of course. Mona sets Femi up with her best friend Linda (Funlola Aofiyebi-Raimi), a fashion designer. The statue of Araromire sits on a shelf above Sola's computer. Mona consults the professor about the statue; he tells her the story about the good luck followed by the devastating bad luck—adding, when she looks distressed, that it is only a fairy tale, folklore. She shares the story, and her anxieties, with Femi.

Things begin to go wrong. Femi's asthma is back. Mona tells Lara to throw out the figurine, but it miraculously reappears on the shelf. When Mona herself tries to throw it into the ocean (they live in a luxurious beach house on an island in commuting distance of Lagos), she collapses, bleeding. Femi's father, a painter and sculptor whose cancer had mysteriously gone into remission for seven years, suddenly dies. Sola is accused of tax evasion and his company's stock crashes, while Femi is fired. Mona is now completely, hysterically convinced the statue is an evil presence in her house. Sola takes it outside and sets it alight. Their son is distressed at the commotion and falls from a window to his death. The statue still sits, unharmed, on the sand. We are now definitely in a horror film. Mona is devastated and sedated with injections. Linda blames Femi's sister Lara for the boy's death and tells her to leave the house. Femi and Sola return to the village of Araromire to return the statue to its shrine, but there, in the remote forest, in the rain, Femi clubs Sola to death. Intercut with this sequence, Lara's suitcase spills open as she is leaving and two more figurines of Araromire fall out. When Femi returns, Linda confronts him and he confesses, laughing demonically: because he knew Mona believed in the power of the figurine, Femi had had his father sculpt multiple copies of it and forced Lara to plant them in order to scare Mona and Sola into breaking up, so he could at last have his true love. But what about the run of misfortunes? she asks. "I wish I could say the whole thing was orchestrated by me, but the truth is, it's all coincidence. You know, like they say, shit happens." He clubs Linda with a copy of the figurine and goes upstairs, where he expires from an asthma attack at the bedside of comatose Mona, while Lara calls the police. A title ends the film, asking, "What do you believe?"

This is a question about how audience members read the puzzle of the movie, meant to jump-start their conversations as they leave the theater. The movie is carefully constructed so it can be read either as an example of supernatural agency by the goddess Araromire or as a tormented and finally psychotic lover's plot that exploits superstition. The two alternative interpretations spiral ironically around one another. (The screenplay is by Kemi Adesoye, from an original concept by Jovi Babs.) So the question becomes, "What is your system of belief?" The movie's refusal to answer the question appears to be a bicultural strategy—a strategy to appeal simultaneously to two different audiences, one of which believes implicitly in the power of indigenous deities or at least is thoroughly used to accepting such power as a premise of the films they watch, and another audience, perhaps better educated, living abroad, or foreign, that might enjoy playing with the notion of exotic spiritual forces but would distance itself from actual belief. The strategy could also be bicultural in aiming at an audience of bicultural people, who are themselves in an unclear relationship to this polarized choice, such issues of belief being, after all, in the dark of a cinema, very complicated matters.[3]

But what is at stake in the difference between the two interpretations? If you believe this is a story of human agency, then it is just the logic of melodrama that curls around everything, subsuming the supernatural: love and betrayal of intimates are the strongest forces in the world. If you believe this is a story of the supernatural power of the goddess Araromire, then what sort of deity is she? Some Nigerians note that they have never heard of a Yoruba deity that behaves as she does, and even within the film, both the voice-over narration at the beginning and the professor call the story of Araromire "folklore" or "a fairy tale"—dismissive terms not normally applied to the Yoruba pantheon. Araromire is not a guardian of ancestral land or morality, as in other films, but a kind of principle of melodrama, the presiding deity of Nollywood: you have really good luck for a while, and then really bad luck—a fate that is meaningless in itself but whose consequences are an occasion for displaying a full range of strong emotions and each individual's moral and spiritual balance or lack of balance. As in *Irapada*, where the protagonist is unambiguously the plaything of an unseen dimension, in *The Figurine* Afolayan's attention is all on the bewildered suffering caused by this unseen dimension, rather than on that dimension itself, and indeed both films seem deliberately to resist giving it determinate form. It hardly matters if the supernatural dimension is now a question rather than clearly determining, if the divine figure is perhaps merely a cultural artifact, perhaps just a device.

The young men Kunle Afolayan plays with his slow, quiet magnetism are settled, married, enmeshed early and deliberately in the web of life, equipped to plumb the depths of loss. As a filmmaker he is a poet of fate and affliction, his plotting full of twists and turns, his attention centered on the betrayals and loyalties of intimate relationships. *Irapada* is swept along in the main current of the great Nigerian river of melodrama, wide and central as the Niger; *The Figurine* also builds to a melodramatic climax, in this case of love and jealousy exacerbated to madness and murder, catatonic grief, cowering subjection, and raw fear.

But while the ending of *Irapada*, with its flood of tears, is ragged and rough as a piece of dramatic construction, in a manner characteristic of Yoruba films, *The Figurine*'s ending is intricately worked and is clearly formed, stylistically and generically, by the conventions of the horror film. As Carol J. Clover illustrates, the Western horror genre turns around a struggle between Black Magic and White Science, with much of the plots devoted to the gradual, reluctant admission by the protagonist that the occult exists at all (Clover 1992). Some protagonists in Nigerian films go through such a process—indeed, Dewunmi in *Irapada* does so. But for the most part, Nigerian protagonists, like Nigerian audiences, already assume the existence of the supernatural and assume that portals to it are easy to find. Therefore (as I have argued elsewhere) it has usually been a mistake to use the Western category of horror to describe Nigerian films in which the occult appears (Haynes 2010b) (though very recently, Western-style Nollywood horror films have come into fashion). In the case of *The Figurine*, the generic shift toward the horror genre might be taken as another sign of accommodation to a transnational audience.

I do not want to exaggerate this point about appealing to a transnational audience. If *Irapada* embodies the aesthetic and the horizon of the Yoruba branch of Nollywood filmmaking while incorporating a strong national dimension, *The Figurine* is both national and transnational. The two films share the national term, and Afolayan is seriously committed to it. *The Figurine* recovers the aspirations of the high-water mark of Nigerian postcolonial culture of the 1970s and 1980s as the film inserts itself into contemporary world cinema culture. We end up in a luxurious, exclusive Lagos waterfront world (a new development and one associated with the return of successful Nigerians from abroad—the Lagos elite had not oriented itself toward the sea in this way before), but in spite of this, lots of Nigerian life gets into the film, as it does not in the decultured films I discussed in the last chapter. It is no accident that *The Figurine* begins in the setting of the National Youth Service Corps, an institution designed to give university graduates a sense of national identity and purpose.

Like *Irapada*, *The Figurine* was shown at international film festivals and triumphed at the Africa Movie Academy Awards. *Irapada* was quickly pirated when it came into the market around the same time and so failed to clear its costs, but Afolayan was riding high, moving into bigger offices and turning into a celebrity. One evening while channel surfing I came across him on the Nigerian *Dancing with the Stars*, doing the cha-cha. In 2011, he told me private investors had offered him $1.5 million to make his next three films—the budget for two dozen normal Nollywood films. This seemed an amazing development, but on reflection, perhaps not so surprising. Investors had been circling around Nollywood, trying to figure out how to get in, and what better investment could they make? The deal promised Afolayan more artistic freedom than perhaps any African filmmaker has ever enjoyed. Confident and full of plans, he started with *Phone Swap*, which he called a light romantic comedy, a minor commercial project.

PHONE SWAP

Then things fell apart. The promised investment never materialized and he had to scramble to finish *Phone Swap* (2012)—adventures detailed in Andrew Rice's profile of Afolayan in the *New York Times Magazine* (2012). The production undertook unprecedentedly ambitious feats: A set of the interior of an airplane was constructed in a warehouse, and Afolayan paid to shoot inside the Lagos airport terminal, flooding it with light and extras at midnight. The whole look of the film is carefully controlled. Rice's article emphasizes how crucial Pat Nebo, the artistic director and set designer, was to the production; the credits also list two directors of photography, a colorist, and a visual effects supervisor. Mobile phones are at the center of the film both as a plot device and thematically, as an illustration of how Nigerians live. They also suggested desperate strategies for getting the film made: BlackBerries dance around the credits (RIM, the company that makes BlackBerries, did not respond with sponsorship as Afolayan hoped); the Nigerian telecommunications company Globacom rescued the production with a grant, and Afolayan himself puts in a cameo appearance wearing the fluorescent green vest of a street vendor, selling Glo recharge cards to the protagonist. Afolayan told Christopher Vourlias the film cost $437,000 to make, of which 40 percent came from corporate sponsorship, 40 percent from personal bank loans, and the rest from his own pocket (Vourlias 2012a).

Phone Swap is a nicely turned, airy entertainment. Akin (Wale Ojo) and Mary (Nse Ikpe-Etim) are opposites. He is a successful businessman from an elite Yoruba family, uptight and friendless, with a reputation at work for being a backstabber. Mary is a scattered, warm Igbo woman, caught up in ordinary social and family life, making a modest living as a dressmaker and designer. They run into one another, literally, in the Lagos airport, the collision sending their identical BlackBerries skittering across the floor. They end up with one another's phones and, after the phones lead them to board planes to one another's destinations, they perforce carry out one another's missions. Mary poses as Akin's personal assistant at a company retreat as part of his plot to take control, while he mediates in a family dispute caused by her ferocious sister, a police officer, who has done violence to her husband's "man thing." He is comically discomforted by the spicy food, communal sleeping arrangements, and mosquitoes of ordinary Nigerian life in her village. She stays with his alcoholic mother (Joke Silva) in her Abuja mansion, the two women charming one another. Mary has just dumped her boyfriend, having discovered he was already married, and Akin has just thrown out his girlfriend, not because she is crude, mercenary, and drunken but because she unforgivably rearranged his furniture without his permission. Akin and Mary fall for one another in the course of their phone conversations and then have to fight off these rivals.

Lockstep dramatic design and crosscutting emphasize the comic symmetries and social and psychological contrasts, but when these reach a slapstick climax the film artfully pivots to affecting emotional depth as Akin and his mother reconcile, with some prompting from Mary. Like the scripting (story and screenplay are by Kemi Adesoye, who wrote *The Figurine*), the acting is stylized, professional, and polished, intending predictable pleasures that are delivered with élan and assurance. The themes of Afolayan's other films—the dislocations of fate, the containment of ethnic and social diversity in a full, familiar national reality—reappear in minor, but not brittle, form. The film aims at light comedy and achieves it, the lightness itself being a sign of maturity.

The response to *Phone Swap* was gratifying. In May 2012 Afolayan showed me, on his phone, the running tally of tickets sold at a multiplex. He complained about the deal he was getting from the cinema, but at least he had solid ticket numbers to look at. *The Figurine*, on the other hand, had been pirated in spite of his best efforts. He kept the film out of the disc market while organizing a massive release as an imported, encrypted DVD with bonus features, selling at a premium price. But before the discs went on sale, university students all across the country already had it on their computers. Afolayan suspects it was leaked by someone who worked on the editing. The company contracted to distribute the DVD was new and untested, and it failed him. He had seen no money since the advance they gave him, and the man he signed the contract with had disappeared. Money came in from other sources in bits and pieces, eventually covering his costs but providing no profit: corporate sponsorship for its premiere in Nigeria; \$75,000 from cinemas in Nigeria, and \$5,000 or \$10,000 per screening in London, Japan, and elsewhere abroad; \$25,000 from Africa Magic for eighteen months' broadcast rights; sale of streaming rights to IbakaTV.com. He wanted to find a DVD distributor for *Phone Swap* but did not know whom to contact.

He was in despair. He had sworn to live and die in Nigeria, making his career there, but he was about to get on a plane to the Cannes Film Festival to pitch his next project, *Dead Alive*, looking for a French or British coproducer. The film had a science fiction dimension, and he wanted partners with CGI experience. And he knew the full international distribution he aimed at would be much more likely if the project had foreign producers with a stake in it from the beginning. But it rankled that his own country would not support him. He was stressed from living on the very edge of the possible. Like other New Nollywood filmmakers, he was practicing the art of filmmaking as if already in a future that hadn't quite arrived yet, willing that future into being by stretching the possibilities.

Postscript, 2013: Toward the Future

> God keep me from ever completing anything. This whole book is but a draught—nay, but the draught of a draught. Oh, Time, Strength, Cash, and Patience.
>
> MELVILLE, *Moby Dick*

On the first leg of a trip to Nigeria in June 2013 I flew British Airways from New York to London. There were no Nigerians I could see on board, but the in-flight entertainment system included two Nollywood films and featured one of a series of documentaries—infomercials, really—about dynamic cities around the world. This one was called *Lagos: Africa's Own Big Apple*. It trumpeted Lagos as "a model megacity for the twenty-first century," the fastest growing city in Africa, an emerging business center. Cosmopolitans were glimpsed golfing, playing polo, jet skiing, enjoying luxury hotels, their children ecstatic on a waterslide. Families visited exotic plants and animals. The current Lagos State governor Babatunde Fashola and his predecessor, Bola Tinubu, introduced segments on plans to address fundamental infrastructural issues: unsnarling traffic with light rail, ferry, and bus projects, providing drinking water for a city of twenty million people. There were computer-generated models of Eko Atlantic, Nigeria's own Dubai of postmodern office and residential towers to be built on landfill off Victoria Island. (That is "Eko," the original name for Lagos, not "Eco"—there are grave concerns about the environmental sustainability of this project.) Fela's son Femi Kuti and others attested to the city's vibrant culture, nightlife, and indomitable spirit.

Nigeria is indeed changing fast. The economy has been growing at nearly 7 percent a year for a decade—not quite a Chinese rate, but truly impressive. The telecommunications sector is the largest in Africa and one of the fastest growing in the world. In 1999, less than 1 percent of the population had access to a telephone; now there are 116 million active cell phone subscriptions. Forty-seven million Nigerians are on the Internet, more than in France.

But, on the ground, things were moving sideways, the basic infrastructural, economic, and political problems far from solved. Electricity is as "epileptic" as ever. More than two-thirds of the population still lives in deep poverty. Twenty million youths have no jobs or job prospects, and the educational system is in sad shape on every level. The Muslim terrorist group Boko Haram feeds on the resulting despair, and the military's response, at once brutal and ineffective, creates new militants. Nigerian pirates, extending their operations west from the Niger Delta along the coast of West Africa, have displaced Somali pirates as the worst threat to international shipping. The World Bank still thinks Nigeria is one of the most difficult places in the world to do business.

2012 saw the worst corruption scandal in Nigeria's history: half the annual budget of the federal government was being stolen by highly placed people scamming the fuel subsidy program. Newspapers also reported that a quarter of a million barrels of oil, $6 billion of oil revenues, disappears each year through an enormous black market infrastructure of clandestine refineries and storage facilities in the Niger Delta, pirates selling seized oil cargos, fleets of trucks moving petrol across Nigeria's borders, and ordinary people as well as organized criminal gangs punching holes in pipelines to get fuel for their own use or small-scale trade. The leaks are literal as well as metaphorical, causing massive environmental damage. The poet and political commentator Odia Ofeimun told me President Jonathan would have already been killed by his political opponents if the Niger Delta, where he is from, were not awash in weapons. If he were killed, the Delta would explode in violence, wrecking the oil economy—a risk no one will take.

In Nollywood, the situation is equally unsettled and contradictory. The future seems to be bursting through everywhere, but the hungriest time is just before the harvest. In 2013 the Nigerian Bureau of Statistics put the value of the film industry at $3.3 billion (the figure was admittedly approximate, based on the 1,844 films produced that year) and claimed that, together with the music industry, it was the second-fastest growing sector of the economy (Bright 2014). But the guy in a shop in Surulere where I go to buy films said only fifteen or eighteen English-language movies are being released every two weeks, a third the number from a year before. (Sixty or so Yoruba films still appear every two weeks.)

I went to see Amaka Igwe, who longed to make a film but had not done so in eight years because she thought the market would not return her investment. She had reverted to her roots in television, busy with plans to launch her own satellite television channel on MultiChoice's DStv, the same South African platform that carries Africa Magic, hoping to begin broadcasting by the end of 2013. (Zeb and Chico Ejiro are also planning a television channel.) The new channel will require staggering amounts of content. All the episodes of her popular pre-Nollywood serial *Checkmate* will be rebroadcast, and her early films *Violated* and *Rattlesnake* will be serialized. Her company is ramping up to produce 1,000 hours of new content a year by 2015, mostly serials, and 5,000 hours by 2017. The aim is to compete globally with Indian and Latin American networks. Chris Ihidero, COO of Amaka Igwe Studios, argues the future is in volume. Africa Magic's success was possible because Nigeria had produced enough films to fill multiple channels, 24/7. "Yes, quality is key. But we should not stupidly, for the sake of quality, abandon volume. The cinema model, where you can only make one film in four years, does not really appeal to a lot of core marketers. . . . Our inroad to the international market at this point is quantity."

I heard a lecture at Pan-Atlantic University by Kene Mkparu and talked with him for a long time afterwards. Mkparu worked for the Odeon cinemas in London, building the audience for Nigerian films there, and then returned to Lagos to start The Filmhouse: A Cinema Development Company with a group of other young Nigerian former Odeon employees. He lectured the assembled filmmakers about how their profits from screenings were declining because the runs were so short; this is because distribution is disorganized and too many films are jockeying for slots. But of course the filmmakers cannot do anything about this. New Nollywood is reproducing on another level old Nollywood's perpetual crisis of overproduction.

By August of 2012 there were twelve Nigerian multiplexes, with 65 screens. Mkparu expected there to be about twenty by the end of 2013 and by 2020, fifty-five cinemas with 275 screens. His company had opened three cinemas in the last six months and planned five a year for the following four or five years. Foreign cinema equipment manufacturers were beginning to take notice of the breakneck speed of these developments.

But Mkparu thought the real money, and the exciting future, was in small community cinemas located in popular neighborhoods or even slums, where there is nothing to do in the evening except drink beer or take your girlfriend to a fast food restaurant. Many people have that kind of money—the beer parlors spill out into the roads. The cinema tickets would cost the same as a bottle of beer. It would be a gold mine.

Everyone around the industry has the same idea, and it seems like an idea whose time has come. Part of its virtue is that the formal sector actors—government, banks, business investors—who have not been able to figure out how to engage with Nollywood would have something clear and relatively straightforward to do: investing in real estate, cinder blocks, and equipment is easier for them and far more reliable than coping with the notorious business practices of the film marketers or making loans directly to uncollateralized filmmakers. Mkparu's company was the first to access the $200 million fund that the government set up in 2010, which sat untouched because the paperwork and guarantees were too difficult for filmmakers to meet (see chapter 2).

A year earlier I had discussed the prospects for community cinemas with Andy Amenechi, newly elected as president of the Directors Guild of Nigeria, and Bond Emeruwa, immediate past president of the DGN and interim chair of the Coalition of Nigerian Guilds and Associations, in the courtyard of Emeruwa's office in Surulere. Amenechi pointed out that the 2006 revision to the federal government's Film Policy—never implemented—calls for the construction of a community cinema in each Local Government Area, of which there are 774. This would be vastly more theaters than exist now but still an exceedingly modest number for a nation of 170 million people. Obviously many Local Government Areas, especially urban ones, could support far more than one theater. Cinemas should be an attractive proposition for government on all levels as a source of tax revenue and employment, Amenechi continued, each cinema generating a little economy of food and drink catering around it and perhaps other entertainment options like a video arcade.

Emeruwa thought the industry will sort itself out into three or so levels. At the top, films by people like Afolayan and Kelani will open their runs at the fancier theaters or abroad before moving down the chain. Emeruwa estimated some forty or fifty films a year could be released at this level. On the middle level, perhaps two or three hundred films a year, or more as theater construction took hold, would be released initially in the community cinemas, then through new media, and finally sold as DVDs with additional features. Below that, the old Nollywood would continue as it has done, releasing new films straight onto VCDs, serving the mass of the population that cannot afford anything else.

Even a partial realization of this dream would transform Nollywood. Much greater and more dependable revenues, mostly freed from the threat of piracy, would permit larger film budgets, and technical and artistic quality would rise accordingly, spurred by the challenge of filling the big screens. Abruptly, the artistic situation would be reversed: instead of struggling to produce decent films on tiny budgets and in a treacherous business environment, the challenge would be to produce enough high-quality work to meet market demand. The process of segmentation of the industry would continue, as it should, but the primacy of the broad popular domestic audience would be restored and, with it, an essentially healthy cultural situation.

The Lagos State government clearly is seriously interested in building community cinemas. The governor took Tunde Kelani and Kunle Afolayan with him on a trip to India to inspect the film industry there. Both filmmakers are on a committee set up to plan community cinemas, though in recent jockeying it seems Mkparu has gotten in front of them with his proposal. In any event, as a sign of its interest in the film sector, the Lagos State government gave both Kelani and Afolayan seed money for the films they are about to shoot.

Kelani has his own plan to build small community theaters on any land he can find. He is tired of waiting for the government to do something and is thoroughly fed up with the market for VCDs. The last film he released as a VCD, *Arugba*, was pirated within three days. One pirate hoped to edge out the competition (seven other pirated versions were available) by including a bonus disc with all of Kelani's previous films—the filmmaker's life's work, given away for free. Kelani has been having a hard time. "It's a very hostile environment," he said, "really challenging, but there are prospects." He won't release his new film *MAAMi* on disc; instead, it's available for Internet streaming, along with several of his other films, on Dobox.com, one of the new challengers to iROKOtv.

Four big undersea fiber optic cables have come ashore in Lagos, with more on the way, but getting broadband the final mile to consumers is proceeding slowly. Streaming whole feature films is still impossible. Kelani is pushing against the limits of the technology, doing everything possible to get online. The Dobox platform serves audiences abroad. He was negotiating to get his films on the mobile phone networks of MTN, which has forty-seven million subscribers in Nigeria, and Etisalat, which has seventeen million. His YouTube channel has had 1,500,000 views. A website for the film he is about to shoot, *Dazzling Mirage*, will post calls for volunteers and experiment with crowdsourcing part of the budget.

The arrival of the fiber optic cables was followed by the arrival in Lagos of Google CEO Eric Schmidt, who came to visit Tunde Kelani in his office. Kelani tried to steer the meeting toward a big hotel, apprehensive about the ordinariness of his street and his lack of air conditioning, but Schmidt insisted, apparently grasping the principle that the coming platforms would be hungry for content and therefore content providers need to be cultivated and understood. So Kelani cleared out his courtyard for the arrival of Schmidt's convoy of white SUVs. Kelani had two generators going behind his office, because of course there was no electricity.

In Google's Lagos office I met Lanre Aina, a tall, soft-spoken, dynamic young man who returned to Nigeria from Boston after getting an MA in telecoms management from Northeastern University. He talked about the fifteen or twenty million Nigerians in the diaspora—the population of a small country. If the Nigerian diaspora were a country, it would be among the best educated in the world: the brain drain of the structural adjustment period exported a whole generation of academics, physicians, and other professionals, and now tens of thousands of Nigerian students go abroad to study and do not come back. As he monitors who is streaming Nigerian content on YouTube, he finds large unexpected pockets of Nigerians, mostly students or young professionals, in Malaysia, Cyprus, and Ukraine.

When YouTube was new, diasporic Nollywood fans uploaded hundreds of Nollywood films in nine-minute segments, out of sheer devotion and a strong sense of community but without authorization. Now, Aina told me, YouTube's Content ID software instantly detects unauthorized posting of content registered to its "Premier Partners" and emails the copyright holder with options for how to proceed: track it, take it down, or monetize it. The technology allows this one sector of Nollywood to be rigorously policed and is already affecting piracy overseas—why bother with a pirated disc when the film is universally available online? As broadband penetration increases in Nigeria, Aina thinks platforms like YouTube can help control this fundamental structural challenge that Nollywood producers have always faced.

Nigerians are always staring at their phones, and Aina spends a lot of time thinking about what they are looking at. Forms shorter than a whole Nollywood movie are getting traction, and not only because of buffering issues. I brought up a conversation I had earlier that morning with King-Richard Ekwegh, editor of an entertainment magazine, who talked about how young people generally feel closer to the bubbling Nigerian music scene than to Nollywood. The music is free on the radio or on YouTube and moves around with them everywhere; often they don't have time to sit down for two hours to watch a film.

Aina talked enthusiastically about the explosion in Nigerian animation—another short form, suitable for YouTube, narrow bandwidth, and mobile phones. On his laptop he showed me a satirical, South Park-ish short by Nnamdi Nwoha, also known as OurOwnArea, poking fun at repatriated Nigerians who think they can insist on American-style civil rights with Nigerian police. In Nigeria, you pay to get your work on television, not the other way around (content creators have to line up their own sponsors), and young filmmakers do not have the money or connections to work this system. Short films on the Internet are a way to get noticed; posting his films on YouTube got Nwoha, a very young man, work doing animation for one of the major banks.

On sporedust.com, Aina pulled up the viral hit "Chicken Core: The Rise of Kings" and a shorter film whose visual style reminded me of manga (young Nigerians have grown up with a lot of Japanese animation) but whose thematics were pure Nollywood: a king, upset that his wife has not provided him with an heir, consults a diviner. Aina had been to visit Sporedust Media, a group of a dozen animators that works in a warehouse near the airport. They are all kinds of people—students, architects, doctors—drawn together by a shared mania; mostly they are young and a number have returned from living (usually studying) abroad. Like Aina himself. As he was walking me out, he said that recently his mother asked him if he would go back to Boston if he had the chance. He would not: Nigeria was his country, and it was booming, flush with creative energies, like that warehouse full of animators.

I met Chike Maduegbuna, whose digital marketing company won a Google-sponsored competition for an Android Web app. The app, AfriNolly.com, provides information on new Nollywood films, including trailers, cinema screening schedules, synopses, cast, and crew—it aims to be the Nigerian Internet Movie Database. The app was downloaded 2.3 million times in its first year; they are aiming at ten to fifteen million. Maduegbuna is frankly not interested in the run-of-the-mill, straight-to-VCD productions, which he does not think are the future of the industry. AfriNolly highlights New Nollywood films, whose sophisticated trailers are central to the app's appeal.

In 2012, looking for a way to expand its scope, AfriNolly got the South African telecoms company MTN to sponsor a short film competition. Bandwidth considerations, as well as a sense of what people would want to watch on their phones, drove the focus on short films, but the effect was to graft a very different constituency onto the Nollywood fan base for whom the app was originally designed. Nollywood does not make short films and has no mechanism for distributing them. The people who entered shorts in the competition are not Nollywood people. Mostly young, in many cases they are trying to get into Nollywood, something that is notoriously difficult to do. AfriNolly helps them to form a community—a deterritorialized community, everything taking place online and mostly through social media. Some of the filmmakers have been to film school abroad, and some still live there. AfriNolly is endeavoring to link Nigeria with its diaspora, Nigeria with South Africa, and the established generation of Nollywood filmmakers with the younger one. In order to level the playing field, AfriNolly created online master classes, one taught by Kunle Afolayan. The impressive array of judges for the competition included filmmakers Tunde Kelani, Emem Isong, and Obi Emelonye; the influential Hollywood executive Franklin Leonard; the founder and director of the African

Film Festival of New York, Mahen Bonetti; and Bongiwe Selane of M-Net. Partly through the influence of the judges, a third constituency joined the Nollywood fans and the young outsiders: international cinema and media mavens, who have been inviting Maduegbuna to address audiences in New York and South Africa.

Maduegbuna espouses net ideology, confident in the ability of a Web app to provide the structures that Nollywood has not been able to create for itself and quietly fierce in his belief in the democratizing, meritocratic force of the Web. Unlike in cliquish Nollywood, you don't need to know anyone to win the AfriNolly short film competition, just as he did not know anyone at Google when his company won their competition. He plans to add user movie reviews to his site, so that direct wikicriticism will force producers to make better films. As it is, he said, producers dismiss negative criticism as springing from an enemy's political agenda, and they can buy good press from mercenary newspaper reviewers or influential bloggers. Maduegbuna used the phrase "creative communities" at the beginning of our conversation. The word "government" never came up. Corporations need to show up wherever people are gathering together, he said, and when they show up, they should be made to foot the bill for the platform.

Corporations still are only connected to Nollywood film production in fleeting and tangential fashion through occasional sponsorships and product placements, but—like everywhere else—the Nigerian cultural landscape is increasingly dominated by corporate brands. Nigerian telecoms companies and breweries sponsor the biggest music and comedy tours and competitions, many of them televised, as well as television talent and reality shows. South African corporations have made serious inroads into Nigeria. Nigeria is the biggest market for the South African telecoms company MTN and for the media conglomerate that owns the satellite broadcasting platform DStv, the content provider M-Net, and the Africa Magic channels, which are the most important packaging and distribution format for Nollywood films. By far the most expensively produced serial on Nigerian television is M-Net's daily soap *Tinsel*, produced in Lagos under close South African supervision. The combination of South African technology and business structures and Nigerian creative talent seems destined to dominate commercial entertainment across the African continent.

The main corporate connection with Nollywood is through brand ambassadorships, which began in 2007 when the Nigerian telecoms company Globacom signed on eight leading actors to participate in their publicity campaigns, soon adding Kunle Afolayan and Funke Akindele. By mid-2013, corporations were spending nearly a billion naira ($66 million) a year on these relationships with Nollywood, music, and sports stars (Alonge 2013). Nollywood is being balkanized by corporate ties: a brand ambassador for one brewery cannot appear at a premiere sponsored by another, for example. Noting that Nollywood stars do not earn enough from acting alone to support the lavish lifestyles they lead, or like to be seen as leading, journalist Funke Osae-Brown did the math on Jim Iyke's ₦23 million ($150,000) deal with Virgin Atlantic: it was worth more than his annual income from acting, if he appeared in twenty films at his market rate of ₦750,000 to ₦1 million ($5,000 to $7,000) per film. Osae-Brown writes, "The brand ambassador is meant to embody the corporate image of the company in appearance, demeanour, values and ethics," but adds, quoting analysts, "some companies and organisations have not tried to achieve a strategic fit between their brands and the chosen ambassadors" (2013). We noticed Jim Iyke playing singularly unpleasant roles in *Goodbye New York* and *The Cat*. The corporate connection is still a work in progress and affects only a few people, and then as celebrities rather than as working filmmakers. Nollywood film production generally continues to be unintegrated with the formal sector. But the formal sector is undoubtedly on the minds of many people in the industry.

Government has, historically, been almost completely irrelevant to Nollywood, but government remains central in the Nigerian imagination, in spite of all its manifest failures. At the time of my visit the federal government had just put another sum of money on the table—₦3 billion (almost $2 million) for entertainment industry training and infrastructure, in addition to the largely untapped $200 million loan fund—and this attracted excited attention and rivalry. The film industry approaches government through its organizations, so the way to the money is through holding offices in the guilds and associations, the politics of which have become correspondingly lively. Since film production slowed, many people have had time to devote to industry politics. In any case, urgent issues do need to be discussed as the future confronts Nollywood, and the endless talk that always surrounded the industry has blossomed.

I found Kunle Afolayan much more buoyant than he'd been in 2012. Driving in his big cream-colored Mercedes sedan from his office in Ikeja to his house further north, he was juggling the radio and two phones. He talked in intimate tones with the fashion designer who was designing the costumes for the film he was about to start shooting, *October 1*, a murder mystery set at the moment of Nigerian independence in 1960. No one in Nigeria has ever tried to make a period film with anything like this level of ambition, and I wondered where he would find old vehicles. As he negotiated Allen Avenue traffic, on the other phone he pulled up photos of a couple of cars from the epoch that he had found here and there and then showed me an architect's drawing of the spectacular house he is building for himself and his young family: a modernist cube with a swimming pool behind and a cinema inside it, fit for a movie star and leading film producer anywhere in the world.

In the comfortable house Afolayan rents now, Bond Emeruwa joined us for goat meat and yam pepper soup and a couple of bottles of red wine. A few days earlier I had watched Emeruwa chairing a big, contentious meeting organized by the marketers. Now he and Afolayan complained of how tired they were of the endless meetings, the endless squabbling in the industry, the endless discussions of the future. No one has been to more meetings than Emeruwa. The two filmmakers both declared that now they just want to make their movies. "They will always need us, they will always come back," Afolayan said. "When the cinemas are built, what will they show? For the Lagos State cinemas we said they should show 70 percent Nigerian. But where are the films? Nigerians will not go the cinema to see rubbish films, no matter how cheap they're showing them." Afolayan talked with satisfaction about all the equipment he has acquired—enough to meet all the needs even of an unprecedentedly large production like the one he was launching into, and he makes good money renting it out. At his office he had shown me a storeroom packed with floodlights and scaffolding for tracking shots. Both office and home had small fleets of vehicles parked in front of them, branded with the logo of his production company, Golden Effects. In the office courtyard was a big flatbed truck he had just imported from Portugal, loaded with an enormous generator, big enough to power any film production or, as he commented, half a town. Yes, Emeruwa said: he used to make cash payments to the villages and neighborhoods where he was shooting films; now he wires them up and gives them electricity from his generator for the days he is around, which is more than they get from the government.

Afolayan was looking back as well as forward. He had used his connection with the governor of Lagos State to get money to redeem four of his father's films, copies of which had been held for unpaid debts in the London laboratory where postproduction work had been done on them in the 1970s. The films have been unavailable in Nigeria for decades, and he plans to release two in theaters, expecting people will be amazed that work of such high quality had been done so long ago in Nigeria. It is no wonder the younger generation has little sense of the history of Nollywood and what preceded it, since there has been no way for them to see those films and television programs.

Earlier in the day, Kelani had also been looking back as well as forward. He told me the story of his recent outburst of anger at a Nollywood film festival in Paris (another sign of the times: the citadel of the other African cinema had hosted its first Nollywood film festival, and a TV channel there had begun broadcasting a steady stream of Nollywood films, dubbed into French). A young Nigerian filmmaker, based abroad, had made the mistake of saying that Kelani and others had come to join Nollywood after *Living in Bondage*. Kelani was incensed at the erasure of the whole rich culture out of which he had come; he is proud of his training at the NTA, of the great television producers he had worked under, who are still alive but largely forgotten. He kept pushing the history of Nollywood back until, laughing, he claimed it was 2,000 years old, an unbroken progressive development of Nigerian culture. He was turning back also to his own formative childhood cultural experiences—to D. O. Fagunwa, whose novels he had read to his grandfather by the light of a hurricane lamp, and to Kola Ogunmola's stage version of *The Palm-Wine Drinkard*, which he'd seen as a student. He was planning to make a short film based on Fagunwa's work for an upcoming conference, and for years he had been nursing the ambition to make a film of *The Palm-Wine Drinkard*. He thinks the community cinemas will be the basis for a revival of Yoruba culture and its classic works of literature and theater. "I know the audience," he said. "They will love such films. Fagunwa is like *The Lord of the Rings* for them. There are more prospects for Nigerian films than ever before, if you do it well. This is the time, really, to start making movies . . ."

NOTES

PREFACE

1. See my literature review (2010a), agenda for research (2010b), and bibliography (2012) of the academic literature on Nigerian and Ghanaian video films.

CHAPTER ONE

1. Uchenunu illustrates the problems facing celluloid filmmakers with a story (drawn from a newspaper account by Oji Onoko) about Eddie Ugbomah's travails in premiering his video film *Aba Women Riots* in 2000. Ugbomah was set to premier the film in Aba, the scene of the important historical event on which the film was based, but as the result of a conversation with the minister of culture and tourism he moved the premier to Abuja. He also had to go back on to location to make changes in the story ordered by the minister. The premiere in Abuja had to be cancelled because of rioting that followed the introduction of Sharia law in some states in northern Nigeria. The minister promised to foot the bill for the rental of the hall, but after long delays, the file with the necessary signature was lost. Ugbomah raised funds to pay the hall rental and arranged another premier, getting members of the National Assembly to lend their prestigious presence to the occasion. As he traveled to Abuja, Ugbomah was held up by armed robbers and his suitcase, with the film in it, was taken at gun point. On the day of the premiere, the ceremonial mace of the National Senate was hidden by a disgruntled official, and the guests of honor had to send their regrets and join the frantic search for the missing mace. On the same day, the government announced a hike in the price of gasoline, which, as usual, provoked widespread disturbances (Uchenunu 2008, 39).

2. Moses Olaiya Adejumo (Baba Sala) said he owed more than half his success to early appearances on NTA Ibadan: "After that we ventured out with our plays, our audience was already made, the television had done it" (Lakoju 1984, 39–40).

3. Shaibu Husseini has systematically interviewed and published biographical data on many of the people involved (2010).

4. Stephen F. Sprague (2002, 173–74) notices a similar heavy emphasis in Yoruba still photography on posed portraiture commemorating a social event rather than landscapes, architecture, objects, or ordinary events.

5. I have seen three rereleases of *Living in Bondage* on VCD. One, from Nnebue's company NEK Video Links, puts each part on three VCD discs. The other two versions, one from NEK and the other from Kingdom Worth Inc., cut down the original film to make each part fit onto two VCDs. In both cases, it is the long sequences of social occasions that are cut.

CHAPTER TWO

1. Susan Vogel is categorical: in Africa, "the aesthetic is fundamentally moral" (1986, 15). This is conspicuously true not only of narrative art forms but of others as well. See, for instance, Robert Farris Thompson's observation about African song and dance "which, however danceable and 'swinging,' remorselessly contrasts social imperfections against implied criteria for perfect living" (1984, xiii) or Vogel's on twentieth century African visual arts: "A similar conception of art—one notably different from Europe's—unites African artists from the beginning of the century until the present. . . . Content, for example, is of prime importance for African artists, critics, and audiences, who tend to share an expectation that works of art will have a readable message or story. . . . That all forms of contemporary African art are seen as functional, or as serving some common good, was one of the most surprising findings of this study. . . . The general consensus is that [art] must honor, instruct, uplift, clarify, or even scold, expose, and ridicule to push people to be what they must be" (Vogel 1991, 16).

2. The opposition of "tradition" and "modernity" in the African context has been trenchantly critiqued by Barber and Waterman (1995) and Marshall (2009), among others. I agree that the opposition is more often misleading than not and that both terms lose their meaning almost entirely when closely examined. I wish we could be rid of them. But we can't, if only because they are built into various fundamental African discourses. "Traditional films" is an alternative name for the cultural epic, a major Nollywood genre. Always enclosing the terms in scare quotes is tiresome, but readers should understand that I assume that traditions always have an invented character.

3. For a while, the National Film and Video Censors Board had three classification symbols to be displayed on films rated for mature audiences only: one plain, one with a machete to indicate "violence," and one with a calabash to indicate the film contained "rituals" (National Film and Video Censors Board 2004b, 17). In 2002–2003, 31 of the 1,784 films classified bore the "rituals" symbol. (Thirty were labeled for "violence.") (National Film and Video Censors Board 2004a, 174)

4. Symbolic elements may resonate in more than one tradition. I had taken the black and red color scheme as an example of the influence of a Christian notion of Hell and the backwards entrance of the cult members as an instance of the reversals that characterize black masses, but the director Chris Obi-Rapu, who was primarily responsible for the design of this scene, pointed out that black and red are the colors associated with Nigerian "native doctors" and fetishism and that when a masquerade enters a room, it does so backwards. When I brought up the absence of caolin face painting, raffia, and the general decor of African shrines, he said the scene was shot in a hurry and without advance preparation.

5. Birgit Meyer develops this theme in her historical account of the Christianizing of the Ewe in Ghana (1999a) and then transposes it into her powerful readings of the Pentecostalite influence over Ghanaian video production in many articles cited below.

6. In many Nollywood films, the representation of rituals and shrines has a plainly ersatz, even cartoonish, character, as if to make it unmistakable that this is not the real thing. Birgit Meyer reports on the anxieties of Ghanaian filmmakers about spiritual forces that may affect the process of filmmaking itself. Shrines they construct as film sets may be invaded by real spirits; the producer and director Michael Akwetey-Kanyi would avoid using real materials, substituting water for alcohol and dyed starch for blood, to minimize this possibility. Demonic forces that did not want to be represented might affect the camera itself (Meyer 2002a, 2003a, 2006a, 2006c).

7. When I tried this interpretation out on Nnebue, he looked blank. Obi-Rapu thought it was possible but that it was also possible that a man talking to himself was a sign of incipient madness.

8. The most famous example of that form, the English late medieval morality play *Everyman*, was the basis for a famous Yoruba traveling theater play, Duro Ladipo's *Eda* (1965), and for Wale Ogunyemi's *Eniyan*, a literary drama in English (1987). The Yoruba traveling theater tradition was born out of plays performed in Christian churches (Clark 1980), as European medieval drama had been. My argument is not for a specific line of influence, only that the southern Nigerian popular arts, Igbo as well as Yoruba, evolved in an environment saturated with homiletic Christian forms that fell on fertile ground, given the African taste for narratives that teach a moral.

9. Poor people wear imported used Western clothes; the wealthy demonstrate their cosmopolitanism as well as their money by switching between Western and African styles, but the embroidered robe is the sartorial pinnacle because of its great expense and its connotations of specifically African social power.

10. *Amadi* was directed by the Yoruba Ola Balogun. Ekwuazi notes that there was only one Igbo celluloid filmmaker, Eddie Ugbomah, who made nine films in English and three in Yoruba but none in Igbo (2000, 132–133).

11. Paul is never shown, as Ogunjiofor, who played the part, had left the production.

12. The Nigerian federal government was in the process of moving hurriedly, propelled by an abrupt decree from Babangida, from Lagos to the new national capital, Abuja, a city under construction in the geographical center of the country. People saw it as a place where corrupt politicians could go about their business untroubled by citizens, its name a watchword for everything that was wrong with national life. Because of the shortage of housing, many men came to work in Abuja without their families and took up with women not their wives, liaisons known as "Abuja marriages."

13. The story is told in Amos Tutuola's *The Palm-Wine Drinkard* (1984, 17–31).

14. Marketer/producers are frequently referred to by the name of their companies, so Kenneth Nnebue is often called "NEK" even by people who know him very well. People in the industry may have trouble recalling the real names of the men known as "Reemmy Jess" or "Infinity." Nollywood directors like to use nicknames: "Da Governor" (Lancelot Imasuen), "Mr. Prolific" (Chico Ejiro), "Mr. Creative" (Emeka Ani). Actors are known by the names of their most famous roles, like"Baba Sala" (Moses Olaiya Adejumo) or "Osuofia" (Nkem Owoh), following a practice already firmly established in the theater.

15. But they are not unionized. Mahmood Ali-Balogun pointed out the consequences to me: since no one on a Nollywood set is working to union rules and everyone is being paid by the job, not by the hour, everyone wants to get the job over with as quickly as possible. Hence there is a general, fluid sharing of tasks such as carrying equipment and props around and setting them up. This partly accounts for the legendary speed and low cost of Nollywood filmmaking.

16. In chapter 7 of *The Pan-African Nation*, Andrew Apter works with a protester's formula "IBB=419" (IBB being Babangida's initials), exploring a "fundamental transformation of value that occurred during IBB's dictatorship, a transformation that produced a national crisis of representation with thoroughgoing political and theoretical implications" (2005, 254) .

CHAPTER THREE

1. As part of the publicity for the 1995 film *True Confession*, Nnebue's NEK Video Links included "bonanza" lottery tickets along with the cassettes and then held a well-publicized drawing in front of the National Theatre, with luminaries in attendance. Prize money of more than half a million naira was given away to winners from the northern, eastern, and western regions of the country, demonstrating the national extent of the new industry's reach. To everyone's surprise, entries also came in from as far away as the Benin Republic, Ghana, and Sierra Leone. It was not clear whether the cassettes circulating abroad were original or pirated. Certainly they were moving through the agency of petty traders, without the knowledge of the producer.

2. With respect to fine arts, Susan Vogel observes that the "desire to make 'nonethnic' art runs through all kinds of 20th century African art except traditional art. Ethnicity, or 'tribalism,' has consistently been seen as divisive in contemporary Africa, and as a sort of throwback to an earlier form of social structure. . . . Artists have taken their inspiration from objects not identifiable with specific ethnic groups, or have deliberately mixed elements from several ethnic traditions" (1991, 26).

3. "Senior girls" is the phrase the film's theme song uses. *Living in Bondage* had used "library" music, but for *Glamour Girls* Nnebue followed what had already become the standard practice, hiring a studio musician to make a theme song that is played repeatedly at key moments in the film.

4. Brian Larkin emphasizes the importance of reaction shots capturing such scandalized responses in what he calls Nollywood's "aesthetics of outrage." *Glamour Girls* is his prime example (Larkin 2008, 186).

5. An undercover journalist's 2014 exposé of a ring trafficking prostitutes to Italy provides a remarkably similar account (Ovuorie 2014).

6. The film was preceded by an advertisement for the authorized Jacuzzi dealer in Nigeria, but the advertisement makes a Jacuzzi seem like plumbing, displayed in a showroom crowded with toilets.

CHAPTER FOUR

1. We need more empirical studies of how Nollywood films are consumed, and by whom. In 2012 Emem Isong commented to me that, unlike Hollywood with its extensive apparatus of audience research, Nollywood has no such thing—filmmakers and marketers must rely entirely

on their instincts and anecdotal evidence to estimate who is buying and watching their films. Onookome Okome and I (Haynes and Okome1998, rpt. in Haynes 2000) called for study of these matters and made some remarks based on conventional wisdom in Nigeria and on the work of contributors to *Nigerian Video Films*, especially Afolabi Adesanya and Brian Larkin. Adesanya contrasts the strong tradition of Yoruba families going out together to see films with the much less enthusiastic attitude of the Igbo, where men tended to leave their women and children alone with the VCR while they went out to sporting events or drinking (Adesanya 2000). Larkin tells the story of the abrupt and dramatic change in Hausa culture, where men were avid cinema-goers but women were considered prostitutes if they set foot there. Film culture was therefore largely closed to women, except for what was broadcast on television, until the advent of VCRs changed the situation entirely—Hausa video films are sometimes called "women's films" (Larkin 2000, see also Larkin 2008). Other studies of audiences include Ajibade 2007; Akoh and Okocha 2011; Akpabio 2007; Alawode 2003; Emasealu 2008; Esan 2011; Lawuyi 1997; Obiaya 2010; Okome 2007b.

2. These matters are complex, of course. Smith points out that Igbo women have roughly equal status with men in premarital sexual and romantic relationships, but after marriage they are subjected to much different and much more restrictive standards as the result of the extended family's interest in their fertility (Smith 2001c).

3. For observations on the difficult relationship of Nollywood to the rest of African cinema, see Haynes 2000, 2011; McCall 2012.

4. Several figure in this book: *Onome*, *Owo Blow, Battle of Musanga*, and *Ikuku.*

5. On the relationship of melodrama as an international form and Nollywood, see also Haynes 2000.

6. Their eldest brother, Peter a.k.a. "Red," became a producer. Zeb and Chico are both married to women named Joy who are partners in their film companies; Chico's Joy is also one of the industry's leading costumiers.

7. I use the word "bourgeois" here and elsewhere in relation to style, but, as Fanon argued in *The Wretched of the Earth*, Africa does not have a proper bourgeoisie to play the historical role of the European bourgeoisie.

8. The exception that proves the rule: *Oduduwa* (2000, dir. Andy Amenechi), which tells the story of one of the Yoruba pantheon of *orishas* in the idiom of the cultural epic. Femi Lasode's film *Shango: The Legendary African King* (1998, begun on celluloid but finished on video) is about Sango's life as a human king before his apotheosis into an orisha.

CHAPTER FIVE

1. These moves don't bear repetition, however. Recently, European and American festival programmers have been discovering that if they "lower their standards" to let Nollywood in, in return they get a large, enthusiastic, and spectacularly dressed audience of Nigerians and other Africans (often there is such a population living in the vicinity)—Nollywood fans, who would not normally attend a film festival. This is good for revenues and brings a jolt of energy and a certain credibility to the festival.

2. Afolabi Adesanya provides a list of films with which Cinecraft was involved (1992, 26).

3. Adepoju is an important figure in Barber 2000.

4. The first part of the film was titled *Ti Oluwa Ni Ile*, contracted in the subsequent parts to *Ti Oluwa Nile*.

5. The Ifa divination system is an essential method of communication with the spiritual realm and is fundamental in Yoruba culture. An Ifa priest (*babalawo* or *iyanifa*) casts a chain or shells; the resulting pattern points to a particular verse of the Ifa corpus, which is then interpreted in light of the occasion of the divination (Abimbola 1977).

6. So in the subtitles of the VCD version. The original VHS version has somewhat different translations, in this case: "'To God belongs all the land,' but also to those who can make a convincing story."

7. Akin Adesokan entitles a chapter "Tunde Kelani's Nollywood: Aesthetics of Exhortation" (2011b, chapter 3).

8. Equivalent to a county.

9. *Efunsetan Aniwura* began as a stage play by Akinwumi Ishola. The traveling theater troupe of Ishola Ogunshola performed versions on stage, television, and celluloid film. Kelani shot the celluloid 1981 film, directed by Bankole Bello. Ishola made changes to the script for this version and for the 2005 video Kelani directed. The rights to this last version belong to Ogunshola's family, so it is not available from Mainframe and is difficult to find.

CHAPTER SIX

1. Heike Becker has a fascinating discussion of the powerful meanings the representations of "tradition" in Nollywood's epics have for educated young people in southern Africa (2013).

2. The films are in English, but often the titles are Igbo names. The early Igbo-language films, conversely, almost all had English titles.

3. Other high-profile slave films include Ndubuisi Okoh's *Ngene* (2000), Kenneth Egbuna's *Kasalama: The Slave Merchant* (2003), Izu Ojukwu's *Sitanda* (2006), and Jeta Amata's *The Amazing Grace* (2006).

4. Perhaps significantly, monarchy was a familiar form around Onitsha and Asaba, Igbo centers of Nollywood.

5. Matthew Brown observes that the NTA version of *Things Fall Apart* includes no such scenes of democratic decision making in the village square. Instead, powerful elders meet repeatedly in private houses to discuss politics (Brown 2014, chapter 3).

6. While the cultural epic is generally seen as an Igbo form, the reality is more complex. As noted, before it was Igboized *Igodo* began as an expression of Bini culture, partly based on Yoruba literary models. Many non-Igbos were involved in the initial burst of epics: The "Isoko Mafia" directors came out in force, especially Chico Ejiro and Fred Amata; others include the Yoruba director Bolaji Dawodu, the Itsikere screenwriter Joe Dudun, and the Ijaw actor Sam Dede. The prolific Bini director Lancelot Imausen soon joined them. The cultures these people came from had various experiences of monarchy. The Kingdom of Benin was a regional power for centuries. The Urhobo/Isoko, on the other hand, suffered as vassals of Benin; the Isoko epic poem *Omofbhon* is about a sadistic Bini king (Azuonye 1995, 71), and the epic founding story of the Urhobo (as retold by the contemporary poet Tanure Ojaide) is of fleeing from a Bini tyrant and finding a new homeland in the creeks further south (Ojaide 1986). See Okpewho's studies of the opposition to tyranny expressed in the epics and folktales of cultures oppressed

by Benin, including the Urhobo, Isoko, Ijaw, and the Igbo living west of the Niger (1998a, 1998b). Monarchy is assumed in Nollywood, but tyrants appear more often than in the Yoruba tradition.

7. Dandaura and Okoli connect the relatively positive representation of diviners in OJ productions with OJ's family's reputation for producing great dibias (2010). Nevertheless, his films are ambivalent.

8. By early 2013 the popular Nollywood Internet streaming site iROKOtv.com had twenty-two films made between 2007 and 2012 with "royal" in their titles. Search terms like "kingdom" or "princess" would have yielded more films in this genre.

9. Beyonce and Tyra are not African names and are clearly inspired by African American celebrities—another convergence of elites, international media celebrity linking the political with the "traditional."

CHAPTER SEVEN

1. This symbolically potent displacement had a practical dimension: the OJ films *Oracle* of the next year (1998) and *Igodo* (1999) were among the productions that pioneered the move of filmmaking out of Lagos to locations in the East.

2. The illegitimacy of the modern state in Africa is a fundamental theme in Africanist history and political thought. See, for instance, Davidson 1992.

3. "It is often said in Nigeria that someone who has wealth, but no house in his hometown to show for it, is not highly regarded. As status and full male adulthood were achieved through relations with kin and dependants, the village remained perhaps not the only, but in many ways the most essential, imagined community for many urban dwellers" (Bersselaar 2005, 63).

4. This colonial dimension is central in Eddie Ugbomah's 1976 celluloid spy thriller *The Mask*, about Benin bronzes looted by the British and held in a museum.

5. John McCall unpacks the meaning of these displays. By leaving the bodies in full view, the Bakassi Boys protected themselves from accusations that they might be using body parts for rituals or selling them. The public spectacles reversed the development Foucault traced in European history from the state staging its power intermittently through public executions to a regime of constant, omnipresent "panoptic" surveillance. The Nigerian state had failed to maintain a centralized regime of surveillance and legal power, so the Bakassi Boys replaced policing with divinatory charms and spectacular violence (McCall 2004, 61).

6. I am grateful to Matthias Krings for pointing out this connection and sharing his poster collection with me. Harnischfeger discusses these posters and an audio cassette of Prophet Eddy's interrogation by the vigilantes that was on sale at the time (2003, n9; 2006, 59–60). Harnischfeger and Baker (2002) both discuss the politics around his execution. Okeke had powerful clients, including Ibrahim Babangida and the governor of Anambra State, who went to Abuja to discuss the case with President Obasanjo. But 10,000 traders demonstrated in favor of the execution and threatened to make the state ungovernable. Harnischfeger argues this was a protest against the corrupt ruling class.

7. Public support for the *Issakaba* movie franchise did not flag. The series came to an end, Sam Dede told me, because of pressure from the censors board, which was campaigning against multipart films. The producer also told him part 4 "was directed at politicians and some people

didn't like it. The last installment wasn't called *Issakaba,* it was *Please Come Back*—like the audience was asking the series to come back. It was a hit."

Dede played the central role in the most popular and important of the films about the Niger Delta militants, *The Liquid Black Gold* (2008). Ambivalence about vigilantism was built into his character in the *Issakaba* films, as McCall argues; in *The Liquid Black Gold* the ambivalence is expressed through a running debate between Dede's character, a noble and articulate leader of armed militants, and his wife, who argues that violence is never the answer and nothing justifies the deaths of innocent members of the community. The film endorses the negotiated compromises reached by the government with at least some of the militant groups. Other films about the Niger Delta militants include *Oil Village* (2001), *Oil Money* (2003), and *Militants* (2007).

CHAPTER EIGHT

1. When Nigerian video films first emerged, the contrast with the rest of African cinema was an inevitable topic, and I addressed it several times: Haynes 1995; Haynes and Okome 1998; Haynes 2000; Haynes 2006, from which parts of this chapter are derived; and Haynes 2011.

2. Chris Dunton, in his catalogue of subjects and themes in Nigerian drama, makes this comment on his list of plays on the "State of the State": "Listed here are plays that deal with corrupt State administration, the oppressive State, the notion of government motivated only/largely by the urge to plunder (categories that overlap). Of all concerns explored by Nigerian dramatists this is the most dominant, providing the major or subsidiary subject-matter in a startlingly large number of plays, dating back to the early 1960s. To one administration after another, military or civilian, this corpus of plays forms a truly remarkable memorial" (Dunton 1998, 284).

3. Filmmakers mostly worry about the State Security Services or offended powerful people, not about the censors board. Only in a few instances has the NFVCB censored a film on political grounds. From its establishment in 1994 to the end of military rule in 1999, according to its own magazine, it approved 1,300 films and refused to pass only seven "in the interest of peace, order, security and stability of the nation and because of patent artistic or structural or cultural defects" (Dosunmu 1999). Paul Ugor reports that from 1994 to 2005 it classified about 4,600 films, completely embargoing only about twenty-five, mostly for explicit sexuality (Ugor 2007, 11–12). On the functioning of the NFVCB see also its own publications, James 2007, and Obiaya 2012.

Perhaps the very existence of a body charged with maintaining the security and integrity as well as morals of the nation has discouraged filmmakers from dealing, except in the safest ways, with ethnic hostilities and with the most explosive national issue: the conflict between the mostly Christian south and the Muslim-dominated north. Nollywood constantly shows spiritual war between Christianity and traditional religions, but conflict between Christians and Muslims is too inflammatory to be touched. (The exception that proves the rule is an Igbo-made film, *Holy Law: Sharia* (2001).) In 2000 Kingsley Ogoro produced a movie about the Nigerian Civil War, the first on this deeply traumatic subject. Originally titled *Guns of Biafra*, it is about an Igbo military officer posted to the north and married to a northern Muslim woman who, as the war breaks out, is forced to flee to the south and takes up arms. The censors board insisted on cuts and, worried by revived talk about Biafra by disgruntled Igbos, forced a change in title, so that the film was released as *The Battle of Love*, pushing it toward romance to blunt its political edge.

4. Kelani and Ishola's first collaboration, *Koseegbe* (1995), is about a customs officer crusading against corruption—in its time, the most direct handling of a political issue, daring to show men in uniform.

5. Kelani regularly shot news footage for the NTA and continues to be accredited as a freelance news cameraman. Working for the BBC, he covered the demonstrations and violence around the annulment of the 1993 election and the deaths of M. K. O. and Kudirat Abiola.

6. On Kelani's run-in with the NFVCB over *Agogo Eewo*, see Haynes 2007c.

7. The first ladies' official, military-backed brand of feminism may have contributed to Tokumbo's character, though some combination of the vixens of international soap operas and the Nigerian troubled obsession with the figure of "senior girls" would be a sufficient basis. This film does not actually seem to be hung up on misogyny, which permeates much of the discourse on "senior girls." Tokumbo's power, though sexualized, is not subsumed by sex, in spite of the number of men attracted to her. Her relationships with the president, Gomez, and Raymond all depend on her intelligence and force of will, not her sexuality. Her sexuality is scandalous, but so is everything else about her. She is full of the most envied and hated qualities—beautiful and rich, arrogant, impious, powerful, independent, sexually uncontrollable—but she is perhaps as much a fantasy projection for women as a male nightmare of women's frightening power.

8. According to Sam Obeakheme, the actor who played the Abacha character in *Stubborn Grasshopper*, the producer of the film spread untrue rumors about arrests for the sake of publicity (Anokam 2010).

CHAPTER NINE

1. Alessandro Jedlowski pointed out to me that the image foreigners have of Nollywood was fixed at this particularly overheated moment in 2007, through journalistic accounts and a trio of good documentary films, *This is Nollywood*, *Nollywood Babylon*, and *Welcome to Nollywood*. Nollywood filmmakers now tend to be indignant at the impression, formed in those frenzied days, that films are shot in a week and postproduction takes two weeks—though the average schedules they give for the more leisurely present are around three times that, still quite remarkable by world standards.

2. Special thanks to Vincent Dubem, Emeka Amakeze, Ugezu J. Ugezu, and to Solomon Apete for letting me see his operation in action.

3. Compare the Yoruba Efe masquerade at the end of *Ti Oluwa Nile* (chapter 5). In his autobiography Olaudah Equiano, remembering his childhood in Igboland in the middle of the eighteenth century, says groups of young men and women performed dance-dramas generally based on a recent event (Equiano 1999, chapter 1, section 3).

4. See Tcheuyap 2011, chapter 1, and the discussion of Baba Sala's 1970s stage play on this theme, *Tokunbo*, in Obafemi 1996, chapter 1.

5. On improvisation in the Yoruba tradition, see Barber 2000 and Adesokan 2009b.

6. Shaibu Husseini describes similar jokes in *Orija Shrine*, one of several Nollywood treatments of the Okija Shrine scandal (Husseini 2005).

7. Bona is hypocritical: he also has not built a house and has abandoned his family in the city. Owoh's characters are usually bad husbands and fathers if they take on these roles at all.

CHAPTER TEN

1. On the global dimensions of Nollywood see Krings and Okome 2013, an excellent volume including an earlier version of this chapter. See also Haynes 2003a, about mostly Ghanaian films made abroad before 2001.

2. It is possible to do without one of these elements—*A Night in the Philippines* does not depend on an expatriate community, and *This America* and *Man on a Mission* have no imported star—but most films have both.

3. Stephanie Okereke's *Through the Glass* (2008) is the strongest instance of this. The setting is entirely American; the Nigerian identity of the character Okereke plays is barely mentioned and has no dramatic significance.

4. For that matter, it is dramatically different from the situation of younger Nigerian writers: nearly all the leading ones live and teach abroad, the immigrant experience is a common subject, debates center on topics like cosmopolitanism or Afropolitianism, and the influence of American MFA programs is clear.

5. I haven't attempted to deal with a whole category of films made with imported Nigerian stars and sometimes directors in other African countries, as those countries attempt to establish their own film industries in imitation of the Nollywood model. See Haynes 2005b.

6. Charles Piot, writing about Togo, describes a disenchantment with postcolonial Africa so intense that a huge percentage of Africans want to leave (2010).

7. But the top-of-the-line production *Dangerous Twins* has shots of both Murtala Muhammed and Heathrow airports. For some remarks on airport scenes in Ghanaian video films, see Dogbe 2003, 237–40.

8. Hamid Naficy writes of exile, "It is a slipzone of anxiety and imperfection, where life hovers between the heights of ecstasy and confidence and the depths of despondency and doubt" (2001, 12).

9. These options lead directly to immersion in the iconography of those professions, already thoroughly developed on Nigerian soil in versions heavily influenced by foreign models, especially gangster films and hip-hop culture. *Man on a Mission* is particularly self-conscious in playing with gangster culture; a major character is called "Dogfather."

10. An *ikenga* (Igbo) is a small statue representing a man's individual strength; *chi* (Igbo) is a person's daimon or spiritual double, and also his or her destiny; *ase* (Yoruba) is the universal life force contained in every individual as well as in objects.

11. *Anchor Baby* (2010) is an exception. A couple without links to an African community overstay their American visas; he is deported and she falls into the hands of white criminals.

CHAPTER ELEVEN

1. See Husseini 2010. Journalists routinely note educational credentials in profiles of movie people. All aspects of the demographics of Nollywood need more thorough investigation. Lillian Ann Auliff noticed in 1997 that "actors of the traveling theatre usually came from the lower ranks of society, while video stars seem to be coming out of the middle and upper classes" (13).

2. For example, the Theatre Arts Department at the University of Port Harcourt has produced an impressive number of Nollywood stars, and its faculty includes the actor Sam Dede

and the film scholar Femi Shaka, but its curriculum remains theater-based. Dede and Shaka proposed an entrepreneurially oriented film studies program designed to train students to function in Nollywood but couldn't get it approved. Institutions trying to educate students for careers in Nollywood include Kwara State University and Pan-Atlantic University.

3. In the public system of higher education tuition is very low, but many families struggle to pay the various fees and living expenses. Students' families may themselves be in need of support; in the films, the burden of paying medical bills for family members often falls on students.

4. *O Le Ku* was quickly followed by *Rampage* (1998), directed by Madu Chikwendu. I have not been able to see this film, which has disappeared from the market. Even the film's director cannot find a copy—an example of the difficulties of constructing a proper history of Nollywood.

5. On the founding and evolution of the Pyrates and the emergence of campus cults out of such confraternities, see Eguavoen 2008 and Bastian 2001. Kelani's film conveyed such an attractive vision of 1970s Nigerian culture that it sparked a revival of fashions and hair styles from that period.

6. A newspaper article reports that some female University of Lagos students put off graduation, preferring their lucrative careers as student prostitutes to the unemployment that awaits them after university. They used to bribe or pressure lecturers to pass them; now they deliberately fail (Mustafa 2010).

7. It is young actors and screenwriters, naturally attuned to the styles of the moment, who have established the new generation's ownership of the genre of campus films. Some are directed by young people, like Rahim Cas Chidiebere's *Before the War*, but mostly the producers and directors are veterans.

8. *Girls Hostel* is one of only two films in my sample with no cults. But according to Bond Emeruwa, who wrote the screenplay and assistant directed, as they filmed on the campus of Rivers State University of Science and Technology, the production was besieged by cultists demanding money. After a tense protracted standoff the filmmakers fled, finishing the film in an Asaba hotel.

9. Compare John McCall's evocation of the dense "landscape of names" in Igbo villages, where places carry the names of ancestors so that "It is impossible to identify a particular place in the village without making reference to these names. They are simultaneously its history and its topography." Everyday experience is saturated with such references, which define and constantly reinforce an individual's sense of identity as being rooted in kin relationships (McCall 2000, 101).

10. The term "capone," universally used in campus films for the leader of a cult, appears to be a conflation of the Italian mafia title "capo" with the surname of the famous American gangster.

11. This is my term, not one in general use.

CHAPTER TWELVE

1. IROKO established itself with twin free Internet channels, one inside YouTube (NollywoodLove.com) and iROKOtv.com. Now they offer only a subscription premium level of iROKOtv.com.

2. Awolowo, mentioned earlier as a hero of the independence era, crystalized an enlightened politics and cultural politics that was at once proudly Yoruba and Nigerian nationalist, with no

sense of contradiction. He is by no means the only figure taking such a position, which sank deeply into the Yoruba popular arts (Barber 1987). "Wazobia" combines the words for "come" in Hausa, Yoruba, and Igbo.

3. The film's English and Yoruba titles are not translations of one another: "Araromire" is the name of the deity and her village, suggesting her power and an indigenous locality; "The Figurine" points to the representation of the deity, which can be transported, duplicated, and falsified.

FILMOGRAPHY

Abeni 1 and 2. 2006. Dir. Tunde Kelani. Perfs. Sola Asedeko, Amzat Abdel Hakim, Jide Kosoko, and Kareem Adepoju. Yoruba and French. VCD. Nigeria. Laha/Mainframe.

Accidental Discharge 1 and 2. 2003. Dir. Teco Benson. Perfs. Hanks Anuku, Ernest Asuzu, Rita Dominic, and Robert Peters. English. VCD. Nigeria. TFP Global Network.

Agbako: The Land of a Thousand Demons. 2000. Dir. Ojiofor Ezeanyaeche. Perfs. Genevieve Nnaji, Sam Dede, Patience Ozokwor, and Steph-Nora Okereke. English. VHS. Nigeria. OJ Productions.

Agba Man. 1992. Dir. Moses Olaiya Adejumo. Perfs. Moses Olaiya Adejumo, Shola Shoremekun, Aduke George, and Bankole Ayodeji. Yoruba. VHS. Nigeria. Amco.

Agogo Eewo/Taboo Gong. 2002. Dir. Tunde Kelani. Perfs. Wale Ogunyemi, Dejumo Lewis, Lere Paimo, and Larinde Akinyele. Yoruba. VCD. Nigeria. Mainframe.

Aiye. 1979. Dir. Ola Balogun. Perfs. Hubert Ogunde, Lere Paimo, Isola Ogunsola, and Jimoh Alliu. Yoruba. Celluloid. Nigeria. Ogunde Films.

Aje Ni Iya Mi/My Mother Is a Witch. 1989. Dir. Hammed Oguntade. Perfs. Shola Ogunsola, Iyabo Ogunsola, Fatai Odua, and Idowu Phillips. Yoruba. VHS. Nigeria. NEK Video Links.

Aki Na Ukwa. 2002. Dir. Amayo Uzo Philips. Perfs. Osita Iheme, Chinedu Ikedezie, Oby Kechere, and Amaechi Muonagor. English. VCD. Nigeria. Kas-Vid.

Amadi. 1975. Dir. Ola Balogun. Perfs. John Chukwu. Igbo. Celluloid. Nigeria. Afrocult.

Amazing Grace, The. 2006. Dir. Jeta Amata. Perfs. Nick Moran, Scott Cleverdon, Fred Amata, and Joke Silva. English and Efik. Celluloid. Nigeria and United Kingdom. Jeta Amata Concepts and Amazing Grace Films.

American Dream. 2006. Dir. Tony Abulu. Perfs. Karibu Fubara, Maryam Basir, Jim Iyke, and Tuvi James. English. DVD. USA and Nigeria. Black Ivory Communications and Royal Pictures Nigeria.

Amina: Unity in Diversity. 1999. Dir. Ndubuisi Okoh. Perfs. Pete Edochie, Olu Jacobs, Kashimu Yaro, and Enebeli Elebuwa. English. VHS. Nigeria. Okija-Amaka Pictures.

Ami-Orun/Birthmark 1 and 2. 1995. Dir. Tunde Alabi-Hundeyin. Perfs. Peju Ogunmola, Shola Fosudo, Clarion Chukwura, and Iya Rainbow. Yoruba. VHS. Nigeria. Dudu Films.

Anchor Baby. 2010. Dir Lonzo Nzekwe. Perf. Omoni Oboli, Sam Sarpong, Terri Oliver, and Michael Scratch. English. DVD. Nigeria and Canada. Alpha Galore Films.

Aristos 1 and 2. 2003. Dir. Tarila Thompson. Perfs. Stephanie Okereke, Steph Nora Okere, Georgina Onuoha, and Ashley Nwosu. English. VCD. Nigeria. Elonel.

Armed Forces. 2000. Dir. Emeka Okpala. Perfs. Jim Iyke, Brenda Paul-Ukpebor, Barbara Odoh-Nnakwe, and Kunle Coker. English. VCD. Nigeria. Christian Dior and Southgate.

Aropin N' Tenia. 1982. Dir. Freddie Goode and Hubert Ogunde. Perfs. Hubert Ogunde, Lere Paimo, Isola Ogunsola, and Oyin Odejobi. Yoruba. Celluloid. Nigeria. Ogunde Films.

Arugba. 2008. Dir. Tunde Kelani. Perfs. Bukola Awoyemi, Segun Adefila, Peter Badejo, and Kareem Adepoju. Yoruba. VCD. Nigeria. Mainframe.

Ashes to Ashes 1 and 2. 2001. Dir. Andy Amenechi. Perfs. BobManuel Udokwu, Justus Esiri, Francis Agu, and Chiega Alisigwe. English. VHS. Nigeria. OJ Productions.

Ayanmo.1988. Dir. Freddie Goode and Hubert Ogunde. Perfs. Hubert Ogunde, Adeyemi Afolayan, Isola Ogunsola, and Oyin Odejobi. Yoruba. Celluloid. Nigeria. Ogunde Films.

Ayo Ni Mo Fe 1 and 2. 1994. Dir. Tunde Kelani. Perfs. Yomi Ogunmola, Bola Obot, Lere Paimo, and Alhaji Kareem Adepoju. Yoruba. VHS. Nigeria. Mainframe.

Babangida Must Go/Maradona. 1993. Dir. Gbenga Adewusi. Perfs. Gbenga Adewusi, Baba Suwe, Pa Kusumu, and Lukuluku. Yoruba. VHS. Nigeria. Bayowa Films.

Back to Africa. 1997. Dir. Tony Abulu. Perfs. Wole Amele, Ella Asad, Jimmy Johnson, and Lanre Hassan. English and Yoruba. VHS. USA and Nigeria. Black Ivory Communication and Even Ezra/Bonag.

Battle of Love. 2000. Dir. Simisola Opeoluwa. Perfs. Segun Arinze, Kanayo O. Kanayo, Rekia Attah, and Ramsey Nouah. English. VHS. Nigeria. Kingsley Ogoro Productions.

Battle of Musanga, The 1 and 2. 1996. Dir. Bolaji Dawodu. Perfs. Alex Usifo, Chika Anyanwu, Chiwetalu Agu, Eucharia Anunobi, and Emeka Ani. English. VHS. Nigeria. Gabosky and Chezkay.

Beautiful Faces 1 and 2. 2004. Dir. Kabat Esosa Egbon. Perfs. Ini Edo, Oge Okoye, and Stephanie Okereke. English. VCD. Nigeria. Kas-Vid.

Before the Rain 1 and 2. 2008. Dir. Ikechukwu Onyeka. Perfs. Van Vicker, Chika Ike, Desmond Elliot, and Tonto Dikeh. English. DVD. Nigeria and Ghana. Sky Movies/Softel and Black Star Entertainment.

Before the War 1 and 2/*Don't Fall the Hands of Lesbians*. 2007. Dir. Rahim Cas Chidiebere. Perfs. Nonso Diobi, Mercy Johnson, Uche Ogbode, and Ony Michael. English and Pidgin. Nigeria. World Choice Movies.

Beginning and the End, The 1 and 2. 2001. Dir. Lancelot Imasuen. Perfs. Clem Ohameze, Zulu Adigwe, Amaechi Muonagor, and Andy Chukwu. English. VCD. Nigeria. OJ Productions/Power Ministry.

Beyoncé, the President's Daughter 1 and 2. 2006. Dir. Frank Rajah Arase. Perfs. Van Vicker, Nadia Buhari, Jackie Agyemang, and Kalsoum Sinare. English. VCD. Ghana. Venus Films.

Billionaire's Club 1–3. 2003. Dir. Afam Okereke. Perfs. Fabian Adibe, Kanayo O. Kanayo, Pete Edochie, and Clem Ohameze. English. VCD. Nigeria. Sunny Collins and Great Movies.

Black Bra 1 and 2. 2005. Dir. Andy Amenechi. Perfs. Nonso Diobi, Oge Okoye, Uche Jombo, and Adaora Ukoh. English. DVD. Nigeria. Annex Merchandise/Sanga.

Black Gold: Struggle for the Niger Delta. 2011. Dir. Jeta Amata. Perfs. Mbong Amata, Mickey Rourke, Tom Sizemore, Vivica Fox, and Hakeem Kae-Kazim. English. Celluloid. Nigeria and USA. Jeta Amata Concepts and Rock City Entertainment.

Black Night in South America . . . Pray Hard Not to Be a Victim 1 and 2. 2007. Dir. Abel Success Erebe. Perfs. Desmond Elliot, Fernanda Fazzi, Eucharia Anunobi, and Charles Dall-Angol. English, Yoruba and Portuguese. DVD. Nigeria. African Oasis and Christian Dior.

Blood Diamonds. 2004. Dir. Teco Benson. Perfs. Zulu Adigwe, Hanks Anuku, Lanre Balogun, and Eunice Becker. English. VCD. Nigeria. Gold Pictures.

Blood Money 1 and 2. 1997. Dir. Chico Ejiro. Perfs. Zach Orji, Kanayo O. Kanayo, Francis Agu, and Francis Duru. English. VHS. Nigeria. OJ Productions.

Blood Sister 1 and 2. 2003. Dir. Tchidi Chikere. Perfs. Omotola Jalade Ekeinde, Genevieve Nnaji, Tony Umez, Patience Ozokwor, and Oge Okoye. English. VCD. Nigeria. Great Movies/Great Future.

Blood Vapour. 1997. Dir. Bolaji Dawodu. Perfs. Nkem Owoh, Dolly Unachukwu, Zach Orji, and Hilda Dokubo. English. VHS. Nigeria. Movielogue Productions.

Bloody Mission. 1998. Dir. Natty Bruce Idigbogu. Perfs. Natty Bruce Idigbogu, Agatha Aluya, Comfort Oleka, and Femi Martins. English. VHS. Nigeria. NBI and Bike.

Blue Sea. 2001. Dir. Chico Ejiro. Perfs. Sandra Achums, Saint Obi, and Ernest Obi. English. VHS. Nigeria. Andy Best Electronics.

Blues for a Prodigal. 1984. Dir. Wole Soyinka. Perfs. Felix Okolo, Femi Euba, Femi Johnson, and Jimi Solanke. English. Celluloid. Nigeria. Ewuro Productions.

Boys from Holland. 2006. Dir. MacCollins Chidebe. Perfs. Chinedu Ikedezie, Osita Iheme, Lilian Njoku, and Oni Michaels. English and Igbo. DVD. Nigeria. Magic Movies/Afric Planet.com.

Broken Pitcher, The. 2008. Dir. Mike Bamiloye. Perfs. Margaret Anenih, Mike Bamiloye, Wunmi Awotoye, and Gloria Bamiloye. English. DVD. USA and Nigeria. Mount Zion Film Productions and Northward Film Productions of RCCG Household of Faith.

Brotherhood of Darkness. 1996. Dir. Andy Amenechi and Bond Emeruwa. Perfs. Patrick Doyle, Zachee Orji, Okechukwu Ogunjiofor, and Dolly Unachukwu. English. VHS. Nigeria. Videosonic.

Campus Queen, The. 2004. Dir. Tunke Kelani. Perfs. Serah Mbaka, Lanre Fasasi, Segun Adefila, and Lere Paimo. English, Yoruba and Pidgin. VCD. Nigeria. Mainframe.

Cat, The 1 and 2. 2004. Dir. Andy Amenechi. Perfs. Jim Iyke, Ini Edo, Tom Njamanze, and Muna Obiekwe. English and Pidgin. DVD. Nigeria. Annex Merchandise/Sanga.

Charge and Bail. 2003. Dir. Prince Emeka Ani. Perfs. Osita Iheme, Chinedu Ikedieze, Amaechi Muonogor, and Tom Njmanze. English. VCD. Nigeria. Cobic and Lucky Star.

Circle of Doom. 1993. Dir. Chris Obi-Rapu. Perfs. Francis Agu, Sandra Damacus, Okechukwu Ogunjiofor, and Kanayo O. Kanayo. Igbo. VHS. Nigeria. Videosonic.

Claws of the Lion. 2005. Dir. Francis Onwochei. Perfs. Keppy Ekpeyong-Bassey, Ekwi Onwuemene, Ashley Nwosu, and Empress Njamah. English. VCD. Nigeria. Francochei Productions.

Close Enemies. 2009. Dir. Lancelot Imasuen. Perfs. Kate Henshawe-Nuttal, Zack Orji, Hakeem Kazee Hakeem, and Oris Erhuero. English. DVD. USA and Nigeria. Afro Media.

College War 1–4. 2010. Dir. Afam Okereke. Perfs. Van Vicker, Mercy Johnson, Jim Iyke, and Emma Ehummadu. English. DVD. Nigeria. Chez.

Columbia Connection 1 and 2. 2004. Dir. Obi Callys Obinali. Perfs. Larry Koldsweat, Osita Iheme, Lilian Bach, and Hanks Anuku. English. DVD. Nigeria. Hallmark Films.

Coming to South Africa 1 and 2. 2004, 2005. Dir. Paul Louwrens. Perfs. Ramsey Nouah, Hakeem Kae-Kazim, Thulani Mengdo, and Jade Hands. English. DVD. South Africa and Nigeria. P. Collins and Emmaco Holdings Films.

Compromise. 1996. Dir. Chika Onukwafor ("Christian Onu"). Perfs. Ifeanyi Azodo, BobManuel Udowku, Kate Henshaw, and Teco Benson. English. VHS. Nigeria. Great Movies and Emmalex.

Computer Girls: The Black Market 1 and 2. 2002. Dir. Chico Ejiro. Perfs. Shan George, Eurcharia Anunobi Ekwu, Charles Okafor, and Franca Aernan. Pidgin and English. VCD. Nigeria. Dux Ventures/Sanga.

Crazy Like a Fox. 2008. Dir. Tony Abulu. Perfs. Angel Fershgenet, Karibi Fubara, Ketura Hamilton, and David Ditto Tawil. English. DVD. USA. Black Ivory Communications.

Crossing Paths 1 and 2. 2008. Dir. John Uche. Perfs. Jiim Iyke, Van Vicker, Kasara Irick, and Courtney Neal. English. DVD. USA. African Movies and Ghawood Angel Productions/ Executive Image.

Crossroad: The Beginning. 1997. Dir. Christyn Michaels. Perfs. Gbenga Richards, Ngozi Nwosu, Emeka Ossai, and Kate Henshawe. English. VHS. Nigeria. Christyn Michaels/ Sungold International.

Dangerous Angels 1 and 2. 2010. Dir. Ikechukwu Onyeka. Perfs. Nonso Diobi, Ini Edo, Tonto Dikeh, and Halima Abubakar. English and Pidgin. Nigeria. De-Zeen.

Dangerous Twins 1–3. 2004. Dir. Tade Ogidan. Perfs. Ramsey Nouah, Danielle Mobarak, Stella Damasus Aboderin, and Norbert Young. English and Pidgin. VCD. Nigeria. Paulo International Concepts and OGD Pictures.

Dapo Junior. 2000. Dir. Tony Dele Akinyemi. Perfs. Saint Obi, Mandy Ooijen, Leonard Odekhiran, and Liz Benson. English and Pidgin. VHS. Netherlands. Imani and Double "A" Entertainment.

Dark Goddess. 1995. Dir. Andy Amenechi. Perfs. Regina Askia, Layi Ashadele, Yinka Craig, and Enebeli Elebuwa. English. VHS. Nigeria. Owoyemi Motion Pictures/Contech Ventures.

Dead End 1 and 2. 1996, 1997. Dir. Chico Ejiro. Perfs. Zach Orji, Liz Benson, Sandra Achums, and Ameze Imarhiagbe. English. VHS. Nigeria. Grand Touch/Amaco and Andy Best.

Deadly Affair: A True Life Story. 1995. Dir. Chico Ejiro. Perfs. Dolly Unachukwu, Sam Loco,

Charles Ifediba, and Jide Kosoko. English, Igbo, and Hausa. VHS. Nigeria. Virgin Organization and Videosonic/Bonag.

Death of the Black President, The. 1983. Dir. Eddie Ugbomah. Perfs. Eddie Ugbomah, Tola Osinubi, Grace Ibok, and Jules Walter. English. Celluloid. Nigeria. Third World Productions.

De Prof 1 and 2. 2006. Dir. Charles Inojie. Perfs. Nkem Owoh, Clem Ohamezie, Rita Arum, and Elder Mugah Njubigbo. English and Pidgin. DVD. Nigeria. Elonel International/Sanga.

Desperadoes: The Story of Derico. 2001. Dir. Izu Ojukwu. Perfs. Alex Usifo, Eucharia Anunobi, Clem Ohamezie, and Sam Dede. English. VHS. Nigeria. Solid Productions.

Devil's Money. 1994. Dir. Anonymous. Perfs. Jagua, Benson, Grace, and Big Abass. Pidgin. VHS. Nigeria. Amaco.

Diabolo. 1991. Dir. William Akuffo. Perfs. Bob Smith Jr., Eunice Banini, Ophylia Ankra, and Nana Asantewaa. English. VHS. Ghana. World Wide Motion Pictures/Alexiboat Productions.

Died Wretched, Buried in N3.2 Million Casket. 1998. Dir. Kenneth Nnebue. Perfs. Tony Umez, Eucharia Anunobi, Rachael Oniga, and Tom Njamanze. English. VHS. Nigeria. NEK Video Links.

Dirty Deal. 1993. Dir. Kenneth Nnebue. Perfs. Chyke Ananaba, Atewe Lucky, Oleh Nnenna, and Carol Okeke. Igbo. VHS. Nigeria. NEK Video Links.

Dollars from Germany 1 and 2. 2004. Dir. Nonso Emekaekwue. Perfs. John Okafor, Mike Mafafa, Fred Ariko, and Sele Kent Sele. Pidgin and English. VCD. Nigeria. Deraco Productions.

Domitilla: The Story of a Prostitute 1 and 2. 1996, 1998. Dir. Zeb Ejiro. Perfs. Nanette Njemanze, Sandra Achums, Kate Henshawe, and Ada Ameli. English and Pidgin. VHS. Nigeria. Zeb Ejiro Productions/Daar Communications.

Dons in Abuja 1 and 2. 2004. Dir. Andy Amenechi. Perfs. Steve Eboh, Pete Edochie, Enebeli Elebuwa, and Colombus Arosanga. English. VCD. Nigeria. OJ Productions.

Dry Leaves. 1997. Dir. Opa Williams. Perfs. Ayo Adesanya, Toun Oni, Albert Egbe, and Segun Arinze. English and Pidgin. VHS. Nigeria. Virgin Organization/Andy Best.

Dubai Runs 1 and 2. 2007. Dir. Mac-Collins Chidebe. Perfs. Eucharia Anunobi, Tony Umez, Ngozi Ezeonu, and Kalu Ikeagwu. English, Igbo, and Pidgin. DVD. Nigeria. Kammadismss and Divine Merchants.

Dust to Dust. 1997. Dir. Fred Amata. Perfs. Fred Amata, Zach Amata, Francis Duru, and Nnena Nwabueze. English. VHS. Nigeria. Joyan Communications.

Dying for the Nation. 2001. Dir. Lancelot Imasuen. Perfs. Emeka Ike, Zach Orji, Ejike Asiegbu, and Patience Ozokwor. English. VHS. Nigeria. NDSS.

Eewo/Taboo. 1989. Dir. Ladi Ladebo. Perfs. Femi Fatoba, Yomi Obileye, Tunde Euba, and Jolade Kilanko. Yoruba. Celluloid. Nigeria. Ladi Ladebo Productions.

Efunsetan Aniwura: Iyalode of Ibadan. 2005. Dir. Tunde Kelani. Perfs. Iyabo Ogunsola, Samson Eluwole, and Toyosi Adesanya. Yoruba. VCD. Nigeria. Isola Ogunsola Film Productions/Golden Link Communications.

Egg of Life 1 and 2. 2003. Dir. Andy Amenechi. Perfs. Pete Edochie, Clarion Chukwura Abiola, Funke Akindele, and Chinelo Ndigwe. English. VCD. Nigeria. OJ Productions.

Emotional Crack. 2003. Dir. Lancelot Imasuen. Perfs. Ramsey Nouah, Dakore Egbuson, Stephanie Okereke, and Emma Ayalogu. English. VCD. Nigeria. Reemmy Jes.

Europe by Road . . . Miles Away from Africa 1 and 2. 2007. Dir. Ikenna Ezeugwu. Perfs. Kevin Bucks, Leo Chimmezie, Chris Onyenso, and Rahim Kas. Pidgin, English, and Igbo. VCD. Nigeria. Project Africa Film and Columbia Production/Time Entertainment.

Evil Passion. 1993. Dir. Chris Obi-Rapu ("Vic Mordi"). Perfs. Ngozi Nwosu, Chizoba Bosah, Nnenna Nwabueze, and Tochukwu Anadi. Igbo. VHS. Nigeria. JBM.

Faculty, The 1–3. 2007. Dir. Ugo Ugbor. Perfs. Ramsey Nouah, Jim Iyke, Oge Okoye, and McMorris Ndubueze. English. DVD. Nigeria. Simony Productions/Franco.

Fatal Desire: A True Life Story. 1995. Dir. Zeb Ejiro. Perf. Sydney Diala. English. VHS. Nigeria. Eclipse/Andy Best.

Fateful Love 1 and 2. 2004. Dir. Simi Opeoluwa. Perfs. Ramsey Nouah, Uche Amah Abriel, Omotola Jalade-Ekeinde, and Paul Obazele. English. DVD. Nigeria. Andy Best Electronics.

Festival of Fire. 1999. Dir. Chico Ejiro. Perfs. Kanayo O. Kanayo, Regina Askia, Saint Obi, and Victoria Inyama. English. VHS. Nigeria. Grand Touch.

Figurine, The/Araromire. 2010. Dir. Kunle Afolayan. Perfs. Kunle Afolayan, Ramsey Nouah, Omoni Oboli, and Funlola Aofiyebi-Raimi. English. DVD. Nigeria. Golden Effects.

Final Account. 2001. Dir. Ndubuisi Okoh. English. VHS. Nigeria. Showers of Blessings Production.

Final Hour 1 and 2. 2007. Dir. Afam Okereke. Perfs. Oge Okoye, Nonso Diobi, Uche Jombo, and Tonto Dikeh. DVD. Nigeria. Simony/Franco.

First Lady: Who Is She? 2000. Dir. Ifeanyi Ikpoenyi. Perfs. Zach Orji, Ernest Obi, and Barbara Udoh. English. VHS. Nigeria. Orange Seed Movies/Cosnoris.

Flesh and Blood: The Jessie Chukwuma Story 1 and 2. 1996, 1997. Dir. Chico Ejiro. Perfs. Ameze Imarhiagbe, Richard Mofe-Damijo, Bassey-Inyang Ekpeyong, and Christy Essien Igbokwe. English. VHS. Nigeria. International Artists/Ami Home Entertainment.

Formidable Force. 2002. Dir. Teco Benson. Perfs. Hanks Anuku, Ernest Asuzu, George Davidson, and Genevieve Nnaji. English. VCD. Nigeria. Reemmy Jes.

419 Connection: Deadly Rose. 2000. Dir. Ralph Nwadike. Perfs. Kanayo O. Kanayo, Barbarah Odoh, Ramsey Nouah, and Kunle Coker. English. VHS. Nigeria. O'King.

Freedom 1 and 2. 1999. Dir. Chico Ejiro. Perfs. Richard Mofe-Damijo, Rita Nzelu, Peter Edochie, and Fayke Aernan. English. VCD. Nigeria. Grand Touch.

Fugitive. 2001. Dir. Moses Ebere. Perfs. Geneveieve Nnaji, Stella Damasus Aboderin, Ramsey Noah, and Rita Dominic. English. VHS. Nigeria. NEK Video Links.

Girls Cot 1–3. 2006. Dir. Afam Okereke. Perfs. Genevieve Nnaji, Rita Dominic, Ini Edo, and Uche Jombo. English. DVD. Nigeria. Simony/Sanga.

Girls Hostel 1 and 2. 2001. Dir. Ndubuisi Okoh. Perfs. Olu Jacobs, Empress Njamah, Alexandra Lopez, and Uche Jombo. English and Pidgin. VHS. Nigeria. Christian Dior and Catwalk Pictures.

Glamour Girls. 1994. Dir. Chika Onukwafor ("Christian Onu"). Perfs. Gloria Anozie, Liz Benson, Jennifer Okereke, and Sola Fasudo. English. VHS. Nigeria. NEK Video Links.

Glamour Girls 2: The Italian Connection. 1996. Dir. Chika Onukwafor ("Christian Onu").

Perfs. Clarion Chukwuru-Abiola, Jennifer Okereke, Zack Orji, and Eucharia Anunobi. English. VHS. Nigeria. NEK Video Links.

Goodbye New York 1 and 2. 2004. Dir. Tchidi Chikere. Perfs. Genevieve Nnaji, Jim Iyke, Rita Dominic, and Chidi Mokeme. English, Pidgin, and Igbo. DVD. Nigeria. A2Z Movies International.

Good Girls Gone Bad 1–4. 2010. Dir. Nonso Emekaekwue. Perfs. Oge Okoye, Nonso Diobi, Chika Ike, and Halimah Abubakar. English and Pidgin. DVD. Nigeria. Great Favour Production/Franco.

Guilty Pleasures. 2009. Dirs. Desmond Elliot and Daniel Ademinokan. Perfs. Ramsey Nouah, Majid Michel, Mercy Johnson, and Nse Ikpe Etim. English. DVD. Nigeria. Royal Arts Academy.

Highway to the Grave. 1999. Dir. Teco Benson. Perfs. Regina Askia, Jide Kosoko, and Helen Ukpabio. English. VHS. Nigeria. Liberty Foundation Gospel Ministry.

Holygans. 1999. Dir. Tony Muonagor. Perfs. Tony Muonagor, Kingsley Ogbonna, Ejike Metusella, and Charles Okafor. Pidgin. VHS. Nigeria. One-Week Productions.

Holy Law: Sharia. 2001. Dir. Ejike Asiegbu. Perfs. Alex Usifo, Ejike Asiegbu, Ibrahim Mandawari, and Rachael Oniga. English. VHS. Nigeria. Kingstream Productions.

Home and Abroad. 2004. Dir. Lancelot Imasuen. Perfs. John Okafor, Victor Oswuagwu, Izoya Isaac, and Rita Azenobor. English and Pidgin. DVD. Nigeria and Germany. Lancewealth Images and Ehizoya Golden Ent./Videofield.

Hostages. 1996. Dir. Tade Ogidan. Perfs. Tope Idowu, Ofuafo Otomewo, Richard Mofe-Damijo, and Bimbo Manuel. English. VHS. Nigeria. OGD Pictures.

Hottest Babes 1 and 2. 2008. Dir. Emeka Nwabueze. Perfs. Oge Okoye, Francis Duru, Chika Ike, and Uche Jombo. English. DVD. Nigeria. Pressing Forward/Black Star Entertainment.

House, The 1 and 2. 2012. Dir. Blessing Ndak. Perfs. Yemi Blaq, Blessing Ndak, Akume Akume, and Vincent Opurum. English. DVD. Nigeria. B2 Entertainment.

Ibu in Campus 1–4. 2011. Dir. Charles Inojie. Perfs. John Okafor, Charles Inojie, Okey Bakassi, and Cynthia Okereke. Pidgin and English. VCD. Nigeria. Great Star.

Ibuka: King of the Forest. 2000. Dir. Lancelot Imasuen. Perfs. Pete Edochie, Sam Dede, Uche Obi Osutule, and Amatu Braide. English. VHS. Nigeria. OJ Productions.

Igodo: Land of the Living Dead. 1999. Dir. Don Pedro Obaseki and Andy Amenechi. Perfs. Pete Edochie, Nobert Young, Sam Dede, and Charles Okafor. English. VHS. Nigeria. OJ Productions.

Ija Ominira/Fight for Freedom. 1979. Dir. Ola Balogun. Perfs. Adeyemi Afolayan, Duro Ladipo, Oyin Adejobi, and Jimoh Alliu. Yoruba. Celluloid. Nigeria. Ade Love and Friendship Motion Pictures.

Ijé, the Journey. 2010. Dir. Chineze Anyaene. Perfs. Genevieve Nnaji, Omotola Jalade-Ekeinde, Ulrich Que, and Jeff Swarthout. English. Celluloid. USA and Nigeria. Xandria Productions.

Ijele: Son of the Masquerade. 1999. Dir. Fred Amata. Perfs. Eucharia Anunobi, Olu Jacobs, Sam Dede, and Sam Loco Efe. English. VHS. Nigeria. Great Movies.

Ikuku/Hurricane 1 and 2. 1995, 1996. Dir. Nkem Owoh and Zeb Ejiro. Perfs. Nkem Owoh, Pete Edochie, Zach Orji, and Sam Loco. Igbo. VHS. Nigeria. Nonks/Andy Best.

Irapada/Redemption. 2007. Dir. Kunle Afolayan and Biodun Aleja. Perfs. Kunle Afolayan, Deola Oloyede, Jotham Ayuba, and Angela Philips. Yoruba. DVD. Nigeria. Golden Effects.

Issakaba 1–4. 2000, 2001. Dir. Lancelot Imasuen. Perfs. Sam Dede, Zulu Adigwe, Chiwetalu Agu, and Pete Eneh. English and Pidgin. VHS. Nigeria. Kas-Vid.

Iwa. 1988. Dir. Lola Fani-Kayode. Perfs. Fr. Joseph Kenny, Fatai Babalola, David Ojedokun, and Wole Amele. Yoruba. Celluloid. Nigeria. Labs Deroy and Cinecraft.

Iya Ibeji Eleran Igbe/Mother of Twins, Seller of Bush Meat. 1997. Dir. Abbey Lanre. Perfs. Aduke Adeyemo, Gbolagade Akinpelu, Dupe Johnson, and Florence Ogunbiyi. Yoruba. VHS. Nigeria. Ogogo/Amazing.

Jaiyesimi. 1980. Dir. Freddie Goode and Hubert Ogunde. Perfs. Hubert Ogunde, Lere Paimo, Olu Omojola, and Sunday Omobolanle. Yoruba. Celluloid. Nigeria. Ogunde Films.

Jenifa 1 and 2. 2008. Dir. Muhydeen S. Ayinde. Perfs. Funke Akindele, Ronke Odusanya, Mosunmola Filani, and Iyabo Ojo. Yoruba and Pidgin. VCD. Nigeria. Olasco Films.

Kasalama: The Slave Merchant. 2003. Dir. Kenneth Egbuna. Perfs. Sam Loco Efe, Chiwetalu Agu, Tom Njemanze, and Emeka Ani. English. VCD. Nigeria. A.J. Films/World Movies Production.

King Jaja of Opobo. 1999. Dir. Harry Agina. Perfs. Haji Bello, Ineye Johnny Dudafa, Enebeli Elebuwa, and Femi Shaka. English. VCD. Nigeria. Sanctus Okereke/Stonecold Pictures.

Kongi's Harvest. 1970. Dir. Ossie Davis. Perfs. Wole Soyinka, Wale Ogunyemi, Femi Johnson, and Dapo Adelugba. English. Celluloid. Nigeria and USA. Francis Oladele/Calpenny.

Koseegbe. 1995. Dir. Tunde Kelani. Perfs. Wole Amele, Toyin Babatope, Faith Eboigbe, and Jide Kosoko. Yoruba. VHS. Nigeria. Mainframe.

Lagos Na Wah!!: Pidgin Comedy 1–3 1994. Dir. Kehinde Soaga. Perfs. James Iroha, Sunday Omobolanle, Kayode Odumosu, and Jide Kosoko. Pidgin. VHS. Nigeria. Topway Productions.

Last Burial: Will His Soul Rest in Peace? 1–3. 2000. Dir. Lancelot Imasuen. Perfs. Clement Ohameze, Eucharia Anunobi, Sam Dede, and Chika Anyanwu. English. VCD. Nigeria. Kas-Vid and Mosco.

Last Flight to Abuja. 2012. Dir. Obi Emelonye. Perfs. Omotola Jalade Ekeine, Jim Iyke, Hakeem Kae-Kazim, and Ali Nuhu. English. DVD. Nigeria. The Nollywood Factory.

Last Girl Standing 1 and 2. 2004. Dir John Uche. Perfs. Jim Iyke, Stepahnie Okereke, Robert Peters, and Empress Njamah. English. VCD. Nigeria. Konia Concept/P. M. O. Global.

Last Messiah, The 1–3. 2007. Dir. Moses Ebere. Perfs. Nkem Owoh, Fabian Adibe, Roy Denani, and Miriam Apolo. Pidgin and English. VCD. Be-Good Ventures/Iyke Merchandise.

Last Prophet. 2001. Dir. Lancelot Imasuen. Perfs. Zulu Adigwe, Ejike Asiegbu, Franca Brown, and Larry Koldsweat. English. VHS. Nigeria. Coruma.

Last Vote, The. 2002. Dir. Andy Amenechi. Perfs. Sam Dede, Olu Jacobs, Acho Ugenyi, and Sandra Achums. English. VHS. Nigeria. I. B. Best Industries.

Lies of Destiny 1 and 2. 1996, 1998. Dir. Madu Chikwendu. Perfs. Franca Brown, Paul Obazele, Joe Nwosu, and Jennifer Okere. English and Igbo. VHS. Nigeria/Ruby Diamond.

Life Incidence: A Day to Destiny 1–4. 2007. Dir. Iyke Odife. Perfs. Jim Iyke, Mike Ezuronye, Ebuba Nwagbo, and Browny Igboegwu. English. DVD. Nigeria. Paulsco Movies/Franco.

Liquid Black Gold, The 1 and 2. 2008. Dir. Ikenna Emma Aniekwe. Perfs. Sam Dede, Justus Esiri, Enebeli Elebuwa, and Gentle Jack. English and Pidgin. VCD. Nigeria. Ossy Affason.

Living in Bondage 1. 1992. Dir. Chris Obi-Rapu ("Vic Mordi"). Perfs. Kenneth Okonkwo, Okechukwu Ogunjiofor, Nnenna Nwabueze, and Kanayo O. Kanayo. Igbo. VHS. Nigeria. NEK Video Links.

Living in Bondage 2. 1993. Dir. Chika Onukwafor ("Christian Onu"). Perfs. Kenneth Okonkwo, Francis Agu, Ngozi Nwaneto, and Rita Nzelu. Igbo. VHS. Nigeria. NEK Video Links.

London Boy, The 1 and 2. 2004. Dir. Simi Opeoluwa. Perfs. Ramsey Nouah, Simone McIntyre, Segun Arinze, and Uche Amah Abriel. English and Pidgin. VCD. Nigeria. Andy Best and House of Macro.

London Forever. 2004. Dir. Chico Ejiro. Perfs. Shan George Nwosisi, Lanre Falana, Lilian Bach, and Rachel Oniga. English. VCD. Nigeria. Grandtouch Pictures/Contech Films.

MAAMi. 2011. Dir. Tunde Kelani. Perfs. Funke Akindele, Wole Ojo, Tamilore Kuboye, and Yinka Davies. English and Yoruba. Digital video. Nigeria. Mainframe.

Made in Cambridge 1 and 2. 2007. Dir. Mac-Collins Chidebe. Perfs. Nkem Owoh, Louisa Nwobodo, Funmi Holder, and Gardiel Onwudiwe. English and Pidgin. VCD. Nigeria. Ossy Affason.

Manko. 2006. Dir. Alhaji Sagir Mohammed. Perfs. Yahaya Alfa, Abdullahi Mohammed Bida, John Gana Muwo, and Jibrin Yikangi. Nupe. VCD. Nigeria. Leo-Shukrah.

Man on a Mission: Making Money Abroad. ND [2008?]. Dir. Romanus Ike Eze. Perfs. Romanus Ike Eze, Coco Xing, Ikenna Stanley, and Frank Ifeanyi. English and Pidgin. DVD. Nigeria. Kingsdome Entertainment.

Mask, The. 1979. Dir. Eddie Ugbomah. Perfs. Eddie Ugbomah, Oladele Osakwe, Fortune Onumajuru, and Moses Ajumobi. English. Celluloid. Nigeria. Edifosa Films.

Militants 1 and 2. 2007. Dirs. Aquiila Njamah and Moses Inwang. Perfs. Banbino Anachina, Monalisa Chinda, Dakore Egbosan, and Justus Esiri. English. VCD. Nigeria. Angel Media Productions.

Mirror Boy, The. 2011. Dir. Obi Emelonye. Perfs. Genevieve Nnaji, Osita Iheme, Fatima Jabbe, and Edward Kagutuzi. English. Digital video. UK. OH Films.

Missing in America. 2004. Dir. Sola Osofisan. Perfs. Uche Ama-Abriel Osotule, Mildred Okopie, Buky Campbell, and Austeen Eboka. English. DVD. USA. Creative Chronicles and Concepts and Buky's Place Enterprises.

Mission to Nowhere 1 and 2. 2008. Dir. Teco Benson. Perfs. Yahseph Ananaba, Sam Dede, Stephanie Okereke, and Jim Roach. English. VCD. Nigeria. TFP Global Network.

Mister Johnson. 1990. Dir. Bruce Beresford. Perfs. Pierce Brosnan, Edward Woodward, Maynard Eziashi, and Hubert Ogunde. English. Celluloid. USA. Avenue Pictures.

Modupe Temi/I Thank God for My Own. 2008. Dir. Daniel Ademinokan. Perfs. Saheed Balogun and Doris Simeon. Yoruba. DVD. Nigeria. Saidi Balogun Film Production.

Mortal Inheritance. 1996. Dir. Andy Amenechi. Perfs. Omotola Jalade-Ekeinde, Kunle Bamtefa, Fred Amata, and Ted Mukoro. English. VHS. Nigeria. Zeb Ejiro/Louis Merchandizing.

Mosebolatan/Hopelessness. 1986. Dir. Adeyemi Afolayan. Perfs. Moses Olaiya Adejumo, Karim Adepoju, Isola Ogunsola, and Tayo Ogunmola. Yoruba. Celluloid. Nigeria. Alawada Movies.

Mr Ibu in London. 2004. Dir. Adim Williams. Perfs. John Okafor, Ishola Oshun, Kareem Adepoju, and Femi Falana. Pidgin and English. VCD. Nigeria. Kas-Vid and Soft Touch Movies.

Mr Lecturer. 2006. Dir. Prince Emeka Ani. Perfs. Nkem Owoh, Sam Loco Efe, Stella Ikwuegbu, and Chidinma Aneke. English and Pidgin. VCD. Nigeria. Konia Concepts.

Muzik Man. 1976. Dir. Ola Balogun. Perfs. George Anderson, James Campbell, Art Alade, and Twins Seven Seven. English. Celluloid. Nigeria. Afrocult.

Naked Girls 1 and 2. 2009. Dir. Cyril Jackson. Perfs. Vincent Opurum, Sean Blessed, Tonto Dike, and Enebeli Elebuwa. English. VCD. Nigeria. Frontmaster.

Narrow Path, The. 2007. Tunde Kelani. Perfs.Sola Asedeko, Seyi Fasuyi, Eniola Olaniyan, and Ayo Badmus.Yoruba. VCD. Nigeria/Benin Republic. Mainframe.

Ngene: The Mistake of the Past Millenium 2000. Dir. Ndubuisi Okoh. Perfs. Kanayo O. Kanayo, Chiyere Wilfred, Ann Ohume, and Prince James Uche. English. VCD. Nigeria. Emeka Obiakunwa/Nwaeze Investments.

Nigerian Girls 1 and 2. 2009. Dir. Dandy Chukwuemeka Echefu. Perfs. Uchel Elendu, Emeka Enyiocha, McMorris Ndubueze, and Udochi Anthony. English. DVD. Nigeria. Golden Movies/Zodiac Films.

Night in the Philippines, A 1 and 2. 2006. Dir. Zeb Ejiro. Perfs. Desmond Elliot, Ibinabo Fiberesima, Marie Eboka, and Ufoma Ejenobor. English. VCD. Nigeria. Zeb Ejiro Productions/Movieland Network.

Nneka, the Pretty Serpent 1 and 2. 1994, 1995. Dirs. Zeb Ejiro and Bolaji Dawodu. Perfs. Ndidi Obi, Okechukwu Ogunjiofor, Rita Nzelu, and Kanayo O. Kanayo. Igbo. VHS. Nigeria. Gabosky and Videosonic.

Nollywood Babylon. 2008. Dirs. Ben Addelman and Samir Mallal. English. DVD. Canada. AM Pictures.

Obee Gbona/Hot Soup. 1997. Dir. Anonymous. Perfs. Moses Olaiya Adejumo, Iya Sala, Adisa Baba, and Oyin Adejobi. Yoruba. VHS. Nigeria. Alawada Movies/Bayowa Films.

Oduduwa. 2000. Dir. Andy Amenechi. Perfs. Peter Fatomilola, Femi Fatoba, Bukky Ajayi, and Pete Edochie. English. VHS. Nigeria. 21st Century African Fox and Ojo Jolu Films.

Odum: A Tale from the Death of the Blue Lake. 1999. Dir. Chico Ejiro. Perfs. Jimi Sholanke, Femi Fatoba, and Nnambi Eze. English. VHS. Nigeria. Amaco.

Oganigwe: My Love Is Your Love. 2000. Dir. Fred Amata. Perfs. Olu Jacobs, Kenneth Okonkwo, Zulu Adigwe, and Amaechi Muonagor. English. VHS. Nigeria. Solid Productions.

Oil Money. 2003. Dir. Neville Ossai. Perfs. Clem Ohameze, Chidi Modeme, Chijioke Abagwe, and Maureen Solomon. English. VHS. Nigeria. Okwuosa-Hand of God Production/Bonag.

Oil Village 1 and 2. 2001. Dir. Kalu Anya. Perfs. Sam Loco Efe, Sam Obiekheme, Sandra Achums, and Nnamdi Eze. English. VHS. Nigeria. Hycromax Investments.

Okada Man. 2002. Dir. Tchidi Chikere. Perfs. Nkem Owoh, Patience Ozokwor, Pete Eneh, and David Ihesie. English and Pidgin. VCD. Nigeria. Sunny Collins/Great Movies.

Okuzu Massacre: The Robbers Revenge. 2001. Dir. John Evah. Perfs. Segun Arinze, Hanks Anuku, Amaechi Muonagor, and Gentle Jack. English. VHS. Nigeria. Grand Touch Pictures/CE-MAX Investment.

Ola: The Morning Sun. 2004. Dir. Andy Amenechi. Perfs. Pete Edochie, Prince James Uche, Nonso Diobi, and Stephanie Okereke. English. VCD. Nigeria. Annex Merchandise.

O Le Ku/This is Serious 1 and 2. 1997. Dir. Tunde Kelani. Perfs. Yemi Shodimu, Feyinkemi Abodunrin, Pauline Dike, and Omolola Amusa. Yoruba. VCD. Nigeria. Mainframe.

Omo Eniyan/Son of Man. 2006. Dir. Muka Ray Eyiwunmi. Perfs. Peju Omobolanle, Muka Ray-Eyiwunmi, Yinka Quadri, and Becky Ajayi. Yoruba. VCD. Nigeria. Muka-Ray Films/Olasco.

One More Man: Who's the Next Victim. 2007. Dir. Ernest Obi. Perfs. Mercy Johnson, Francis Duru, Sylvia Ezeokafo, and Tony Ezimadu. English and Pidgin. VCD. Nigeria. Meena Pictures/Onye-Eze.

Onome 1 and 2. 1996, 1997. Dirs. Chico Ejiro and Opa Williams. Perfs. Uche Osotule, Olu Jacobs, Zach Amata, and Sam Loco. English. VHS. Nigeria. Consolidated Fortunes.

Oracle. 1998. Dir. Andy Amenechi. Perfs. Pete Odochie, Charles Okafor, Saint Obi, and Ejike Asiegbu. English. VHS. Nigeria. OJ Productions.

Orija Shrine 1 and 2. 2004. Dir. Tchidi Chikere. Perfs. Patience Ozokwor, Ejike Asiegbu, Enebele Elebuwa, and Clem Ohameze. English. VCD. Nigeria. Sunny Collins/Great Movies.

Oroki: Osun Osogbo Festival. 1996. Dir. Tunde Kelani. English and Yoruba. VHS. Nigeria. Mainframe.

Orun Mooru/Heaven Is Hot. 1982. Dir. Ola Balogun. Perfs. Moses Olaiya Adejumo, Deji Bankole, Twins Seven Seven, and King Sunny Ade. Yoruba. Celluloid. Nigeria. Alawada Movies.

Ose Sango/Sango's Wand. 1991. Dir. Afolabi Adesanya. Perfs. Kola Oyewo, Karimu Adepoju, Jide Kosoko, and Olatunbosun Odunsi. Yoruba. Celluloid. Nigeria. A- Productions.

Osuofia in London 1 and 2. 2003, 2004. Dir. Kingsley Ogoro. Perfs. Nkem Owoh, Mara Derwent, Charles Angiama, and Cynthia Okereke. English and Pidgin. VHS. Nigeria. Kingsley Ogoro Productions.

Other Side of Life, The. 2003. Dir. Femi J. Babatunde. Perfs. Ahmed Eddie Bangura, Julian Bezi, Willie Ali II, and Paul Oliver. English. DVD. USA. TFT Entertainment.

Outkast. 2001. Dir. Chico Ejiro. Perfs. Hank George, Sandra Achums, Lilian Bach, and Bob-Manuel Udokwu. English and Pidgin. VHS. Nigeria. Grand Touch.

Out of Bounds. 1997. Dir. Tade Ogidan. Perfs. Richard Mofe-Damijo, Lilian Amah, Rachael Oniga, and Steve Rhodes. English. VHS. Nigeria. Whitewater Productions/Outrage Pictures.

Owo Blow 1–3. 1996, 1998. Dir. Tade Ogidan. Perfs. Femi Adebayo, Taiwo Hassan, Rachael Oniga, and Yinka Quadri. Yoruba. VHS. Nigeria. First Call.

Pestilence. 2004. Dir. Mlemchukwu Prospect. Perfs. BobManuel Udokwu, Sam Loco Efe, Larry Koldsweat, and Pete Eneh. English. VCD. Nigeria. Ulzee Films.

Phone Swap. 2012. Dir. Kunle Afolayan. Perfs. Wale Ojo, Nse Ikpe-Etim, Joke Silva, and Lydia Forson. English, Pidgin, Yoruba, and Igbo. Digital video. Nigeria. Golden Effects.

President's Daughter, The. 2000. Dir. Chico Ejiro. Perfs. Regina Askia, Kunle Coker, Ashley Nwosu, and Paul Obazele. English. VHS. Nigeria. Infinity.

Princess Tyra 1 and 2. 2007. Dir. Frank Rajah Arase. Perfs. Van Vicker, Jackie A. Appiah, Kofi Adjorlolo, and Kalsoum Sinare. English. VCD. Ghana. Venus Films/Sanga.

Prof and Den-Gun, The. 2007. Dir. Amayo Uzo Philips. Perfs. Sam Loco Efe, Uche Ogbuagu, Ini Edo, and Charles Awurum. English and Pidgin. VCD. Nigeria. Reemmy Jes.

Prostitute, The. 2001. Dir. Fred Amata. Perfs. Omotola Jalade-Ekeinde, Segun Arinze, Elder Maya, and Nkechi Asiegbu. VHS. Nigeria. Kinglsey Ogoro/Ossy Affason.

Rampage. 1998. Dir. Madu Chikwendu. Perf. Monalisa Chinda. VHS. Nigeria. Cash Nwachukwu.

Rattlesnake 1 and 2. 1995, 1996. Dir. Amaka Igwe. Perfs. Okey Igwe, Nkem Owoh, Francis Duru, and Ebele Uzochukwu. Igbo. VHS. Nigeria. Moving Movies/Crystal Gold.

Red Matchet 1 and 2. 2000. Dir. Zeb Ejiro. Perfs. Zach Orji, Alex Usifo, Regina Askia, and Prince James Uche. English. VCD. Nigeria. Hycromax Investments.

Return of Beyoncé 1 and 2. 2006. Dir. Frank Rajah Arase. Perfs. Van Vicker, Nadia Buhari, Jackie Agyemang, and Kalsoum Sinare. English. VCD. Ghana. Venus Films.

Return of Jenifa 1 and 2. 2011. Dirs. Muyhdeen S. Ayinde and Lekan Oropo. Perfs. Funke Akindele, Ireti Osayemi, and Eniola Badmus. Yoruba. VCD. Nigeria. Olasco Films.

Rise and Fall of Dr. Oyenusi, The. 1976. Dir. Eddie Ugbomah. Perfs. Eddie Ugbomah, Enebeli Elebuwa, Moses Ajumobi, and Leke Ajao. English. Celluloid. Nigeria. Edifosa Films.

Rising Sun. 2003. Dir. Tchidi Chikere. Perfs. Genevieve Nnaji, Kenneth Okonkwo, and Chinwe Owoh. English. VCD. Nigeria. Oakfil and Emmason.

Rituals. 1997. Dir. Andy Amenechi. Perfs. Peter Edochie, Kanayo O. Kanayo, Charles Okafor, and Sola Fosudo. English. VHS. Nigeria. NEK Video Links.

Royal Palace 1 and 2. 2007. Dir. Andy Amanechi. Perfs. Olu Jacobs, Patience Ozokwor, Bob-Manuel Udokwu, and Chinyere Wilfred. English. VCD. Nigeria. Valesco.

Rush Hour 1 and 2. 2007. Dir. Afam Okereke. Perfs. Tonto Dikeh, Nonso Diobi, Oge Okoye, and McMorris Ndubueze. English. DVD. Nigeria. Simony/Franco.

Saving Alero. 2002. Dir. Tade Ogidan. Perfs. Bukky Ajayi, Francis Onwochei, Ayo Adesanya Hassan, and Bimbo Akintola. English. VCD. Nigeria. OGD Pictures.

Saworoide/Brass Bells. 1999. Dir. Tunde Kelani. Perfs. Koya Oyewo, Lere Paimo, Kunle Bantefa, and Bukky Wright. Yoruba. VCD. Nigeria. Mainframe.

7 *Kilometers* 1 and 2. 2007. Dir. Prince Ben Markson Jr. Perfs. Ebube Nwagbo, Columbus Irosanga, Walter Angar, and Geraldine Ekeocha. English. VCD. Nigeria. Onye-Eze.

Shame. 1996. Dir. Chico Ejiro. Perfs. Richard Mofe-Damijo, Liz Benson, Shola Fosudo, and Peter Ejiro. English. VHS. Nigeria. OJ Productions.

Shango: The Legendary African King. 1998. Dir. Femi Lasode. Perfs. Wale Adebayo, Bunmi Sanya, and Rachael Oniga. English. Celluloid and DVD. Nigeria. Even-Ezra.

Shehu Umar. 1976. Dir. Adamu Halilu. Perfs. Umaru Ladan and Assad Yasin. Hausa. Celluloid. Nigeria. Federal Film Unit.

Sherikoko 1 and 2. 2010. Dir. Amayo Uzo Philips. Perfs. Funke Akindele, John Okafor, Chizzy Alichi, and Charles Awurum. Pidgin and English. VCD. Nigeria. Onye-Eze.

Sitanda. 2006. Dir. Izu Ojukwu. Perfs. Justus Esiri, Bimbo Manuel, Stephanie Okereke, and Ali Nuhu. English. VCD. Nigeria. Amstel Malta Production/Digital Jungle Studios Production.

Six Demons: The Final End-Time Warning. 2004. Dir. Teco Benson. Perfs. Justus Esiri, Tina Amuziam, Mary Okolo, and Nora Roberts. English. VCD. Nigeria. TFP Global Network/ Reemmy Jes.

Slave. 1999. Dir. Chico Ejiro. Perfs. Kanayo O. Kanayo, Uche Obi-Osotule, Emeka Ossai, and Omotola Jalade-Ekeinde. English. VCD. Nigeria. Grand Touch and Infinity.

South Connection 1 and 2. 2004. Dir. Andy Chukwu. Perfs. Kanayo O. Kanayo, Pat Attah, Chidi Mokeme, and Pete Edochie. English. VCD. Nigeria. OJ Productions.

Staff of Odo, The. 2005. Dir. Sunday Nnajiude. Perfs. Fabian Adibe, Patience Ozokwor, Nkiru Sylvanus, and Pete Edochie. English. VCD. Nigeria. Mauri Production.

State of Emergency 1 and 2. 2000. Dir. Teco Benson. Perfs. Saint Obi, J.T. Tom West, and Bimbo Manuel. English. VHS. Nigeria. Ossy Affason.

Strange Ordeal. 1996. Dir. Jimi Odumosu. Perfs. Shola Fosudo, Edyth-Jayne Azu, Jide Kosoko, and BobManuel Udukwu. English. VHS. Nigeria. Centre Stage.

Stubborn Grasshopper: Loved Power, Died in Power 1 and 2. 2001. Dir. Simisola Opeoluwa. Perfs. Sam Obiakhme, Lanre Balogun, Clems Ohameze, and Ramsey Noah. English. VHS. Nigeria. Hycromax Investments.

Super Babes 1 and 2. 2008. Dir. Emeka Nwabueze. Perfs. Oge Okoye, Francis Duru, Chika Ike, and Uche Jombo. English. DVD. Nigeria. Pressing Forward/Black Star Entertainment.

Taboo. 1993. Dir. Chris Obi-Rapu ("Vic Mordi"). Perfs. Kenneth Okonkwo, Rosemary Honnah, Daniel Oluigbo, and Ngozi Nwaneto. Igbo. VHS. Nigeria. Sage.

Tango with Me. 2010. Dir. Mahmood Ali-Balogun. Perfs. Genevieve Nnaji, Joseph Benjamin, Bimbo Manuel, and Joke Silva. English. Celluloid. Nigeria. Mahmood Ali-Balogun.

Tears for Love. 1995. Dir. Chico Ejiro. Perfs. Keppy Ekpeyong-Bassey, Kanayo O. Kanayo, Ameze Imarhiagbe, and Fred Amata. English. VHS. Nigeria. Virgin Organization.

Tenant, The. 2009. Dir. Lucky Ejim. Perfs. Lucky Ejim, David Braughn, Richard Collier, and Jude Idaba. English. Celluloid. Canada. Broken Manacles Entertainment.

Things Fall Apart 1–13. 1986. Dir. David Orere. Perfs. Pete Edochie, Elizabeth Okaro, and Justus Esiri. English. Television broadcast and VCD. Nigeria. Peter Igho.

30 Days: Hell Hath No Fury. 2006. Dir. Mildred Okwo. Perfs. Genevieve Nnaji, Joke Silva, Segun Arinze, and CBA. English. DVD. USA and Nigeria. Native Lingua Films and Temple Productions.

This America. 2005. Dir. Bethels Agomuoh. Perfs. Oliver Oscar Mbamara, Bethels Agomuoh, Angelinah Ada, and Rena Anakwe. English. DVD. USA. African Film Company/United African Artists.

This Is Nollywood. 2007. Dir. Franco Sacchi. English. DVD. USA. Eureka Film Productions/ California Newsreel.

Through the Glass. 2008. Dir. Stephanie Okereke. Perfs. Stephanie Okereke, Garrett McKechnie, Ranier L. Kenny, and Pascal Atuma. English. DVD. USA and Nigeria. Next Page/ Social Movies.

Thunderbolt/Magun. 2001. Dir. Tunde Kelani. Perfs. Uche Obi-Osotule, Lanre Balogun, Buki Ajayi, and Larinde Akinleye. English. VCD. Nigeria. Mainframe.

Time Up . . . No Place to Hide. 2001. Dir. Lancelot Imasuen. Perfs. Kanayo O. Kanayo, Emma Oga, Justus Esiri, and Chiwetalu Agu. English. VHS. Nigeria. Moviemates.

Ti Oluwa Nile/The Earth is the Lord's 1–3. 1993, 1994, 1995. Dir. Tunde Kelani. Perfs. Kareem Adepoju, Dele Odule, Lekan Oladepo, and Jide Oyegunle. Yoruba. VHS. Nigeria. Mainframe.

Toronto Connection 1 and 2. 2007. Dir. Amayo Uzo Philips. Perfs. John Okafor, Sam Loco Efe, Charles Awurum, and Chiege Alusigwe. Pidgin and English. DVD. Nigeria. Darlington Okonkwo Production and Goodlife Production.

True Confession. 1995. Dir. Kenneth Nnebue. Perfs. Liz Benson, Shola Fosudo, Jennifer Okere, and Zach Orji. English. VHS. Nigeria. NEK Video Links.

Vendor. 1988. Dir. Ladi Ladebo. Perfs. Abu-Lo, Yemi Ajibade, Yinka Akerele, and Art Alade. Yoruba. Celluloid. Nigeria. Ladi Ladebo Productions.

Vigilante. 1988. Dir. Adedeji Adesanya. Perfs. Wole Amele, Olu Jacobs, Sam Loco Efe, and Toun Oni. English. Celluloid. Nigeria. A- Productions.

Violated: A Tale of Secrets 1 and 2. 1996. Dir. Amaka Igwe. Perfs. Ego Boyo, Richard Mofe-Damijo, Joke Silva, and Kunle Bamtefa. English and Pidgin. Nigeria. Moving Movies/Crystal Gold.

War Front 1 and 2. 2004. Dir. Teco Benson. Perfs. Festus Aguebor, Sam Dede, Steve Eboh, and Enebeli Elebuwa. English. VCD. Nigeria. Reemmy Jes.

Welcome to Nollywood. 2007. Dir. Jamie Meltzer. English. DVD. USA. National Black Programming Consortium/Cinema Guild.

Western Union 1 and 2. 2007. Dirs. Stanley Solomon Phillips and Prince Sam Onyejuwa. Perfs. Monalisa Chinda, Kester Peters, Precious Craoke, and Jim Lawson. English. VCD. Germany and Nigeria. Uche 10 and Damek Comm. Network.

White Castle 1 and 2. 2011. Dir. Okey Zubelu Okoh. Perfs. Olu Jacobs, Mercy Johnson, Chika Ike, and Anni Macauley. English. VCD. Nigeria. Social Movies/iROKOtv.

Yankee Boys 1–4. 2008. Dir. Moses Ebere. Perfs. Jim Iyke, Emeka Ike, Ramsey Nouah, and Gentle Jack. English. Nigeria. True Pictures and Mega Movies.

Yankee Girls 1 and 2. 2008. Dir. Moses Ebere. Perfs. Rita Dominic, Stella Damasus, and Omotola Jalade-Ekeinde. English. DVD. Nigeria. Mega Movies/Executive Image.

BIBLIOGRAPHY

Abimbola, Wande. 1977. *Ifa Divination Poetry*. New York: NOK.

Abone, Kasie. 2009. "Living in Bondage: How I Was Cheated out of a Project I Created." *Saturday Champion*, April 25, 18–19, 30.

Abu-Lughod, Lila. 2002. "The Objects of Soap Opera: Egyptian Television and the Cultural Politics of Modernity." In *The Anthropology of Media: A Reader*, edited by Kelly Askew and Richard R. Wilk, 376–93. Boston: Blackwell.

Achebe, Chinua. 1983. *The Trouble with Nigeria*. Enugu: Fourth Dimension.

———. 1994a. *No Longer at Ease*. New York: Anchor. First published 1960.

———. 1994b. *Things Fall Apart*. New York: Anchor. First published 1959.

Adamu, Abdalla Uba. 2005. *Passage to India: Media Parenting and Changing Popular Culture in Northern Nigeria*. Kaduna, Nigeria: Informart.

———. 2007a. "Currying Favour: Eastern Media Influences and the Hausa Video Film." *Film International* 5 (4): 77–89.

———. 2007b. *Transglobal Media Flows and African Popular Culture: Revolution and Reaction in Muslim Hausa Popular Culture*. Kano: Visually Ethnographic Productions.

———. 2010. "The Muse's Journey: Transcultural Translators and the Domestication of Hindi Music in Hausa Popular Culture." *Journal of African Cultural Studies* 22 (1): 41–56.

Adejunmobi, Moradewun. 2002. "English and the Audience of an African Popular Culture." *Cultural Critique* 50:74–103.

———. 2003. "Video Film Technology and Serial Narratives in West Africa." In *African Video Film Today*, edited by Foluke Ogunleye, 51–68. Manzini, Swaziland: Academic Publishers.

———. 2004. *Vernacular Palaver: Imaginations of the Local and Non-Native Languages in West Africa*. Bristol, UK: Multilingual Matters.

———. 2005. "Reading Video Film and Narrative Commerce in West Africa." *Canadian Review of Comparative Literature* 32 (3–4): 280–301.

———. 2012. "Nollywood and New Templates for Minor Transnational Film." Paper presented at the Society for Cinema and Media Studies Conference, Boston, March 21–25.

Aderinto, Saheed. 2012. "Representing 'Tradition,' Confusing 'Modernity': Love and Mental Illness in Yoruba (Nigerian) Video Films." In *Mental Illness in Popular Media: Essays on the Representation of Disorders*, edited by Lawrence Rubin, 256–69. Jefferson, NC: MacFarland.

Adesanya, Afolabi. 1990a. "Borrowing a leaf." *Guardian*, September 23. Rpt. in *Reel Views: A Collection of Essays and Reviews on the Nigerian and African Film Industry*, 37–38. Jos: Nigerian Film Corporation, 2012.

———. 1990b."Film: Language and Elitism." *Guardian*, July 8. Rpt. in *Reel Views*, 39–43.

———. 1992. *The Nigerian Film/TV Index*. Lagos: A-Productions.

———. 2000. "From Film to Video." In *Nigerian Video Films*, edited by Jonathan Haynes, 37–50. Athens: Ohio University Press.

Adesokan, Akin. 2008. "Alade Aromire: an Innovator's Legacy." *Nigerians in America*. Accessed September 12, 2012. www.nigeriansinamerica.com/articles/3123/1/Alade-Aromire-An-Innovators-Legacy/Page1.html.

———. 2009a. "Excess Luggage: Nigerian Films and the World of Immigrants." In *The New African Diaspora*, edited by Isidore Okpewho and Nkiru Nzegwu, 401–22. Bloomington: Indiana University Press.———. 2009b. "Practising 'Democracy' in Nigerian Films." *African Affairs* 108/433:599–619.

———. 2011a. "Anticipating Nollywood: Lagos Circa 1996." *Social Dynamics* 37 (1): 96–110.

———. 2011b. *Postcolonial Artists and Global Aesthetics*. Bloomington: Indiana University Press.

———. 2012. "Nollywood and the Idea of the Nigerian Cinema." *Journal of African Cinemas* 4 (1): 81–98.

Afigbo, A. E. 1972. *The Warrant Chiefs: Indirect Rule in Southeastern Nigeria, 1891–1929*. London: Longman.

Agbaegbu, Tobs. 1999. "Otokoto: Two Years After." *Newswatch* June 24. Accessed July 2, 1999. http://www.afbis.com/newswatch/Otokoto-Two%20Years%20After.htm (site discontinued).

Ajayi, I. A., H. T. Ekundayo, and F. M. Osalusi. 2010. "Menace of Cultism in Nigerian Tertiary Institutions: The Way Out." *Anthropologist* 12 (3): 155–60.

Ajibade, Babson. 2007. "From Lagos to Douala: The Video Film and Its Spaces of Seeing." *Postcolonial Text* 3 (2): 1–14. http://postcolonial.org/index.php/pct/article/view/524/418.

Akoh, Ameh Dennis, and Mary Okocha. 2011. " 'No, I Don't Watch Nigerian Films': Reception and Popularity of Nollywood Films among Select Nigerian University Students." In *Nollywood and Theatre for Development (TFD): Exploring the Bridges of Interaction*, edited by Samuel Ayedime Kafewo, 564–84. Zaria: Society of Nigerian Theatre Artists (SONTA).

Akpabio, Eno. 2007. "Attitude of Audience Members to Nollywood Films." *Nordic Journal of African Studies* 16 (1): 90–100.

Alawode, Sunday Olayinka. 2003. "Video Cassette Recorder (VCR) Uses among Families in Urban Lagos." *Nigerian Journal of Communications* 2 (1–2): 20–32.

Allen, Robert C., ed. 1995. *To Be Continued. . . . Soap Operas around the World*. London: Routledge.

Alonge, Osagie. 2013. "Endorsement Fever Grips Nigeria." *Nigerian Entertainment Today* 3 (26) (July 1–7): 1–2.

American Embassy Abuja. 2007. "Nigeria's PDP—When is a party not a party?" *WikiLeaks*. Accessed December 4, 2014. http://wikileaks.org/cable/2007/10/07ABUJA2232.html.

Anokam, Sam. 2010. "Playing Sani Abacha Made Me—Sam Obeakheme, actor." *Nigeria Films*, June 19. Accessed January 5, 2014. http://www.nigeriafilms.com/news/7994/1/playing-sani-abacha-made-me-sam-obeakheme-actor.html.

Apter, Andrew. 2005. *The Pan-African Nation: Oil and the Spectacle of Culture in Nigeria*. Chicago: University of Chicago Press.

Armes, Roy. 2008. *Dictionary of African Filmmakers*. Bloomington: Indiana University Press.

Ashforth, Adam. 1998. "Reflections on Spiritual Insecurity in a Modern African City (Soweto)." *African Studies Review* 41 (3): 39–67.

Auliff, Lillian Ann. 1997. *The Evolution of the Yoruba Video Industry and Its Potential for Development Communication*. Ames: Iowa State University Research Foundation.

Ayorinde, Steve. 1997. "Video Rage and Money Rake." *Guardian*, January 2, 25.

———. 1999. "Weed on the Path of Quality Movie." *Guardian*. January 7. Accessed December 4, 2009. http://www.ngrguardiannews.com/arts/an736101.htm (site discontinued).

Azuonye, Chukwuma. 1995. "*Igbo enwe eze*: Monarchical Power versus Democratic Values in Igbo Oral Narratives." In *Power, Marginality and African Oral Literature*, edited by Graham Furniss and Liz Gunner, 65–82. Cambridge: Cambridge University Press.

Baker, Bruce. 2002. "When the Bakassi Boys Came: Eastern Nigeria Confronts Vigilantism." *Journal of Contemporary African Studies* 20 (2): 223–44.

Bakhtin, Mikhail. 1968. *Rabelais and His World*. Cambridge: MIT Press.

———. 1981. *The Dialogic Imagination: Four Essays*. Austin: University of Texas Press.

Balogun, Francoise. 1987. *Cinema in Nigeria*. Enugu, Nigeria: Delta.

Barber, Karin. 1982. "Popular Reactions to the Petro-Naira." *Journal of Modern African Studies* 20 (3): 431–50.

———. 1987. "Popular Arts in Africa." *African Studies Review* 30 (3): 1–78.

———. 1991. *I Could Speak Until Tomorrow: Oriki, Women, and the Past in a Yoruba Town*. Edinburgh: Edinburgh University Press.

———. 2000. *The Generation of Plays: Yoruba Popular Life in Theater*. Bloomington: Indiana University Press.

Barber, Karin, and Christopher Waterman. 1995. "Traversing the Global and the Local: Fuji Music and Praise Poetry in the Production of Contemporary Yoruba Popular Culture." In *Worlds Apart*, edited by Daniel Miller, 240–62. London and New York: Routledge.

Barrot, Pierre, ed. 2009. *Nollywood: The Video Phenomenon in Nigeria*. Bloomington: Indiana University Press.

Basden, George Thomas. 1966. *Among the Ibos of Nigeria*. New York: Barnes and Noble.

Bastian, Misty L. 1993. "'Bloodhounds Who Have No Friends': Witchcraft and Locality in the Nigerian Popular Press." In *Modernity and Its Malcontents: Ritual and Power in Postcolonial Africa*, edited by Jean Comaroff and John Comaroff, 129–66. Chicago: University of Chicago Press.

———. 1997. "Married in the Water: Spirit Kin and Other Afflictions of Modernity in Southeastern Nigeria." *Journal of Religion in Africa* 27 (2): 116–34.

———. 2001. "Vulture Men, Campus Cultists, and Teenage Witches: Modern Magics in Nigerian Popular Media." In *Magical Interpretations, Material Realities: Modernity, Witchcraft, and the Occult in Postcolonial Africa*, edited by Henrieta L. Moore and Todd Sanders, 71–96. London: Routledge.

Bayart, Jean-Francois. 1993. *The State in Africa: The Politics of the Belly*. New York: Longman.

Bayart, Jean-Francois, Stephen Ellis, and Béatrice Hibou. 1999. *The Criminalization of the State in Africa*. Oxford: James Currey.

Becker, Heike. 2013. "Nollywood in Urban Southern Africa: Nigerian Video Films and Their Audiences in Cape Town and Windhoek." In *Global Nollywood*, edited by Matthias Krings and Onookome Okome, 179–98.

Bersselaar, Dmitri van den. 2005. "Imagining Home: Migration and the Igbo Village in Colonial Nigeria." *Journal of African History* 46:51–73.

Boughedir, Ferid. 1983. "Les grandes tendances du cinéma en Afrique noire." *CinémAction* 26:48–57.

Bourdieu, Pierre. 1977. *Outline of a Theory of Practice*. Cambridge: Cambridge University Press.

Bourgault, Louise M. 1995. *Mass Media in Sub-Saharan Africa*. Bloomington: Indiana University Press.

Box Office Mojo. 2012. "Yearly Box Office." Accessed June 6, 2012. http://boxofficemojo.com/yearly.

Bright, Jake. 2014. "Nollywood: The New Business of African Film." *This is Africa*. May 7. Accessed July 2, 2014. http://www.thisisafricaonline.com/Business/Nollywood-The-new-business-of-African-film.

Brooks, Peter. 1976. *The Melodramatic Imagination: Balzac, Henry James, and the Mode of Excess*. New Haven: Yale University Press.

Brown, Matthew H. 2014. "The Long Nollywood Century: Colonial Cinema, Nationalist Literature, State Television, and Video Film." PhD dissertation, Department of African Languages and Literature, University of Wisconsin-Madison.

Carwile, Christy. 2014. "Dancing a Pan-African Future: Inventive Dance Traditions in Ghana." Paper delivered at the African Studies Association Annual Meeting, Indianapolis, Indiana, November 20–23.

Charry, Eric, ed. 2012. *Hip Hop Africa: New African Music in a Globalizing World*. Bloomington: Indiana University Press.

Clark, Ebun. 1980. *Hubert Ogunde: The Making of Nigerian Theatre*. Oxford: Oxford University Press.

Clover, Carol J. 1992. *Men, Women, and Chainsaws: Gender in the Modern Horror Film*. Princeton: Princeton University Press.

Comaroff, Jean, and John Comaroff, eds. 1993. *Modernity and Its Malcontents: Ritual and Power in Postcolonial Africa*. Chicago: University of Chicago Press.

———. 1999. "Occult Economies and the Violence of Abstraction: Notes from the South African Postcolony." *American Ethnologist* 26 (2): 279–303.

———. 2000. "Millennial Capitalism: First Thoughts on a Second Coming." *Public Culture* 12:291–343.

Cooper, Frederick. 1981. "Africa in World History." *African Studies Review* 24 (2/3): 1–86.

Dandaura, Emmanuel S. and Obi Okoli. 2010. "Nigerian Home Video and the Imaging of Igbo Leadership Values and Cultural Identity." In *Theatre, Culture, and Re-imaging Nigeria*, edited by Emmanuel Samu Dandaura and Alex Chinwuba Asigbo, 63–74. Keffi: Society of Nigerian Theatre Artists.

Davidson, Basil. 1992. *The Black Man's Burden: Africa and the Curse of the Nation-State.* London: James Currey.

Diawara, Manthia. 1992. *African Cinema: Politics & Culture.* Bloomington: Indiana University Press.

Dogbe, Esi. 2003. "Elusive Modernity: Portraits of the City in Popular Ghanaian Video." In *Leisure in Urban Africa*, edited by Paul Tiyambe Zeleza and Cassandra Rachel Veney, 227–48. Trenton: Africa World Press, 2003.

Dosunmu, G. K. 1999. "Board's Management Deserves a Pat on the Back." *Classifier* 3 (1–3): 17.

Drewal, Henry John, ed. 2008. *Mami Wata: Arts for Water Spirits in Africa and its Diaspora.* Bloomington: Indiana University Press.

Drewal, Henry John, and Margaret Thompson Drewal. 1983. *Gelede: Art and Female Power among the Yoruba.* Bloomington: Indiana University Press.

Drewal, Henry John, John Pemberton III, and Rowland Abiodun. 1989. *Yoruba: Nine Centuries of African Art and Thought.* New York: Center for African Art and Harry N. Abrams.

Dunton, Chris. 1998. *Nigerian Theatre in English: A Critical Bibliography.* London: Hans Zell.

Ebeogu, Afam. 1987. "The Adventures of the 'Masquerade' Drama Group." *Nigeria Magazine* 55 (2): 1–12.

Eguavoen, I. 2008. "Killer Cults on Campus: Secrets, Security, and Services among Nigerian Students." *Sociologus* 58 (1): 1–25.

Ehirim, Chuks. 1997. "Otokoto Drama." *TheNEWS.* November 3, 28.

Ejike, Bob. 2005. "Nollywood and Electronics Traders." *Nigerians in America.* March 6. Accessed August 16, 2005. http://www.nigeriansinamerica.com/articles/583/1/Nollywood-And-Electronics-Traders/ (site discontinued).

Ejiogu, Ben. 2005. "Moses Eberegbulam Osuji (1929–2005)." *Guardian*, 55.

Ekunno, Mike. 2011. "Nollywood and the New Cinema." *Next.* Accessed December 4, 2012. http://234next.com/csp/cms/sites/Next/ArtsandCulture/5659940-147/story.csp (site discontinued).

Ekwuazi, Hyginus. 1991. *Film in Nigeria.* 2nd ed. Jos: Nigerian Film Corporation.

———. 2000. "The Igbo Video Film: A Glimpse into the Cult of the Individual." In *Nigerian Video Films*, edited by Jonathan Haynes, 131–47. Athens: Ohio University Press.

———. 2008a. "Development Communication: Towards an Assessment of the Nollywood Practice." *International Journal of Multi-Disciplinary Scholarship* 3–5:190–206.

———. 2008b. "Nollywood: History as Economic Determinism or as an Accident in Evolutionary Trends/Creative Process." *International Journal of Multi-Disciplinary Scholarship* 3–5:135–42.

Elegbeleye, O. S. 2005. "Personality Dimension to University Campus Cult Membership." *Anthropologist* 7 (2): 127–35.

Ellis, Stephen. 2001. *The Mask of Anarchy: The Destruction of Liberia and the Religious Dimension of an African Civil War*. New York: New York University Press.

———. 2008. "The Okija Shrine: Death and Life in Nigerian Politics." *Journal of African History* 49:445–66.

Emasealu, Emmanuel C. 2008. "The Audience Factor in Nollywood." *International Journal of Multi-Disciplinary Scholarship* 3–5:143–52.

Enwerem, Father Iheanyi. 1997. "The Money-Magic Phenomenon: A Study of Ritual Killings in Contemporary Nigeria." Unpublished manuscript.

Equiano, Olaudah. 1999. *The Life of Olaudah Equiano, or Gustavus Vassa, the African*. Mineola, NY: Dover.

Esan, Oluyinka. 2009. *Nigerian Television: Fifty Years of Television in Africa*. Princeton: AMV Publishing.

———. 2011. "Audience Appreciation of Nigerian Films (Nollywood)." In *Valuing Films: Shifting Perceptions of Worth*, edited by Laura Hubner, 121–48. New York: Palgrave Macmillan.

Fagunwa, D. O. 1982. *Forest of a Thousand Daemons*. Translated by Wole Soyinka. New York: Random House.

Fair, Austin. 2003. "NEK Video's Boss Loses N40m to Fraudsters." *Daily Times*, June 6, 11.

Fair, Laura. 2009. "Making Love in the Indian Ocean: Hindi Films, Zanzibari Audiences, and the Construction of Romance in the 1950s and 1960s." In *Love in Africa*, edited by Jennifer Cole and Lynn M. Thomas, 58–82. Chicago: University of Chicago Press.

Fanon, Frantz. 1964. *The Wretched of the Earth*. New York: Grove.

Fortes, Meyer. 1978. "Parenthood, Marriage, and Fertility in West Africa." *Journal of Development Studies* 14 (4): 121–48.

Frank, Barbara. 1995. "Permitted and Prohibited Wealth: Commodity-Possessing Spirits, Economic Morals, and the Goddess Mami Wata in West Africa." *Ethnology* 34 (4): 331–46.

Fuglesang, Minou. 1994. *Veils and Videos: Female Youth Culture on the Kenyan Coast*. Stockholm: Department of Social Anthropology, Stockholm University.

Gandy, Matthew. 2005. "Learning From Lagos." *New Left Review* 33:36–52.

———. 2006. "Planning, Anti-Planning, and the Infrastructure Crisis Facing Metropolitan Lagos." *Urban Studies* 43 (2): 371–96.

Garritano, Carmela. 2008. "Contesting Authenticities: The Emergence of Local Video Production in Ghana." *Critical Arts* 22 (1): 21–48.

———. 2013. *African Video Movies and Global Desires: A Ghanaian History*. Athens: Ohio University Press.

Geschiere, Peter. 1997. *The Modernity of Witchcraft: Politics and the Occult in Postcolonial Africa*. Charlottesville: University Press of Virginia.

Green-Simms, Lindsey. 2012a. "Hustlers, Home-wreckers, and Homoeroticism: Nollywood's *Beautiful Faces*." *Journal of African Cinemas* 4 (1): 59–79.

———. 2012b. "Occult Melodramas: Spectral Affect and West African Video-Film." *Camera Obscura* 27 (2): 25–59.

Green-Simms, Lindsey, and Unoma Azuah. 2012. "The Video-Closet: Nollywood's Gay-Themed Movies." *Transition* 107:32–49.

Griswold, Wendy. 2000. *Bearing Witness: Readers, Writers, and the Novel in Nigeria*. Princeton: Princeton University Press.

Guyer, Jane. 1993. "Wealth in People and Self-Realization in Equitorial Africa." *Man* 28: 243–65.

———. 2004. *Marginal Gains: Monetary Transactions in Atlantic Africa*. Chicago: University of Chicago Press.

Hallen, Barry. 2000. *The Good, the Bad, and the Beautiful: Discourse About Values in Yoruba Culture*. Bloomington: Indiana University Press.

Harneit-Sievers, Axel. 1998. "Igbo 'Traditional Rulers': Chieftaincy and the State in Southeastern Nigeria." *Afrika Spectrum* 33 (1): 57–70.

Harnischfeger, Johannes. 2003. "The Bakassi Boys: Fighting Crime in Nigeria." *Journal of Modern African Studies* 41 (1): 23–49.

———. 2006. "State Decline and the Return of Occult Powers: The Case of Prophet Eddy in Nigeria." *Magic, Ritual, and Witchcraft* 1 (1): 56–78.

Haynes, Jonathan. 1992. *The Social Relations of Jonson's Theater*. New York: Cambridge University Press.

———. 1995. "Nigerian Cinema: Structural Adjustments." *Research in African Literatures* 26 (3): 97–119.

———, ed. 1997. *Nigerian Video Films*. Ibadan: Kraft Books. Revised and expanded edition, Athens: Ohio University Press, 2000.

———. 2000. "Introduction." In *Nigerian Video Films*, edited by Jonathan Haynes, 1–36. Athens: Ohio University Press.

———. 2002. "Devaluation and the Video Boom: Economics and Thematics." In *Money Struggles and City Life: Devaluation in Ibadan and Other Urban Centers in Southern Nigeria, 1986–1996*, edited by Jane I. Guyer, LaRay Denzer, and Adigun Agbaje, 207–17. Portsmouth, NH: Heinemann.

———. 2003a. "Africans Abroad: A Theme in Film and Video." *Africa & Mediterraneo* 45: 22–29.

———. 2003b. "Mobilizing Yoruba Popular Culture: Babangida Must Go." *Africa* 73 (1): 122–38.

———. 2005a. "Cultural Epic: A Nigerian Video Film Genre." Paper presented at the African Studies Association Annual Meeting, Washington, DC, November 17–20.

———. 2005b. "Nollywood: What's in a Name?" *Guardian* (Lagos), July 3, 56, 58. Rpt. *Film International* 28 (5.4) (2007): 106–8.

———. 2006. "Political Critique in Nigerian Video Films." *African Affairs* 105 (421): 511–33.

———. 2007a. "Nnebue: The Anatomy of Power." *Film International* 28 (5.4): 30–40.

———. 2007b. "Nollywood in Lagos, Lagos in Nollywood Films." *Africa Today* 54 (2): 130–50.

———. 2007c. "TK in NYC: An Interview with Tunde Kelani." *Postcolonial Text* 3 (2). Accessed December 4, 2007. http://postcolonial.org/index.php/pct/article/view/659/409.

———. 2010a. "A Literature Review: Nigerian and Ghanaian Videos." *Journal of African Cultural Studies* 22 (1): 105–20.

———. 2010b. "What Is to Be Done? Film Studies and Nigerian and Ghanaian Videos." In *Viewing African Cinema in the Twenty-First Century: Art Films and the Nollywood Video Revolution*, edited by Mahir Saul and Ralph A. Austen, 11–25. Athens: Ohio University Press.

———. 2011. "African Cinema and Nollywood: Contradictions." *Situations* 4 (1): 67–90.

———. 2012. "A Bibliography of Academic Work on Nigerian and Ghanaian Video Films." *Journal of African Cinemas* 4 (1): 99–133.

———. 2013. "Nollywood Screenwriting: Notes toward a Literary History." Paper presented in the Distinguished Faculty Lecture Series, Faculty of Arts, University of Ibadan, June 24.

Haynes, Jonathan, and Onookome Okome. 1998. "Evolving Popular Media: Nigerian Video Films." *Research in African Literatures* 29 (3): 106–28. Rpt. from *Nigerian Video Films*, ed. Jonathan Haynes, 21–44, 1997.

Henderson, Richard M. 1972. *The King in Every Man: Evolutionary Trends in Onitsha Igbo Society and Culture*. New Haven: Yale University Press.

Human Rights Watch and Centre for Law Enforcement Education. 2002. *The Bakassi Boys: The Legitimization of Murder and Torture*. Human Rights Watch Reports 14.5(A). Accessed June 6, 2012. http://www.hrw.org/reports/2002/nigeria2/.

Husseini, Shaibu. 2005. "Orija Shrine: Tales of a Dreaded Forest in Pictures." *Guardian*, January 27, 66.

———. 2010. *Moviedom: Nollywood Narratives*. Lagos: All Media International.

Ifeka, Caroline. 2006. "Youth Cultures and the Fetishization of Violence in Nigeria." *Review of African Political Economy* 110:721–36.

"In Ijebu, Age-Long Myths Crash." 1997. *Guardian on Sunday*, April 5.

Iwenjora, Fred. 2001. "Living in Bondage Was a Rejected Stone—Nek." *Weekend Vanguard*, October 27.

James, Ademola. 1999. "Warning Notice: The Need for a New Direction in Nigerian Film Content." Memorandum. National Film and Video Censors Board. A.15/Vol. 1. July 14.

———. 2007. *The Making of Nigeria's Film and Video Revolution*. Lagos: Publicomm Associates.

Jedlowski, Alessandro. 2013. "From Nollywood to Nollyworld: Processes of Transnationalization in the Nigerian Video Film Industry." In *Global Nollywood and Beyond: Transnational Dimensions of an African Video Film Industry*, edited by Matthias Krings and Onookome Okome, 25–45. Bloomington: Indiana University Press.

Jeyifo, Biodun. 1984. *The Yoruba Popular Travelling Theatre of Nigeria*. Lagos: Nigeria Magazine.

Johnson, Rev. Samuel. 1921. *The History of the Yorubas*. Lagos: C. S. S. Bookshops.

Jones, G. I. 1970. "Chieftaincy in the Former Eastern Region of Nigeria." In *West African Chiefs: Their Changing Status under Colonial Rule and Independence*, edited by Michael Crowder and Obaro Ikime, 312–24. Ile-Ife: University of Ife Press.

Klein, Debra L. 2007. *Yoruba Bata Goes Global: Artists, Culture Brokers, and Fans*. Chicago: University of Chicago Press.

Krings, Matthias, and Onookome Okome, eds. 2013. *Global Nollywood: Transnational Dimensions of an African Video Film Industry*. Bloomington: Indiana University Press.

Kupoluyi, Biodun. 2004. "War against Pirates: Gbenga Adewusi Beaten, Police Harassed." *Sunday Punch*, September 19. Accessed December 4, 2004. http://www.odili.net/news/source/2004/sep/19/516.html (site discontinued).

Lakoju, Tunde. 1984, "Popular (Travelling) Theatre in Nigeria: The Example of Moses Olaiya Adejumo (Alias Baba Sala)." *Nigeria Magazine* 149:35–46.

Larkin, Brian. 1997. "Indian Films and Nigerian Lovers: Media and the Creation of Parallel Modernities." *Africa* 67 (3): 406–40.

———. 2000. "Hausa Dramas and the Rise of Video Culture in Nigeria." In *Nigerian Video Films*, edited by Jonathan Haynes, 209–41. Athens: Ohio University Press.

———. 2003. "Itineraries of Indian Cinema: African Videos, Bollywood, and Global Media." In *Multiculturalism, Postcolonialism, and Transnational Media*, edited by Ella Shohat and Robert Stam, 170–92. New Brunswick, NJ: Rutgers University Press.

———. 2004. "Degraded Images, Distorted Sounds: Nigerian Video and the Infrastructure of Piracy." *Public Culture* 16 (2): 289–314. Rpt. in Larkin 2008.

———. 2008. *Signal and Noise: Media, Infrastructure, and Urban Culture in Northern Nigeria*. Chapel Hill, NC: Duke University Press.

Lasode, Obafemi. 1994. *Television Broadcasting: The Nigerian Experience (1959–1992)*. Ibadan: Caltop.

Lawuyi, B. Olatunde. 1997. "The Political Economy of Video Marketing in Ogbomosho, Nigeria." *Africa* 67 (3): 476–90.

Lebeau, Yann. 1999. "Permissivité et violence sur les campus Nigérians." *Politique Africaine* 76:173–80.

———. 2008. "Universities and Social Transformation in Sub-Saharan Africa: Global Rhetoric and Local Contradictions." *Compare* 38 (2): 139–53.

Leu, Bic. 2011. "Nollywood and the New Cinema." *Finding Nollywood*. January 3. Accessed January 5, 2011. http://findingnollywood.com/2011/01/03/234next-nollywood-and-the-new-cinema/.

Lindfors, Bernth. 2004. *Recovering Letters, Discovering Numbers: Literary and Statistical Studies*. Trenton, NJ:Africa World Press.

Mamdani, Mahmood. 1996. *Citizen and Subject: Contemporary Africa and the Legacy of Late Colonialism*. Princeton: Princceton University Press.

Marshall, Ruth. 2009. *Political Spiritualities: The Pentecostal Revolution in Nigeria*. Chicago: University of Chicago Press.

Martin, Angela. 1982. *African Films: The Context of Production*. London: BFI.

Martins, Rotimi. 2001. "NFVCB on Videos of Violence." *ThisDay*, April 2.

McCall, John C. 2000. *Dancing Histories: Heuristic Anthropology with the Ohafia Igbo*. Ann Arbor: University of Michigan Press.

———. 2002. "Madness, Money, and Movies: Watching Nigerian Popular Videos with the Guidance of a Native Doctor." *Africa Today* 49 (3): 78–94.

———. 2004. "Juju and Justice at the Movies: Vigilantes in Nigerian Popular Videos." *African Studies Review* 47 (3): 51–67.

———. 2007. "The Pan-Africanism We Have: Nollywood's Invention of Africa." *Film International* 5 (4) (28): 92–97.

———. 2012. "The Capital Gap: Nollywood and the Limits of Informal Trade." *Journal of African Cinemas* 4 (1): 9–23.

Meyer, Birgit. 1998. "The Power of Money: Politics, Occult Forces, and Pentecostalism in Ghana." *African Studies Review* 41 (3): 15–37.

———. 1999a. "Popular Ghanaian Cinema and 'African Heritage.'" *Africa Today* 46 (2): 93–114.

———. 1999b. *Translating the Devil: Religion and Modernity among the Ewe in Ghana*. Trenton, NJ: Africa World Press.

———. 2002a. "Occult Forces on Screen: Representation and the Danger of Mimesis in Popular Ghanaian Films." *Etnofoor* 15 (1–2): 212–21.

———. 2002b. "Pentecostalism, Prosperity, and Popular Cinema in Ghana." *Culture and Religion* 3 (1): 67–87.

———. 2003a. "Ghanaian Popular Cinema and the Magic in and of Film." In *Magic and Modernity: Interfaces of Revelation and Concealment*, edited by Birgit Meyer and Peter Pels, 200–22. Stanford: Stanford University Press.

———. 2003b. "Visions of Blood, Sex, and Money: Fantasy Spaces in Popular Ghanaian Cinema." *Visual Anthropology* 16 (1): 15–41.

———. 2004. "'Praise the Lord': Popular Cinema and Pentecostalite Style in Ghana's New Public Sphere." *American Ethnologist* 31 (1): 92–110.

———. 2005a. "Mediating Tradition: Pentecostal Pastors, African Priests, and Chiefs in Ghanaian Popular Films." In *Christianity and Social Change in Africa*, edited by Toyin Falola, 275–304. Durham: Carolina Academic Press.

———. 2005b. "Religious Remediations: Pentecostal Views in Ghanaian Video Movies." *Postcripts* 1 (2–3): 155–81.

———. 2006a. "Impossible Representations: Pentecostalism, Vision, and Video Technology in Ghana." In *Religion, Media, and the Public Sphere*, edited by Birgit Meyer and Annelies Moors, 290–312. Bloomington: Indiana University Press.

———. 2006b. "Prayers, Guns, and Ritual Murder: Power and the Occult in Ghanaian Popular Cinema." In *The Power of the Occult in Africa*, edited by Jim Kiernan, 182–205. Berlin: LIT Verlag.

———. 2006c. "Religious Revelation, Secrecy, and the Limits of Visual Representation." *Anthropological Theory* 6 (4): 431–53.

———. 2007. "Pentecostalism and Neo-Liberal Capitalism: Faith, Prosperity, and Vision in African Pentecostal-Charismatic Churches." *Journal for the Study of Religion* 20 (2): 5–28.

———. 2010a. "Ghanaian Popular Video Movies between State Film Policies and Nollywood." In *Viewing African Cinema in the Twenty-First Century*, edited by Mahir Saul and Ralph A. Austen, 42–62. Athens: Ohio University Press.

———. 2010b. "'Tradition and Colour at Its Best': 'Tradition' and 'Heritage' in Ghanaian Video-Movies." *Journal of African Cultural Studies* 22 (1): 7–23.

Miller, Jade. 2012. "Global Nollywood: The Nigerian Movie Industry and Alternative Global Networks in Production and Distribution." *Global Media & Communication* 8 (2): 117–33.

Moretti, Franco. 2000. "Conjectures on World Literature." *New Left Review* 1:54–68.

Mustafa, Lolade. 2010. "Sex for Cash Booms in Varsities." *P. M. News*, December 28. Accessed December 29, 2010. http://www.nigeriafilms.com/news/9413/7/sex-for-cash-booms-in-varsities-unilag-shuts-femal.html.

Naficy, Hamid. 2001. *An Accented Cinema: Exilic and Diasporic Filmmaking*. Princeton: Princeton University Press,

National Film and Video Censors Board. 2002, 2004a, 2006. *Film & Video Directory in Nigeria*. Vols. 1 and 2 edited by Ferdinand O. Abua; vol. 3 edited by D. R. Gana and Clement D. Edekor. Abuja: National Film and Video Censors Board.

———. 2004b. *Code of Ethics and Production for Film Makers in Nigeria*. Abuja: National Film and Video Censors Board.

———. 2007. *Comprehensive Document on the Distribution, Exhibition, and Marketing of Films and Video Works in Nigeria*. Abuja: National Film and Video Censors Board.

Nnebue, Kenneth. 1997. "Production and Distribution of Video Films: An Alternative to Cine Films." Paper presented at the Nigerian Film and Video Workshop, Kaduna, April 8.

"No Human Heads, No Crown." 2002. *NewsWatch*, July 1. Accessed September 11, 2004. http://www.newswatchngr.com/editorial/prime/2002/01072002/ngr10701114555.htm (site discontinued).

Nolte, Insa. 2004. "Identity and Violence: The Politics of Youth in Ijebu-Remo, Nigeria." *Journal of Modern African Studies* 42 (1): 61–89.

Novia, Charles. 2012. *Nollywood till November: Memoirs of a Nollywood Insider*. Bloomington: AuthorHouse.

Nwagbara, Charles. 2004. "Delta Big Boys & Babes Who Rule the Movie Industry." *Nollywood News*. Accessed June 6, 2005. http://www.modernghana.com/moviethread2/32/6/ (site discontinued).

Obadare, Ebenezer. 2007. "White-Collar Fundamentalism: Interrogating Youth Religiosity on Nigerian University Campuses." *Journal of Modern African Studies* 45 (4): 517–37.

Obafemi, Olu. 1996. *Contemporary Nigerian Theatre: Cultural Heritage and Social Vision*. Bayreuth, Germany: Eckhard Breitinger.

Obaseki, Don Pedro. 2009. "Nigerian Video as the 'Child of Television.'" In *Nollywood: The Video Phenomenon in Nigeria*, edited by Pierre Barrot, 72–76. Bloomington: Indiana University Press.

Obiaya, Ikechukwu. 2010. "Nollywood on the Internet: A Preliminary Analysis of an Online Nigerian Video-Film Audience." *Journal of African Media Studies* 2 (3): 321–38.

———. 2012. "Restructuring the Nigerian Video Film Industry." PhD dissertation, Department of Communications, Universidad de Navarra.

Obiechina, Emmanuel. 1971. *An African Popular Literature: A Study of Onitsha Market Pamphlets*. Cambridge: Cambridge University Press.

Official Site of King Jaja of Opobo: The African Epic Movie of the Millenium. 2000. Accessed July 3, 2005. http://www.ngex.com/entertainmnet/movies/kingjaja/kingjaja.htm (site discontinued).

Ogundele, Wole. 2000. "From Folk Opera to Soap Opera: Improvisations and Transformations in Yoruba Popular Theater." In *Nigerian Video Films*, edited by Jonathan Haynes, 89–130. Athens: Ohio University Press.

Ogunleye, Foluke. 2003a. "Christian Video Film in Nigeria: Dramatic Sermons through the Silver Screen." In *African Video Film Today*, edited by Foluke Ogunleye, 105–28. Manzini, Swaziland: Academic Publishers.

———. 2003b. " 'That We May Serve Him Without Fear': Nigerian Christian Video Film and Battle against Cultism." *International Journal of Humanistic Studies* 2:16–27.

———. 2014. "Audio-Visual Griots: On the Historiography of the Indigenous Yoruba Video Film in Nigeria." In *Auteuring Nollywood: Critical Perspectives on "The Figurine,"* edited by Adeshina Afolayan, 237–56. Ibadan: University Press.

Ogunyemi, Wale. 1979. *Langbodo*. Ikeja: Thomas Nelson.

———. 1987. *Eniyan: A Morality Play*. Ibadan: Ibadan University Press.

Oha, Obododimma. 2000. "The Rhetoric of Nigerian Christian Videos: The War Paradigm of *The Great Mistake*." In *Nigerian Video Films*, edited by Jonathan Haynes, 192–99. Athens: Ohio University Press, 2000.

———. 2001. "The Visual Rhetoric of the Ambivalent City in Nigerian Video Films." In *Cinema and the City*, edited by Mark Shiel and Tony Fitzmaurice, 195–205. Oxford: Blackwell.

———. 2002. "Yoruba Christian Video Narrative and Indigenous Imaginations: Dialogue and Duelogue." *Cahiers d'études africaines* 165:121–42.

Ojaide, Tanure. 1986. *Labyrinths of the Delta*. Greenfield Center, NY: Greenfield Review Press.

Ojo, J. D. 1995. *Students' Unrest in Nigerian University: A Legal and Historical Approach*. Ibadan: IFRA/Spectrum.

Okome, Onookome. "*Onome*: Ethnicity, Class, Gender." In *Nigerian Video Films*, edited by Jonathan Haynes, 148–64. Athens: Ohio University Press, 2000.

———. 2003. "Writing the Anxious City: Images of Lagos in Nigerian Home Video Films." *Black Renaissance/Renaissance Noire* 5 (2): 65–75.

———. 2007a. " 'The Message Is Reaching a Lot of People': Proselytizing and Video Films of Helen Ukpabio." *Postcolonial Text* 3 (2): 1–20. Accessed December 4, 2010. http://postcolonial.org/index.php/pct/article/view/750/419.

———. 2007b. "Nollywood: Spectatorship, Audience, and the Sites of Consumption." *Postcolonial Text* 3 (2): 1–21. Accessed December 4, 2010. http://postcolonial.org/index.php/pct/article/view/763/425.

———. 2013. "Reversing the Filmic Gaze: Comedy and the Critique of the Postcolony in *Osuofia in London*." In *Global Nollywood*, edited by Matthias Krings and Onookome Okome, 139–57. Bloomington: Indiana University Press.

Okome, Onookome, and Jonathan Haynes. 1995. *Cinema and Social Change in West Africa*. Jos: Nigerian Film Corporation.

Okoye, Gab Onyi. 2004. "Creating an International Marketing Network for Made-in-Nigeria Film and Video Works." *Vanguard* , October 30. Accessed November 1, 2004. www.vanguardngr.com/articles/2002.features/fe530102004.html (site discontinued).

Okpewho, Isidore. 1998a. "African Mythology and Africa's Political Impasse." *Research in African Literatures* 29 (1): 1–15.

———. 1998b. *Once Upon a Kingdom: Myth, Hegemony, and Identity*. Bloomington: Indiana University Press.

Olaoluwa, Senayon. 2011. "Igwe!!! Igbo Monarchy, Paradox, and Cultural Passage in Nollywood: Some Preliminary Notes." Paper delivered at Reading and Producing Nollywood: An International Symposium, University of Lagos, March.

Olaoluwa, Senayon, and Adewole Adejayan. 2011. "Thierry Henry as *Igwe*: Soccer Fandom, Christening, and Cultural Passage in Nollywood." *Journal of African Cinemas* 3 (1): 25–42.

Oloruntoba-Oju, Taiwo. 1990. "The Language Question in African Film Aesthetics: Truly the Dead End?" Paper presented at the Society of Nigerian Theatre Artists Conference, Katsina-Ala.

Olusola, Segun. 1986. "Film-TV and the Arts—The African Experience." In *Mass Communication in Nigeria: A Book of Readings*, edited by O. E. Nwuneli, 161–78. Enugu: Fourth Dimension.

Omozokpia, Chris. 1997. "Thema '97: A Night of Surprises." *Post Express*, March 29, 29.

Onishi, Norimitsu. 2002. "Step aside, L. A. and Bombay, for Nollywood." *New York Times*, September 16. Accessed January 6, 2009. http://www.nytimes.com/2002/09/16/world/step-aside-la-and-bombay-for-nollywood.html.

Oreh, O. O. 1985. "*Masquerade* and Other Plays on Nigerian Television." In *Mass Communication, Culture, and Society in West Africa*, edited by F. O. Ugboajah, 108–12. New York: Hans Zell.

Osae-Brown, Funke. 2013. "Firms Invest N500m in Celebrities for Brand Reach." *Nigerian Entertainment Today*, March 6. Accessed March 7, 2013. http://thenet.ng/2013/03/firms-invest-n500m-in-nigerian-celebrities-for-brand-reach/.

Ovuorie, Tobore. 2014. "Investigation: Inside Nigeria's Ruthless Human Trafficking Mafia." *Premium Times*, January 23. Accessed January 24, 2014. http://premiumtimesng.com/app/humantrafficking/.

Peel, J. D. Y. 2000. *Religious Encounter and the Making of the Yoruba*. Bloomington: Indiana University Press.

Pfaff, Françoise. 1996. "Eroticism in Sub-Saharan African Film." In *African Experiences of Cinema*, edited by Imruh Bakari and Mbye Cham, 252–61. London: British Film Insitute.

Piot, Charles. 2010. *Nostalgia for the Future: West Africa after the Cold War*. Chicago: University of Chicago Press.

Pratten, David. 2008. "'The Thief Eats His Shame': Practice and Power in Nigerian Vigilantism." *African Studies Review* 78 (1): 64–83.

Ricard, Alain. 1983. "Du théâter au cinéma yoruba: Le cas nigérian." *CinémAction* 26:160–67.

Rice, Andrew. 2012. "A Scorsese in Lagos." *New York Times Magazine*, February 26, 26–31.

Ryan, Connor. 2013. "Yoruba Video Comedies: You Don't Know Lagos." *African Studies Review* 56 (1): 215–19.

Shaka, Femi Okiremuete. 2003. "History, Genres, and Nigeria's Emergent Video Film Industry." *Black Renaissance/Renaissance Noire* 5 (2): 51–64.

———. 2004. *Modernity and the African Cinema*. Trenton: Africa World Press.

Simone, AbdouMaliq. 2004. *For the City Yet to Come: Changing African Life in Four Cities*. Durham: Duke University Press.

Sinclair, John, Elizabeth Jacka, and Stuart Cunningham. 1996. *New Patterns in Global Television: Peripheral Vision*. Oxford: Oxford University Press.

Smith, Andrew. 2001. "Reading Wealth in Nigeria: Occult Capitalism and Marx's Vampires." *Historical Materialism* 9:39–59.

———. 2009. "Nigerian Scam E-Mails and the Charms of Capital." *Cultural Studies* 23 (1): 27–47.

Smith, Daniel Jordan. 2001a. "'The Arrow of God': Pentecostalism, Inequality, and the Supernatural in Southeastern Nigeria." *Africa* 71 (4): 587–613.

———. 2001b. "Ritual Killing, 419, and Fast Wealth." *American Ethnologist* 28 (4): 803–26.

———. 2001c. "Romance, Parenthood, and Gender in a Modern African Society." *Ethnology* 40 (2): 129–51.

———. 2004. "The Bakassi Boys: Vigilantism, Violence, and Political Imagination in Nigeria." *Current Anthropology* 19 (3): 429–55.

———. 2007. *A Culture of Corruption: Everyday Deception and Popular Discontent in Nigeria*. Princeton: Princeton University Press.

———. 2009. "Managing Men, Marriage, and Modern Love: Women's Perspectives on Intimacy and Male Infidelity in Southeastern Nigeria." In *Love in Africa*, edited by Jennifer Cole and Lynn M. Thomas, 157–80. Chicago: University of Chicago Press.

Soyinka, Wole. 1989. *Aké: The Years of Childhood*. New York: Vintage.

———. 2003. *Death and the King's Horseman*. New York: Norton.

Sprague, Stephen F. 2002. "Yoruba Photography: How the Yoruba See Themselves." In *The Anthropology of Media*, edited by Kelly Askew and Richard R. Wilk, 172–86. Boston: Blackwell.

Spronk, Rachel. 2009. "Media and the Therapeutic Ethos of Romantic Love in Middle-Class Nairobi." In *Love in Africa*, edited by Jennifer Cole and Lynn M. Thomas, 181–203. Chicago: University of Chicago Press.

Sreberny-Mohammadi, Annabelle, and Ali Mohammadi. 1994. *Small Media, Big Revolution: Communication, Culture, and the Iranian Revolution*. Minneapolis: University of Minnesota Press.

Tcheuyap, Alexie. 2011. *Postnationalist African Cinemas*. Manchester: Manchester University Press.

Thomas, Lynn M., and Jennifer Cole. 2009. "Thinking through Love in Africa." In *Love in Africa*, edited by Jennifer Cole and Lynn M. Thomas, 1–30. Chicago: University of Chicago Press.

Thometz, Kurt, ed. 2001. *Life Turns Man Up and Down: High Life, Useful Advice, and Mad English*. New York: Pantheon.

Thompson, Robert Farris. 1984. *Flash of the Spirit: African & Afro-American Art & Philosophy*. New York: Vintage.

Tudesq, André-Jean. 1992. *L'Afrique noire et ses télévisions*. Paris: Anthropos/INA.

Tunstall, Jeremy. 1977. *The Media Are American*. London: Constable.

Tutuola, Amos. 1984. *The Palm-Wine Drinkard*. New York: Grove.

Uchenunu, Ambrose O. 2008. "The Decline of Cinema in Nigeria." *International Journal of Multi-Disciplinary Scholarship* 3–5:26–43.

Ugor, Paul. 2007. "Censorship and the Content of Nigerian Home Video Films." *Postcolonial Text* 3 (2): 1–22. Accessed November 5, 2007. http://postcolonial.org/index.php/pct/article/view/518/403.

Ukadike, Frank Nwachukwu. 1994. *Black African Cinema*. Berkeley: University of California Press.

Ukah, Asonzeh F.-K. 2002. "Reklame Für Gott: Religiöse Verbung in Nigeria." In *Afrikanische Reklamekunst*, edited by Tobias Wendl, 148–53. Wuppertal: Peter Hammer.

———. 2003. "Advertising God: Nigerian Christian Video-Films and the Power of Consumer Culture." *Journal of Religion in Africa* 33 (2): 203–31.

———. 2005. "The Local and the Global in the Media and Material Culture of Nigerian Pentecostalism." In *Entreprises Religieuses Transnationales En Afrique De L'ouest*, edited by Laurent Fourchard, André Mary, and René Otayek, 285–313. Paris: Karthala.

———. 2011. "Mediating Armageddon: Popular Christian Video-Films as a Source of Conflict in Nigeria." In *Displacing the State: Religion and Conflict in Neoliberal Africa*, edited by James Howard Smith and Rosalind I. J. Hackett, 209–39. Notre Dame: University of Notre Dame Press.

Usman, Evelyn. 2013. "Why We Prefer Live Human Beings—Suspected Human Parts Dealer." *Vanguard*, June 13, 6.

Utoh-Ezeajugh, Tracie Chima. 2008. "Beyond the Negativisation Syndrome: Nigerian Video Films and National Image Laundering." *International Journal of Multi-Disciplinary Scholarship* 3–5: 249–58.

Uwugiaren, Iyobosa. 1997. "A Cover-Up & a Battle with Ghost." *TheNEWS*, October 27, 14–21.

Vasagar, Jeevan. 2006. "Welcome to Nollywood." *Guardian* (UK), March 23. Accessed May 12, 2006. http://www.theguardian.com/film/2006/mar/23/world.features.

Vogel, Susan. 1986. *The Aesthetics of African Art: The Carlo Monzino Collection*. New York: Museum for African Art.

———. 1991. "Introduction: Digesting the West." In *Africa Explores: 20th Century African Art*, edited by Susan Vogel and Ima Ebong, 14–31. New York: Center for African Art.

Vourlias, Christopher. 2010. "Nigerian Helmer Leads 'New Nollywood':Afolayan's 'The Figurine' Gets Critical Kudos and Strong B. O." *Variety*, June 5. Accessed June 6, 2010. http://www.variety.com/article/VR1118020218?refCatId=13.

———. 2012a. "Helmer is Hot, in More Ways Than One: Former Banker Afolayan Shakes Up Nigerian Pic Biz." *Variety*, June 2. Accessed August 7, 2012. http://www.variety.com/article/VR1118054917?refcatid=3762.

———. 2012b. "Nigerian Directors Target Bigscreen: Biz Shifting from Low-Budget to Competitive Pics." *Variety*, May 5. Accessed August 7, 2012. http://www.variety.com/article/VR1118053553?refcatid=1278.

Watts, Michael J. 1994. "Oil as Money: The Devil's Excrement and the Spectacle of Black Gold." In *Money, Power, and Space*, edited by Stuart Corbridge, Nigel Thrift, and Ron Martin, 406–45. Cambridge: Blackwell.

Williams, Raymond. 1977. *Marxism and Literature*. Oxford: Oxford University Press.

INDEX OF NAMES

Page numbers in italics refer to figures and tables.

INDEX OF SUBJECTS

Page numbers in italics refer to figures and tables.